Guang Shen

Regulation of Cross-border Establishment in China and the EU

A Comparative Law and Economics Approach

intersentia

METRO

Ius Commune Europaeum

Intersentia Ltd
Sheraton House | Castle Park
Cambridge | CB3 0AX | United Kingdom
Tel.: +44 1223 370 170 | Fax: +44 1223 370 169
Email: mail@intersentia.co.uk
www.intersentia.com | www.intersentia.co.uk

Distribution for the UK and Ireland:
NBN International
Airport Business Centre, 10 Thornbury Road
Plymouth, PL6 7PP
United Kingdom
Tel.: +44 1752 202 301 | Fax: +44 1752 202 331
Email: orders@nbninternational.com

Distribution for Europe and all other countries:
Intersentia Publishing nv
Groenstraat 31
2640 Mortsel
Belgium
Tel.: +32 3 680 15 50 | Fax: 32 3 658 71 21
Email: mail@intersentia.be

Distribution for the USA and Canada:
International Specialized Book Services
920 NE 58th Ave. Suite 300
Portland, OR 97213
USA
Tel.: +1 800 944 6190 (toll free) | Fax: + 1 503 280 8832
Email: info@isbs.com

Regulation of Cross-border Establishment in China and the EU
A Comparative Law and Economics Approach

ISBN 978-1-78068-414-7
D/2016/7849/100
NUR 828

British Library Cataloguing in Publication Data. A catalogue record for this book is available from the British Library.

Regulation of Cross-border Establishment in China and the EU
A Comparative Law and Economics Approach

ACKNOWLEDGEMENTS

The following thesis, while an individual work, profited from the advice and comments of several people. First, I would like to express my gratitude to my supervisors Prof. Michael Faure and Dr. Niels Philipsen. Their insights and expertise, from the initial to the final level, allowed me to complete my project on schedule.

Besides my supervisors, I would like to thank the members of the reading committee: Prof. Anthony Ogus, Prof. Hildegard Schneider, Prof. Oswald Jansen and Dr. Xu Guangdong, for their constructive and thoughtful feedback on my research.

In addition to the academic assistance above, my sincere thanks go to those lawyers, businessmen and officials who helped me carry out the empirical research for this book. Without their support, it would not be possible to provide deep insights into the reality of the inter-provincial establishment in China.

I must also acknowledge my colleagues at the Law Faculty of Maastricht University for creating a pleasant working environment. Special appreciation goes out to my METRO colleagues for the stimulating discussions and for all the fun we had in the past four years.

Since my study at the China-EU School of Law laid a solid foundation for my PhD research, I also would like to thank the professors from Europe who fly to Beijing to teach. In particular, I want to express my appreciation to Prof. Remco van Rhee and Dr. Jackson Maogoto for encouraging me to pursue PhD research in Europe.

I also wish to thank my parents for supporting me throughout drafting this dissertation. They instilled in me, from an early stage, the desire to do a doctorate.

Finally, I recognize that this research would not have been possible without the monetary support of the China Scholarship Council.

CONTENTS

PART I. LEGAL ANALYSIS

LIST OF ABBREVIATIONS

AIC	Administration for Industry and Commerce
ALL	Administrative License Law
AML	Anti-Monopoly Law
APL	Administrative Procedural Law
ARL	Administrative Reconsideration Law
AUCL	Anti-Unfair Competition Law
BEPA	Bureau of European Policy Advisers
CAAC	Civil Aviation Administration of China
CBRC	China Banking Regulatory Commission
CCCPC	Central Committee of the Communist Party of China
CEN	European Committee for Standardisation
CFLP	China Federation of Logistics and Purchasing
CIRC	China Insurance Regulatory Commission
CJEU	Court of Justice of the European Union
CJV	Contractural Joint Venture
CPC	Communist Party of China
CPPCC	Chinese People's Political Consultative Conference
CSRC	China Securities Regulatory Commission
DRC	Development and Reform Commission
ECJ	European Court of Justice
EEC	European Economic Community
EJV	Equity Joint Venture
EMU	Economic and Monetary Union
ESCAP	Economic and Social Commission for Asia and the Pacific
EU	European Union
FDA	Food and Drug Administration
FDI	Foreign Direct Investment
FIE	Foreign Invested Enterprise
FIHC	Foreign Invested Holding Company
GAQSIQ	General Administration of Quality Supervision, Inspection and Quarantine
GDP	Gross Domestic Production
IPO	Initial Public Offering

JSLC	Joint Stock Limited Company
JV	Joint Venture
JVC	Joint Venture Company
LLC	Limited Liability Company
LLP	Limited Liability Partnership
MEP	Ministry of Environmental Protection
MOFCOM	the Ministry of Commerce
NDRC	National Development and Reform Commission
NPC	National People's Congress (China)
OLS	Ordinary Least Squares
One-person LLC	One-person Limited Liability Company
PRC	People's Republic of China
PWC	PricewaterhouseCoopers
RACR	Regulation on the Administration of Company Registration
RMB	the renminbi
SAIC	State Administration of Industry and Commerce
SASAC	State-funded Assets Supervision and Administration Commission
SAT	State Administration of Tax
SEA	Single European Act
SERC	State Electricity Regulatory Commission
SFDA	State Food and Drug Administration
SME	Small and Medium Enterprise
SOE	State-Owned Enterprise
TEC	Treaty Establishing the European Community
TEEC	Treaty Establishing the European Economic Community
TEU	Treaty on European Union
TFEU	Treaty on the Functioning of the European Union
UK	United Kingdom
US	United States
USCBC	US-Chna Business Council
VAT	Value Added Tax
WFOE	Wholly Foreign Owned Enterprise
WTO	World Trade Organization

Chapter 1

INTRODUCTION

1. Societal Problems

It has been pointed out in the literature that enterprises in China usually encounter barriers when they invest across provinces.[1] For example, an empirical study by the Development Research Center of the State Council (2004) demonstrated that businesses in China may be confronted with some barriers in the process of inter-provincial investment, including more stringent capital requirements than those made by national law.[2] According to another (more recent) study, protectionist measures are taken by local authorities, which lead to restrictions on the inter-provincial establishment of companies and market segmentation.[3]

Despite the above research, there appears to be limited research on how, in practice, rules on the inter-provincial establishment of companies are applied. That being said, the impact of regulation on the inter-provincial establishment of companies should not be underestimated. In 2013, the Communist Party of China announced that it would 'tidy up and annul all sorts of regulations and methods that impede the national unified market and fair competition.'[4] Usually, the regulation of inter-provincial establishment on the one hand restricts expansion across provincial borders, while on the other hand it can deter the entry of unqualified companies into local markets.

In contrast to the creation of entry barriers, as discussed above, local authorities sometimes compete with each other to attract investment by non-local businesses. There may even be destructive competition between provinces or regions. For example, Wei and Bi demonstrate that Chinese firms in certain

1 See, for example, Boyreau-Debray & Wei 2004, p. 6.

2 Li *et al.* 2005, p. 104.

3 Xia, Lu & Yu 2011, p. 65.

4 中共中央关于全面深化改革若干重大问题的决定（全文），Decision of the Central Committee of the Communist Party of China (CCCPC) on Some Major Issues Concerning Comprehensively Deepening the Reform. The document can be obtained in English from <www.china.org.cn/chinese/2014-01/17/content_31226494_3.htm> (last accessed 8 October 2014).

industries tend to relocate their factories from Eastern China to regions with weaker environmental regulation in Central China and Western China. Based on this tendency, it is reasonable to presume that local authorities in Western China and Central China have powerful incentives to engage in a race to the bottom in environmental standards on establishment.[5] The issue of the race to the bottom will be discussed in detail in Chapter 6. Whether or not local officials create entry barriers to non-local firms depends on the specific context, e.g. whether the region concerned is developed or backward.

Ensuring easier inter-provincial establishment can benefit China. Cross-provincial investment by firms has been recognized as one form of capital mobility across provinces in China.[6] A World Bank country study pointed out that in a market economy that China was moving towards, capital mobility played a crucial role in achieving efficient resource allocation, if investment could be made in the ideal location and for the most efficient use.[7] The expansion of China's internal market may become a more significant ingredient for its economic development in the future.[8]

Facilitating cross-border establishment is also important in other federal jurisdictions, such as the EU. In recent times, Mario Monti, the former Commissioner for Competition of the European Commission, recognized establishing a stronger single market as one of the priorities to boost the economy of the EU. In particular, he held that the single market for services is of crucial significance for economic development.[9] In 2006, the EU adopted the Services Directive 2006/123 to tap into the potential of the market in services that accounts for almost 70 per cent of the EU's GDP.[10] The Services Directive has removed some barriers created by regulations of Member States. Their removal is bound to significantly facilitate cross-border investment in the market for services in the longer run.[11] Nevertheless, further efforts are needed to break down obstacles inside the services market, according to Federica Mustilli and Jacques Pelkmans.[12] The development of the internal market can cause us to question whether China can learn something from the EU experience.

2. Scientific Relevance

One can find a large body of theoretical economic literature that examines the effects of competition between jurisdictions on regulatory standards.[13] However,

5 Wei & Bi 2011, p. 73 and 74.
6 Boyreau-Debray & Wei 2004, p. 6.
7 The World Bank 1994, p. 4.
8 Naughton 2003, p. 207. See also Philipsen *et al.* 2016.
9 Monti 2010.
10 Barnard 2008, p. 326.
11 Mustilli & Pelkmans 2013, p. 26.
12 Mustilli & Pelkmans 2013, p. 3. See also Philipsen *et al.* 2016. This report studies the free movement of lawyers and finds some concrete barriers to the cross-border establishment for legal professions, e.g. language, pension system, the requirements of local bars, etc.
13 Van den Bergh 2010, p. 76.

whether regulatory competition will lead to a race to the bottom or rather a race to the top is still a highly disputed issue.[14] It is unclear in which circumstances a race to the bottom or a race to the top will occur.[15] This thesis will seek to contribute to the literature by examining the conditions under which Chinese local governments create entry barriers to non-local firms.

3. Research Questions

In the light of the observations in section 1, this research sets out to examine to what extent regulation of the inter-provincial establishment of companies in China can be considered as serving a public interest or private interest goal. Moreover, this research will study the extent to which lessons can be learned from economic theory and the EU experience for the regulation of inter-provincial establishment. In order to answer these main research questions, they will be divided into several sub-questions.

Part I (Legal Analysis) will first focus on China and answer Question 1: *What regulations exist in China concerning the inter-provincial establishment of companies and how they are enforced?* Part I will then shift attention to the EU and examine Question 2: *How does the EU regulate the cross-border establishment of companies?*

Part II (Theoretical Framework) will turn to Question 3 concerning a law and economics analysis of regulation: *what does economic theory teach us about regulation of the cross-border establishment of companies in a multi-level jurisdiction?*

Following the line of the reasoning of the economic theory presented earlier, Question 4 will be addressed in Part III (Economic Evaluation): *to what extent can the regulation of inter-provincial establishment in China be considered as serving public interest or private interest purposes?* Part III (Economic Evaluation) will also answer Question 5: *whether regulating inter-provincial establishment at central level or local level should be preferred in China?*

Finally, this thesis will examine: *to what extent can the EU experience in regulating the cross-border establishment of companies be a source of inspiration for China* (Question 6)?

The structure of the thesis, to be discussed in more detail in section 4 below, is based on these research questions.

4. Methodologies

This thesis uses an economic analysis of regulation and applies it to the specific case of the cross-border establishment of businesses. Moreover, a comparative law and economics approach is adapted to the inter-provincial establishment of companies in China and the cross-border establishment of companies in the EU. Furthermore, interviews are held to examine the extent to which regulation of inter-provincial establishment in China can be considered as serving the goals of public interest or private interest.

14 Eger & Schüller 2007, p. 11.
15 Van den Bergh 2000, p. 445.

Chapters 2 and 3 of the book provide a legal analysis of the existing provisions on the inter-provincial establishment of companies in China and the cross-border establishment of companies in the EU respectively. The objective of analysing the rules on inter-provincial establishment in China is to reveal (potential) barriers hindering this activity and the cause of these barriers. The discussion on the regulation of the EU aims to show how the EU removes obstacles to the cross-border establishment of businesses.

Part II of the dissertation focuses on the economic literature with respect to regulating the cross-border establishment of companies at central level in a multi-level jurisdiction. Chapter 4 of Part II describes economic theory in the field of regulating business establishment in a single-level jurisdiction. The arguments in favour of regulation on public interest grounds and other explanations for regulation following from the private interest approach are addressed there. Moreover, this chapter, from an economic standpoint, considers some regulatory instruments in the process of business establishment. Thereafter, Chapter 5 of Part II offers the economic theory concerning the regulation of the cross-border establishment of companies in a multi-level jurisdiction. Chapter 5 first investigates the arguments for differentiating between requirements for the cross-border establishment of companies and general rules on the establishment of companies on public interest grounds, and other explanations for this distinction as identified via the private interest approach. Next, adopting the economics of federalism, Chapter 5 addresses public interest reasons to support regulating cross-border establishment at central level and reasons against it on the basis of public choice analysis.

Chapter 6 applies the economic analysis presented in Chapter 5 to the current regulation in China. The aim is to examine the extent to which the regulation of cross-provincial establishment in China can be considered as serving public interest or private interest purposes. Apart from the existing empirical evidence, an analysis of interviews on the formation of companies across provinces is provided, with the aim of finding out whether some of the arguments put forward by the private interest approach can be backed.

Chapter 7 adopts a comparative law and economics approach to the regulation of cross-provincial establishment in China and the regulation of the cross-border establishment of companies in the EU. The aim of this comparison is to examine whether China can learn something from the EU experience with market integration. Since the institutional differences between the European and Chinese legal systems appear very distinct, Chapter 7 will take a careful look at the particular institutional features of these two regimes.

5. Structure

This thesis consists of three parts. The current regulation is presented in Part I. Chapter 2 discusses the rules governing inter-provincial establishment in China, examines their implementation, explores existing solutions to cope with the barriers to inter-provincial establishment, and investigates their enforcement effects. Chapter 3 first analyses the evolution of the EU internal market and then discusses the regulation of the cross-border establishment of companies in the EU. Moreover, to reflect the practice of the freedom of establishment, remaining barriers to this freedom are considered, as well as the possible ways to cope with these obstacles.

Part II presents an economic analysis of the regulation of the cross-border establishment of companies in a multi-level jurisdiction. Chapter 4 demonstrates that in a single-level jurisdiction, licensing requirements and minimum capital requirements in the set-up process can deal with externalities and information problems, but may benefit certain interest groups, e.g. incumbents. Chapter 5 first applies the theory of Chapter 4 to the cross-border establishment of companies. Next, an economic analysis of regulating cross-border establishment at central level is offered. The main arguments in favour of centralization of the regulation of cross-border establishment appear to be economies of scale and trans-boundary externalities. However, the centralization may profit some interest groups at the expense of others.

The regulation of inter-provincial establishment in China is reviewed in the light of the economic literature presented in Chapter 6 of Part III. More specifically, this chapter explores arguments for distinguishing between requirements for the inter-provincial establishment of companies and general rules on the establishment of companies on public interest grounds and other explanations for the differentiation following from the private interest approach. Moreover, the extent to which regulating inter-provincial establishment at central level can be considered as serving public interest or private interest goals is examined. Based on the above analysis, this chapter also provides policy recommendations on whether the inter-provincial establishment of companies in China should be regulated at central level or local level.

The differences between the regulation of cross-provincial establishment in China and the EU regulation of the cross-border establishment of companies are analysed in Chapter 7, adopting a comparative law and economics approach.

PART I

LEGAL ANALYSIS

Part I

Part I describes the current regulation. After presentation of the regulation of cross-provincial establishment in China (Chapter 2), attention will turn to the EU regulation of the cross-border establishment of companies (Chapter 3).

Chapter 2

REGULATION OF THE INTER-PROVINCIAL ESTABLISHMENT OF COMPANIES IN CHINA

1. Introduction

This chapter considers (potential) barriers hindering the inter-provincial establishment of companies in China. It elaborates the rules governing such establishment, examines their implementation in practice, explores existing solutions to tackle the obstacles to inter-provincial establishment, and investigates their enforcement effects. The objective of Chapter 2 is to demonstrate whether the obstacles stem from the legal provisions themselves or from the implementation of the rules on the inter-provincial establishment for companies.

Sections 2, 3 and 4 of this chapter discuss the rules on the establishment of a domestic company, the rules on the establishment of Foreign Invested Enterprises (FIEs) and the rules on the inter-provincial establishment for companies in China, respectively.[1] The elaboration of these provisions aims to examine whether the legal barriers for the establishment of companies in China can be erected according to law in the books.

Section 5 and section 6 study the actual situation of the inter-provincial establishment for domestic companies and FIEs in China, respectively. This chapter focuses only on the application of the rules on the inter-provincial establishment for companies. The aim is to analyse whether the execution of the rules can lead to barriers to the inter-provincial establishment of companies.

Section 7 interprets the laws coping with administrative monopolies in China. It is designed to evaluate whether such laws can ensure freedom in the inter-provincial establishment of companies in China. The interpretation and enforcement of the rules governing this establishment are also studied in this section. This is because the research on the effectiveness of the anti-monopoly rules

1 FIEs refer to the companies that are established in China according to Chinese law and whose capital contributions are made by foreign investors solely or made by Chinese and foreign investors together. Domestic companies are the companies that are set up in China following Chinese law and whose capital is contributed by Chinese investors only. Together FIEs and domestic companies constitute Chinese companies.

can certainly reveal the real situation whether companies can establish businesses in another province freely. Moreover, how the rules on the inter-provincial establishment for companies are applied in practice can be examined.

Based on the analysis in the preceding sections, section 8 provides original ideas on the possible causes for the occurrence of obstacles to the inter-provincial establishment of companies in China. The reasons are viewed from two perspectives: the provision and the implementation of national law in China.

Section 9 outlines the important changes in regulation of establishment brought by the reform measures of 2013. The social background of this amendment is also pointed out. Moreover, section 8 explains that (probably due to opposition from central regulators) such changes have been instituted in a pilot project rather than in the whole nation at once.

Chapter 2 comes to its conclusion in section 10. This section sums up the rules regarding the establishment of companies in China and their implementation in practice. Moreover, an overview is presented of the rules coping with administrative monopolies and the actual effect of the rules. Lastly, it points out why the cross-provincial establishment of companies is hindered.

The main research of Chapter 2 was completed in November 2015. As a result, the relevant Chinese legislation was incorporated until November 2015.

2. Rules Concerning the Establishment of Domestic Companies

When setting up a company in China, one needs to differentiate between the types of company first. The establishment of FIEs and of domestic companies is regulated by different laws. The domestic companies are governed by the Chinese Company Law (Amended 2005) (hereinafter the Company Law). According to Article 218 of this law, limited liability companies and joint stock limited companies funded by foreign investors shall be governed by the Company Law. But where there are otherwise different provisions in any law regarding foreign investment, such provisions shall prevail. This section details the rules on the establishment of domestic companies.

According to the Company Law, to establish domestic companies lawfully, it is necessary to comply with the establishment process strictly and satisfy substantial conditions provided in laws and regulations based on their legal forms. The basic requirements of the incorporation of domestic companies are provided in Articles 23 and 77 of the Company Law.

Article 23 of the Company Law prescribes the conditions for the establishment of a limited liability company (LLC). They relate to the number of shareholders that must meet the statutory requirement; the amount of capital contribution made by the shareholders that has to reach the statutory minimum amount of the registered capital; the articles of association that must be formulated jointly by shareholders; the company has a name and its organizational setup conforms to that of a LLC; and the company owns a domicile. The provisions governing the establishment of LLCs in the Company Law apply to the setting up of one-person limited liability companies and solely state-funded companies, unless it provides different regulations for the latter two types specifically.[2]

For the establishment of a joint stock limited company (JSLC), the conditions are laid down in Article 77: the number of initiators meets the statutory requirement; the capital stock subscribed for and raised by the initiators satisfies the minimum amount of the statutory capital; shares are issued and the preparatory work is done in accordance with the conditions provided in laws; the articles of association are made by the initiators, and are adopted at the establishment meeting when stock floatation is used to set up the company; the company has a name, and its organizational setup complies with that of a JSLC; the company owns a domicile.[3] Capital requirements for JSLCs established by stock floatation and promotion are slightly different.[4]

The remainder of this section elaborates on substantive conditions and procedural requirements for the establishment of a domestic company. In practice, licensing requirements can also be involved in the establishment of domestic companies since the incorporation of some domestic companies in particular industries is subject to approvals. Therefore, rules on the licensing for the incorporation of a domestic company are also explained in section 2 where the establishment process is described. The purpose of this section is to examine whether there are legal barriers to the establishment of a domestic company.

Below, this section first explains the substantive conditions. According to Articles 23 and 77 of the Company Law, the incorporation of a domestic company needs to meet three main conditions related to initiators, capital contribution and the company's articles of association.

2.1. *Initiator Requirements*

Initiator requirements are composed of initiator numbers and initiator qualifications. Initiators refer to shareholders of both a LLC and a JSLC who have established these companies.[5] Requirements on capital and initiators in the

2 Arts. 58 and 65 of the Company Law (2005). The English version of the Company Law is available at: <www. fdi.gov.cn> (last accessed 17 April 2016).

3 *Ibid.*, Art. 77.

4 According to Art. 78 of the Company Law (2005), the establishment of a company by promotion means that the initiators establish a company by subscribing for all of the shares that should be issued by the company. The establishment of a company by stock floatation has the meaning that the initiators establish a company by subscribing for some of the shares that should be issued by the company and offering the remaining shares to the general public or to particular objects for subscription.

5 The Company Law does not name shareholders of a LLC who have established the LLC initiators. However, initiators in the Company Law, in the Chinese scholars' opinion, mean anyone who participates in the establishment of companies, makes capital contributions, signs articles of association, and shoulders legal responsibilities. Mi 2008, p. 11.

Company Law, as Blaze and Chan argue, are strongly reminiscent of those found in standard Western company codes.[6]

2.1.1. Initiator Numbers

There should be no less than 2 but not more than 50 initiators for a LLC.[7] A one-person limited liability company and a solely state-funded company should only have one shareholder.[8] A JSLC should be established by not less than 2 but not more than 200 initiators, more than half of whom must have a domicile in China.[9] Their main responsibility is to make capital contribution. Initiators in a LLC must make a full capital contribution when they subscribe.[10] All shares should be subscribed for by initiators in a JSLC that are set up by way of promotion. For those established by way of stock floatation, their initiators must subscribe for some shares.[11] Moreover, initiators in a JSLC are also responsible for undertaking the preparatory activities.[12]

2.1.2. Initiator Qualifications

For a solely state-funded company, only the Chinese state can be a shareholder. The State-funded Assets Supervision and Administration Commission (SASAC) and its institutions at local levels perform the functions of initiators.[13] For other legal forms, generally, both legal persons and natural persons can be initiators. Other laws and regulations should be referred to when determining initiator qualifications in a particular situation. The Company Law includes no provisions regarding initiator qualifications.

First, the following groups and individuals are not entitled to be initiators in any case. Civil servants, according to Article 53 of the Civil Servant Law (2005), must not participate in any profit-making activity or hold a concurrent position in any profit-making organization.[14] For a certain period after civil servants' retirement or resignation this restriction still applies, if the profit-making activity or organization relates to their original work.[15] Moreover, prosecutors and judges have no initiator qualifications. The Judges Law (2001) and the Prosecutors Law (2001) prohibit the involvement of prosecutors and judges in profit-making activities.[16] Furthermore, the Communist Party of China (CPC) and state organs at and above county levels and their officials cannot be engaged in business activities according

6 Blazey & Chan 2008, p. 250.
7 Art. 24 of the Company Law (2005).
8 *Ibid.*, Arts. 58 and 65.
9 *Ibid.*, Art. 79.
10 *Ibid.*, Art. 28.
11 *Ibid.*, Art. 78.
12 *Ibid.*, Art. 80.
13 *Ibid.*, Art. 65.
14 公务员法（2005年）第53条，Art. 53 of the Civil Servant Law (2005).
15 *Ibid.*, Art. 102.
16 中国法官法（2001年修订）第32条，Art. 32 of the Judges Law (revised 2001)，中国检察官法（2001年修订）第35条，Art. 35 of the Prosecutors Law (revised 2001).

to the Notice on the Establishment of Economic Entities by the CPC and State Organs and the Participation in Business Activities by Officials of the CPC and State Organs (1992).[17]

Second, local Administrations for Industry and Commerce (AICs) impose different restrictions on initiator qualifications of other groups and individuals. A case in point is that in Hangzhou bank clerks, active military personnel and students studying at school (except those permitted to do business by school authorities) cannot be initiators. In Beijing, the local AIC lists different market players whose qualifications are not permitted.[18] Therefore, it is necessary to check with every individual region's stipulations when setting up a company there.

2.2. *Capital Requirements*

Among the capital matters dealt with are minimum capital requirements, capital forms and capital contribution.

2.2.1. Minimum Capital Requirements

Minimum capital requirements are 30,000 RMB for LLCs, 100,000 RMB for one-person LLCs and 5,000,000 RMB for JSLCs.[19] When a higher minimum capital requirement for a LLC and a JSLC is stipulated by any law or regulation, such stipulation must be followed.[20] This is usually the case for companies that engage in the business of securities, insurance, futures and intermediary services. For a JSLC set up by way of stock flotation, the shares subscribed for by the initiators must not be less than 35 per cent of the total shares. However, if laws and administrative regulations have different requirements, such provisions must prevail.[21]

2.2.2. Capital Forms

For both a LLC and a JSLC, rules on capital forms are the same. Capital contributions can be made to non-monetary properties as long as they can be transferred and assessed on the basis of currency.[22] No less than 30 per cent of the registered capital paid by all the shareholders should be in the form of currency.[23] In

17 规定见于《中共中央办公厅、国务院办公厅，　关于党政机关兴办经济实体，　党政机关干部，从事经营　活动问题的通知》　(1992年6月26日). It is stipulated in the Notice on the Establishment of Economic Entities by CPC and State Organs and the Participation in Business Activities by Officials of CPC and State Organs (26 June 1992).

18 Mi 2008, p. 19.

19 Arts. 26, 59 and 81 of the Company Law (2005).

20 *Ibid.*, Arts. 26 and 81.

21 *Ibid.*, Art. 85.

22 *Ibid.*, Art. 27.

23 *Ibid.*, Arts. 27 and 83.

practice, in Xinping Mi's opinion, non-monetary properties that cannot be contributed to may be listed by local AICs.[24]

2.2.3. Capital Contributions

JSLCs established by stock floatation are required to pay registered capital in single instalments.[25] Likewise, one-person LLCs are asked to pay a capital contribution in a lump sum.[26] JSLCs established by promotion and LLCs may pay off their contributions in two years from companies' establishment dates, though all their capital must be subscribed at one time. As for an investment company, the period could be prolonged to five years.[27] It is a necessity that capital contributions made by shareholders are checked by a lawfully established capital verification institution.[28]

2.3. *Articles of Association*

For a solely state-funded company, its articles of association must be created by the SASAC. They can also be drafted by its board of directors, which should be submitted to this institution for approvals.[29]

Other companies need to formulate their articles of association themselves, which will be checked by the AICs. Articles 25 and 82 of the Company Law stipulate items that must be stated in the companies' articles of association. For a LLC, they are 'the name, domicile, business scope and registered capital of the company, names of shareholders, forms, amount and date of capital contribution made by shareholders, the organizations of the company and its formation, their functions and rules of procedure, the legal representative of the company and other matters deemed necessary by shareholders.'[30] For a JSLC, their articles of association must specify 'the name and domicile of the company, the business scope of the company, the form of company establishment, total shares, value of each share, and the amount of registered capital of the company, the name of every initiator, the shares which they have subscribed for, the form and date of capital contribution, the composition, authorities, term of office and rules of procedure of the board of directors, the legal representative of the company, the composition, authorities, term of office and rules of procedure of the board of supervisors, the methods for profit distribution of the company and liquidation methods, the methods for issuing notices or public announcements of the company and other matters deemed

24 米兴平，公司设立的合法性问题研究，中国人民大学，博士学位论文，2008，页19. Mi 2008, p. 19.
25 *Ibid.*, Art. 81 of the Company Law (2005).
26 *Ibid.*, Art. 59.
27 *Ibid.*, Arts. 26 and 81.
28 *Ibid.*, Art. 29.
29 *Ibid.*, Art. 66.
30 *Ibid.*, Art. 25.

necessary by the meetings of shareholders.'[31] As Yue Wu argues, these items are mandatory. If any of the items are stated illegally or omitted from a company's articles of association, the articles of association will be null and void. The establishment of that company will be invalidated.[32]

The AICs should check the above items. If they do not comply with the provisions of laws and administrative decrees, companies will not be registered by the AICs, according to Article 10 of the Regulations on the Administration of Company Registration (Revised 2005) (hereinafter the RACR).[33] In practice, as Xiaomeng Li (2006) remarks, the AICs usually only see whether the articles of association records all the items and their contents are not checked.[34]

Table 1. Rules concerning the establishment of a domestic company in China

Legal Forms	Categories	Initiator requirements		Capital requirements			Articles of association
		Initiator numbers	Initiator qualifications	Minimum capital requirements	Capital forms	Capital contribution	
LLC	LLC (except one-person and solely state-funded LLCs)	Not less than 2 but not more than 50	Both legal persons and natural persons can be initiators, except civil servants, prosecutors, judges, the CPC and state organs at and above county level and their officials. Local AICs may impose other restrictions.	30,000 RMB. The threshold may be set higher by other laws and administrative regulations	Currency shall not be less than 30%. Capital forms can be non-monetary properties that could be transferred and assessed.	Contributions can be paid off in two years since companies' establishment dates	It must be formulated according to Art. 25 of the Company Law and checked by the AICs.
	One-person LLC	One	The same as above	100,000 RMB. The threshold may be set higher by other laws and administrative regulations	The same as above	Contributions must be paid off in a lump sum.	The same as above

31 *Ibid.*, Art. 82.

32 Mi 2008, p. 19.

33 中华人民共和国公司登记管理条例（2005年修订）第10条.

34 Li 2006, p. 38.

	Solely state-funded LLC	One	It should be the Chinese state. The SASAC and its local institutions perform the functions of initiators	The same as above	The same as above	The same as LLC (except one-person and solely State-funded LLCs)	It must be drafted by the SASAC or by its board of directors and approved by the SASAC
JSLC	JSLC estab-lished by promotio n	Not less than 2 but not more than 200	The same as LLC (except one-person and solely State-funded LLCs)	5,000,000 RMB. The threshold may be set higher by other laws and administra-tive regulations	The same as above	The same as LLC (except one-person and solely State-funded LLCs)	It must be formulated according to Art. 82 of the Company Law and checked by the AICs.
	JSLC estab-lished by stock floatation	The same as above	The same as LLC (except one-person and solely State-funded LLCs)	The same as above	The same as above	Contri-butions must be paid off in a lump sum.	The same as above

2.4. *Procedural Requirements*

After satisfying capital, initiators and articles of association requirements, there are still formalities necessary for a valid establishment. The World Bank Group (2008) lists 14 steps that a LLC must go through before it can be incorporated in China.[35] This section adopts this model. However, this section only focuses on the provision of acquiring a notice of pre-approval of the company name and applying for establishment registration for their significance and complexities; other steps for incorporation will only be introduced from a more general perspective.

2.4.1. Steps to Incorporate a LLC

The World Bank Group (2008) notes that 14 steps to incorporate a LLC include pre-registering a company name, opening a preliminary bank account, verifying paid-in

[35] The World Bank Group 2008, p. 10.

capital with an auditing firm, registering with the local AIC, obtaining approval to make a company seal, making the company seal, obtaining an organization code certificate, registering with the local statistics bureau, registering with state and local tax bureaus, opening an official company bank account, getting approval for purchasing receipts and invoices, purchasing receipts and invoices, registering with a local labour center and registering with a local social security center.[36]

2.4.2. Acquiring a Notice of Pre-approval of the Company Name

All Chinese Companies should apply for prior approval of the company name in accordance with the Measures for the Implementation of Administration of Enterprise Name Registration, the Provisions for Administration of Enterprise Name Registration and the Regulation of the Administration of Company Registration. If the establishment of a company needs to be examined and approved or its business scope includes any field subject to examinations and approvals stipulated by laws and administrative regulations, applications for the company name pre-approval must be made before such examinations and approvals.[37] For these applications, the following documents should be submitted: an application for the prior approval of the name of the company, the certificate of the entrustment of agency or the designation of representatives by all shareholders and any other document as required by the AICs.[38] All shareholders must sign and seal the completed applications with the information required.[39] The provisions must be conformed to when filling in the information. Moreover, a LLC must indicate the words 'limited liability company' or 'limited company' and a JSLC must indicate 'joint stock limited company' or 'joint stock company' in their company names respectively.[40] These forms should be submitted to the AICs by the agents entrusted by all investors, partners, and collaborators or the representatives designated by them.[41] The agents can use mail, email, fax etc. or go directly to the AICs.[42]

2.4.3. Applying for Establishment Registration

For the establishment of a company, the most important step is to file an application for establishment registration. In China, a company can obtain its business license after it first makes the establishment registration application and, second, relevant authorities accept it.[43] After obtaining this license, it is legally set up. In this

36 *Ibid.*

37 企业名称登记管理实施办法(2004修订)第22条， Art. 22 of the Measures for the Implementation of Administration of Enterprise Name Registration (Revised 2004).

38 公司登记管理条例（2005修订）第17条， Art. 17 of the RACR (2005).

39 *Ibid.*, Art. 23.

40 Art. 8 of the Company Law (2005).

41 Art. 23 of the Measures for the Implementation of Administration of Enterprise Name Registration (Revised 2004).

42 *Ibid.*, Art. 24.

43 Art. 7 of the Company Law (2005); Art. 3 of the RACR (Revised 2005).

procedure, administrative agencies play a significant role in deciding whether to approve this application. Therefore the following section will introduce the rules on how a company can finish this application and then present the situation on how administrative authorities exercise their power of approval.

2.4.3.1. Rules on How to Fulfil Establishment Registration

As is provided in the Regulation on the Administration of Company Registration, to acquire a business license for a LLC, these items need to be registered: name, business scope, registered capital and residence of the company, name of the legal representative, type of enterprise, term of operation and names of the shareholders of a LLC as well as the amount, time and form of contributions as subscribed and actually paid.[44] A LLC should submit the following list of files: the application form for establishment signed by the legal representative of the LLC, the document certifying the representation authorization or the entrusted agency relations, articles of association, the certificate of capital verification prepared by a verification organization, the files certifying the transfer of the property title of non-monetary properties if the initial capital contribution is made in such properties, the identity cards of natural person shareholders and the identity documents of other shareholders, the certificate for the commission, appointment and election of the directors, supervisors and managers with their names and addresses specified, the appointment documents and the identity certificates for the legal representative of the LLC, the notice for the prior approval of the company's name, the proof of the company's residence and other documents as requested by the AICs.[45] It is necessary to go through an approval process and obtain approval documents before applying for the establishment registration if the establishment of a company is subject to an approval stipulated by any law, regulation or the decisions of the State Council.[46] On its website, the SAIC clarifies the notion of other documents. The submission for the relevant files of approvals or the copies of licenses is requested if the aforementioned legislation stipulates that the establishment of a one-person limited liability company should be approved. It is also mandatory to submit the relevant documents of approval or the copies of licenses or the certificates of permission when the business scope of companies for registration application includes the items subject to approval before registration in accordance with laws, administrative regulations and the State Council decisions.[47]

Compared to LLCs, JVCs must also go through the same company registration procedures for their establishment with only a few differences with regard to the documents requested. First, in the case that a JVC is set up by stock floatation making public stock offers, it must provide the approval documents issued by the

44 Art. 9 of the RACR (Revised 2005).

45 *Ibid.*, Art. 20.

46 Art. 9 of the RACR (Revised 2005) and Art. 6 of the Company Law (2005).

47 国家工商行政管理总局，公司设立登记说明, the SAIC, Explanation of the Registration for the Establishment of Companies, available at: <www.saic.gov.cn/zwgk/xzxk/qyhzdj/> (last accessed 6 April 2016).

China Securities Regulatory Commission (CSRC) to the AICs. Second, when laws, administrative regulations and the State Council decisions stipulate that the establishment of a JVC is subject to approval, the submission of the relevant approval files or the copies of license is necessary. Third, the identity documents of initiators or their identity cards in the circumstances that they are natural persons must be submitted.[48]

Among all the items needed to be registered, the business scope is relatively important. Scopes of business are composed of licensed operations and general operations.[49] Authorities impose more control over licensed operations. To obtain approval is a necessity if a company's business scope covers any field subject to approval in accordance with laws and regulations.[50] AICs can refuse to register the licensed operations of a company, unless relevant examination and approval authorities allow its licensed operations first. AICs also register restrictions on the operating period of licensed operations if the relevant authorities impose such limits. The company may conduct business within the operating period.[51] Articles 4, 6 and 9 of the Investigating, Handling and Banning Unlicensed Business Operations Procedures (2003) provide legal consequences concerning companies' engagement in licensed operations with no approval.[52] Regarding the general operations registrations, companies can make direct applications to AICs in accordance with the regulation.[53]

The above analysis finds that a company may need to obtain licenses before the business can apply for establishment registration. They consist of the licenses for public stock offers made by a JVC launched by stock floatation, for licensed operations, and for the establishment of certain types of companies. A licensing regime has also been established for the establishment registration of companies by the SAIC.[54]

The following sections (from 2.4.3.2 to 2.4.3.4) elaborate on how most of these licenses are regulated.[55] The only exception is the licensing regime for public stock offers made by a JVC launched by stock floatation. Moreover, section 2.4.3.5 interprets the remedies for businesses if their reasonable application for these licenses is refused.

48 *Ibid.*

49 企业经营范围登记管理规定（2004）第4条，Art. 4 of the Administration of Registration of the Scope of Business of Enterprises (2004).

50 Art. 12 of the Company Law (2005).

51 Art. 5 of the Administration of Registration of the Scope of Business of Enterprises (2004).

52 无照经营查处取缔办法(2003). Measures for Investigating, Punishing and Banning Unlicensed Business Operations (2003).

53 Art. 6 of the Administration of Registration of the Scope of Business of Enterprises (2004).

54 国家工商行政管理总局，公司设立登记说明, the SAIC, Explanation on the Registration for the Establishment of Companies, available at: <www.saic.gov.cn/zwgk/xzxk/qyhzdj/> (last accessed 6 April 2016).

55 As demonstrated by Chinese scholars, the distinction between the concepts of administrative approval and an administrative license is very complicated in China. However, the ALL adopts the approach that they in fact mean the same thing. Thus administrative license in this thesis also refers to administrative approval. See Wang 2007, p. 60 and 61.

The licensing system for the public stock offers is excluded from this discussion due to the lack of relevant rules in this regard. Information is only available about what documents are required for this licensing item and what agencies are empowered to grant licenses. Article 12 of the Securities Law (2005) lists the necessary files.[56] Moreover, the Department of Unlisted Public Company Supervision under the China Securities Regulatory Commission is authorized to approve the application for establishing a company limited by shares in the way of public offering.

As shown in a blog by Mr. Jiao, a Chinese lawyer, these public stock offers have rarely been used in practice. This may be because implementing regulations concerning these offers have not been made.[57] Interviews with some Chinese lawyers confirmed this.[58]

2.4.3.2. Obtaining Approval for the Establishment of a Company

It is mandatory to go through an approval process and obtain relevant documents before applying for the establishment registration if the establishment of a company needs to be approved according to any law, regulation or the decision of the State Council.[59] Usually, this occurs when establishing a company in industries relating to national safety, public interest and other vital interests that are governed by the competent authorities for these businesses. Moreover, one explanation from the SAIC states that the submission of the relevant documents of approval or the copies of license are requested if laws, administrative regulations and the State Council decisions stipulate that the establishment of a one-person limited liability company is subject to approval.[60]

56 The application for share offer and the following documents must be submitted to the securities regulatory authority under the State Council: (1) The articles of association of the company; (2) The sponsors' agreement; (3) The names or title of the sponsors, the number of shares subscribed for by the sponsors, the forms of capital contributions and the capital verification certificate; (4) The prospectus; (5) The names and addresses of the banks accepting subscription money on behalf of the company; and (6) The names of the underwriting agencies and related agreements. Where a sponsor is engaged in accordance with the provisions of this Law, the letter of sponsorship issued by the sponsor must also be submitted. Where the incorporation of the company must be reported for approval in accordance with the provisions of laws or administrative regulations, the relevant approval document must also be submitted. (The English text of the Securities Law is available at: <www.accaglobal.com/content/dam/acca/global/pdf/ChinaSecuritiesLaw2006.pdf> (last accessed 6 April 2016).

57 Available at: <http://blog.sina.com.cn/s/blog_4920711101011lek.html> (last accessed 6 April 2016).

58 Chapter 6 will provide an analysis of interviews on the formation of companies across provinces in China.

59 Arts. 20 and 21 of the RARC (Revised 2004) and Art. 6 of the Company Law (2005).

60 国家工商行政管理总局，公司设立登记说明, the SAIC, Explanation of the Registration for the Establishment of Companies, available at: <www.saic.gov.cn/zwgk/xzxk/qyhzdj/> (last accessed 6 April 2016).

However, it is not clear at which government agency a specific category of company should apply for a license. Businesses are only informed that these approvals are controlled by the competent authorities for certain industries, either at central level or at local level. Therefore, some scholars try to identify what types of licenses are required for what types of companies at academic level. In 2006, Ping Jiang and Guoguang Li summarized 110 categories of the approvals for establishment. They found that the allocation of authority for the approvals may be decided by the importance of a specific license or the geographic scope of the potential company's business. For example, the State Food and Drug Administration (SFDA) governs the licensing for the establishment of companies making dietary supplements; by contrast, local relevant authorities control the licensing for the setting up of those manufacturing veterinary medicine. Moreover, the State Electricity Regulatory Commission (SERC) approves the establishment of companies supplying power across regions; in contrast, the approval for the setting up of other power supply enterprises is governed by local authorities.[61]

Moreover, at policy level, attempts have been made to identify the number of licenses required for the establishment of companies and what types of corporations are subject to these licenses in practice. Article 88 of the Regulations on the Administration of Company Registration (Amended 2005) (the RARC) prescribes a relevant responsibility for the SAIC. Where it is prescribed by any law, administrative regulation, or the decisions of the State Council that the establishment of a company should be reported for approvals or where any item within the business scope of a company should be approved before the registration of the company, the SAIC will formulate and publicize the Catalogue of Pre-administrative License for the Registration of a Company according to the same rules.[62] The Catalogue of Pre-administrative License for the Registration of a Company can provide information on how many categories of companies are required to apply for pre-administrative licenses. Pre-administrative licenses seemingly refer to the licenses that applicants must obtain before they can apply for other licenses. In the context of the establishment for companies, this term means the license to approve the establishment of a company and the license for licensed operations that businesses should obtain prior to making applications for the establishment registration. It should be noted that pre-administrative licenses used in Chinese law are not another kind of license. They are licenses regulated by the Administrative License Law (ALL). If applications for pre-administrative licenses are denied, remedies that will be discussed in section 2.3.4.5 have to be used against each pre-administrative license. Apparently, this catalogue made by the SAIC turns out to be more authoritative than the summary made by Jiang and Li (2006) in the preceding paragraph.

However, the SAIC has not yet finished this catalogue. In 2004, it created the 2004 Catalogue of Pre-administrative License for the Registration of a Company to

61 Jiang & Li 2006, p. 24, 27 and 31.

62 The translation of the RARC's provisions in this chapter largely relies on the English version, available at: <http://tradeinservices.mofcom.gov.cn/en/b/2005-12-18/17120.shtml> (last accessed 6 April 2016).

facilitate the implementation of the ALL (the 2004 Catalogue). The civil servants of the AICs administrating the registration at local levels could refer to the 2004 Catalogue, but it was not publicized as an official document. In 2006, the SAIC wrote a new draft of the Catalogue of Pre-administrative License for the Registration of a Company for discussion purposes. However, no final document was formulated. These files also provide different levels and different agencies for the approvals of the establishment of companies as the summary made by Jiang and Li. Zhaohui Huang (2010) notes that the license items in the 2004 Catalogue do not meet the requirements provided by current legislation. Some laws and regulations as the legal basis for these items have been amended or abolished. Moreover, some governmental departments governing these licenses have been merged and some agencies do not exist any longer. The catalogue which was subsequently formulated in 2006 does not have enough authority and also shares the same problem as the 2004 Catalogue.[63] In Zhou's opinion, no legal documents can show how many licensing items are pre-administrative licenses for companies.[64] This may deter the establishment of companies if the range for pre-administrative licenses is wrongfully enlarged. Moreover, as Zhou points out, many items of administrative licenses lack implementation procedures. That is why an official at the enterprises registration branch of the SAIC has asked for an instant improvement.[65]

2.4.3.3. *The Approval for Licensed Operations*

It is not clear exactly for which business activities a company is required to apply for a license. The scope of licensed operations is decided in accordance with the ALL since this law provides what matters are subject to licensing. This section discusses for what matters license systems can be established and who can exercise this licensing power. Moreover, it introduces a mechanism that can decrease the types of activities for which licensing regimes can be created.

First, one needs to consider Articles 12 and 13 of the ALL to know for what matters licensing systems can be set up. Article 12 of this law prescribes for which matters licensing may be required. These relate to: '(1) the special activities that directly bear on state security, public security, macro-economic control, ecological environment protection, and those directly related to the human health, safety of life and property, which must be approved according to the legal requirements; (2) the development and utilization of limited natural resources, allocation of public resources and the market entry of the special trades that directly concern public interest, which need to be entitled with special rights; (3) the vocations and trades that provide public services and directly relate to the public interest, which requires a high reputation, special conditions or skills; (4) the important equipment, facilities, products, articles that directly concern public security, human health, the safety of life and property, which must be examined and approved by means of inspection,

63 Huang 2010, p. 52.

64 Zhou 2010, p. 39.

65 *Ibid.*

testing, and quarantining according to the technical standards or criteria; (5) the establishment of enterprises or other institutions, which need to address the question of their capacity to be a subject of law; (6) other matters, for which administrative licenses may be established in accordance with the laws and regulations.'[66]

However, according to Article 13 of the ALL, administrative licenses may not be established for the activities in Article 12, if '(1) citizens, legal persons or other institutions can decide upon them by themselves, or (2) the market competition mechanism can regulate them effectively, or (3) trade organizations or intermediary institutions can regulate them by themselves, or (4) administrative organs can govern them through ex post regulatory controls or by other administrative methods'.

As Yuan Li notes, the two articles aim to reduce the types of administrative licenses. Even for the license regimes that may be established, government agencies are still encouraged to avoid the creation of administrative licenses.[67]

Articles 12 and 13 of the ALL do not provide a clear definition for what matters licensing regimes can be established. If one reads Article 12 in Chinese, it seems the Chinese authorities can establish licensing regimes for almost every matter as they would like. The following section interprets the two provisions individually.

According to Qing Zhang, the scope of Article 12 of the ALL permits a certain extent of discretion for the Chinese lawmakers to apply administrative licenses. He remarks that the activities in Item (1) of Article 12 could create large externalities, which can hardly be internalized. A case in point is the activities that can affect public security. Moreover, some of the matters in this item can cause irreparable damage, e.g., the activities that could harm human health or life.[68] Despite Zhang's remarks, it is still difficult to define the activities in Item (1). As Yafeng Zu argues, national security and other legal concepts in this catalogue are unclear and inconsistent. They need to be considered and defined specifically in each legislative, administrative and judicial procedure for certain licenses. It is not possible to determine from the ALL what matters could be included in these definitions. Zu

66 The translation of the ALL in this chapter is mostly based on the English version of this law available at: <www.fdi.gov.cn/pub/FDI_EN/Laws/GeneralLawsandRegulations/-BasicLaws/P020060620319981258285.pdf> (last accessed 6 April 2016). It should be pointed out that the official translation of Art. 12(5) is 'the establishment of the enterprises or other institutions, which needs to determine a subject qualification' (企业或其他组织的设立等，需要确定主体资格的事项). In other cases, some terms have been changed.

67 Li 2003, p. 92.

68 Zhang 2008a, p. 109. Externalities are effects of economic activities that can influence the manufacturing conditions or third parties' utility level. Moreover, such influence comes into existence outside the market. Externalities are one type of market failures. Market failures arise where the market, as a basic way to allocate resources in an economy, does not always function well due to the lack of certain conditions. In case of these failures, regulations can be used to advance the efficiency of allocation. This is the public interest approach of regulation (Den Hertog 2003, p. 9, 13 and 15).

cannot find them by referring to available judicial cases either.[69] Duanhong Chen also holds that all the matters in Item (1) are some examples of public interest and their definitions are not consistent. They can only be defined in the context of legislation, administration and the administration of justice.[70] In practice, the interpretation on the National People's Congress (NPC) website for the ALL provides examples for this item. For instance, this explanation lists the restriction on goods exports for national security as a matter in Item (1).[71]

Item (2), in Zhang's opinion, means government franchising, a particular type of administrative license. With an aim to optimize the use of resources, this license is usually used to impose quantitative restrictions and create substantive requirements for the suppliers engaging in the matters of this item.[72] Kewen Wang agrees that Item (2) means government franchising. The nature of this franchising is to sell the right of property owned by the Chinese state and to entitle individuals, companies etc. with these rights. This characteristic distinguishes government franchising from licensing systems that can be created for the matters in Item (1) and (3) to (6) of Article 12. With regard to the terms used in Item (2), he thinks that only 'the development and utilization of limited natural resources' can be relatively easily defined and he cannot give definite meanings for other phrases in this item. Considering that the ALL does not give definitions for the other terms, he argues that it is very hard to use Item (2) precisely. For example, it is not sure whether Item (2) shall be applied to license plate numbers in practice. Some local authorities such as the Shanghai government consider license plate numbers as public resources in Item (2); in contrast, other cities do not regard them as such resources.[73]

The activities in Item (3), as Zhang argues, refer to professional services. According to him, in unregulated markets, such services may create the problems of externalities and information asymmetry.[74] Here he implicitly points out that because of externalities and information asymmetry; it is justifiable to establish a licensing regime for the matters listed in Item (3).[75]

69 祖亚锋，行政许可的规范分析，Yafeng Zu, Norm Analysis of Administrative Licenses, available at: <http://article.chinalawinfo.com/Article_Detail.asp?ArticleId=32470> (last accessed 6 April 2016).

70 Chen 2004, p. 33.

71 中国人大网，法律问答与释义，Questions, Answers and Explanations of Laws, available at: <www.npc.gov.cn/npc/flsyywd/xingzheng/2004-10/26/content_337759.htm#> (last accessed 6 April 2016).

72 Zhang 2008a, p. 109.

73 Wang 2011, p. 84, 86 and 87.

74 Zhang 2008a, p. 109.

75 Of course, the view is widely accepted that licenses are a possible remedy to deal with externalities. As summarised from the law and economics literature by Niels Philipsen, licensing is used to remedy market failures e.g. information asymmetry and negative externalities when it can improve the quality of service (see Philipsen 2011, p. 205). Negative externalities refer to the costs of market transactions that affect other parties except those involved in the transaction. A primary example of negative externalities is air pollution (Ulen & Cooter 2011, p. 39). Information asymmetry can be caused by the offer of professional services. Specifically, these service receivers usually do not know the information of these services, while lawyers or doctors own relevant knowledge (Philipsen 2003, p. 15).

Zhang's remarks can be further specified. Professional services are generally experience goods or even trust goods, such as the services provided by lawyers, doctors or accountants. In addition, their qualities usually cannot be assessed by clients. Therefore, information asymmetry and externalities may appear. As a result, these providers are asked to have a good reputation and special skills to deal with these problems.[76]

Following the above argument, Zhang explains the reasons for creating a licensing system for the facilities, products and equipment in Item (4). He states that the articles in this item may create large externalities and cause irreparable damage when those facilities, products and equipment are directly linked to public security and human health.[77]

With regard to the matter in Item (5), Qing Zhang disagrees with establishing a licensing system for the establishment of companies. Instead, he prefers using registration to govern the mentioned establishment rather than licensing. According to Zhang, the administration for the establishment of companies is not intended for solving the problem of market failure. This administration is designed to collect relevant information for governments, so the authorities can reduce the administrative costs created by taxing or other supervision methods. The aim in the last sentence could be achieved through registration with relatively low cost. This is because, as he mentions, registration does not ask government officials to evaluate whether a potential company can conduct certain activities or can do business in a certain field. Neither does it require this company to satisfy many criteria. He further remarks that even if the Chinese government may need to use licensing sometimes to tackle the problem of market failure, licensing still cannot be utilized to govern the establishment of companies.[78] Here it should be pointed out that his concept of registration is different from the establishment registration for companies that is governed by the SAIC and its local agencies. From his text, one could conclude that the registration mentioned by him means the recording of relevant information for the establishment of a company by officials. In reality, the SAIC establishes a licensing system for the establishment registration of companies. This licensing regime is called registration in China.

Article 12(6) seems to leave open the possibility of creating licensing systems for almost everything. When remarking on this item, the interpretation of the NPC website admits that the provision of other matters makes the indefinite scope more confused.[79] Zhang also expresses his concern that this item could make the provision of the first five items meaningless. Licensing regimes could still be

76 The concept of experience goods is introduced by Nelson. Experience goods are such products whose qualities cannot be judged by consumers before purchasing (Nelson 1970, p. 312). Trust goods have the characteristics that it is hard for purchasers to make a judgment about their qualities even after purchasing or using. This is because such evaluating asks for certain expertise (Darby & Karni 1973, p. 68 and 69).

77 Zhang 2008a, p. 109.

78 *Ibid.*

79 中国人大网，法律问答与释义, Questions, Answers and Explanations of Laws, available at: <www.npc.gov.cn/npc/flsyywd/xingzheng/2004-10/26/content_337759.htm#> (last accessed 6 April 2016).

established for other matters as well as the activities of Items (1) to (5). As he further argues, this may be because the lawmakers of the ALL worry that the five items cannot cover all the matters needing licensing. Another possible reason is that the legislators want to reserve more power for themselves.[80]

Summarising the comments by Zhang and other scholars on Article 12, it is not clear for what matters licensing systems can be created. The following part continues to discuss Article 13. Then it should be clear for what matters licensing regimes are not necessary.

It seems that Article 13(1) prefers self-regulation to licensing. The interpretation of the ALL on the website of the NPC does not provide a clear definition for Item (1) of Article 13 and only gives some examples. This explanation notes that it is not necessary to create a licensing regime for the employment of nurses by individuals according to Item 1. This activity is a matter that can be decided upon by individuals.[81] Qing Zhang remarks that Item (1) is ambiguous and unnecessary. This is because from a legal perspective, all activities can be determined by individuals, legal persons or other organizations, unless it is otherwise provided by laws or regulations (e.g., legislation requiring administrative licenses). As he suggests, maybe the Chinese legislator wants to apply Article 13(1) only when natural persons and legal persons can make the best decision. According to these lawmakers, citizens etc. with the necessary information can make optimal choices only in some cases. Based on his understanding, he proposes a more clear expression: 'citizens, legal persons or other institutions can make better decisions than governments'.[82]

Item (2) of Article 13, in Niels Philipsen's view, refers to competition being preferable to public regulation. As shown by the ALL provision itself, it seems at least in writing, the Chinese legislator takes the market as a primary solution to many problems. The importance attached to the market mechanism can to some extent also to be found in the 2008 Anti-Monopoly Law (AML).[83] As argued by Qing Zhang, Article 13(2) seems to show that market mechanisms and self-regulation are to be preferred over administrative licenses. However, he remarks that, before making this provision, the lawmakers need to identify the situation in which self-regulation should be chosen rather than licensing. The preference of administrative licenses over self-regulation is justifiable only in cases where the legislators can achieve the objectives of supervision more easily through self-regulation rather than by using administrative licenses. Therefore, he struggles to understand why Article 13(2) chooses self-regulation as the only alternative and without any justification.[84]

80 Zhang 2008a, p. 109.

81 中国人大网，法律问答与释义, the Website of the NPC, Questions, Answers and Explanations of Laws, available at: <www.npc.gov.cn/npc/flsyywd/xingzheng/2004-10/26/-content_337759.htm#> (last accessed 6 April 2016).

82 Zhang 2008a, p. 109.

83 Philipsen 2010, p. 217. The Chinese name for the 2008 Anti-Monopoly Law (AML) is 反垄断法（2008).

84 Zhang 2008a, p. 109.

Philipsen takes Item (3) as a rule that self-regulation by professional associations is preferable to public regulation. But this preference is not reasonable in circumstances where interest groups seek rents by affecting political decisions. This rent-seeking behaviour usually prohibits the achieving of social welfare.[85] Thus the legislator of the ALL still needs to clarify the context where the choosing of self-regulation is justifiable.

In both the opinion of Philipsen and Zhang, the preference for ex post measures over licensing in Item (4) cannot be fully proven by the fact that ex post supervision measures could provide an effective solution to the problem discussed by this item. As Philipsen suggests, the social and administrative costs for regulation should be considered. As a result, the optimal regulatory method can be chosen. This is because this regulatory instrument should be the least interventionist regulatory method that requires regulation to be both justifiable and proportionate. Article 13(4) turns out to be unclear without mentioning this cost.[86] According to Zhang, another reason to choose ex post measures is that this measure has more advantages than administrative licenses, besides the provision of an effective method prescribed in Item (4). If ex post measures can lead to more social costs than licensing, licensing should not be abandoned. Moreover, Zhang recognizes the value of ex post non-regulatory measures such as private law remedies, besides ex post regulatory controls. He proposes a more precise wording for Item (4): '(administrative organs) can govern (the aforementioned activities and products) better through ex post regulatory controls or ex post non-regulatory measures'.[87]

Although there are many discussions on Article 13, the meaning of this article is not very clear. As demonstrated by Shilin Li, because it is hard to define the matters in the first three items in Article 13, the legal value of this provision is doubtful.[88]

Moreover, there is widespread criticism about the usage of 'may be' in Articles 12 and 13, except the interpretation of the items in these two provisions. Wei Liu notes that the term 'may be' in Article 12 of the ALL grants authorities the power to decide whether licenses for the items of this provision need to be set up. Therefore, the establishment of these licensing regimes is left to their discretion, which does not relate to the provision made by national law and administrative regulations. Considering 'may be' is also used in Article 13 of this law, he holds that it is not clear for which items licenses should in fact be established according to regulations. Thus, he is not sure whether the ALL aims to set its limits on items that can be governed by licensing or loosens the control over licensing.[89] Concluded by the interpretation on the NPC website, the usage of 'may be' in Article 13 of the ALL indicates that legislators are still finding ways to set the scope for establishing

85 Philipsen 2010, p. 207 and 217.
86 *Ibid.*, p. 218.
87 Zhang 2008, p. 109.
88 Li 2008, p. 69.
89 Liu 2006, p. 88.

administrative licenses. It also shows that the current provision is flexible, which asks for improvement through a combined use with specific legislation.[90]

Even after analysing Articles 12 and 13 carefully and reading the academics' interpretation, it is not completely clear for what items licensing systems can be created. Most noticeably, Article 12(6) seems to allow administrative agencies to extend licensing regimes to almost every matter, which can undermine other items in this provision.

In addition, the vagueness of some concepts in Articles 12 and 13, in Shoulong Mao's opinion, permits administrative agencies at both national and local levels high discretion in interpreting the two articles. This can cause conflicts in practice and make these rules ineffective.[91] Moreover, because of the use of 'may be' in these two provisions, the question of for what matters licensing is necessary, turns out to be vaguer if Articles 12 and 13 are read together.

Second, the ALL prescribes which authorities have the power to set up licensing regimes for the activities provided by Articles 12 and 13. At state level, according to Article 14(1) of the ALL, the NPC and its Standing Committee have the authority to create administrative licenses by means of laws. Where laws are not passed, the State Council can establish administrative licenses by means of administrative regulations. Moreover, Article 14(2) reads that 'where necessary, the State Council may establish administrative licenses by adapting the way of releasing decisions. After their implementation, except for the matters under temporary administrative licenses, the State Council shall prepare a timely proposal for the NPC and its Standing Committee to make laws or make administrative regulations by itself.'

'Where necessary' here means that for the governance of certain activities licensing regimes will be established, but there is no time to create these systems by means of laws and administrative regulations, according to the explanation given on the NPC website.[92]

At local levels, provided by the first part in Article 15(1) of the ALL, the People's Congress and its Standing Committee at provincial level and the People's Congress and its Standing Committee of relatively large cities may create administrative licenses by making local regulations for the activities in Article 12.[93] By relatively large cities is meant those cities where the governments of provinces

90 中国人大网，法律问答与释义，the Website of the NPC, Questions, Answers and Explanations of Laws, available at: <www.npc.gov.cn/npc/flsyywd/xingzheng/2004-10/26/content_337759.htm#> (last accessed 6 April 2016).

91 《中国经济周刊》毛寿龙：行政许可法的缺憾——中国人民大学行政管理学系主任毛寿龙教授, China Economic Weekly, Soulong Mao: the Defects of the ALL-an Interview with Prof. Mao, the Head of Administrative Management Department of Renmin University of China, available at: <http://theory.people.com.cn/GB/40764/55938/55941/3939671.html> (last accessed 6 April 2016).

92 中国人大网，法律问答与释义，Questions, Answers and Explanations of Laws, available at: <www.npc.gov.cn/npc/flsyywd/xingzheng/2004-10/26/content_337759.htm#> (last accessed 6 April 2016).

93 Provinces, autonomous regions and direct-controlled municipalities are all provincial regions in China.

and autonomous regions are located, cities where special economic zones are situated and any other relatively large cities approved by the State Council.[94] The pre-condition for the above creation of licensing systems is that the NPC, its Standing Committee and the State Council have not established licensing systems for the mentioned matters by means of laws and administrative regulations.

The second part in Article 15(1) of the ALL regulates the situation that the NPC and its Standing Committee, the State Council, the People's Congress and its Standing Committee at provincial level and the People's Congress and its Standing Committee of relatively large cities have not created licensing regimes for the activities in Article 12 of the ALL. In this context, if it is essential to establish an administrative license immediately for the need to conduct administrative management for these activities, the governments at provincial level may establish temporary administrative licenses by passing government rules. Temporary administrative licenses can only be implemented for one year. After this period, if it is still imperative to establish a licensing regime for these activities, a proposal will be sent to the People's Congress and its Standing Committee at the same level. The People's Congress and its Standing Committee at provincial level then consider whether a licensing system should be created for these activities by making local regulations. In the opinion of the legislators of the ALL, the exercise of licensing power by the governments at provincial level is necessary because of the major differences among different provinces and the new problems arising in different regions.[95]

In short, Article 15(1) of the ALL states that the People's Congress and its Standing Committee at provincial level, the People's Congress and its Standing Committee of relatively large cities and the governments at provincial level can establish licensing regimes under the conditions discussed above. However, their licensing power is limited by Article 15(2) of the same law.

The first section of Item (2) in Article 15 confirms for what matters administrative licenses cannot be established by the local authorities in the last paragraph. The matters include 'the qualifications of the citizens, legal persons or other institutions that shall be determined by state'. Moreover, the local authorities shall not 'establish administrative licenses and pre-administrative licenses for the establishment and registration of enterprises or other institutions'. Pre-administrative licenses, as discussed previously to interpret the Catalogue of Pre-administrative License for the Registration of a Company, means the licenses for the establishment of a company and the license for licensed operations. They are governed by the ALL. Registration is a licensing system created by the SAIC, as demonstrated in the previous part where Article 12 of the ALL is explained.

94 According to Art. 63 of the Legislation law (2000) (立法法) (2000), relatively large cities mean cities where the governments of provinces and autonomous regions are located, cities where special economic zones are situated and any other relatively large cities approved by the State Council.

95 中国人大网，法律问答与释义, Questions, Answers and Explanations of Laws, available at: <www.npc.gov.cn/npc/flsyywd/xingzheng/2004-10/26/content_337759.htm#> (last accessed 6 April 2016).

Furthermore, as noted by the second section of Item (2), the administrative licenses established by the local authorities 'shall not hinder the individuals or enterprises of other regions from dealing in production and business and providing services in one region, and shall not restrict the commodities of other regions from entering into the market of the local regions.'

In summary, Article 15(1) of the ALL defines that some local authorities can establish licensing regimes for the matters in Article 12, where other authorities provided by the item (1) have not established such regimes. However, the local organizations can set up regional blockades through the licensing, as Aiping Gu argues. Thus, Article 15(2) of the same law has been made to prevent interference by local authorities in the development of China's unified market.[96]

No authorities can require administrative licenses besides those agencies mentioned above in Articles 14 and 15. According to Article 17 of the ALL, no administrative license shall be set in any other regulatory document except for the provisions of Articles 14 and 15.

Third, it is possible to reduce the number of matters for which licensing regimes can be established. Article 20(1) of the ALL states that 'the establishment authority of administrative licenses shall periodically evaluate the administrative licenses it sets. If it considers that an already established administrative license can be solved through any of the methods listed in Article 13 of the same law, it shall modify the provision for the establishment of the administrative license or abolish it in time.' Here readers should be reminded that the methods in Article 13 refer to self-regulation, market mechanisms and those ex post measures discussed preciously, whose meanings are unclear. According to the explanation provided on the NPC website, Article 20(1) regulates the licensing regimes that have been established by licensing authorities.[97] An example of the licensing systems subject to Article 20(1) is provided here. As already mentioned, the SCRC establishes a licensing regime for the establishment of subsidiaries by securities companies. In accordance with Article 20(1), the SCRC can replace this licensing system with self-regulation. That means securities companies are allowed to decide whether or not to establish a subsidiary by themselves in the future after this replacement.

According to Article 21 of the ALL, 'where based on the economic and social development of its administrative area, a government at provincial level considers a license on economic affairs established by administrative regulations can be solved through the methods in Article 13, it may stop implementing it within its area upon reporting to and obtaining the approval of the State Council'. The NPC stresses four points in this article: the licensing systems in Article 21 are the licensing regimes (1) that are already created by the State Council and (2) that are only governing economic affairs; (3) only a provincial government can submit the report and (4) the condition to use this article is that the methods in Article 13 can replace the

96 Gu 2006, p. 23.

97 中国人大网，法律问答与释义, Questions, Answers and Explanations of Laws, available at: <www.npc.gov.cn/npc/flsyywd/xingzheng/2004-10/26/content_337759.htm#> (last accessed 6 April 2016).

licensing systems.[98] The replacement by Article 13 means that for the activities for which licensing systems have already been established, in the future, individuals, companies etc. no longer need licenses and the criteria provided for by Article 13 such as self-regulation apply.

In Yuan Li's opinion, Articles 20(1) and 21 of the ALL can make licensing systems established according to the ALL adapt to new changes in practice. It can downsize the Chinese administrative licensing system in accordance with the present situation.[99]

The three issues discussed in this section turn out to be complicated to businesses. Therefore, it should be mentioned that the Catalogue of Pre-administrative Licenses for the Registration of a Company has to be drafted by the SAIC. From this document, companies can see the number and types of licensed operations in practice. In other words, the document can show for what activities licensed operations are required.

2.4.3.4. The Establishment Registration of Companies

For the establishment registration of companies, an administrative license has been established by the SAIC according to the ALL, the Company Law and the RACR.[100] Article 12(5) of the ALL states that an administrative license may be created for the establishment of the enterprises or other institutions, that needs to determine a subject qualification. Article 6 of the Company Law and Article 3 of the RACR provide that the establishment of a company shall be subject to establishment registration.

Chapter two of the RACR prescribes the jurisdictions of the AICs at different levels over the establishment registration of companies. At national level, according to Article 6 of this regulation, the SAIC should take charge of the registration of the following companies: (1) a company, for which the SASAC of the State Council performs the functions and duties of a capital contributor, as well as a company, which is established by the investment of the aforesaid corporation that holds more than 50 per cent shares therein; (2) a foreign-funded company; (3) a company subject to the registration of the SAIC according to relevant laws, administrative regulations, or decisions of the State Council; and (4) any others that are requested to be registered by the SAIC according to the provisions of the SAIC.

According to Article 7 of the RARC, the AIC at the level of province should take charge of the registration of the following corporations within the administrative jurisdiction of these authorities: (1) a company, for which the provincial SASAC undertakes the functions and obligations of a capital contributor, and a company, which is set up by the investment of the aforementioned one that owns more than 50 per cent shares therein; (2) a company established by the

98 *Ibid.*

99 Li 2003, p. 92.

100 国家工商行政管理总局，公司设立登记说明， the SAIC, Explanation on the Registration for the Establishment of Companies, available at: <www.saic.gov.cn/zwgk/xzxk/qyhzdj/> (last accessed 6 April 2016).

investment of a natural person that is subject to the registration of the AIC at the level of province; (3) a company that is required to be registered by the AIC at the level of province according to relevant laws, administrative regulations, and decisions of the State Council; and (4) any others subject to the registration of the AIC at the level of province as authorized by the SAIC.

Article 8 of the RARC regulates the AIC of a city (region) divided into districts, the sub-administration of the mentioned AIC at the level of district, the AIC of a county and the sub-administration of the AIC of a direct-controlled municipality.[101] They will take charge of the registration of the following companies within their administrative jurisdiction: (1) any company other than those as prescribed in Articles 6 and 7 of the RARC; and (2) a company subject to the registration as authorized by the SAIC or the AIC at the level of province. The specific jurisdiction over registration as provided by Article 8 will be decided by the AIC at the level of province. However, the agency of a city (region) divided into districts will take charge of the registration of a JSLC.

2.4.3.5. Remedies of the Refusal of a License Application

A reasonable application for licenses shall be approved according to Article 38(1) of the ALL. The Article 38(1) reads that 'where an applicant (for an administrative license) meets the statutory requirements and standards, the administrative organ shall make a written decision about the approval of the administrative license.'

In the case that businesses' applications for licenses are refused, companies could seek remedies in accordance with Article 38(2) of the ALL. This item states that where the administrative organ makes a decision about the non-approval of the administrative license in accordance with the law, it shall give explanations and inform the applicant that it is entitled to apply for administrative reconsideration or to file an administrative lawsuit. Therefore, a business can either make an application for administrative reconsideration or bring an administrative lawsuit if their applications for licenses are denied.

First, a right to apply for administrative reconsideration is regulated by the Administrative Reconsideration Law (ARL) (1999).[102] According to Article 6(8) of the ARL, citizens, legal persons and other organizations may apply for administrative reconsideration according to this law if they consider administrative organs fail to deal with their applications for a number of items, while the applications meet the requirements as prescribed by law. These items cover such documents as permits, licenses and qualification certificates, or examination and approval and registration of affairs concerned.

Article 9 of the ARL sets the time limit within which a business can apply for administrative reconsideration. According to Article 9(1), citizens, legal persons and other organizations who consider that certain specific administrative acts infringe

101 The names of these authorities have been changed to make them understandable in English.

102 The English text of the Administrative Procedure Law (1989) used in this chapter is obtained from: <www.npc.gov.cn/englishnpc/Law/2007-12/12/content_1383912.htm> (last accessed 6 April 2016). In a few cases, the English written material has been modified.

upon their lawful rights or interests may apply for administrative reconsideration within 60 days from the date when they came to know about such administrative acts, except where the time limit for application is more than 60 days as prescribed by law. Moreover, as stated by Article 9(2), in the case of delay in applying within the statutory time limit occasioned by force majeure or for other justifiable reasons, the counting of the days will be resumed from the date when the obstacle is removed. Specific administrative acts are a concept that is contrary to abstract administrative acts under Chinese law, in Bixin Jiang's opinion. Generally, it is held that 'administrative rules and regulations, regulations, or decisions and orders with general binding force formulated and announced by administrative organs' in Article 12(2) of the Administrative Procedure Law (the APL) (1989), refer to abstract administrative acts.[103] Specific administrative acts are aimed at a certain individual or a business and only have binding force over that particular person. Though a distinction between the two kinds of administrative acts is not very sharp as demonstrated by Jiang,[104] it is widely accepted that administrative acts dealing with license applications belong to specific administrative acts.

Articles 12, 13, 14 and 15 of the ARL provide which agency an applicant can apply to for administrative reconsideration. Articles 12 and 14 seem to govern the reconsideration application concerning the licenses for the establishment of a business. According to Article 12(1), when refusing to accept a specific administrative act taken by the department of a government at or above the county level, the applicant may choose to apply to the government at the same level or to the competent department at a higher level for administrative reconsideration. Article 12(2) notes that when refusing to accept a specific administrative act taken by the administrative organ that exercises vertical leadership over the customs, banking, national tax and foreign exchange administration or by a state security organ, the applicant shall apply to the competent department at a higher level for administrative reconsideration. According to Article 14, when refusing to accept a specific administrative act taken by a department under the State Council or by a provincial government, the applicant should apply to the said departments or government for administrative reconsideration. When refusing to accept a decision made after administrative reconsideration, the applicant may bring an administrative lawsuit before a court, or apply to the State Council for arbitration, which will give a final ruling in accordance with this law.

Article 28(3) of the ARL formulates the rules according to which a refusal to a license application should be altered. In accordance with this provision, if a specific administrative act is taken in one of the following circumstances, a decision must be made to have it nullified or changed or confirm that it is illegal; in that case, the defending party will be ordered to take another specific administrative act within a time limit: (1) The main facts are not clear and essential evidence is inadequate; (2) The basis is used incorrectly; (3) Statutory procedures were violated; (4) Authority is

103 行政诉讼法（1989）. Jiang 2009a, p. 15.

104 Bixin Jiang, Review of Administrative Decisions of Government by Chinese Courts, available at: <www.aihja.org/images/users/1/files/china.en.0.pdf> p. 4 (last accessed 6 April 2016).

exceeded or power is abused; or (5) The act is obviously inappropriate. Moreover, as provided by Article 28(4) of the ARL, where an administrative reconsideration organ orders the defending party to take another specific administrative act, it must not take the same or basically the same specific administrative act on the basis of the same facts or reasons. The meaning of the defending party in Article 28 is defined by Article 10 of the same law. According to Article 10, when a citizen, legal person or other organization refuses to accept a certain specific administrative act taken by an administrative organ and applies for administrative reconsideration, the said administrative organ is the defending party to the application.

Article 5 of the ARL allows applicants for administrative reconsideration to bring a suit if they reject the decision taken after administrative reconsideration. According to this provision, in the case of such refusal, a citizen, legal person or other organization may, in accordance with the APL, file an administrative lawsuit before a court, with the exception of those decisions that are final as prescribed by law.

Second, the APL governs an administrative lawsuit brought by a company. Article 11 of the APL lays down the scope of accepting cases of administrative litigation. According to Item (4) of this article, courts must accept suits brought by legal persons against refusal by an administrative organ to issue a permit or license, which the legal persons consider themselves legally qualified to apply for, or the failure of that administrative agency to respond to the application.

Article 37 of the APL explains the relation between making an application for administrative reconsideration and bringing an administrative lawsuit by an individual, a business or any other institution. As provided in Article 37(1), generally, a natural person, a legal person or any other organization can either file a lawsuit or apply for administrative reconsideration. According to this provision, a citizen, a legal person or any other organization may, within the scope of cases acceptable to courts, apply to an administrative organ at the next higher level or to an administrative organ as prescribed by the law or regulations for reconsideration first. Anyone who refuses to accept the reconsideration decision then may bring a suit before a court. A citizen, a legal person or any other organization may also bring a suit directly before a court without undergoing reconsideration. There is an exception to Article 37(1) made by Article 37(2). As prescribed in the latter provision, in circumstances where, according to relevant provisions of laws or regulations, a citizen, a legal person or any other organization must first apply to an administrative organ for reconsideration and then bring a suit before a court, the provisions of the laws or regulations will apply.

Article 41 stipulates that the following requirements must be met when a suit is brought: (1) The plaintiff must be a citizen, a legal person or any other organization that considers a specific administrative act to have infringed upon his or its lawful rights and interest; (2) There must be a specific defendant or defendants; (3) There must be a specific claim and a corresponding factual basis for the suit; and (4) The suit must fall within the scope of cases acceptable to courts and the specific jurisdiction of the court where it is filed.

Article 54(4) provides for the circumstances in which a specific administrative act can be annulled or partially annulled by judgment, or the defendant may be required by judgment to undertake a specific administrative act anew. The conditions refer to one of the following circumstances: (1) inadequacy of essential evidence; (2) erroneous application of the law or regulations; (3) violation of legal procedure; (4) exceeding authority; or (5) abuse of powers.

According to Article 55, a defendant who has been judged by a court to undertake a specific administrative act anew must not, based on the same fact and reason, undertake a specific administrative act essentially identical with the original act.

According to Article 58, a company is entitled to file an appeal against a judgment or an order of first instance by a court within the time limit provided for by this article.

2.5. *Summary*

As discussed above, the establishment of a domestic company in China needs to meet the requirements on initiators, capital and articles of association. Moreover, it is necessary to undergo a series of procedures. Among them, applying for establishment registration is very important but also very complex.

For this establishment, licensing regimes have been created for public stock offers made by a JVC launched by stock floatation, licensed operations, the establishment for certain types of companies and establishment registration. All the four systems are regulated by the ALL.

According to the provision on substantive conditions and steps for the establishment of a domestic company, no legal obstacles can be erected for such incorporation. Moreover, entry barriers can hardly be created by the above licensing regimes based on the ALL provisions themselves. First, it is unlikely that a reasonable application for the four types of licenses could be rejected according to the rules of the ALL. Second, companies can use administrative reconsideration and judicial review as remedies where their applications are refused.

However, Article 12(6) of the ALL permits licensing authorities to establish licensing systems for other matters besides these items provided for in Item (1) to (5) of this article. If Article 12(6) was mis-used, it would still be likely to create licensing regimes for almost everything. As a result, entry barriers can be erected by means of licensing.

Moreover, it is possible that the practical application of the licensing rules can be a cause of entry barriers. Therefore, section 5 examines the actual use of licensing through analysing existing empirical studies to find out whether the licensing systems constitute barriers for the establishment of domestic companies.

3. Regulations on the Establishment of FIEs

Section 2 has shown that most of the legal rules for the establishment of a domestic company do not allow the erection of entry barriers for such incorporation. Only Article 12(6) of the ALL can be abused in the sense of creating such obstacles.

Section 3 continues to discuss the rules on the establishment of FIEs in China to examine whether the creation of legal obstacles for setting this up is also a rare circumstance.

Three forms of FIEs are mainly used by foreign investors in China, i.e. wholly foreign owned enterprises (WFOEs), equity joint ventures (EJVs) and contractual joint ventures (CJVs). The Catalogue for the Guidance of Foreign Investment Industries (Amended 2011) (hereinafter the Catalogue) provides which types of FIEs can be chosen for a particular industry.[105] Moreover, there may be restrictions on the form of investment set out by regulations governing a specific industry.[106] After references are made to the Catalogue and the regulations for a particular industry, it can be decided whether the establishment of a WFOE, EJV or CJV is allowed for this business.

The provisions governing the incorporation of a WFOE, EJV and CJV can be divided into two items: rules on capital requirements and on establishment processes. While the regulations on capital requirement vary depending on the form of FIEs, the requirement on the establishment procedures of the three investment vehicles are almost the same. One vital stage for this process is to obtain licenses.

The licensing requirement can vary due to classification made by the Catalogue, being shown in sections 3.3 and 4.2. It groups all activities and sectors into encouraged, restricted and prohibited categorizations. Any activities or sectors not mentioned by the Catalogue are permitted.

The following section examines the provision on capital requirement of a WFOE and a Joint Venture (JV) respectively and discusses the process for the establishment of an FIE. Much emphasis is given to the license acquisition.

3.1. *Capital Requirement of a WFOE*

Three points concerning the capital requirement of a WFOE should be mentioned: the amount of registered capital, capital forms and capital contribution. This classification of capital requirement also applies to a CJV or an EJV.

3.1.1. The Amount of Registered Capital

According to Dan Harris (2012), an experienced attorney, the registered capital of a WFOE is the actual expenses used by this investment vehicle to pay its start-up costs of plant, machinery etc. The amount of the registered capital for each WFOE is different. However, according to most Chinese regulators, the registered capital of a WFOE is hoped to amount to its operating expenditure for the first three years at least. Authorities of some regions have set a minimum capital requirement for the

105 The Catalogue is called《外商投资产业指导目录（2011年修订）》 in Chinese. The English text of this document is available at: <www.fdi.gov.cn/pub/FDI_EN/Laws/-GeneralLawsandRegulations/MinisterialRulings/P020120427348389211538.pdf> (last accessed 6 April 2016).

106 Herbert Smith LLP, China Investment Guide 2012, p. 7, available at: <www.atilimfuar.-com/en/belge/investment_guide_china.pdf> (last accessed 6 April 2016).

establishment of a WFOE. For instance, a minimum registered capital of US $150,000 is required by the districts of Shanghai municipality. Moreover, it is possible for the companies engaging in certain businesses to have a higher registered capital requirement.[107] More precisely, the engagement mentioned means the business scope of the companies. Thus, in sum, the amount of the registered capital of a WFOE is decided by the business scope, the location and the financial needs of the initial operation of this WFOE.

3.1.2. Capital Forms

According to Articles 27 and 179 of the Company Law (2005), the capital contributions of a WFOE can be made in cash and non-cash. Capital contributions in cash of a WFOE should be no less than 30 per cent of its total registered capital. As provided in Article 27(2) of the Detailed Rules for the Implementation of the Law on Wholly Foreign-owned Enterprises (Revised 2001) (hereinafter the Detailed Rules for WFOEs), 'Upon the approval by the examination and approval authority, the foreign investor may also make its/his capital contribution with their profits in RMB from any other enterprises it/he established in China'.[108]

In terms of non-monetary capital contributions, 'a foreign investor may make its/his investment in convertible foreign currencies or with machinery and equipment, industrial property rights and proprietary technologies by evaluating their values', as stipulated in Article 27(1) of the Detailed Rules for WFOEs. Moreover, according to Article 2 of the Interim Provisions on Investment by Equity Interest in respect of Foreign-invested Enterprises (2012) made by MOFCOM (hereinafter the Equity Interest Investment Provisions), the equity interest of one Chinese company can be used to make contributions to the registered capital of an FIE if conditions stipulated are met.

As prescribed in Article 28 of the Detailed Rules for WFOEs, 'the machinery and equipment to be used as capital contribution by a foreign investor should be those needed for production of the wholly foreign-owned enterprise.' 'The evaluation of the aforesaid machinery and equipment should not be higher than the normal price of the same machinery and equipment in the international market at that time.' 'For any foreign investor making its/his capital contribution with machinery and equipment, it/he shall submit an inventory of the aforesaid machinery and equipment, including descriptions, types, quantities and evaluation, to the examination and approval authority, together with the application for establishment of the wholly foreign-owned enterprise as an attachment.'

According to Article 29 of the Detailed Rules for WFOEs, 'the industrial property rights and proprietary technologies to be used as capital contribution by the foreign investor shall be owned by the foreign investor.' 'The aforesaid industrial property rights and proprietary technologies must be evaluated

107 Dan Harris, Forming a China WFOE: How Long Will That Be Going On?, available at: <www.chinalawblog.com/2012/12/forming-a-china-wfoe.html> (last accessed 6 April 2016).

108 This legislation is called 外资企业法实施细则（2001修订）in Chinese. The English version of this law is available at: <www.fdi.gov.cn> (last accessed 6 April 2016).

according to international principles of evaluation and the evaluated value shall not exceed the registered capital of the wholly foreign-owned enterprise by 20 per cent.' 'Detailed information of the industrial property rights and proprietary technologies evaluated to be used as capital contribution, including copies of certificates of the title, validity of the title, technical performances and basis and standards of evaluation, shall be submitted to the examination and approval authority as an attachment to the application for the establishment of the wholly foreign-owned enterprise.'

The use of equity interest for capital contributions has more complicated rules. Articles 4 and 19 of the Equity Interest Investment Provisions deal with the general conditions of the equity interest that can be contributed to the registered capital of an FIE. Article 19 states that capital contributions in the form of equity interest must conform with the state tax administration regulations.

According to Article 4, the equity interest to be contributed by an investor for the establishment of an FIE (hereinafter the investee enterprise) must be transferable and the investor must have a clean title to the equity interest. Contributions of equity interest will not be permitted in any of the following cases: '(1) the registered capital of the enterprise whose equity interest is to be contributed has not been fully paid up; (2) the equity interest to be contributed is pledged or frozen; (3) the constitutional documents of the enterprise whose equity interest is to be contributed impose restrictions on equity transfer; (4) the enterprise whose equity interest is to be contributed (in case such enterprise is an FIE) fails to pass the annual inspection for the preceding year; (5) the enterprise whose equity interest is to be contributed is a real estate enterprise, a foreign-invested holding company or a foreign-invested venture capital (private equity) investment enterprise; or (6) regulatory approvals required for the relevant equity transfer have not been obtained'.[109]

Moreover, if the equity interest of certain particular types of companies is used for capital contributions, other relevant articles of the Equity Interest Investment Provisions will automatically be complied with. According to Article 16, the use of the equity interest of domestic listed companies must comply with the relevant provision in terms of state security administration, security exchange and security registration and settlement.

Article 20 regulates the contributions of equity interest that involve the administration of the state-owned asset of an enterprise and the administration of the state stock of a listed company. These capital contributions shall conform to the relevant provision managing state-owned assets.

Article 23 governs the contributions in the form of the equity interest of a Foreign Invested Holding Company (FIHC). Relevant provisions shall be followed

[109] Art. 4 of the Interim Provisions on Investment by Equity Interest in respect of Foreign-invested Enterprises (商务部关于涉及外商投资企业股权出资的暂行规定) (2012) is largely based on an article, available at: <www.nortonrose.com/knowledge/publications/71989/-prc-legal-updater-issue-32> (last accessed 6 April 2016).

that administer the establishment of a FIHC by foreign investors when making such contributions.[110]

Two steps need to be followed if the equity interest is used for capital contributions. First, according to Article 6 of the Equity Interest Investment Provisions, it is necessary for a Chinese appraisal institution to evaluate the equity interest before using the equity interest to contribute.

Second, the equity interest contributor or the investee enterprise is required to submit a list of documents and apply for approval, as provided in Article 10. These files include: (1) an application for capital contributions in the form of equity interest and an agreement for such capital contributions; (2) proof of lawful ownership of the equity interest to be used to make capital contributions; (3) the corporate business license of the enterprise whose equity interest is contributed (a copy); (4) the approval certificate of an FIE, a copy of this certificate and the proof of passing the joint yearly inspection of an FIE, where the enterprise whose equity interest is contributed is an FIE; (5) equity appraisal reports finished by appraisal firms; (6) legal opinions on Items (4) and (5) given by law firms and the lawyers appointed by these firms; (7) other documents in terms of the establishment or the change of an FIE required according to laws, administrative regulations and rules for foreign investment; (8) relevant approval documents, where the equity interest transference of the enterprise whose equity interest is contributed shall be approved according to laws, administrative regulations or the decisions of the State Council; and (9) other documents required by approval authorities.[111]

Article 5 provides for the requirements for relevant enterprises after capital contributions have been made in the form of equity interest. These companies refer to the investee enterprise, the enterprise whose equity interest is contributed and the enterprise whose stock is held directly or indirectly by the first two enterprises. All these corporations shall conform to the Catalogue, the Provisions on Guiding the Orientation of Foreign Investment (2002) and other relevant provisions in terms of foreign investment.[112]

In short, the capital forms of a WFOE can be both currency and non-currency. The non-cash contributions of a WFOE can be in the form of machinery and equipment, industrial property rights, proprietary technologies and equity interest. MOFCOM has recently made regulations on the use of equity interest as capital contributions.

110 According to Art. 1 of the Regulations on the Establishment of a FIHC by Foreign Investors (关于外商投资举办投资性公司的规定) (2004), the FIHC means a WFOE, CJV or EJV set up to make direct investments in the PRC.

111 The translation of Items (1), (2), (5) and (6) considers the article FIEs face new regulations for capital contributions in the form of equity by Elvin Ye and Henry Song, available at: <http://cblj.com/cblj/correspondent/1f7bc179c218ece5abe6f6ae91b1cdae.pdf> (last accessed 6 April 2016).

112 The Provisions on Guiding the Orientation of Foreign Investment 指导外商投资方向规定 (2002).

3.1.3. Capital Contributions

Rules on the capital contributions of a WFOE deal with two issues: the time limit of and the verifications of capital contributions. As provided in Article 30(1) of the Detailed Rules for a WFOE, 'the time limit for a foreign investor to make its/his capital contribution should be explicitly indicated in both the application for the establishment of the wholly foreign-owned enterprise and the articles of association of the enterprise'. 'The foreign investor may make its/his capital contribution by instalments, provided that the last instalment is to be paid within 3 years of the date of issuance of the business license. Among them, the first instalment should not be less than 15 per cent of the total subscribed capital contribution of the foreign investor and should be paid within 90 days from the date of issuance of the business license of the wholly foreign-owned enterprise.'

According to Article 32 of the Detailed Rules for WFOEs, 'for each instalment made by the foreign investor, the wholly foreign-owned enterprise shall invite a Chinese certified accountant to make verification and prepare a capital verification report, which shall be submitted to the examination and approval authority and the administration for industry and commerce for filing.'

3.2. *Capital Requirement of a JV*

3.2.1. The Amount of Registered Capital

The amount of registered capital for a JV is determined in the same way as the amount of registered capital for a WFOE. According to Dezan Shira & Associates (2011), the quantity of registered capital for a JV is decided by three elements. These factors include the establishment place and the business scope of a JV and the financial support for the operation of a JV until a JV can fund itself.[113] Therefore, the amount of the registered capital varies in each case. It is impossible to give a fixed sum for the registered capital of a JV.

3.2.2. Capital Forms

The capital forms of a JV have some common points with the capital forms of a WFOE, but a JV has more variable rules on the forms than a WFOE. This is because most issues of a JV are governed by cooperation contracts. Moreover, a CJV receives fewer restraints on capital forms than an EJV. Since there is more free will for partners to a CJV to make the contracts, a CJV turns out to be very flexible, as demonstrated by Dezan Shira & Associates (2011).[114]

First, like a WFOE, cash, machinery and industrial property right can be contributed to a JV. These forms are provided by Article 18 of the Rules for the Implementation of the Law on CJVs (Revised 2001) (hereinafter the Implementation

113 Dezan Shira & Associates 2011, p. 27.
114 *Ibid.*, p. 37.

Rules for CJVs) and Article 22 of the Regulations for the Implementation of the Law on EJVs (Revised 2011) (hereinafter the Implementation Regulations for EJVs).[115]

Second, parties to a JV should make its contract covering capital form issues and it is possible for a JV to have its own requirements on these forms. Moreover, besides the rules provided by the contract, the capital forms of a JV are still subject to other conditions laid down in the Implementation Regulations for EJVs and the Implementation Rules for CJVs.

The autonomy of a CJV to regulate the capital forms can be shown in the following provisions. Article 3 of the Implementation Rules for CJVs grants approved agreements, contracts and articles of association of CJVs the effectiveness to govern the operations and business activities of CJVs. As noted by Article 10(4), the contracts of CJVs pre-empt the approved agreements and the articles of associations of CJVs. According to Article 12(3), the contracts of CJVs should include total investment, registered capital, investment by each partner or forms and terms of cooperation. Therefore, CJVs can make requirements on capital forms by themselves.

However, it should be pointed out that the conditions for capital forms provided by contracts of CJVs are still subject to approval. As stated by Article 11 of the Implementation Rules for CJVs, contracts of CJVs shall enter into force as of the date of the issuance of the establishment approval documents by examination and approval departments.

Moreover, the Implementation Rules for CJVs stipulate two rules for the capital forms of a CJV. First, according to Article 18(2), if the capital forms contributed by the Chinese parties to a CJV are state fixed assets, these state properties must undergo assets assessment in accordance with related laws and administrative regulations or provisions. Second, as noted by Article 19, the property or the property rights used for contributions must be owned by parties to a CJV and must not be mortgaged or guaranteed through other means.

Like a CJV, an EJV is also required to regulate the capital forms in the contract of this EJV, as provided in Article 11(3) of the Implementation Regulations for EJVs. Moreover, as noted by Article 5, an EJV has the right to do business independently within the scope of the provisions of Chinese laws, administrative regulations, and the agreement, contract and articles of association of this EJV. Furthermore, according to Article 14, the contract of an EJV will also become effective after the approval by examination and approval authorities.

Moreover, as mentioned above, the capital forms of an EJV still need to conform to a set of rules provided by the Implementation Regulations for EJVs. These conditions are very similar to the requirements for the capital forms of a WFOE. According to Article 24, 'the machinery, equipment and other materials contributed by the foreign party (to EJVs) should be those necessary for the

115 The Regulations for the Implementation of the Law on Sino-foreign Equity Joint Ventures (中外合资经营企业法实施条例) (Revised 2011) and the Regulations for the Implementation of the Law on Sino-foreign Equity Joint Ventures (2001) (中外合作经营企业法实施细则) (Revised 2001). The English version of the two documents is available at: <www.fdi.gov.cn> (last accessed 6 April 2016).

production of the joint venture.' 'The price of the machinery, equipment and other materials referred to in the preceding paragraph should not be higher than the current international market price for similar equipment or materials.'

As provided in Article 25, 'the industrial property or proprietary technologies contributed by the foreign party to (EJVs) as investment shall meet one of the following conditions: (1) capable of improving markedly the performance and quality of existing products and raising productivity or (2) capable of notable savings in raw materials, fuel or power.'

According to Article 26, 'foreign parties (to EJVs) who contribute industrial property or proprietary technologies as investment shall present relevant documentation concerning the industrial property or proprietary technologies, including photocopies of the patent certificates or trademark registration certificates, statements of validity, their technical characteristics, practical value, the basis for calculating the price and the price agreement signed with the Chinese partners All these serve as an annex to the contract.'

Article 27 provides that all the capital forms in Articles 24, 25 and 26 need to be approved. According to Article 27, 'the machinery, equipment or other materials, industrial property or proprietary technologies contributed by foreign parties as investment will be subject to examination and approval authority for approval.'[116]

Third, as discussed in section 3.1.2, equity interest can be used to contribute for FIEs. The capital contributions to JVs in the form of equity interest are certainly governed by the Equity Interest Investment Provisions.

Fourth, a land use right is another capital form available to a JV. Unlike a WFOE, a JV is jointly established by foreign and domestic investors and Chinese investors can make contributions in the form of a land use right. A land use right as a capital form is laid down in Article 18 of the Implementation Rules for CJVs and Article 22 of the Implementation Regulations for EJVs.

In summary, the capital forms of a JV can be cash, machinery, industrial property rights and equity interests, which are the same as capital forms of a WFOE. Moreover, Chinese parties to a JV can use land use rights to contribute. Although the provision on the forms is complicated, entry barriers can hardly be created.

3.2.3. Capital Contributions

Like a WFOE, two points should be discussed concerning the capital contributions of a JV, i.e. the time limit of and the verifications of capital contributions. According to Article 11 of the Implementation Regulations for EJVs and Article 12 of the Implementation Rules for CJVs, the time limit will be provided in the contracts of a JV. After the contracts are approved, parties to JVs are bound by the time limit.

Article 29 of the Implementation Regulations for EJVs and Article 22 of the Implementation Rules for CJVs lay down the responsibility for parties to JVs to

116 Like a CJV, state owned assets can also be contributed to an EJV. However, no provision of the Implementation Regulations for EJVs states that the state owned assets as capital contributions for an EJV must be assessed.

verify their capital contributions. According to these two provisions, the parties must get their contributions verified after the capital contributions to JVs are made.

3.3. *Procedural Requirements for the Establishment of an FIE*

Besides the capital requirement, the incorporation of either a JV or a WFOE is required to complete a set of procedural steps. The US Chamber of Commerce (2012) reviews and presents the necessary process for the inbound FDI in China.[117] This section chooses and discusses the general steps for the forming of an FIE from that report. The establishment of an FIE engaging in certain service industries has different procedural requirements.[118] The process to incorporate such an investment vehicle is not explained in this section.

3.3.1. Steps to Establish an FIE

According to the US Chamber of Commerce, a general process to incorporate an FIE in China consists of pre-registering a company name, receiving site-related opinion letters, obtaining project approval of Development and Reform Commissions (DRCs), commerce department approval and license of industry regulators (if necessary) and registering with the local AIC. After registration, an FIE still needs to acquire an organization code certificate, get a permission to make company seals, register with the tax authority, register for foreign exchange and apply for registration with the Import and Export Consignees associated with Customs. It should be pointed out that to incorporate an FIE in different industries or in different administrative regions can result in a modification of the above process.[119] Moreover, the investment in certain service industries has different procedural requirements.[120] The general crucial steps to establish an FIE are interpreted as follows.

3.3.1.1. The DRC Project Approval

As demonstrated by the US Chamber of Commerce, an applicant for establishing an FIE usually should submit its report for a foreign investment project to the local DRCs for approval. This document will be passed to the NDRC where this project should be considered by the NDRC.[121]

According to Article 5 of the Interim Measures for the Administration of Examining and Approving Foreign Investment Projects (2004) (hereinafter the

117 The US Chamber of Commerce, China's Approval Process for Inbound Foreign Direct Investment: Impact on Market Access, National Treatment and Transparency, available at: <www.uschamber.com/sites/default/files/reports/020021_China_InvestmentPaper_hires.pdf> p. 15-31 (last accessed 6 April 2016).

118 *Ibid.*, p. 32.

119 *Ibid.*, p. 31.

120 *Ibid.*, p. 18.

121 *Ibid.*, p. 23.

Interim Measures), the report submitted to the NDRC should contain: '(1) the name of the project, the time limit of operation and the fundamental information of an investor; (2) the construction scale, main construction projects and products of the project, main technologies and techniques adopted, the target markets of products and the planned number of workers; (3) the construction site of the project, the demands of resources such as land, water and energy, and the amount of consumption of main raw materials; (4) the evaluation of impacts on the environment; (5) the prices involving public products or services; and (6) the total investment amount of the project, the registered capital and the amount of contribution of each party, the mode of contribution and the financing schemes, and the equipment needed to be imported and the price thereof.'[122]

Moreover, as prescribed by Article 6, the report submitted to the NDRC should be accompanied by the following documents: (1) the business license of the Chinese party (if any) and foreign party of the investment project, the certificate of commercial registration and the latest financial statements of each investor (including the balance sheet, the profit and loss statement and the cash flow statement), and the certificate of capital credit issued by the bank of deposit; (2) the letter of intent to invest; (3) the financing letter of intent issued by a bank; (4) 'the written evaluation and suggestions about the impact on environment issued by a provincial or the State administrative department in charge of environmental protection'; (5) 'the written suggestions regarding the selection of sites issued by a provincial planning department'; (6) 'the written suggestions regarding a preliminary examination of land use of the project issued by the administrative department for state land and resources of a province or the state'; (7) 'in case the contribution is state-owned assets or the right of land use, a confirmation document issued by relevant competent departments is required'.

Furthermore, according to the US Chamber of Commerce, a written application in the form stipulated must be filed with the local DRCs. This report will assess energy conservation of a project based on the plan's potential energy needs.[123]

Articles 3 and 4 of the Interim Measures provide for the relevant examination and approval organs for a particular type of foreign investment projects. According to Article 3, the NDRC should examine and approve the application reports of encouraged projects and permitted projects with a total investment (including the increased amount of capital, similarly hereinafter) of US $100 million or more.[124] The

122 This legislation is called外商投资项目核准暂行管理办法 (2004) in Chinese. The English text is available at: <www.fdi.gov.cn/pub/FDI_EN/Economy/Investment%20Environment/FDI%-20in%20China/Examination%20and%20Approval/t20060422_24925.htm> (last accessed 6 April 2016). As shown in the report of the US Chamber of Commerce, Arts. 5, 6, 8, 9 and 12 of the Interim Measures also apply to the local DRCs.

123 The US Chamber of Commerce, China's Approval Process for Inbound Foreign Direct Investment: Impact on Market Access, National Treatment and Transparency, available at: <www.uschamber.com/sites/default/files/reports/020021_China_InvestmentPaper_hires.pdf>, p. 25 (last accessed 6 April 2016).

124 The concept of a total investment of a WFOE is defined in Art. 19 of the Detailed Rules for the WFOE. According to Orrick LLP, a total investment of an FIE refers to the whole amount of →

NDRC will also evaluate and approve the application reports of restricted projects with a total investment of US $50 million dollars or more. Among all the application reports mentioned above, some projects must be reported to the State Council for verification after the examination and approval by the NDRC. These plans include those encouraged projects and permitted projects with a total investment of US $500 million or more and those restricted projects with a total investment of US $100 million or more.

As provided in Article 4(1), the local DRCs should examine and approve encouraged projects and permitted ones with a total investment lower than US $100 million and restricted projects with a total investment lower than US $50 million. However, restricted projects will be subject to the examination and approval of the provincial DRCs and the power to examine and approve such projects will not be transferred to a lower-level department. According to Article 4(2), in case that, according to relevant laws and regulations, the local governments have otherwise formulated rules for examining and approving projects listed in Article 4(1), such rules must prevail.[125]

According to Articles 8 and 9 of the Interim Measures, under the conditions stipulated, the NDRC should seek opinions when examining and approving a project. As provided in Article 8, 'if it is necessary to solicit the opinions of the department of the State Council in charge of the industry concerned, the NDRC shall issue a letter soliciting opinions to the administrative department of industry of the State Council and attach relevant materials at the same time. The department of the State Council in charge of industries concerned shall submit written opinions to the NDRC within 7working days after acceptance of the said materials.'[126]

In accordance with Article 9, 'the NDRC shall entrust a qualified consultation organization to assess the key issues that need to be evaluated and demonstrated within 5 working days after acceptance of an application report. The entrusted consultation organization shall put forward an appraisal report to the NDRC within the prescribed time limit.'

Article 12 lays down the conditions for the NDRC to examine and approve a project. The criteria include: (1) complying with the laws and regulations of the State and the prescriptions of the Catalogue and the Catalogue of Priority Industries for Foreign Investment in the Central-Western Region (Revised 2008); (2) complying with the requirements of middle-term and long-term plans of the national economy and social development, the industry plans and the policies for the adjustment of industry structure; (3) complying with the public interest and related anti-monopoly prescriptions of the State; (4) complying with the requirements of plans of land use, general planning of cities and policies of environmental protection; (5) complying with the requirements of technological and technical standards set down

the registered capital of an FIE and the capital that the FIE is allowed to borrow. Orrick LLP, Foreign investment in China: an introduction, p. 3, available at: <www.orrick.com/Events-and-Publications/Documents/4520.pdf> (last accessed 6 April 2016).

125 The classification of DRCs' project approving authority according to Arts. 3 and 4 is shown in Table 2 at the end of section 2.3.1.1.

126 The industry concerned means the field of the FDI.

by the State; (6) complying with the related prescriptions of the national capital project management and the management of foreign debts.[127]

Some drawbacks of the above rules should be pointed out. First, according to the US Chamber of Commerce, standards provided by Article 12 turn out to be broad. The use of such criteria makes the creation of barriers to market entry possible.[128] These standards are also vaguely defined. As a result, provisions such as Article 12 offer a broad range for limiting the FDI.[129] Moreover, as demonstrated by the OECD in 2003, the economic criteria of the NDRC to approve FDI then was not precise and specific in such a manner that foreign companies can fulfil them with efforts. As a result, it can be argued that the criteria were hard to understand.[130] Likewise, the conditions of Article 12 are not precisely laid down in such a way that foreign investors can strive to conform to them. Thus, it can also be demonstrated that Article 12 appears opaque.

Second, some terms in Articles 9 and 3 do not have clear definitions. For example, the duration for the consultation in Article 9 has not been specified by the Interim Measures, neither has the time limit for the State Council to approve a project in Article 3.[131] Moreover, the key issues mentioned in Article 9 appear to be unclear. To have an exact meaning of this term, other documents need to be referred to. However, it seems that there is no such document. In other words, whether a matter belongs to the key issues fully depends on the discretion of the NDRC.

Table 2. The division of DRCs' project approving authority based on total investment volume (Units: a million US $)

Authorities	Encouraged projects	Permitted projects	Restricted projects
NDRC	total investment amount ≥100 (if a project has a volume bigger than or equal to 500, it should also be reported to the State Council for verification)	the same as encouraged projects	total investment amount ≥50 (if a project has a volume bigger than or equal to 100, it should also be reported to the State Council for verification)
Provincial DRCs			total investment amount<50
Provincial DRCs or other local provincial DRCs	total investment amount<100	the same as encouraged projects	

127 The legal status of the two catalogues is the rules of the departments under the State Council that are binding legislative acts. The first catalogue is applicable to all regions in the PRC, while the second catalogue is applicable to the Central-Western region.

128 The US Chamber of Commerce, China's Approval Process for Inbound Foreign Direct Investment: Impact on Market Access, National Treatment and Transparency, available at: <www.uschamber.com/sites/default/files/reports/020021_China_InvestmentPaper_hires.pdf> p. 27 (last accessed 6 April 2016).

129 *Ibid.*, p. 57.

130 OECD 2003, p. 22.

131 The US Chamber of Commerce, China's Approval Process for Inbound Foreign Direct Investment: Impact on Market Access, National Treatment and Transparency, available at: <www.uschamber.com/sites/default/files/reports/020021_China_InvestmentPaper_hires.pdf> p. 26 (last accessed 6 April 2016).

The project approving power of provincial DRCs and of other local DRCs may vary in different regions due to Article 4(2) of the Interim Measures.

3.3.1.2. *The Commerce Department Approval*

After the approval of an investment project by the DRC, the application to establish an FIE shall be submitted for a commerce department's approval and examination. In practice, the commerce department will be the authorities at the corresponding level of the DRC.

The incorporation of a CJV, EJV or WFOE is required to submit a list of documents to the commerce authority. The submission of the following files is necessary for all the three types of the FDI, as shown by the US Chamber of Commerce and relevant legislation governing each type of the FIEs: '(1) a written application for formation of the FIE; (2) a feasibility study report; (3) articles of association; (4) the project approval opinion issued by DRC; (5) authority opinions regarding site-related land-use rights, zoning, and environmental impact.'[132] For a specific type of FDI, the commerce department also demands other documents.

According to Article 10 of the Detailed Rules for the WFOE, other files for the establishment of a WFOE consist of '(4) The name list of legal representative (or candidates for the future board of directors) of the wholly foreign-owned enterprise; (5) The legal documents and credit certificates of the foreign investor; (6) The written reply of the local people's government at county level or above at the place where the wholly foreign-owned enterprise is to be located; (7) A list of articles and materials that will be imported; and (8) other documents required.' Moreover, if two foreign investors or more jointly apply for establishment of a wholly foreign-owned enterprise, they must submit a copy of the contract by and between them.

As provided in Article 7 of the Implementation Regulations for EJVs, it is mandatory to submit the following remaining documents to incorporate an EJV: (1) the agreement and the contract of an EJV signed by representatives authorized by the parties to an EJV; (2) a list of candidates for chairperson, vice-chairperson and directors nominated by the parties to an EJV; (3) 'other documents required by the examination and approval authority'.[133]

According to Article 7 of the Implementation Rules for CJVs, the submission of other files is required for the establishment of a CJV: (1) the agreements and contracts of a CJV; (2) 'the partners' business licenses, registration documents, capital credibility reports and other valid documents of the legal representatives. If a partner is a foreign natural person, the partner must also present valid documents on their identification, biographical data and capital credibility'; (3) 'a roster of the

132 *Ibid.*, p. 27. Art. 7 of the Rules for the Implementation of the Law on Chinese-foreign Contractual Joint Ventures; Art. 10 of the Detailed Rules for the Implementation of the Law on Wholly Foreign-owned Enterprises (Revised 2001) and Art. 7 of the Regulations for the Implementation of the Sino-Foreign Equity Joint Venture Enterprise Law.

133 Parties to an EJV mean foreign and Chinese investors who make contributions to set up an EJV.

Chairman and Deputy Chairmen of the Board of Directors, members of the Board of Directors or a name list of the Chairman and Deputy Chairmen of the Joint Management Committee and members of the Joint Management Committee'; and (4) 'other documents as deemed necessary by the examination and approval departments'.[134]

Reasons to refuse an application for the commerce department approval can be found in Article 5 of the Detailed Rules for a WFOE, Article 9 of the Implementation Rules for CJVs and Article 4 of the Implementation Regulations for EJVs. For any EJV, CJV or WFOE, its application for the commerce department approval will be denied if the enterprise may (1) damage China's sovereignty or social and public interest, (2) violate Chinese laws and regulations or (3) pollute the environment.

The approval for a WFOE can also be refused if the establishment of a WFOE may result in (1) the failure to conform to the requirements of national economic development of China or (2) the endangerment of the national security of China.

For a CJV, if other incidents happen that are against laws, administrative regulations and national industrial policies, its approval cannot be obtained either.

For an EJV, there are two other reasons to deny its approval: (1) nonconformity with the requirements of the development of the national economy of China and (2) obvious inequity in the agreements, contracts and articles of association signed, impairing the rights and interests of one party of an EJV.

According to the US Chamber of Commerce, the standards to assess the applications for the commerce department approval turn out to be broad. The breadth of these criteria allows officials to make discretionary decisions that can violate relevant WTO commitments. As part of China's WTO obligations, China must avoid 'trade-distorting conditions on investment', accord national treatment and market access to foreign investors in some areas and ensure transparency of the approval for investment.[135]

3.3.1.3. The Approval of Industry Regulators (if Necessary)

Chinese authorities administrating some industries have established licensing regimes for certain business activities. Therefore, an FIE focusing on these industries should apply for and obtain a license before they can register with the AIC. In Section 2.4.3.4, rules relating to approvals for licensed operations of a domestic company have been discussed. These provisions apply to an FIE that needs to make applications for a license to engage in these businesses. It should be noted that these

[134] According to Art. 2 of Law on Chinese-Foreign Contractual Joint Ventures, parties to a CJV mean foreign and domestic investors who are part of a contractual joint venture contract to establish a JVC.

[135] The US Chamber of Commerce, China's Approval Process for Inbound Foreign Direct Investment: Impact on Market Access, National Treatment and Transparency, available at: <www.uschamber.com/sites/default/files/reports/020021_China_InvestmentPaper_hires.pdf> (last accessed 6 April 2016).

rules mainly govern for what matters licensing systems can be created and what authorities can establish such regimes.

Of course, the defects of the rules discussed in section 2.4.3.4 can also affect the approval of the industry regulators for the establishment of an FIE. Article 12(6) of the ALL providing for what matters licensing systems are necessary has been proven not to be ideal. This item notes that licensing regimes can be established for other matters except those listed in the preceding items of Article 12. If Article 12(6) is abused, licensing systems can still be set up for almost every situation. As a result, entry barriers can be erected for the establishment of an FIE.

3.4. *Summary*

As interpreted above, an FIE can be established if the capital requirements are met and the relevant procedure is completed. Though the requirements may differ depending on whether an FIE is a CJV, an EJV or a WFOE, the establishment process is almost the same for the three types of FIEs.

The capital requirements can be divided into the rules on the amount of registered capital, capital forms and capital contributions. Important steps to establish an FIE include the DRC project approval, the commerce department approval and the approval of industry regulators if required. If an application for any of the mentioned approval is denied, no FIE can be established.

According to the rules on the capital requirements, it seems hard to create entry barriers for the establishment of an FIE. However, there is a probability that such barriers can be erected based on the opaque rules governing the above approval. First, concerning the approval of industry regulators, there is a possibility for the authorities to abuse Article 12(6) and create licensing systems for almost every matter.

Second, the criteria for the DRC project approval and the commerce department approval share the characteristics of being too broad and granting the approval authorities too much discretion. According to the American Chamber of Commerce in China (hereinafter AmCham China), the evaluation standard for approval should be more exact so that the transparency of the FDI approval procedure could be expected. For example, the concepts of 'public interest' or 'obvious unfairness' with unclear meanings in legislation can be defined.[136]

Third, it is likely that the actual use of licensing can cause entry barriers, which are examined in section 6 by analysing existing empirical research. It should be noted that the DRC project approval, the commerce department approval and the approval of industry regulators are all licensing systems created according to the ALL.

136 AmCham China, the 2012 China Business Climate Survey Report, p. 78, available at: <http://web.resource.amchamchina.org/cmsfile/2012/03/26/c46fc22667c5eeb231748808a9244027.pdf> (last accessed 6 April 2016).

4. Rules on the Inter-provincial Establishment for Companies in China

Having discussed the provisions for the establishment of domestic companies and FIEs, section 4 goes on to examine rules in a particular situation, i.e. the setting up of Chinese companies across provinces. The following discussion serves the purpose of studying the provisions applying to the inter-provincial establishment of a Chinese company and whether the creation of entry barriers for cross-provincial incorporation is possible based on these legal rules.

Together FIEs and domestic companies constitute Chinese companies and the inter-provincial establishment for these two types of companies is subject to different sets of rules. Section 4 begins with the elaboration of the rules of the inter-provincial establishment by domestic companies.

4.1. *Rules on the Inter-provincial Establishment by Domestic Companies*

Under Chinese law, the establishment by domestic companies across provinces can take the form of either wholly owned or joint venture subsidiaries. In other cases, only the way of branches could be chosen. This is because the Company Law stipulates that for a company, the locus of its main office will be regarded as its domicile.[137] Moreover, according to the Company Registration Regulation, the number of company residences registered with the company registration organ can only be one and it must be within the jurisdiction of the organ.[138] Furthermore, more clearly, as provided in the Reply from the SAIC to the Issue of the Registration Management for Additional Premises (2000), in accordance with the mentioned rules in the Company Registration Regulation, the premises set up by companies outside their residences shall be registered as branches since the Company Registration Regulation does not include premises in the items for company registration.[139]

4.1.1. Rules in Terms of Establishing Subsidiaries

According to Article 14 of the Company Law, a company may establish subsidiaries. Subsidiaries are considered as legal entities under Chinese law and the setting up for them needs to satisfy all the substantial conditions and follow all the procedures required for the establishment of companies.[140] The rules on the establishment of a domestic company in China were discussed in section 2.

Moreover, for the subsidiaries engaging in industries such as insurance and securities, their establishment is required to comply with specific conditions. For example, to deal with the issue of securities' acts of establishing subsidiaries, the

137 Art. 10 of the Company Law (2005).

138 Art. 12 of the RACR (Revised 2004).

139 《国家工商行政管理局关于企业增设经营场所是否要登记管理有关问题的答复工商企字[2000]第103号》, the Reply from the State Administration for Industry and Commerce to the Issue of the Registration Management for Additional Premises (2000 No. 103).

140 Art. 14 of the Company Law (2005).

SCRC formulates the Provisions for Trial Implementation on Establishing Subsidiary Companies by Securities Companies (2008). This legislation explicitly stipulates that certain substantial conditions must be met and a list of documents must be submitted for such establishment.[141] Correspondingly, the Commission sets the rules in terms of approving administrative licenses for setting up these subsidiaries.[142] Licensing of the establishment of subsidiaries is certainly subject to the relevant rules of the ALL, which were explained in section 2.

4.1.2. Rules Regarding Establishing Branches

Article 14 of the Company Law provides that a company may set up its branches. Compared to subsidiaries, branches do not enjoy the status as legal persons and setting them up does not require the same process as for establishing companies. However, for the branches involved in certain businesses e.g., insurance, securities etc., their establishment is required to meet the additional conditions set by competent authorities governing these industries. For instance, for setting up branches by the securities companies, they must meet the conditions stipulated in the Provisions for Trial Implementation on Establishing Branches by Securities Companies (2008).[143]

In terms of the procedural requirements, it is necessary for a company to make an application for registration of its branches with the AICs and acquire business licenses.[144] The registration items cover their names, business sites, leading members and business scopes.[145] On the website of the SAIC, materials necessary for this application are listed. They are the application form for establishment signed by the legal representative of the company, the document certifying the representation authorization or the entrusted agency relations, articles of association, the certificate for the commission of the branch managers and the copies of their identity cards, the copy of the counterpart of the company's business license, and the certificate for using the premises of the branches.

Moreover, where in accordance with laws, administrative regulations and the State Council decisions, companies' business scope for registration application includes the items subject to approval before registration, other files are required to

141 中国证监会,《证券公司设立子公司试行规定》(2012年修订)第5、6条。the CSRC, Arts. 5 and 6 of the Provisions for Trial Implementation on Establishing Subsidiary Companies by Securities Companies (2012).

142 中国证监会，证券公司设立审批 (2015), the CSRC, Approvals for Setting up Securities Companies, available at: <www.csrc.gov.cn/pub/zjhpublic/G00306205/201104/-t20110414_194368.htm> (last accessed 6 April 2016).

143 中国证监会《证券公司分公司监管规定（试行）》第3、6条, the CSRC, Arts. 3 and 6 of the Provisions for Trial Implementation on Establishing Branches by Securities Companies (2008).

144 Art. 14 of the Company Law (2005).

145 Art. 47 of the RACR.

be submitted. These files are the relevant documents of approval, the copies of licenses or the certificates of permission.[146]

Furthermore, the submission for the relevant documents of approval or for the copies of licenses is necessary, if the aforementioned legislation stipulates that the establishment of branches is requested to be approved. This application can be either filed simultaneously when setting up a company or after it. In the second circumstance, the application shall be filed within 30 days from the date on which the decisions for establishing branches are made. In the case that approvals are required, the application should be made in 30 days starting from the date when they are given.[147]

4.1.3. Policies to Facilitate the Cross-regional Establishment of Branches and Subsidiaries

In some cases, the previously mentioned requirement to apply for registration and approval is likely to be replaced by other simple procedures when establishing branches and subsidiaries. Certain measures have been proposed to assist the cross-regional establishment of companies in some industries, especially those whose success relies largely on a national network. They can be seen in the following documents targeting service industries. However, these documents can only be considered as the policies of the Chinese government rather than as legislation.

First, in accordance with the 2007 Opinions of the State Council concerning Accelerating the Development of the Service Sector (hereinafter the 2007 Opinions), the inter-regional establishment of some service companies is facilitated to a large extent. The opinion asks governments of all provinces, autonomous regions, and municipalities directly under State Council, and all ministries, commissions and directly subordinate authorities under the State Council to lower the threshold for the entry of general service industries in terms of registered capital and registration with industrial and commercial administration authorities, considering the actual situations. For the service enterprises running chains, the formalities for the registration and business approvals (of their chain stores) could be completed by the companies' headquarters for all of their chains.[148] According to some experts, the essence of the release for the 2007 Opinions is that the completion of the formalities for all the approvals by the headquarters could reduce the duplication of administrative examinations and approvals and the obstacles for chain operations

146 国家工商总局，《分公司设立登记提交材料》, the State Administration of Industry and Commerce, Materials for the establishment registration of branches, available at: <www.saic.gov.cn/ywbl/bszn/nzdjzn/200902/t20090224_11945.html> (last accessed 6 April 2016).

147 *Ibid.*

148 《国务院关于加快发展服务业的若干意见》(2007), the Opinions of the State Council concerning Accelerating the Development of the Service Sector (2007).

caused by local protectionism. It is hoped that the Chinese companies can rapidly run their inter-regional chains, enjoy scale advantages, and lower their costs.[149]

Second, the General Office of the State Council puts forward its opinions agreed with the State Council to promote the sound development of the logistics industry in Opinions of the General Office of the State Council on the Policies and Measures for Promoting the Sound Development of the Logistics Industry (2011) (hereinafter the 2011 Opinions). According to this document, measures will be taken to get rid of regional blockades, facilitate the establishment for legal persons and branches of logistics enterprises and encourage these enterprises to carry out network operations across regions. With regard to the examination and approval procedures implemented by the transportation, public security, environmental protection, quality control, and fire authorities, it is necessary to further standardize them with an aim to shorten the processing time and improve the processing efficiency. For the qualifications not mandatorily applied for by legal persons in accordance with the laws and the approvals of the State Council, the branches can obtain them through making records at their local relevant departments, as long as the headquarters of the logistics companies have acquired them. Moreover, after the headquarters complete the procedures of the registration and approvals for all of its branches, they can go directly to local AICs for registration without undergoing the examination and transformation procedures of such registrations as usual.[150]

Third, the Implementation Opinion on Encouraging and Guiding Private Investment into the Industry of logistics based on the opinions of the General Office of the State Council (2012) (hereinafter the Implementation Opinion) stresses the same points mentioned in the second document.[151] The Implementation Opinion is addressed to the local administrative agencies involved in the administration of the logistic industry such as the SAIC and agencies for governing approvals (e.g., the SCRC).

The above documents clearly reveal the Chinese central government's wish to prevent local protectionism in the establishment of companies through avoiding the

149 超市周刊，《连锁经营行政门槛降低采取总部统一报批制》，Supermarket Weekly, Lowering the Administrative Threshold for Chain Operations, Implementing the policy that formalities of approvals can be completed by the headquarters, available at: <www.cszk.com.cn/n3890c35.aspx> (last accessed 6 April 2016).

150 《国务院办公厅关于促进物流业健康发展政策措施的意见》(国办发 (2011) 38号)，Opinions of the General Office of the State Council on the Policies and Measures for Promoting the Sound Development of the Logistics Industry (No. 38, 2011).

151 《国家发展和改革委员会、公安部、财政部、国土资源部、交通运输部、铁道部、商务部、中国人民银行、国家税务总局、国家工商行政管理总局、中国银行业监督管理委员会、中国证券监督管理委员会关于鼓励和引导民间投资进入物流领域的实施意见》（发改经贸[2012]1619号），National Development and Reform Commission (NDRC), Ministry of Finance, Ministry of Land and Resources, Ministry of Public Security, Ministry of Transport, Ministry of Railways, Ministry of Commerce, the People's Bank of China, State Administration of Taxation, State Administration for Industry and China Banking Regulatory Management Committee and China Securities Regulatory Commission : the Implementation Opinions on Encouraging and Guiding Private Investment into the Industry of logistics (the Bureau of Economy and Trade of the NDRC (2012) No. 1619).

abuse of the approvals and registration powers by local authorities. The remaining question is whether the policies can be enforced. As an official from the National Development and Reform Commission (NDRC) points out, the implementation opinion, as a guiding document, clarifies the policies for encouraging the entry of private capital to the logistics industry in the next stages, but the point is that whether it could be implemented effectively.[152] Moreover, according to AmCham China, the influence of these measures of the 2011 Opinions will depend on their effective enforcement by the government organizations concerned.[153]

However, a report finished by the China Federation of Logistics and Purchasing (CFLP) shows that the 2011 Opinions has been unsatisfactorily implemented. These policies do not reach their potential aims. More specifically, many regions require that only subsidiaries could be established in those particular areas. They do not allow the establishment of branches. Some areas demand additional requirements for the setting up in those specific areas. In some cases, companies are asked to affiliate with other enterprises or organizations, to do business on certain sites only, limit their vehicles to a restricted number or pay operation deposits. Some do not accept the qualifications and certificates obtained by companies' headquarters and a new registration application is still necessary for establishing subsidiaries and branches. The policies enjoyed by the headquarters are not applied to them. Other districts still implement local protectionism measures, set entry barriers and restrict the establishment of companies coming from other places in these districts.[154]

The prohibition on the establishment of branches mentioned above was introduced because branches do not pay all of their enterprise income tax to the tax authorities in the areas where they are located. According to the No. 57 Notice of the State Administration of Tax (SAT) (2012), branches do not have an independent accounting condition. Branches pay the enterprise income tax in advance monthly or quarterly to the local tax authorities where they are set up. After the end of a tax year, the headquarters of the branches shall make a final settlement for the tax already paid by the headquarters and all the branches. For the corporation headquarters and the local businesses, any deficiency must be repaid and any excess payment reimbursed. Moreover, all the local areas where branches are established can only receive 50 per cent of all the tax that is paid by the

152 新华网，发展改革委谈鼓励和引导民间投资进入物流领域实施意见, Xinhua Net, Thoughts of the National Development and Reform Commission on the Implementation Opinions on Encouraging and Guiding Private Investment into the Industry of logistics, available at: <http://news.xinhuanet.com/fortune/2012-07/29/c_112560452.htm#> (last accessed 6 April 2016).

153 AmCham China, American Business in China: 2012 White Paper, p. 218, available at: <www.amchamchina.org/whitepaper2012> (last accessed 6 April 2016).

154 中国物流与采购联合会,《关于"物流国九条"政策落实情况的调查报告》， 2012年3月15日，页19, the China Federation of Logistics and Purchasing, 'A Report on the Survey for the Implementation Result of Opinions of the General Office of the State Council on the Policies and Measures for Promoting the Sound Development of the Logistics Industry', 15 March 2012, p. 19, available at: <www.cflp.org.cn/lhhkx/201203/20/180106.shtml> (last accessed 6 April 2016).

headquarters and all the branches together. The tax revenues which are mentioned, are shared among all the local regions. As demonstrated by civil servants of tax authorities in Beijing and Chengdu, a particular local region where a specific branch is located usually can only receive some of the enterprise income tax revenues generated by this branch. They also pointed out that the branch did not pay any enterprise income tax to the local authority before the implementation of this notice on 1 January 2013.[155]

By contrast, a subsidiary pays all of its enterprise income tax to the tax authority in the local area where it is established. A subsidiary has an independent accounting status and it should be treated as independent taxpayers.[156] That is why local governments usually welcome the establishment of subsidiaries rather than branches.

If a company is permitted to establish subsidiaries only, it can bring disadvantages to the business in the following situation. Sometimes, a company is profit-making, but its newly established subsidiary may make a loss. Under Chinese tax law, the income of a company cannot be used to balance the loss of its subsidiary. In this case, the enterprise income tax paid by the incorporation cannot be reduced even if the subsidiary is in a loss-making position. In contrast, if a company sets up a branch and this local business is crippled by losses, the enterprise income tax paid by the incorporation can be decreased. The reason is that the profit of a company can be reduced since the revenue can be used to balance the loss of its branch.

Considering the implementation of the Opinion, the CFLP proposes some urgent suggestions to facilitate the establishment of branches and subsidiaries in one area by companies having their headquarters in other places. Local authorities should permit companies to establish branches and cancel the requirements on affiliation. It is also profitable to strengthen the administration of qualifications for the logistics industry, simplify the process to get relevant certifications and qualifications. For those mandatory certifications and qualifications, branches and subsidiaries should be allowed to use them across China. Moreover, the policies advantageous to their headquarters should also be executed for the branches and subsidiaries equally and another application should be avoided.[157]

The measures of the 2007 Opinions to facilitate the expansion of chain businesses are not enforced in certain areas at all. For example, as reported in Zhongshan Business Daily, the headquarters of Youchebang, a chain enterprise for

155 I am grateful to the two officials. They kindly explained independent accounting conditions and the No. 57 Notice of the State Administration of Tax (SAT) (2012) to me.

156 异地成立分公司如何缴纳所得税？How to Pay Income Tax for Branches Established in Other Places?, available at: <www.zjtax.net/newsDetail_3250.html> (last accessed 6 April 2016).

157 中国物流与采购联合会,《关于"物流国九条"政策落实情况的调查报告》, 2012年3月15日, 页25, the China Federation of Logistics and Purchasing, 'A Report on the Survey for the Implementation Result of Opinions of the General Office of the State Council on the Policies and Measures for Promoting the Sound Development of the Logistics Industry', 15 March 2012, p. 25, available at: <www.cflp.org.cn/lhhkx/201203/20/180106.shtml> (last accessed 6 April 2016).

car maintenance, cannot use its approvals for the branches established by the company in Zhongshan city in 2013. Instead, these new shops are still asked to acquire the permission from relevant agencies by the local AIC. The branches are refused registration by the AIC without obtaining these approvals.[158] However, the 2007 Opinions allow the bases of chain businesses to acquire the qualifications for all these divisions that are accepted by the local authorities at the seat of the branches. Furthermore, a representative from the AIC of Hangzhou also demonstrates that such policies are not adopted in that municipality.

4.1.4. Summary

As elaborated on above, the inter-provincial establishment of subsidiaries by a domestic company is subject to the same rules that apply for the incorporation of a domestic company. The cross-provincial establishment of branches by a domestic company requires an application for registration with the AICs and for licenses in some cases.

It seems as if legal barriers are unlikely to be created in the case of cross-provincial establishment, according to the law in the books. However, Article 12(6) of the ALL can be an exception. As mentioned before, there is a possibility that Article 12(6) can be abused, thus, allowing licensing systems to be set up at random.

Moreover, the actual interpretation and enforcement of legal requirements may hinder the inter-provincial incorporation of a domestic company. First, there are reports that some legal rules governing the cross-provincial establishment are violated, and as a result, companies have difficulties. Second, some policies to facilitate this establishment are not fully implemented.

In section 5, the results of some earlier empirical research will be discussed. The question, after all, is whether the actual application of the legal rules leads to considerable barriers to inter-provincial establishment by a domestic company.

4.2. *Rules on Inter-provincial Establishment by FIEs*

An established FIE can expand its business across provincial borders by establishing either branches or subsidiaries. This section starts by discussing the rules concerning the inter-provincial establishment of branches by an FIE.

4.2.1. Rules in Terms of Establishing Branches

According to Sinovantage (2012), an investment consulting company, an FIE can establish its branches in China after the registered capital of the FIE has been fully

158 中山商报，连锁企业落户中山遭遇前置审批，工商部称弄错概念， Zhongshan Business Daily, Zhongshan Authorities Impose Pre-administrative Licenses Requirements on Companies Setting up Businesses, the AIC Takes the Confusion about the Concepts of Branches and Chain Businesses as an Excuse, available at: <www.zsnews.cn/news/2013/-01/29/2353015.shtml> (last accessed 6 April 2016).

paid and verified.[159] There is no registered capital requirement for a branch set up by an FIE.[160] That means that as long as steps stipulated are finished, a branch can be established. According to the US Chamber of Commerce, the procedure for the establishment of a branch in most domains includes pre-registering a company name, receiving site-related opinion letters, obtaining the DRC project approval, registering with the AICs and filing for registration with a commerce department. After this process, the branch may need to register with other administrative organizations such as tax authorities if required.[161]

The above process for the establishment of a branch has roughly the same steps necessary for the incorporation of an FIE in China. For example, as demonstrated by Chris Devonshire-Ellis, the establishment of a WFOE branch and the creation of a WFOE have almost the same application process.[162] Only two different points should be mentioned.

First, registering with the AICs requires a registration both where an FIE is located and where a branch of the FIE is established. By contrast, the establishment of an FIE in China only asks for filing a registration with the AIC where the FIE is incorporated.

Second, companies wanting to establish branches need to file registrations with a commerce authority instead of applying for a commerce department license. Such requirement makes a difference to businesses. In the first case, officials are asked to record this setting up, while they can deny a license if the second governing method is used. As provided in Article 1 of the Circular of the Ministry of Commerce on Further Improving Examination and Approval of Foreign Investment (2009), the establishment of a branch by an FIE is subject to record keeping and administration. Specifically, the FIE should directly go through the formalities for filing at the competent commercial authority where the FIE is registered.[163]

4.2.2. Rules in Terms of Establishing Subsidiaries

The inter-provincial establishment of subsidiaries by FIEs is governed by the Provisional Regulations Governing Investment within the Territory by Foreign

159 Patrick K. Abotsi (Sinovantage Investment Consulting Limited), Setting up a Branch of Your WFOE at a Second Location in China: an Overview, available at: <www.sinoinvest.hk> p. 3 (last accessed 6 April 2016).

160 Dezan Shira & Associates, China Branch Offices and RO-WFOE 'Conversions', available at: <www.china-briefing.com/news/2012/06/18/china-branch-offices-and-ro-wfoe-conversions.html> (last accessed 6 April 2016).

161 The US Chamber of Commerce, China's Approval Process for Inbound Foreign Direct Investment: Impact on Market Access, National Treatment and Transparency, p. 36 and 37, available at: <https://www.uschamber.com/sites/default/files/documents/files/-020021_China_InboundInvestment_Cvr.pdf> (last accessed 6 April 2016).

162 Dezan Shira & Associates 2011, p. 56.

163 商务部关于进一步改进外商投资审批工作的通知 (2009). The English version of this document is available at: <http://sa2.mofcom.gov.cn/article/shangfuting/200904/20090406140607.-shtml> (last accessed 6 April 2016).

Investment Enterprises (2000) (hereinafter the Regulations for Reinvestment).[164] According to Article 1 of the Regulations for Reinvestment, this document regulates the investment activities of FIEs. Article 2 interprets establishing enterprises through investment within the territory of China as one way of such investment by FIEs. As provided in Article 3(3), FIEs can establish subsidiaries in restricted, permitted or encouraged foreign investment fields only. As demonstrated in the section on the establishment of FIEs, the categories of the investment fields are regulated by the Catalogue.

However, the Regulations for Reinvestment do not regulate the investment that is made by investment companies established by foreign investors. As prescribed in Article 2(2) of the Regulations for Reinvestment, the inter-provincial incorporation of subsidiaries by such companies is governed by the Provisional Regulations on the Establishment of Investment Companies by Foreign Investors (1995) and other related provisions. In fact, the aforementioned legislation has lapsed. At present, such incorporation is regulated by other legislation. Most important rules are provided in the Provisions of the Ministry of Commerce on the Establishment of Investment Companies by Foreign Investors (Revised 2004), the Supplementary Provisions on the Establishment of Investment Companies by Foreign Investors (2006) and the Provisions Concerning the Administration of Foreign-funded Business-starting Investment Enterprises (2003).[165]

It should be mentioned that some provisions in the Regulations for Reinvestment have been annulled since the enactment of the Company Law and other regulatory documents. However, the Regulations for Reinvestment have not yet been amended. As a result, the rules on the inter-provincial establishment by FIEs appear not as clear as the regulations for the cross-provincial establishment by domestic companies.

The establishment of subsidiaries by FIEs needs to meet capital conditions and satisfy procedural requirements. Both the conditions and the requirements can be different, based on which types of FIEs start the subsidiaries and the business scope of the subsidiaries.

164 The Provisional Regulations Governing Investment within the Territory by Foreign Investment Enterprises (外商投资企业境内投资的暂行规定) (2000) is available in English at: < www.lehmanlaw.com/resource-centre/laws-and-regulations/foreign-investment/-provisional-regulations-governing-investment-within-the-territory-by-foreign-investment-enterprises-2000.html> (last accessed 6 April 2016). Some provisions discussed in this chapter have been modified considerably.

165 In this paragraph, the four pieces of legislation concerning the establishment of investment companies by foreign investors are 关于外商投资举办投资性公司的暂行规定（1995），关于外商投资举办投资性公司的规定（2004修订）， 商务部关于外商投资举办投资性公司的补充规定（2006） and 外商投资创业投资企业管理规定（2003年第2号）in sequence.

4.2.2.1. *Capital Requirements*

FIEs can establish either wholly owned or joint venture subsidiaries. The rules on the capital requirements for the establishment depend on what types of companies open the subsidiaries.

The incorporation of subsidiaries solely by a WFOE or jointly by WFOEs has the same capital requirements as the establishment of WFOEs. According to Article 2 of the Law on WFOEs (2000), WFOEs in this law refers to those enterprises established in China by foreign investors exclusively with their own capital. However, WFOEs defined by this law exclude branches set up in China by foreign enterprises and other foreign economic organizations.[166] As a result, WFOEs regulated by the Law on WFOEs (2000) include the mentioned subsidiaries. Therefore, the rules on the capital requirements of WFOEs discussed previously certainly apply to such subsidiaries.

The capital requirements for the formation of subsidiaries by FIEs and foreign investors jointly are subject to the same rules as EJVs. As provided in Article 1 of the Law on EJVs (Revised 2001), an EJV means any enterprise incorporated by foreign investors and Chinese companies, enterprise or other economic organizations.[167] Since FIEs are Chinese companies, the subsidiaries established by FIEs and foreign investors, of course, belong to EJVs governed by the Law on EJVs (Revised 2001). Thus, these subsidiaries should meet the same capital requirements as EJVs.

The formation of subsidiaries by FIEs, by WFOEs and domestic companies or by FIEs and domestic companies jointly share the same rules on capital requirements as EJVs. Unlike the above two situations about the establishment, this application of the rules for EJVs is not explicitly provided in any law. Instead, the use of such rules is justified by the following fact. The subsidiaries mentioned are incorporated through contributing capitals. Moreover, the contribution is, in essence, made by both foreign and domestic investors. According to the Law on EJVs (Revised 2001), an EJV is also established by domestic and foreign investors through contributing capitals. That is why it is necessary for the subsidiaries discussed in this paragraph to satisfy the same capital requirements as EJVs.[168]

In short, the capital requirements for FIEs to establish subsidiaries differ in the above three situations. Where a WFOE establishes subsidiaries by itself or jointly with other WFOEs, the WFOEs should follow the capital requirements for the formation of WFOEs. In the other two cases, the capital requirements for the establishment of EJVs should be satisfied.

In addition, the contributions for the establishment of subsidiaries should not be made in the fund in RMB obtained from the settlement of exchange by FIEs. This rule is provided in the Notice on the Relevant Operating Issues concerning the

166 The Law on the WFOEs (2000), 外资企业法（2000）. The English text of this law is available at: <www.fdi.gov.cn> (last accessed 6 April 2016).

167 The Law on the EJVs (Revised 2001), 中外合资经营企业法（2001年修订）. The English version of this law is available at: <www.fdi.gov.cn> (last accessed 6 April 2016).

168 WFOEs are certainly a type of FIEs. However, FIEs mentioned in this paragraph only include CJVs and EJVs.

Improvement of Administrating the Payment and Settlement of the Foreign Currency Capital of FIEs (2008), which is issued by the State Administration of Foreign Exchange.[169] According to this regulation, the mentioned fund in RMB can only be used for certain business scopes approved by governmental agencies. Furthermore, unless otherwise provided, such a fund cannot be contributed to by incorporate subsidiaries.

Lastly, it should be remembered that an FIE does not need to acquire any qualification to establish subsidiaries. This provision is laid down in the Notice of the SAIC about Executing the Executive Opinions on Some Issues Concerning the Application of Law Governing the Examination, Approval and Registration of Foreign-funded Companies (2006).[170]According to this notice, the qualification refers to the requirements provided in Articles 5 and 6 of the Regulations for Reinvestment. Articles 5 and 6 ask an FIE to meet certain conditions before being able to make investment in China. Article 5 provides that (1) the registered capital of FIEs has been fully paid in; (2) FIEs commence to make profit and (3) FIEs conduct business lawfully and have no record of illegal operations. According to Article 6, the aggregated investment amount of FIEs shall not exceed 50 per cent of their own net assets. Although the Regulations for Reinvestment have not been amended, Articles 5 and 6 of this legislation have expired due to the 2006 document.

4.2.2.2. *Procedural Requirements for the Establishment of Subsidiaries*

The procedural requirements to incorporate a subsidiary depend on the category of the business this company engages in. The establishment of a subsidiary in the permitted and encouraged investment fields has similar simple rules. By contrast, the provisions governing the incorporation of a subsidiary in the restricted industries are more complicated. The following section starts to explain how to create a subsidiary in the restricted investment fields.

According to Article 9 of the Regulations for Reinvestment, any FIEs establishing subsidiaries in the field of restricted foreign investment industries will apply to a commercial authority. The authority will be the provincial commerce department of the place where the subsidiary is to be located.

Moreover, as also prescribed in Article 9, certain documents must be submitted to the commerce department.[171] Among them, the articles of association

[169] 国家外汇管理局关于完善外商投资企业外汇资本金支付结汇管理有关业务操作问题的通知（2008).

[170] 《国家工商总局关于实施〈关于外商投资的公司审批登记管理法律适用若干问题的执行意见>的通知》(2006).

[171] These files include (1) the unanimously approved resolution of the board of directors of the FIEs about the establishment of their subsidiary; (2) the copies of the approval certificate and the business license of the FIEs, (3) the articles of association of the subsidiary and (4) other documents required by laws, regulations and rules.

should mention a list of items.[172] Moreover, the Investors must sign and seal in the articles of association of the subsidiary.

According to Article 10, the provincial commerce department shall ask for the opinions of the national or provincial administrative department in charge of the business scope of the subsidiary. After obtaining the consent or dissent from the industry regulator, the provincial commerce department shall issue a written reply within 10 days. As a potential problem for Article 10, the relation between the opinions and the decision of the commerce department is unclear. In other words, the question is whether the commercial authority can deny the applications to establish subsidiaries if the industry regulator has the dissent.

As provided in Article 11, in the case where the provincial commerce department has made a positive reply to the FIEs, the FIEs should apply for the business registration to an AIC upon the approval reply. It is provided that the AIC will be the authority at the place where the subsidiary is to be located. The AIC should rely on the relevant regulations of the Company Registration Regulation to decide to permit the registration or not. If the registration is permitted, the business license of the subsidiary should be issued.

Articles 9 to 12 regulate how the provincial commerce department approves the application of establishing subsidiaries by FIEs. However, according to Article 22, MOFOCM is responsible for the approval, if the subsidiary belongs to the FIE in the fields that should be approved by MOFCOM. In this case, the provincial commerce department must forward the application to MOFCOM.

As provided in Article 12, within 30 days from the establishment of the subsidiary, the FIE starting the subsidiary should submit certain documents to the original examination and approval authority for their records. The authority refers to the administrative departments that approve the incorporation of the FIE. The documents for filing include: (1) the filing form for the investment of the FIE; (2) the business license (copy) of the subsidiary; (3) the provincial commercial department's reply to approve the establishment of the subsidiary, in a case where the business scope of the subsidiary includes the field belonging to the restricted category.

The above section discussed the process for setting up a subsidiary in the restricted industries. How to create a subsidiary corporation in the permitted and encouraged fields is explained as follows. According to Article 7, any FIE incorporating a subsidiary in these two types of foreign investment industries must apply to the AIC of the place where the subsidiary is to be situated. Moreover, the

172 The articles of association should contain information about (1) the name and the domicile of the subsidiary; (2) the business scope and the proportion of the subsidiary's output to be sold domestically and internationally; (3) the registered capital of the subsidiary; (4) the name of the investors of the subsidiary; (5) the rights and the obligations of the investors; (6) the contribution method and amount of the investors; (7) the conditions for the transfer of capital contributions; (8) the organisations of the subsidiary and their formation method, authority and rules of procedure; (9) the legal representative of the subsidiary; (10) the dissolution reasons and the liquidation method of the subsidiary and (11) other matters deemed necessary by the investors.

following documents must be submitted: (1) the unanimously approved resolution of the board of directors of the FIE about the establishment of the subsidiary; (2) the copies of the approval certificate and the business license of the FIE and (3) other documents required by laws, regulations and rules.[173]

As provided in Article 8, the AIC shall decide to permit the registration or not by taking the Company Law and the Company Registration Regulation as criterion. If the registration is permitted, the AIC should issue a business license to the subsidiary and add 'Invested by the FIE' in the 'Enterprise Type' column of the license.

After the two steps provided in Articles 7 and 8, the FIE incorporating the subsidiary needs to meet the requirements of Article 12. Briefly, Article 12 asks the FIE to report the establishment of the subsidiary corporation for recording. Article 12 has been interpreted in detail above.

In conclusion, the incorporation of subsidiaries by FIEs in different industries has different rules. For establishment in restricted areas there is a requirement to obtain approval from commerce departments, while there is no such requirement for the incorporation in the encouraged and permitted fields. Of course, the formation of subsidiaries in the all the areas shares certain steps, e.g., registering with the AIC.

Nevertheless, whether or not approval by a commerce agency is necessary can vary in practice. As argued by Xiaodong Zhang and Mei Li, the sector groups in the Catalogue are not well defined and can be interpreted rather flexibly.[174] According to AmCham China, these categories can even conflict with each other. For example, 'outsourcing' falls in encouraged categories and the services are 'outsourced' are listed, according to AmCham China. However, some of these services are also mentioned in restricted or prohibited categories.[175]

4.2.3. Summary

FIEs can either set up a branch or subsidiary to expand their business in China. The formation of a branch requires a set of steps, most of which are the same as those for FIEs. No capital requirement has been imposed by any law for the incorporation of branches by FIEs.

There are both capital and procedural requirements for the establishment of subsidiaries by FIEs. The capital requirements are laid down in the relevant legislation on the incorporation of FIEs. The procedural steps depend on the field the subsidiaries engage in. The subsidiaries whose business belongs to the encouraged and permitted investment categories should be registered with certain

173 Art. 7 asks for the submission of other documents by the FIE. However, it is not necessary for the FIE to fulfil the requirements currently. This is because such files are used to demonstrate the qualification provided by Arts. 5 and 6 and these two provisions have lapsed.

174 Zhang & Li 2003, p. 6.

175 AmCham China, American Business in China, 2013 White Paper, p. 176, available at: <http://web.resource.amchamchina.org/cmsfile/2013/04/23/bdc6b202456080c09530a66d8c5ea48d.pdf> (last accessed 6 April 2016).

authorities. For the subsidiary corporations operating in restricted investment areas, it is important to apply for registration and obtain approval. Most of the steps are those required for the incorporation of FIEs.

Some of the barriers to the formation of FIEs can also be erected for the establishment of new businesses by FIEs. This is because there are some similar requirements for the expansion of FIEs and the establishment of FIEs, as summarised above. To be specific, the barriers can be imposed due to the rules providing the criteria for the DRC project and the commerce department approval. This provision turns out to be general and allows the authorities to use very wide discretion, which is discussed in the section about establishing FIEs. Such wide discretion can deny the approval, as a result of which FIEs cannot incorporate subsidiaries and branches. In addition, again, Article 12(6) of the ALL can play a potential role in creating barriers.

Moreover, it is unclear how the industry regulators' views can influence the establishment of subsidiaries by FIEs. According to Article 10 of the Reinvestment Regulation, there is a possibility that the application for commerce department licenses can be denied based on the opinions of the industry regulators. However, it is unclear what views held by the industry regulators can be a reason for this rejection. If Article 10 is misused, obstacles can be erected for this formation.

Furthermore, it is likely that in some cases, the establishment of subsidiaries in a specific area has to be approved by the commerce department, while in other cases the incorporation of subsidiaries in the same field does not require the same licenses. This is because there is some conflicting business classification in the Catalogue.

Finally, it is likely that entry barriers can be erected through the exercise of licensing. It should be mentioned that the DRC project and the commerce department approval are all licensing regimes created according to the ALL. The use of licensing is examined in section 6.

5. The Reality of Cross-provincial Establishment by Domestic Companies

Sections 2, 3 and 4 have considered the rules concerning the incorporation of a domestic company, the establishment of FIEs and the inter-provincial establishment for companies in China. Logically, the application of these provisions ought to be studied to have a complete and in-depth examination on the possible barriers for this establishment. However, the following sections examine the facts about inter-provincial establishment for companies in China and focus on the interpretation and enforcement of the rules governing this establishment only.

This section concentrates on the situation concerning domestic businesses, whereas the facts about the FIEs are dealt in with section 6. As explained in section 4, cross-provincial incorporation by the two types of companies is governed by two different sets of rules. A separate discussion can provide a clear understanding about the formation in practice.

According to the rules for the inter-provincial establishment for domestic companies in China, as long as the requirements of both the procedures and substantial conditions are met, a company can be successfully set up in different provinces in China. However, many reports show that the problem of local protectionism hinders the setting up in practice. The Business Daily mentions that local protectionism is serious in some regions, implementing differentiated policies towards local companies and those from outside. It seriously hinders the operation of big chains across different areas.[176] According to an article from the China Youth Daily, local protectionism has been the biggest barrier to a unified national market. One research conducted by MOFCOM shows that chain stores are especially confronted with the resistances from various sides when trying to set up branches in different areas.[177] A report finished in 2011 reveals that local protectionism still poses difficulties for the development of pharmacy chains across regions.[178] Moreover, as discussed in a meeting organised by the Ministry of Culture in 2012, eliminating the country's local protectionism is still one of the first priorities for developing café chains.[179] Thus, in this section, the types of problems for the establishment will be categorized based on relatively detailed cases for individual companies. It will also examine whether the Chinese authorities create these barriers, more specifically, which government agency at which level places obstacles in the way of companies trying to become established outside their regions.

5.1. *Classification of Barriers Faced by Companies*

5.1.1. Abuse of Administrative Powers

As shown in practice, the administrative powers of local government agencies are sometimes abused to hinder the setting up of companies. The problem of imposing additional requirements can be easily identified in the establishment of café chains. For example, the Beijing Youth Daily indicates that the development of café chains is obstructed by local protectionism. One manager of a cafés chain complains that even if licenses for national application are used to set up cafés in local regions,

176 每日商报, 汽车用品连锁经营的优缺点及注意事项, Business Daily, Advantages and Disadvantages of the Chain Operation for the Production of Cars and Relevant Matters Needing Consideration, available at: <http://info.auto-a.hc360.com/2010/12/-060841312596.shtml> (last accessed 6 April 2016).

177 中国青年报, 地方保护主义已成全国统一市场的最大障碍，2004年6月23日, 参见, available at: <http://big5.china.com.cn/chinese/law/592681.htm> (last accessed 6 April 2016), Local Protectionism Has Been the Biggest Barrier to a Unified National Market, the China Youth Daily, 23 June 2004.

178 政策助推连锁药店行业加快整合升级, Policies to Promote the Integration and Upgrade of Drugstore Chains. Available at: <http://blog.vsharing.com/zhuantifenxi/A1647868.html> (last accessed 6 April 2016).

179 内蒙古自治区文化厅市场处, 全国文化市场管理工作会议暨全国网吧连锁推进工作阶段总结会精神传达提纲（2012年1月）, Market Department of Culture Bureau of Inner Mongolia Autonomous Region , the Outline on the Spirit of the National Culture Market Management Working Conference and the Summary Session of the Development of Café Chains (January 2012). Available at: <www.qb5200.com/content/2015-12-28/224142.html> (last accessed 6 April 2016).

there are still many key issues that need to be considered and solved. As a result, opportunities are lost in many cases. Because of the seriousness of the protectionism, companies coming from outside have to meet some additional thresholds, causing difficulties for setting up their business there when trying to enter the local market.[180]

Moreover, according to an article from the 21st Century Business Herald, there are too many formalities, necessary for a valid setting up, which are imposed by various administrative agencies ranging from ministries to the local government's cultural departments and even the cultural inspection team at county level.[181] Furthermore, as demonstrated by the Zhongguancun Online, local protectionism usually takes various forms. The café chains have to deal with the endless reviews, inspections and approvals of the authorities for public security, industry and commerce, health etc. In addition, there are too many 'competent' authorities. The owners of these cafés have to cope with the 'interim measures' and 'provisional regulations' of governments at all levels, besides the remaining 'red-tape documents'.[182]

5.1.2. Under-enforcement of State Regulations and Policies

Another problem for the inter-provincial establishment of companies is that the relevant national rules and policies are seldom followed by local authorities. Abundant cases can be found in pharmacy sectors.

First, policies to allow the inter-provincial establishment of certain companies are rarely enforced. A case in point is the difficulties for establishing pharmacy chains in different provinces. As reported in the Beijing Morning Post, even though relevant national administrative agencies have announced the cancelation of the restrictions on the inter-provincial establishment of pharmacy chains, some enterprises still cannot overcome barriers of local protectionism to set up new shops. Many pharmacy chains are usually subject to interference from local governments when setting up their inter-regional shops there. In the process of establishing a new branch, a domestic pharmacy chain in a southern city received a notice from the local drug administrative bureau that its application for establishment could not be approved even after all the requirements regarding capital, personnel and shop site were met. The simple reason was that there was already a pharmacy within 500 metres of the potential location of the branch. The

180 北京青年报,《连锁网吧"鸡肋"式生存文化部欲靠免税救场》， 2005年1月17日，Beijing Youth Daily, The Café Chains Have Difficulties Surviving, but Businesses are unwilling to Abandon Their Operations. The Ministry of Culture Wants to Cut Tax to Support the Market, 17 January 2005.

181 21世纪经济报 (记者: 雷中辉), 连锁网吧鸡肋式生存文化部救场三年免税, 2005年1月16日，The café Chains Have Difficulties Surviving, but Businesses are unwilling to Abandon Their Operations. The Ministry of Culture Supports the Market by Cutting Tax. 21st Century Business Herald (journalist: Zhonghui Lei), 16 January 2005.

182 中关村在线, 网吧连锁: 前途有些光明道路绝对曲折, 2006年09月06日，Zhongguancun Online, the Café Chains: a Cautiously Optimistic Future, but Absolutely Difficult to Develop, 6 September 2006.

establishment of the branch there would not meet the requirement for the planning of pharmacies' sites. However, unexpectedly, a local company successfully set up a pharmacy on the same site just two weeks later.[183]

Moreover, according to Nanfengchuan, in a research paper on circulation by the Guangdong government almost all the pharmaceutical chain enterprises consider local protectionism as the most severe problem for their further development and their first priority is committed to breaking it. Nevertheless, the article on Nanfengchuan does not indicate at which level administrative agencies create this obstacle. As shown in the same article, with the satisfaction of all the other requirements, the 999 company which is registered in Guangdong province, and is one of the biggest pharmaceutical corporations in China, still cannot establish its shops in Nanchang as the local Food and Drug Administration (FDA) refused to deal with its license application promptly. The authority explained that it turned out to be time-consuming to get it processed. It planned to study the 999's situation and discuss it first with the chamber of commerce, the local pharmaceutical company and related pharmaceutical stores at first. Only after these steps, could relevant policies and regulations be made.[184]

Furthermore, one article of the Nan Fang Daily shows that the official in charge of the SFDA strongly criticized the local blockade measures taken by some regions that hinder the chain store operations directly or indirectly. According to him, certain regions explicitly prohibit the establishment of pharmaceutical chain stores there. Some reject the applications of such operations for the reason that 'no acceptance for the applications is allowed during the time for changing certificates', 'the horizontal management system is not ready for the mentioned acceptance', 'the local area has not yet started to accept those applications' etc. Some explain that 'the administrative agencies use the current period to improve their management' and 'there are too many local pharmaceutical retailers already' and prolong the approval process deliberately. Others resist processing the applications by publicly stating that 'our local retailers cannot do business and survive if your stores are set up here'.[185]

The reasons for the problems of enforcement have been discussed. According to a report of Nanfengchuan, as an insider points out, though the SFDA explicitly allows certain pharmaceutical companies to set up chain stores in other provinces,

183 鄢晨，走好，连锁药店！, 北京晨报, 2001年11月8日， Chen Ye, Wish a Good Development to Drugstore Chains, Beijing Morning Post, 8 November 2001. In the study of European scholars, especially in their research on the Internal Market, the pharmacy is often considered as a profession. However, it could also be treated as a category of business. That is why the barriers faced by pharmacies are included here to show whether there is freedom of establishment for companies in China. This point is also made in the introduction chapter of this thesis.

184 袁卫东、毛译敏, 谁在阻击药业连锁, 南风窗 2001.11下， 页7. Weidong Yuan, Yimin Mao, Who is Blocking the Pharmaceutical Chain, Nanfenchuang, (11) 2001, p. 7.

185 连锁还是封锁？国家药监局负责人痛斥地方保护主义(新华社供稿)，《南方日报》，2001年9月03日, 参见人民网, Chain Operation or Blockade? The Official in Charge of the State Food and Drug Administration Criticized Severely Local Protectionism （sources: Xinhua News Agency）, Nan Fang Daily, 3 September 2001.

their establishment is hindered by the local FDAs at county level. This is because the local authorities have the power to deal with their applications for such establishment in their regions and they usually do not approve them in an independent and unbiased manner. Their officials are very likely to become the managers of the local pharmaceutical companies and conflicts of interest may arise among the local FDAs, the local pharmaceutical companies and the offices of local governments for the pharmaceutical industry. Unfortunately, the provincial FDAs, which are only responsible for management, cannot implement the policy allowing the establishment of chain stores.[186]

Second, acquiring approval turns out to be extremely difficult in some circumstances. One vice chief editor of the China Chain Magazine indicates that when entering a new provincial market in the Northeast of China, a home appliances chain enterprise cannot obtain its business licenses for more than one year because of the obstacles set by a local retailer and relevant local authorities.[187]

5.2. *Xia, Lu and Yu's Essay on the Creation of Obstacles for the Inter-provincial Establishment by Local Governments*[188]

Xia, Lu and Yu (2011) analyse the relation between the political connections of chairmen and general managers in Chinese listed companies and the inter-provincial establishment of branches and subsidiaries by these corporations. They first hypothesize that (1) companies with political ties are more likely to invest in cross-provincial establishment than those without the political connections and (2) corporations having political relations with central governmental agencies are more likely to engage in this establishment than those without such relationships. Later, they collect data and use an OLS regression analysis to test and confirm their hypotheses. They conclude that Chinese companies registered in a provincial region are faced with certain obstacles when they try to establish their subsidiaries and branches in another provincial area. Moreover, local governments are to a certain extent responsible for these barriers. This section interprets the data in their research, discusses their conclusion and explains how they draw their conclusion.

Their data is collected mainly from the initial public offering (IPO) reports submitted by Chinese listed companies between 1997 and 2003, which is convincing. To begin with, they choose the companies that used the offering during that time, but exclude those whose ownership is indeterminate, those whose general

186 袁卫东、毛译敏，谁在阻击药业连锁，南风窗2001.11下， 页7. Weidong Yuan, Yimin Mao, Who is Blocking the Pharmaceutical Chain, Nanfenchuang, (11) 2001, p. 7.

187 陈岳峰，地方保护主义将扼杀民族企业，Yuefeng Chen, Local Protectionism Would Stifle National Enterprises, available at: <http://blog.sina.com.cn/s/blog_54f00a1e0100088n.html> (last accessed 6 April 2016).

188 Xia, Lu & Yu 2011. Xia is a scholar from Shanghai Jiao Tong University. Lu currently conducts research at Fudan Univeristy and Zhejiang University and Yu works at Shanghai University of Finance & Economics and the University of British Columbia. The authors receive funding from some top research foundations in China, for example, the National Natural Science Foundation of China and a key research base of the Chinese Ministry of Education.

managers and chairmen have unknown government backgrounds and those that do not establish subsidiaries and branches. Second, they categorize them into companies not controlled by governments, those controlled by central government and those controlled by local governments.

Their set of data includes 64 companies which were not government controlled at the end of the year for the IPO. This information shows that in the first place, branches, subsidiaries and associated enterprises established by them in mainland China outside the provincial regions where they have their registered offices account for 32 per cent of them in the mainland. Second, in terms of their political relations, 20 per cent of their general managers and chairmen have served in governmental agencies. 19 per cent of their general managers and chairmen's highest position ranking is lower than or equal to county level. 2 per cent of their highest posts rank equal to or above assistant department or bureau level. 3 per cent of them have had official experience at central government departments. However, on average their positions are lower than governors at county level. Moreover, more than half of them have not had government posts. Third, the writers list other elements that may affect the inter-provincial establishment, e.g., the average number of branches and subsidiaries established by those companies. They try to remove the influence of the other factors over the establishment with the aim of studying the relationship between political relation and the setting up only.[189]

With regard to 158 companies controlled by local governments, the authors demonstrate first that until the end of that year, 20 per cent of their branches, subsidiaries and associated enterprises in the mainland are established outside the provincial areas where their registered offices are located. Second, concerning their political relations, 40 per cent of their general managers and chairmen have had official experience in governmental departments. 27 per cent of them have held high positions which were lower than or equal to county level. 13 per cent have held high posts ranking equal to or above assistant department or bureau level. 2 per cent of them have held positions in central government departments. However, similar to the above group of companies, their positions are lower than leading cadres at county level on average and more than half of them have not had government positions.

In terms of 75 companies controlled by central government, by the end of the year for the IPO, they had set up 50 per cent of their branches, subsidiaries and associated enterprises in the provincial regions of mainland China where their registered offices are not located. Then, with regard to their political relations, 40 per cent of their general managers and chairmen have had official experience in governmental departments. 27 per cent of them have had highest positions lower than or equal to county level. 13 per cent of their highest posts ranking is equal to or above assistant department or bureau level. 2 per cent of them have held positions at central government departments. However, again, their positions are lower than governors at county level on average with more than half of them having no government positions.

[189] Therefore, the chapter does not provide their data on those factors.

Moreover, Xia, Lu and Yu explicitly reveal the information for the selected Chinese listed companies as a whole. To start with, branches, subsidiaries and associated enterprises set up by them in mainland China outside the provincial regions where their registered offices are situated amount to 32 per cent of them in the mainland. Second, regarding their political relations, 35 per cent of their general managers and chairmen have held offices in governmental agencies. 22 per cent of them have held highest positions lower than or equal to county level. There are 13 per cent of them having had highest posts equal to or above assistant department or bureau level. 6 per cent of them have had official experience at central government agencies. However, like all the categories mentioned, on average their positions are lower than administrators at county level. Moreover, more than half of them have not had government posts.[190]

Based on the above information, they use a mathematical model and an OLS regression analysis to verify their hypothesis. Relying on the application of the model and regression, they detail their findings on the relationship between the political connections of managers and a chairman in a company and the inter-provincial investment the business makes. Their discoveries can be interpreted from two perspectives.

First, they compare the likelihood of the three different categories of companies establishing branches or subsidiaries in other provinces. Corporations controlled by central government are more likely to start these two kinds of local businesses than companies not controlled by government. Moreover, it is most unlikely that companies controlled by local governments will incorporate branches or subsidiaries in other provincial regions.

Second, they explain how important the political ties of managers and directors are for the inter-provincial establishment of branches and subsidiaries by each type of company. Enterprises controlled by central government do not benefit from the political connections of their senior managers and directors in the corporations' cross-provincial establishment. A possible reason could be that these companies can manage with the obstacles created for the establishment of their branches and subsidiaries in another province because they have central government support. The political relation is not important to them according to the authors.

By contrast, it is mainly enterprises controlled by local governments which profit from these political connections, but only when their managers and directors have been senior officials e.g., heads of department under provincial governments or at equivalent levels. However, the political experience held by the leaders of these corporations in central governmental agencies does not help in setting up a local business in another provincial area. In Xia, Lu and Yu's view, this is probably because the barriers to the cross-provincial establishment of branches and subsidiaries are created by the local government of that particular district and not by industrial policies. The policies appear to be made by national authorities.

190 Xia, Lu & Yu 2011, p. 132-134.

Likewise, the official experience of managers and chairmen at departments of central government could facilitate companies not controlled by governments to incorporate branches and subsidiaries in other provinces. However, if these leaders in this category of corporations have only held official positions in the provinces where the headquarters of the companies are located, their political experience is unlikely to influence the cross-provincial establishment.[191] According to the writers, this is probably because most of the leaders' posts are only equal to the assistant department or bureau levels. If those provinces prevent the headquarters from establishing local companies in other provincial areas, the managers and directors are very likely to obey that restriction.

Very few researches have previously studied the fragmentation of China's capital market from the perspective of inter-provincial establishment by Chinese companies, according to Xia, Lu and Yu. So, these authors have contributed substantially to reveal the problem of the cross-provincial establishment and its causes from an economic standpoint. However, empirical research on what treatment investors from other provinces receive is still needed so that their needs could well be addressed on the basis of this study. Moreover, the authors focus on listed companies only. Small and medium sized enterprises with less attention from governments may be confronted with more barriers when setting up their branches in other provinces. According to a report from the European Union Chamber of Commerce in China, the system under which enterprises operate is weighted against small and medium enterprises (SMEs) and favours big companies, though attempts have been made by the Chinese government to enhance the business environment for SMEs.[192] It is advisable to study the treatment they receive. To do so, reliable statistics are important.

5.3. *Restrictions on the Freedom of Establishment Created by Various Authorities at Local Levels*

Both the news reports and economic studies reveal that the Chinese authorities set up barriers for the cross-provincial establishment of companies. The following part is designed to further explore which institutions cause this problem.

5.3.1. The Hampering of the Freedom of Establishment by Licensing Authorities

As remarked by Yin Yang and Lei Han (2006), local governments, in recent years, usually take disguised measures to restrict the entry of commodities and enterprises from other places to local areas by abusing the power to establish licenses, which leads to market barriers. Also, there is an excessive granting of licenses without effective administration. Together with other ways, local protectionism has become stricter in order to realise a high Gross Domestic Production (GDP) in local

191 *Ibid.*, p. 128 and 131.

192 The European Union Chamber of Commerce in China, 'European Business in China Position Paper 2011/2012', p. 69, available at: <www.europeanchamber.com.cn/en/chamber-publications> (last accessed 6 April 2016).

regions.[193] The view of Yang and Han should be taken critically since they do not provide any empirical evidence for their above statement. Moreover, it is difficult to determine what 'an excessive granting of licenses' means. This term may refer to the situation as follows within the context of their essay. Local authorities license unqualified goods such as fake products made by companies in their local regions, although the licensing agencies know the commodities are of poor quality. On the one hand, the inferior goods with licenses could be sold in other places; as a result, the health of the citizens in other regions may be affected. On the other hand, the local producers of the shabby products could contribute to the tax revenues of the authorities governing the area where the manufacturers are situated.

According to available information, licensing authorities for licensed operations and for the establishment of companies and AICs for company establishment registration engage in erecting obstacles to the establishment. Nevertheless, there is not much data, especially for the first two sorts of agencies.

First, the AIC's implementation of company establishment registration is often interfered with by local authorities. Weidong Yang (2005) explains that theoretically, there should be no unlawful interference with company registration from local administrative authorities, but in practice, under the name of 'assistance to the local development', local governments usually interfere with this registration.[194] The Administration of Company Registration (Revised 2005) clearly provides that the SAIC shoulders the responsibility of company registration in the whole of China and its company registration departments at a higher level lead such departments at a lower level.[195] However, in reality, local authorities usually ask local AICs to stop approvals for registration applications from a certain type of company, raise or lower the standards for approvals and alter the conditions for approvals. As a result, a vice governor of the Jiangsu AIC complains that it is difficult to perform the AICs' duties according to law. To win cooperation and support from local governments, AICs have to follow their instructions in some cases.[196] This partly proves Feng's statement that the direct or indirect involvement of AICs in local protectionism and administrative-monopolies happens often.[197] More precisely, licensing is abused by AICs to set up obstacles for the establishment of companies in the context of this part.

In addition, the above problem may become worse. According to document No. 48 (2011) of the General Office of the State Council, at and below county levels, the leadership by AICs' company registration departments of their lower

193 Yang & Han 2006, p. 19.

194 Yang 2005, p. 31.

195 公司登记管理规定（2005年修订）第4条，Art. 4 of the on the Administration of Company Registration (Revised 2005).

196 Yang 2005, p. 31.

197 冯兴元，地方保护主义问题与地方政府行为的规则框架，"中央与地方关系的法治化"国际学术研讨会论文集，2007年1月6日，北京，页113. Xingyuan Feng, 'Local Protectionism and Skeleton of Rules of Local Governmental Action', essays from International Symposium on the legalization of the relationship between the central and local governments, Beijing, 6 January 2007, p. 114.

departments was transferred to the local governments in 2011. It means that those local governments can guide and supervise company registration of AICs in their respective administrative regions. They can appoint or remove civil servants of AICs, evaluate their work and reward or penalize them. By contrast, the AICs at the next higher level can only provide professional guidance. Moreover, the local governments have been the only financial source for AICs in their regions. Zeyuan Zuo's essay (2012) shows that scholars have pointed out that under such funding and leadership mechanisms, local protectionism would be more severe.[198] In essence, local governments, to a certain extent, can control company registration. Since in Chinese law, registration is a necessary and final step to setting up a company, this control would certainly influence such establishment.

Second, there is evidence that the licensing authorities for licensed operations are involved in creating local protectionist barriers to the inter-provincial establishment for companies. A typical example is that the government agencies administrating the trade of pig slaughtering increase the difficulty for companies to obtain the licenses for this licensed operation. This problem is well illustrated by the following case.

Jintao Liu, the vice president of the Shuanghui Group, says when the conglomerate tries to establish new factories in other provinces, the group always meets different kinds of unreasonable barriers to entry and other obstacles. These hurdles are sometimes erected by the small meat producing plants that monopolise local markets. Sometimes these obstacles are created by the offices of local governments who regulate slaughter and who act in collusion with local companies. According to the journalist of this article, governments are responsible for regulating market access to the pig-slaughtering industry. Considering the practical situation of local regions, local governments at different levels usually make relevant supervision methods. The power of formulating the local rules can make the creation of economic rents for local authorities possible. In practice, these offices often set up local protectionism barriers, regardless of what the Regulation on the Administration of Pig Slaughtering (Revised 2008) clearly provides. According to this regulation, the authorities supervising pig slaughtering must respect the principle of benefiting the flow of market.[199]

The local protectionism obstacles set by the regulators for pig slaughtering mentioned above certainly relate to the use of licensing for licensed operations. This business is a licensed operation and the offices have the authority to decide on the

198 卓泽渊，消除地方保护主义的法律措施, Zeyuan Zuo, 'Legal Methods to Erase Local Protectionisms', available at: <www.juristical.com/fyjj/188_2.html#> (last accessed 6 April 2016).

199 双汇集团与山西焦煤联姻背后：突围地方保护, 来源：新金融观察, The Hidden Reason for the Cooperation between the Shuanghui Group and the Shanxi Coking Coal Group: Breaking Local Protectionism, Sources: Innovative Finance Observation, available at: <http://news.xiancn.com/content/2012-06/24/content_2626162.htm> (last accessed 6 April 2016). The Regulations on the Administration of Pig Slaughtering (Revised 2008) is called 生猪屠宰管理条例(2008年修订) in Chinese. The paragraph is a literal translation of that essay included in Innovative Finance Observation.

granting of licenses for the slaughtering industry. If the application for that licensed operation is denied, no new plants can be set up by the Shuanghui Group.

Third, the local FDAs at county level, as the licensing authorities for the establishment of pharmacy chains, are liable to hamper this incorporation. Earlier section 4 has illustrated that these local authorities create difficulties in businesses' process of setting up these chains in different regions. Nevertheless, the superior authorities at the level of the provinces intend to execute the SFDA's policy, but they have no means to apply practical measures.

In sum, it can be drawn from the above research that licensing is used as a major way to erect barriers. Licensing barriers have been created by some authorities responsible for the establishment registration of companies and licensed operations. Moreover, the establishment of companies in some industries is subject to government approval and the relevant licensing authorities have also erected entry barriers in some cases. However, existing information does not reveal at which level authorities erect barriers.

Moreover, even the discretion for licensing may be abused by the refusal to grant a license. Ogus and Zhang (2005) demonstrate that the licensing partly relies on the judgment of officers. Even when the criterion has been detailed, it is still possible for them to have some discretion in making decisions.[200]A certain extent of discretion appears beneficial for officials to deal with different situations. However, possibly, they may wrongly use it for other purposes.

According to Ogus and Zhang, to obtain licenses has a big impact on business activity, and businesses particularly consider it as a main barrier to investment.[201] The impact of licensing on the freedom of businesses will also be taken into account in the latter section elaborating the ALL.

5.3.2. The Possibility for other Institutions to Impose Barriers

Bill K.P. Chou (2009) notes that all the Chinese governments ranging from the level of province to township until that year could exercise some sort of power for the establishment of business licenses. However, no case or explanation is provided.[202] Moreover, not enough information can be found to study his argument.

Nevertheless, existing data can demonstrate that subordinate bodies of the licensing authorities are very likely to be involved in setting up the barriers in practice. As demonstrated by an article from the People's Daily Online, in Huangpu District of Shanghai City, numerous governmental agencies delegate the power to accept, evaluate and approve licensing applications to their interior organizations and even to public institutions. For instance, the Bureau of Health gives its licensing authority to its sanitation monitoring stations. In a similar way, culture inspecting teams and community culture stations are permitted to exercise this power for the

200 Ogus & Zhang 2005, p. 125 and 126.

201 *Ibid.*, p. 124.

202 Chou 2009, p. 162.

Bureau of Culture.[203] This is similar to café chains that have to cope with formalities imposed by the cultural inspection team at county level for their establishment. Thus, it could be argued that licensing may be abused by local authorities' subdivisions, as a result of which, the obstacles are created.

6. The Practice of the Cross-provincial Establishment by FIEs

The cross-provincial establishment by FIEs presents a more complicated situation than such incorporation by domestic companies. On the one hand, some examples show that licensing authorities at both national and local levels create difficulties for such formation. On the other hand, there are cases where regional governing agencies for this incorporation facilitate the inter-provincial formation of companies. Specifically, some local authorities support FIEs in obtaining licenses and others offer some other favourable conditions.

Considering the above complexity, this section has a different structure from section 5. It studies the difficulties for FIEs to obtain licenses for their cross-provincial establishment and examines the measures taken to ease such formation. In addition, it specifies what agencies adopt these actions.

6.1. *Difficulties to Obtain Licenses*

Relevant reports demonstrate that the difficulties for FIEs to acquire licenses increase so that the expansion of these businesses is obstructed. The troubles are not only shown in general surveys of the foreign chambers of commerce in China, but are also reflected in specific examples concerning individual company's establishment across regional borders.

In the 2012 China Business Climate Survey Report, AmCham China lists licensing as one major obstacle for FIEs to make investment or open new businesses in China.[204] In total, 390 members of AmCham China responded to the survey.[205] 68 per cent of the participants in this empirical research find that their expansion and investment pace have slowed down because of licensing requirements.[206] The US-China Business Council (USCBC) also mentions that foreign companies expand slowly because of licensing procedures.[207]

203 陆晓钧，行政许可法实施中出现的几个问题，中国人大，2004年24期. Xiaojun Lu, Some Problems Arising From the Implementation of the ALL, Zhongguo Renda, No. 24, 2004.

204 AmCham China, the 2012 China Business Climate Survey Report, p. 15, available at: <http://web.resource.amchamchina.org/cmsfile/2012/03/26/c46fc22667c5eeb231748808a9244027.pdf> (last accessed 6 April 2016).

205 *Ibid.*, preface.

206 *Ibid.*, p. 17.

207 The US-China Business Council, the 2012 China Business Environment Survey Results, available at: <https://www.uschina.org/info/members-survey/> p. 8 (last accessed 6 April 2016).

As demonstrated by 37 per cent of the interviewees, it has become more difficult to acquire their licenses.[208] In the 2011 survey of AmCham China, answering 'which licenses are difficult to obtain', 42 per cent of 434 members of AmCham China mentioned new business licenses, 34 per cent named new product licenses, and 25 per cent new expansion licenses.[209]

Certain types of troubles concerning licensing acquisition are also touched upon. For instance, 71 per cent of respondents note that there is unequal treatment in granting licenses to domestic and foreign ventures.[210] In addition, the lack of consistency and fairness in licensing practices discourages the investment of FIEs.[211] Nevertheless, 60 per cent of the firms surveyed show obtaining licenses is very or extremely important to their operation e.g. adding branches, retail networks etc.[212]

6.1.1. Imposing Licensing Requirements in Excess of Authority

Specifically, first, when considering approving licensing applications, relevant governmental agencies exceed their legal authority to impose requirements that vary in different cases.[213] Both central and local authorities can be seen to exercise their licensing power in this way.

With regard to central authorities, as a primary case, the official from the China Insurance Regulatory Commission (CIRC) publicly states that foreign-invested insurance companies can only make one branch application at one time.[214] In AmCham China's view, this means if they apply for several branches at a time, such applications will not be considered.[215] According to Foreign Banks in China 2012, a survey conducted by PricewaterhouseCoopers (PWC), foreign invested bank

208 AmCham China, The 2012 China Business Climate Survey Report, p. 15, available at: <http://web.resource.amchamchina.org/cmsfile/2012/03/26/c46fc22667c5eeb231748808a9244027.pdf> (last accessed 6 April 2016).

209 AmCham China, The 2011 China Business Climate Survey Report, p. 18, available at: <http://www.chinaglobaltrade.com/sites/default/files/american-chamber-of-commerce-china-business-climate-survey.pdf> (last accessed 6 April 2016).

210 *Ibid.*, p. 16.

211 AmCham China, The 2012 China Business Climate Survey Report, p. 17, available at: <http://web.resource.amchamchina.org/cmsfile/2012/03/26/c46fc22667c5eeb231748808a9244027.pdf> (last accessed 6 April 2016).

212 AmCham China, The 2011 China Business Climate Survey Report, p. 16, available at: <http://www.chinaglobaltrade.com/sites/default/files/american-chamber-of-commerce-china-business-climate-survey.pdf> (last accessed 6 April 2016).

213 AmCham China, The 2012 China Business Climate Survey Report, p. 55, available at: <http://web.resource.amchamchina.org/cmsfile/2012/03/26/c46fc22667c5eeb231748808a9244027.pdf> (last accessed 6 April 2016).

214 *Ibid.*, p. 57.

215 中国美国商会，外资险企在华业务依然限制重重, AmCham China, There are still Numerous Restrictions on Foreign-funded Insurance Companies' Business in China, available at: <http://magazine.caijing.com.cn/2011-06-07/110739522.html> (last accessed 6 April 2016).

managers interviewed also complained about the impossibility of obtaining simultaneous branch licenses.[216]

However, according to AmCham China, the CIRC should allow such submission by foreign-funded insurance companies. This is because the Insurance Law (2009) does not prohibit foreign-funded insurance ventures from submitting applications for establishing several branches at one time.[217] There is no difference in the legal requirements for approving branches of a foreign-invested or a domestic insurance company either. Nevertheless, in practice, the domestic businesses can make multiple applications at one time, as reflected by AmCham China.[218]

As shown by another example, a foreign invested bank planning to open branches in some coastal areas learns from the banking regulators that such establishment is allowed. In spite of this statement, the agencies ask this financial institution to establish an extra entity in a remote or in an inland city, according to an employee from this bank. The business had to fulfil such a requirement and the additional bank outlet made a loss for two years. As demonstrated by the financial profession, the banking authorities propose such extra conditions for obtaining approval and foreign invested banks certainly cannot refuse their suggestions.[219]

The final recognizable problem is that the China Banking Regulatory Commission (CBRC) processes foreign-invested banks' licensing applications for establishing branches with low efficiency and sets high barriers to entry. For example, it once asked these banks to invest at least 0.2 billion RMB for each branch they wanted to form. Therefore, industry insiders once held that the expansion of foreign-invested banks was significantly affected by the licensing practice of this state agency. Nevertheless, not all businessmen agree with this thought. For instance, it took the Development Bank of Singapore less than 6 months to open for business in Chongqing, as reflected by its manager.[220]

In terms of local licensing agencies, additional unlawful requirements made by them can be noticed easily in the retail industry. According to China Business, to increase local tax revenues, they set the precondition for local market entry that

216 PWC, Foreign Banks in China 2012, available at: <www.pwccn.com/webmedia/-doc/634781336834535403_fs_foreign_banks_china_jul2012.pdf> p. 41 (last accessed 6 April 2016).

217 *Ibid.* Other legal documents regulating this establishment of branches do not make such requirements either. See the Detailed Rules for the Implementation of the Administrative Regulation on Foreign-funded Insurance Companies (外资保险公司管理条例实施细则) (Revised 2010) and the Administrative Regulation on Foreign-funded Insurance Companies (外资保险公司管理条例) (Revised 2013).

218 *Ibid.*, p. 250.

219 唐君燕（华夏时报），铁面监管下外资行很纠结 "潜规则"避无可避, Yanjun Tang (China Times), The Foreign Funded Banks are Troubled by Strict Supervision, They Have no Way to Avoid Unwritten Rules, available at: <http://finance.eastmoney.com/news/-1355,2010092597581375.html> (last accessed 6 April 2016).

220 谈佳隆, 外资银行为何跑不赢中资银行？, 中国经济周刊, 2012年第17期, Jialong Tan, Why Foreign-invested Banks cannot Win a Competition with Domestic Rivals? China Economic Weekly, 2012 (17), available at: <http://paper.people.com.cn/zgjjzk/html/2012-04/30/content_1045209.htm?div=-1> (last accessed 6 April 2016).

foreign invested retailers should pay a tax to the regions where their shops operate.[221] Thus, local authorities usually require these firms to take the form of subsidiaries or to move their headquarters to regions administrated by these agencies. In other circumstances, these departments ask for the building of distribution centers in their areas, as strings attached to these FIEs' establishment.

For example, the Guangzhou government offered such terms for Wal-Mart China's expansion in its region, though Wal-Mart China's investment is welcomed, according to one former commercial official. Specifically, this FIE had to either relocate its headquarters or accounting center to Guangzhou or create an independent management system for all of its branches in Guangzhou. Without meeting these conditions, Wal-Mart China would not be allowed to set up supermarkets in Guangzhou city.[222]

It is due to tax reasons that the Guangzhou authority imposed this requirement of relocation. According to a renowned financial professional, Wal-Mart China sets up an accounting center for all its branches and locates it in Shenzhen, the municipality where Wal-Mart China's headquarter is situated. Therefore, the financial flows of all the outlets are calculated in Shenzhen.[223] Moreover, these local shops only pay sales tax to the local tax authorities where their business is located whose amounts are rather small. Other taxes, such as the enterprise income tax and the value added tax (VAT) are paid to the Shenzhen region.[224]

One provincial governmental officer even stated that his region was tricked into stimulating Wal-Mart China's investment, as revealed by one insider. This is because the tax contribution made by one Wal-Mart shop to his area amounted to only about 1 million RMB.[225] Apparently, his region may have offered preferential terms to attract Wal-Mart China's establishment, with an expectation to increase tax revenues. Nevertheless, the real tax contribution disappointed him. That is why he made the above statement.

221 进入中国12年终辗转进广州，沃尔玛区域突围，2007年12月17日，来源：中国经营报，With the Twists and Turns for 12 Years After its Entry into China, Wal-Mart Finally Opens up Markets in Guangzhou, 17th December 2007, sources: China Business, available at: <http://bj.house.sina.com.cn/mansion/2007-12-17/1008229736.html> (last accessed 6 April 2016).

222 周芳，被拒13年，沃尔玛终以妥协得进广州，经理日报，2009年11月8日，Fang Zhou, After Being Kept out of Guangzhou for 13 Years, Wal-Mart China Finally Enters into this Market through Compromising, JingLi Ribao, 8 November 2009, available at: <http://cjb.newsscc.org/html/2009-11/08/content_735222.htm> (last accessed 6 April 2016).

223 刘林鹏，重庆释放沃尔玛被捕员工，绿色猪肉导致损失近亿，每日经济新闻，2012年5月2日，Penglin Liu, Chongqing Authority Releases Wal-Mart 's Employees Arrested, Green Pork Causes Almost 0.1 Billion RMB Losses, National Business Daily, 2 May 2012.

224 黄清燕，迎合地方政府，沃尔玛设数十子公司加速扩张，2010年3月18日，来源:每日经济新闻，Qingyan Huang, By Winning the Acceptance of Local Governments, Wal-Mart Accelerates its Expansion for Dozens of Branches, 18 March 2010, sources: National Business Daily.

225 孙欣，沃尔玛的羁绊，中国企业家，2008 (21), Xin Sun, the Barriers for Wal-Mart, China Entrepreneurs, 2008 (21), available at: <www.iceo.com.cn/renwu/34/1999/1130/-174785.shtml> (last accessed 6 April 2016).

Wal-Mart China's way to pay taxes means, in the case of establishing shops in Guangzhou, that Wal-Mart China could profit from these outlets, according to Zhou. In contrast, Guangzhou could not benefit from the tax receipts of these shops.[226]

However, Wal-Mart China refused to move its headquarters. As reported by China Business, this rejection also put it in real difficulties with the Guangzhou municipality; as a result, the firm had difficulties to establish branches in the city.

Thus, with twists and turns, this firm could not open its shops in Guangzhou until the 12th year after Wal-Mart's entry into China.[227] According to Fang Zhou, an agreement was reached for the establishment of Wal-Mart China's Guangzhou outlet that this municipality can receive all the business tax revenues of this shop. To realize this aim, Wal-Mart China's supermarkets in Guangzhou can only be corporations whose capital is subscribed by this FIE and local firms together. In other words, Wal-Mart China is prevented from setting up branches in Guangzhou.[228]

In fact, Guangzhou is not the only place where Wal-Mart China's expansion is hamstrung, as shown by China Business.[229] Due to the location of its headquarters, other regions, apart from Shenzhen, opposed Wal-Mart China's establishment of branches in these areas firmly, as pointed out by one expert in the retail field.[230] For instance, in both Shanghai and Hangzhou, this FIE experienced the problem of adding a distribution center.[231] In Wal-Mart China's process to establish its first store in Shanghai, it was confronted with great hurdles. Besides normal establishment conditions, the Shanghai authority also asked it to set up a distribution center there as a string attached. Wal-Mart China's expansion was

226 周芳，被拒13年，沃尔玛终以妥协得进广州，经理日报，2009年11月8日，Fang Zhou, After Being Kept out of Guangzhou for 13 Years, Wal-Mart China Finally Enters into this Market through Compromising, JingLi Ribao, 8 November 2009, available at: <http://cjb.newssc.org/html/2009-11/08/content_735222.htm> (last accessed 6 April 2016).

227 进入中国12年终辗转进广州，沃尔玛区域突围，2007年12月17日，来源：中国经营报，With the Twists and Turns for 12 Years After its Entry into China, Wal-Mart Finally Opens up Markets in Guangzhou, 17 December 2007.

228 周芳，被拒13年，沃尔玛终以妥协得进广州，经理日报，2009年11月8日，Fang Zhou, After Being Kept out of Guangzhou for 13 Years, Wal-Mart China Finally Enters into this Market through Compromising, JingLi Ribao, 8 November 2009, available at: <http://cjb.newssc.org/html/2009-11/08/content_735222.htm> (last accessed 6 April 2016).

229 进入中国12年终辗转进广州，沃尔玛区域突围，2007年12月17日，来源：中国经营报，With the Twists and Turns for 12 Years After its Entry into China, Wal-Mart Finally Opens up Markets in Guangzhou, 17 December 2007.

230 刘林鹏，重庆释放沃尔玛被捕员工，绿色猪肉导致损失近亿，每日经济新闻，2012年5月2日，Penglin Liu, Chongqing Authority Releases Wal-Mart 's Employees Arrested, Green Pork Causes Almost 0.1 Billion RMB Losses, National Business Daily, 2 May 2012.

231 李纬娜，沃尔玛、家乐福谁赢得中国市场？，财经，2007年7月22日，Weina Li, Who Will Win Chinese market: Carrefour or Wal-Mart?, Caijing, 22-7-2007. The Asia Case Research Centre, the University of Hong Kong, Wal-Mart Stores: "Every Day Low Prices" in China, available at: <https://hbr.org/product/wal-mart-stores-everyday-low-prices-in-china/HKU590-PDF-ENG> (last accessed 6 April 2016).

stopped in Shanghai after stating that such a requirement is unacceptable.[232] In 2003, the Shanghai municipality denied this firm's investment project for the reason that no hypermarket building was allowed within the city's outer-ring road.[233]

Obviously, in the above case, the Shanghai authority wanted to increase its tax revenues generated from the operation of a distribution center there, as demonstrated by a study from Hong Kong University. Based on its experience, Wal-Mart China lists local protectionism as one of the most serious problems for expanding its business in China. An analysis from Hong Kong University also holds that local administrative agencies usually create difficulties for the establishment of companies in their regions for their own interest.[234]

Moreover, according to a domestic commercial venture's manager, some regions not only become less eager to attract Wal-Mart, but also support local enterprises more in building shops. The reason is that these outlets contribute all their tax revenues to regional authorities.[235] How local public officers in China behave depends on whether businesses have enough clout that the public servants must accommodate their interests.[236]

Other foreign funded retailers are also likely to encounter entry barriers for the tax reason as Wal-Mart China. For instance, METRO China cannot enter certain regional markets either due to the same tax payment method as the American invested supermarket, as confirmed by one former experienced employee from METRO China.[237]

As concluded by Xin Sun, Wal-Mart China comes into conflict with local governments that cannot be easily compromised. This conflict has been the third element restricting this FIE's expansion apart from the influence of MOFCOM and

232 The Asia Case Research Centre, the University of Hong Kong, Wal-Mart Stores: "Every Day Low Prices" in China, available at: <https://hbr.org/product/wal-mart-stores-everyday-low-prices-in-china/HKU590-PDF-ENG> (last accessed 6 April 2016).

233 进入中国12年终辗转进广州，沃尔玛区域突围，2007年12月17日，来源：中国经营报，With the Twists and Turns for 12 Years After its Entry into China, Wal-Mart Finally Opens up Markets in Guangzhou, 17 December 2007.

234 The Asia Case Research Centre, the University of Hong Kong, Wal-Mart Stores: "Every Day Low Prices" in China. Because Wal-Mart China is an FIE, local protectionism here may also refer to the obstacles faced by the Foreign Direct Investment. Local protectionism is commonly used to mean the barriers created in the process of this investment and the future development of FIEs. For example, see MOFCOM, Overview of the FDI in China, available at: <http://english.mofcom.gov.cn/aarticle/topic/bizchina/fdiinchina/200406/20040600233643.html> (last accessed 6 April 2016).

235 孙欣，沃尔玛的羁绊，中国企业家，2008 (21)，Xin Sun, the Barriers for Wal-Mart, China Entrepreneurs, 2008 (21), available at: 〈www.iceo.com.cn/renwu/34/1999/1130/-174785.shtml> (last accessed 6 April 2016).

236 Smith 2013, p. 1029.

237 进入中国12年终辗转进广州，沃尔玛区域突围，2007年12月17日，来源：中国经营报，With the Twists and Turns for 12 Years After its Entry into China, Wal-Mart Finally Opens up Markets in Guangzhou, 17 December 2007.

of local retailers.[238] According to the National Business Daily, the only reason for such frustration is that these regions cannot profit from Wal-Mart China's operation in terms of tax receipts.[239] This is because most of this FIE's tax is paid at its headquarters, as shown by China Business. Thus, as a key, local governments refuse to grant licenses for this firm to add networks, keeping Wal-Mart China from opening outlets in many cities.[240]

6.1.2. The Delay in Granting Licenses

Second, taking too long time to grant licenses is another problem. What is even worse is that companies are not informed how long it takes before they can get an approval. According to the US-China Business Council, companies have continuing troubles in obtaining licenses necessary for business. For example, it takes months to approve licenses for businesses in certain industries though regulations set the limit of weeks. Regulators have different opinions, as a result, making application for and acquiring approvals can be confusing and delayed.[241] As another example, more than one year after applying for domestic licenses, some foreign invested logistics and express delivery companies still do not know when their applications will be approved or not. These licenses are necessary for the companies to establish branches.[242] Therefore, the inability to obtain them can undermine expansion.

Moreover, Amcham China criticizes the slowness and futility of the approval procedure for foreign-funded financial services providers to expand their business and branch networks.[243]As demonstrated in the interviews of PWC, foreign banks' development is restricted in China as their applications for expansion are processed comparatively slowly.[244] According to the China Times, the refusal to grant licenses in time prevents foreign invested banks from opening branches according to

238 孙欣，沃尔玛的羁绊，中国企业家，2008 (21)，Xin Sun, the Barriers for Wal-Mart, China Entrepreneurs, 2008 (21), available at: <www.iceo.com.cn/renwu/34/1999/1130/-174785.shtml> (last accessed 6 April 2016).

239 沃尔玛: 妥协于中国消费模式？每日经济新闻，Wal-Mart: Compromising itself by Accepting Chinese Comsuming Model? National Business Daily, available at: <http://news.yipu.com.cn/shAngye/cs/229423.html> (last accessed 6 April 2016).

240 进入中国12年终辗转进广州，沃尔玛区域突围，2007年12月17日，来源：中国经营报，With the Twists and Turns for 12 Years After its Entry into China, Wal-Mart Finally Opens up Markets in Guangzhou, 17 December 2007, sources: China Business, available at: <http://bj.house.sina.com.cn/mansion/2007-12-17/1008229736.html> (last accessed 6 April 2016).

241 The US-China Business Council, The 2011 China Business Environment Survey Results, available at: <www.linkingmarket.com/files/201111081942080.china_uscouncil_survey_-2011.pdf> p. 9 (last accessed 6 April 2016). This empirical study does not show licensing officials of which industries take such a long time to make licensing decisions. Therefore, one cannot find relevant laws to know the deadline to grant licenses in these trades.

242 AmCham China, The American Business in China 2012 White Paper, p. 218, available at: <www.amchamchina.org/whitepaper2012> (last accessed 6 April 2016).

243 *Ibid.*, p. 161.

244 PWC, Foreign Banks in China 2012, available at: <www.pwccn.cn> p. 10 (last accessed 6 April 2016).

commercial requirements. As pointed out by a professional from these banks, no laws or regulations set limits on what business a foreign invested banking group can conduct. However, relevant government departments can constrain the foreign invested banks' business development through controlling the time of approval. In addition, no way can be taken by the banks to change the situation. As a result, some applications for approval made by 2010 cannot be considered until 2013. Because of the problem to acquire approvals, the difficulties to establish outlets have been the most important impediment to these banking ventures. By contrast, their domestic competitors can incorporate branches almost freely.[245]

6.1.3. Variable Licensing Practice

Third, according to AmCham China, local authorities have large discretion to implement the rules concerning licensing. Thus, the practice of licensing may vary greatly between different regions.[246]The respondents to the 2012 survey by the British Chamber of Commerce in China and the China-Britain Business Council also state that licenses vary in enforcement in different areas and municipalities in China. In addition, the process to decide the granting of licenses lacks transparency.[247] As mentioned in a seminar of AmCham China, the application of governmental internal files makes licensing opaque to foreign companies and variable licensing conditions are another problem.[248] Moreover, unclear approval process and contradictory enforcement by state and local authorities cause a belief that licensing systems may not treat FIEs fairly. This result is drawn from the 2011 China Business Environment Survey by the USCBC.[249]

245 唐君燕（华夏时报）, 铁面监管下外资行很纠结 "潜规则"避无可避, Junyan Tang (China Times), the Foreign Funded Banks are Troubled by Strict Supervision, They Have no Way to Avoid Unwritten Rules, available at: <http://finance.eastmoney.com/news/-1355,20100925975813 75.html> (last accessed 6 April 2016).

246 AmCham China, The American Business in China 2012 White Paper, p. 16, available at: <www.amchamchina.org/whitepaper2012> (last accessed 6 April 2016).

247 The British Chamber of Commerce in China and the China-Britain Business Council, The British Business in China – 2012 Business Climate Survey, available at: <www.cbbc.org/guide/downloads/2012_china_business_climate_survey> p. 20 (last accessed 6 April 2016).

248 AmCham China, License to Expand – a 2012 Business Climate Survey Event 25 April 2012, available at: <www.amchamchina.org/article/9560> (last accessed 28 September 2013). This discussion focuses on licensing subjects. The speakers include a partner and senior vice president for Larkin Trade International, the CEO of BabyCare, the Chief Representative China, MetLife and a partner of WilmerHale.

249 The US-China Business Council, The 2011 China Business Environment Survey Results, available at: <https://www.uschina.org/public/documents/2011/10/membership_survey_-english.pdf> p. 9 (last accessed 6 April 2016).

6.1.4. The Increased Difficulties to Acquire Licenses from MOFCOM in the Retail Field

Fourth, to ensure equal competition, MOFCOM tightens up requirements for granting foreign contributed retailers licenses. According to Guoxiong Huang (2008), a high ranking counsellor at MOFCOM, the failure to acquire MOFCOM's approval has been the bottleneck for the FIEs to open outlets. Moreover, according to Xin Sun, the inability to obtain MOFCOM's approval constitutes one of the most significant barriers for Wal-Mart's expansion.

MOFCOM's tightening up on licensing is because of its different opinion from local authorities towards the expansion of Wal-Mart China. Most of the local authorities welcome the establishment of new shops by Wal-Mart China in local areas to boost local economies and gain political achievement. In contrast, the attitude of MOFCOM about the further development of foreign retailers becomes moderate gradually. The national authority abolishes the super national treatment to foreign investment and tries to level the playing field for foreign and local retailers. As a result, the benefit of all is expected to be balanced.[250]

In sum, some FIEs encounter difficulties to acquire licenses for their inter-regional formation of branches. Licensing requirements with strings attached and lengthy licensing processes constitute the main possible reasons.

In addition, national industry regulators can be recognized to erect obstacles for FIEs' licenses acquisition in some cases. Moreover, there is evidence for the barriers created by local authorities. In particular, local governments play an important role in denying foreign invested retailers' access to local markets.

6.2. *Local Authorities' Support to Acquire Licenses*

Contrary to the barriers described above, some local authorities assist FIEs in obtaining licenses. The following text shows such a phenomenon and recognizes that through two possible ways local governments grant this preferential treatment. Moreover, it also discusses why local governmental agencies give assistance in license acquisition.

6.2.1. Local Agencies' Preference for Granting Licenses to FIEs

In practice, some FIEs are treated preferentially in their licensing applications, as shown by some reports. Such treatment can be identified e.g. in the auto and the retail industries.

Concerning the car industry, local governments tend to prefer FIEs to domestic firms in stages such as granting licenses for land use, according to an anonymous worker from a car manufacturer. Such local practice can allow FIEs to

[250] 孙欣，沃尔玛的羁绊，中国企业家，2008 (21)，Xin Sun, the Barriers for Wal-Mart, China Entrepreneurs, 2008 (21)，available at: <www.iceo.com.cn/renwu/34/1999/1130/174785.-shtml> (last accessed 6 April 2016).

expand smoothly and represent many challenges to domestic firms, though there is no licensing requirement for non-local firms to build car-making plants. Based on this phenomenon, Cao (2013) thinks that there seems to be governmental favouritism over foreign capital in car industry.[251]

Moreover, some domestic companies have plans to establish new firms, but a lot of licensing barriers have been erected for their expansion, as mentioned by the above employee. Many domestic firms experience the same difficulties for the Volvo project operated by Geely. According to an expert from the China Association of Automobiles Manufacturers, Geely, as a firm controlled by a Chinese partner, cannot gain strong support from relevant Chinese agencies. As a result, numerous chances for the Volvo plan are estimated to have been wasted, with the opening of new factories by other FIEs continually.[252]

As stated by Cao, the different treatment can be a reason why numerous factories are set up by foreign invested car makers, while domestic auto producers expand rarely. Therefore, the above anonymous worker suggests that governmental agencies should notice the threat of unchecked expansion of foreign capital. Moreover, they ought to assist domestic firms in clearing the way for development rather than creating barriers.[253]

Regarding the retailing field, establishment funded by FIEs seems to be encouraged and accepted all the time. For instance, according to one general manager of a leading Chinese retail enterprise from Guangzhou, the company has difficulties to establish its shopping center in another city. Relevant departments of that municipality deliberately erect obstacles. Moreover, the local government leader refuses the manager's request to explain his views. By contrast, a competing multinational corporation wanting to build a center in that region is favoured by the local authorities.[254]

As another example, Homemart, a Chinese construction material outlet chain, also faces obstacles created by local governments and its investment to open new shops in the local areas was rejected. Contrary to the treatment received by this domestic company, B&Q was welcomed by the local authorities to start a business there.[255]

Furthermore, in 2007, Carrefour China established its Chongqing supermarket near to a hypermarket formed by Beijing Hualian Ltd in Chongqing. The Beijing company petitioned the Standing Committee of the Chongqing People's Congress

251 曹婷，外资扩张凶猛，谁为自主担忧，中国汽车报，2013年6月14日，Ting Cao, Foreign Invested Auto Makers Expand Rapidly, Who has Concern about Domestic Producers? China Automotive News, available at: <www.cnautonews.com/tt/201306/t20130614_205431.htm> (last accessed 6 April 2016).

252 *Ibid.*

253 *Ibid.*

254 田爱丽，地方政府为沃尔玛等"超国民待遇"开绿灯，第一财经日报，2009年3月6日，Aili Tian, Local Governments Give the Green Light to Super National Treatment for Wal-Mart and other FIEs, China Business News, 6th Mar. 2009, available at: <www.p5w.net/news/-cjxw/200903/t2205628.htm> (last accessed 6 April 2016).

255 *Ibid.*

to ask relevant regulators to coordinate and solve this problem. Nevertheless, it failed to stop Carrefour China's operation.[256]

Carrefour China's establishment next-door to the domestic rival may be illegal due to the following provision. According to Wei Shi (2004), the establishment of big commercial shopping centers in cities usually refers to the Guiding Opinion on the Commerce Outlet Planning in Urban Areas (2001) at that time.[257] As noted by this document, the creation of such networks should avoid high concentration and redundant construction and the situation of present merchandising outlets should be taken into account. The number of commodity networks should also be determined rationally.

Moreover, MOFCOM transfers its licensing power for FIEs in the retail sector to provincial authorities, giving a profound stimulus to these FIEs' expansion. According to Yong Jiang, taking this event as a golden opportunity to obtain political success, local governments are prompted to lure investment for a new round. The transfer also stimulated Carrefour and other FIEs to make plans and set ambitious goals to expand their operations.[258] This is because the local licensing authorities are much easier to deal with than the MOFOCOM.[259] Partly due to this delegation of power, since 2008, Wal-Mart China has opened over a dozen wholly-owned subsidiaries in various provinces, according to Qingyan Huang (2010).[260]

6.2.2. Recognizable Ways to Support FIEs' License Obtainment

Other articles point out local authorities' approaches to support FIEs in acquiring licenses. Of course, these reports can demonstrate again that sometimes such assistance is offered by these agencies.

First, one particularly noticeable way is side-stepping the licensing authority to permit the establishment of FIEs in local regions. Such examples mostly occurred in the retail field at the beginning of the 21st century.

As reflected by one official from the Liaoning government, the Shenyang municipality exceeded its authority in approving Carrefour China to open a new hypermarket in Shenyang. However, according to laws, the establishment of a retail

256 *Ibid.*

257 关于城市商业网点规划工作的指导意见(2001). 石薇，中国近期可能出台对大型商业网点发展的限制政策，中新社，2004年5月25日. Wei Shi, China may Unveil Restrictive Policies on the Development of Big Commerce Centers Recently, China News Agency, 25 May 2004.

258 Jiang 2009b.

259 孙欣，沃尔玛的羁绊，中国企业家，2008 (21), Xin Sun, the Barriers for Wal-Mart, China Entrepreneurs, 2008 (21), available at: <www.iceo.com.cn/renwu/34/1999/1130/-174785.shtml> (last accessed 6 April 2016).

260 黄清燕，迎合地方政府，沃尔玛设数十子公司加速扩张，2010年3月18日，来源:每日经济新闻, Qingyan Huang, By Winning the Acceptance of Local Governments, Wal-Mart Accelerates its Expansion for Dozens of Branches, 18 March 2010. Contrary to the barriers faced by FIEs demonstrated in section 5.1, section 5.2 shows that these ventures sometimes are treated preferentially for their establishment. Reasons for this treatment are provided by existing reports, which are also summarized in this chapter. Empirical legal research on the inter-provincial establishment of companies in China also tries to explain the favour in Chapter 5.

shop by FIEs should obtain the approval from the State Council at that time. Though the Shenyang authority fully understands this requirement, it still exercises its approval authority illegally for economic considerations. The reason is that the incorporation of the branch there can generate huge tax revenues and numerous jobs for the government.[261]

The Shenyang authority's way to help the expansion of foreign retailers is very common in China, according to the same officer. Many local governments, especially those in the coastal provinces in Southeast China, go beyond their power to approve the opening of foreign invested retail companies in their local areas. The explanation for the illegal approval is simple and almost the same: the foreign investment can bring in big benefits for the local areas.[262] To attract investors, local authorities even often make local regulations that conflict with state law.[263]

A large number of foreign retail companies make full use of the local authorities' policies and successfully set up stores across different regions in China. As for Carrefour China, two other outlets in Chongqing and Dalian were established by the French giant in the same way as the shop in Shenyang. By profiting from the illegal approval of local governments, Carrefour China boasted of having 27 hypermarkets in China in 2000.[264]

Moreover, another 216 foreign invested retailers also benefited from making approval beyond local governments' authorities such as Wal-Mart, Trust Mart, Parkson and Ito Yokado. As a result, nearly 300 foreign invested commercial enterprises operated in China by the year 1999 and only 21 of them were approved by national authorities.[265]

Nevertheless, measures have been taken to prohibit the local governments from approving the expansion of foreign invested retail businesses beyond their authorities. The efforts are first reflected in legal documents made in 1997. Emphasized in the Urgent Circular of the General Office of the State Council Concerning the Immediate Termination of the Unauthorized Local Approval of Foreign Invested Commercial Enterprises (1997), only the State Council can approve the incorporation of the foreign invested commercial companies.[266] As provided in the Notice on the Check-up and Rectification of Non-pilot Foreign-funded

261 中国青年报，地方越权审批放水外资零售进驻——关注"家乐福"事件，China Youth Daily, Local authorities go beyond their Power to Approve the Opening of Foreign Retail Shops-Focusing on the Carrefour Incident, available at: <http://news.hexun.com/2013-02-04/150910434.html> (last accessed 6 April 2016). Though not indicated in this article, it can be known that the Carrefour shop established in Shenyang is a branch opened by Carrefour China according to another essay, available at: <www.linkshop.com.cn/Club/-dispbbs.aspx?rootid=258740> (last accessed 6 April 2016).

262 *Ibid.*

263 Peerenboom 2001, p. 207.

264 中国青年报，地方越权审批放水外资零售进驻——关注"家乐福"事件，China Youth Daily, Local authorities go beyond their Power to Approve the Opening of Foreign Retail Shops-Focusing on the Carrefour Incident, available at: <http://news.hexun.com/2013-02-04/150910434.html> (last accessed 6 April 2016).

265 *Ibid.*

266 国务院办公厅关于立即停止地方自行审批外商投资商业企业的紧急通知（1997）.

Commercial Enterprises (1997), the foreign invested commercial companies who form branches without the approval of the State Council should be checked-up and rectified.[267]

Moreover, as stressed in the Circular of the General Office of the State Council on the Situation of Checking-up and Rectifying Non-pilot Foreign-funded Commercial Enterprises (1998), local governments should be prevented from approving foreign invested enterprises beyond their authority.[268] According to the Circular on the Immediate Termination of Approving Foreign Invested Commercial Enterprises beyond Authorities or in a Disguised Manner (2000), it is wrong that local governments exceed their authorities to make the approval of the establishment of branches of those enterprises. Such practice should be stopped immediately.[269] As pointed out in the Notice on Further Enhancing the Check-up and Rectification of Non-pilot Foreign-funded Commercial Enterprises (2001), the unauthorized approval of foreign invested enterprises and their branches still happens in some local areas. Therefore, the regulation made in 1998 is not satisfactorily implemented.[270]

However, these rules that aim to correct the illegal approval of the establishment of foreign invested enterprises achieve nothing in their implementation. Most of the companies even expand more rapidly. As a reason for the provisions' practical effects, the local authorities go their own ways and do not enforce the national rules for increasing local regions' tax revenues and employment.[271] In fact, according to Weina Li, they have been Carrefour's best partner to bypass policy restrictions.[272]

Second, FIEs' licensing obligation for expansion can be influenced, due to local agencies' discretion in classifying investment plans under different categories. This is because only these FIEs establishing subsidiaries in the restricted industries of the Catalogue are required to acquire licenses. Rules on this establishment have been explained in section 4.2.2.

For example, as demonstrated by Liwen Jiang, in practice, the classification in the Catalogue for this field is not strictly followed at all. According to the Catalogue, some business of the real estate sector belong to the encouraged catalogue and some are included in the restricted catalogue. However, local authorities can decide which catalogue a particular real estate project can be put in. In particular, the

267 国务院办公厅关于清理整顿非试点外商投资商业企业有关问题的通知（1997).

268 国务院办公厅关于清理整顿非试点外商投资商业企业情况的通知 (1998).

269 国家经济贸易委员会、对外贸易经济合作部、国家工商行政管理局, 关于, 立即停止, 越权审批和变相设立, 外商投资商业企业, 的通知（2000).

270 国家经济贸易委员会、对外贸易经济合作部、国家工商行政管理总局, 关于, 进一步做好, 清理整顿, 非试点外商投资商业企业, 工作的通知（2001).

271 中国零售商：第二次起跑，A Second Round of Competition Stars for the Chinese retailers, available at: <http://elab.icxo.com/htmlnews/2005/01/25/560253.htm> (last accessed 6 April 2016).

272 李纬娜，沃尔玛、家乐福谁赢得中国市场？财经，2007年7月22日. Weina Li, Who Will Win Chinese market: Carrefour or Wal-Mart, Caijing, 22 July, 2007.

government agencies in second-tier or third-tier cities have few limits on what business a foreign invested real estate company can engage in in their regions.[273]

Moreover, Xiaodong Zhang and Mei Li argue that encouraged sectors and permitted ones usually get mixed up on purpose. In other words, local licensing officials can decide whether a project is encouraged or permitted in order to develop the local economy, grant a favour etc.[274]

6.2.3. Reasons to Assist FIEs with the Acquisition of Licenses

As pointed out in AmCham China's workshop, there are still obstacles for obtaining a license, though progress has been made since China's accession to the WTO. It is necessary for FIEs to show their definite contribution to the market and industry sites they want to operate in. One of extra optimum practices can be the execution of FIE's information about their way to benefit local communities. Moreover, drawing support from regional governments can accelerate license permission due to their ability to help and coordinate the application procedure. Local authorities are willing to give such assistance since they might want to increase employment and attract capital, whereas the State Council might not.[275]

This argument can be proved by Wal-Mart China's experience. Local authorities usually expect it to generate tax revenues and bring other benefits; in return, strong support in granting licenses can be provided. Moreover, the building of supermarkets by this FIE in local places itself is considered as a political success.

To begin with, tax payment is crucial to Wal-Mart China's expansion. For example, the opening of Wal-Mart China's shop in Chongqing will definitely make tax contributions to the Chongqing city, according to one officer from this region. Otherwise, it would be impossible for this municipality to pay much attention and thought to promote this establishment. Moreover, recruiting a Fortune 500 firm's investment is surely to increase tax receipts and employment for Guiyang city, as confirmed by one administrator responsible for attracting investment for this district. Because Wal-Mart China satisfies this expectation, this retailer successfully builds two shopping malls in Guiyang.[276]

Thus, to win local governments' support, this FIE has decided to change its tax payment method, according to Wal-Mart China's partner.[277] As confirmed by this venture's Tianjin branch, the business tax and the VAT of its supermarkets are paid

273 姜立文，中国房地产市场外资准入的法律分析, Liwen Jiang, the Legal Analysis of the Entry to the Chinese Real Estate Market for Foreign Capital, available at: <www.wecomesh.com/-news/waizi023.htm> (last accessed 6 April 2016).

274 Zhang & Li 2003, p. 6.

275 AmCham China, License To Expand – A 2012 Business Climate Survey Event 25 April 2012, available at: <www.amchamchina.org/article/9560> (last accessed 6 April 2016).

276 文静，美国销售模式不适合中国国情, 沃尔玛变通开跑, 21世纪经济报道, 2005年4月26日. Jing Wen, The American Selling Model does not Suit Chinese Situation, Wal-Mart Changes its Strategies and Starts to Accelerate its Expansion, 21st Century Business Herald, 26 April 2005.

277 赵谨，沃尔玛变阵破中国困局，改变选址和缴税方式，新华网，2005年4月29日. Jin Zhao, to Change its Poor Situation in China, Wal-Mart Modifies its Strategy in terms of Location Selection and Tax Payment, Xinhua Net, 29 April 2005.

to the areas where these businesses are run. Nevertheless, Wal-Mart China's enterprise income is still taxed by Shenzhen authority. This is why currently, Wal-Mart China can enter Shanghai and other regions in which this firm has never conducted business.[278]

Second, Wal-Mart China's other contributions to local districts can also be noticed. Apart from changing its tax payment mechanism, Wal-Mart China does not mind participating in PR activities any more as before, as argued by Jing Wen. According to one of Wal-Mart China's PR managers (2005), this firm spends a lot on public service events and allocated over 10 million RMB last year. Moreover, it is said that this FIE also assists one local agriculture bureau in selling a large quantity of unmarketable farm produce.[279]

Third, as reported by the Economic Observer, the opening of shops by Carrefour and Wal-Mart means administrative achievement to local officials. This is because, in China, these enterprises stand for Global 500, advanced management and good services. To commercial estate developers, they are also most valued clients.[280]

Therefore, because of the various kinds of measures beneficial to local governments, Wal-Mart China begins to win their support, according to Jing Wen. For instance, one head for a Chongqing commercial section shows that the Chongqing government completely supports this firm in building shops in Chongqing. This authority provides one-stop service for Wal-Mart China to obtain all necessary licenses and certificates.[281] As a result, Wal-Mart China's expansion speed is nearly more than 6 times faster, while three years ago it only built 2 shopping centers yearly, according to Li (2005).[282]

To sum up, local governments support FIEs in acquiring licenses for their establishment in some sectors. One obvious way for giving this support is going beyond their licensing authorities. In addition, there are reports that some municipal governments offer such assistance. Other support is also provided by city

278 厉林, 加速布局体制变通, 沃尔玛中国财富柳暗花明？中国经营报, 2005年5月23日. Lin Li, By Accelerating the Change of its Expansion Strategy, can Wal-Mart Have Turnaround in Fortune Making in China? China Business, 23 May 2005. As also mentioned in this article, to cater for local authorities, the branches of Carrefour China pay all sorts of their tax to the districts where they are situated. It should be reminded that, according to section 5.1, other cities except Wal-Mart China's headquarter usually oppose its establishment in their areas, because this investment cannot contribute financially to them considerably.

279 文静, 美国销售模式不适合中国国情, 沃尔玛变通开跑, 21世纪经济报道, 2005年4月26日. Jing Wen, The American Selling Model does not Suit Chinese Situation, Wal-Mart Changes its Strategies and Starts to Accelerate its Expansion, 21st Century Business Herald, 26 April 2005.

280 经济观察报, 《商业大店法》背后的纠葛, The Economic Observer, the Conflicts behind the Large Stores Law, available at: <www.18108.com/news.asp?nid=780> (last accessed 6 April 2016).

281 文静, 美国销售模式不适合中国国情, 沃尔玛变通开跑, 21世纪经济报道, 2005年4月26日. Jing Wen, The American Selling Model does not Suit Chinese Situation, Wal-Mart Changes its Strategies and Starts to Accelerate its Expansion, 21st Century Business Herald, 26 April 2005.

282 厉林, 加速布局体制变通, 沃尔玛中国财富柳暗花明？中国经营报, 2005年5月23日. Lin Li, By Accelerating the Change of its Expansion Strategy, Can Wal-Mart Have Turnaround in Fortune Making in China? China Business, 23 May 2005.

governments such as preferential conditions concerning tax and land. Moreover, FIEs are usually expected to generate benefits such as tax receipts for this favourable treatment.

Moreover, it is interesting to learn from the same sources that some domestic companies experience difficulties in their cross-regional incorporation. Such information can also demonstrate the findings explained in section 5.

6.3. *Local Authorities' Assistance other than License Obtaining Facilitation*

Apart from the support in granting licenses, local governmental agencies can also offer other assistance to foreign funded retailers. Indeed, the conditions provided by local authorities are so good that super national treatment is deemed to be given.

Local governments can assist FIEs in establishing firms through a wide variety of methods. According to Yong Jiang, for political achievement, local governments manage to attract foreign funded retailers by lowering their operation cost in ways of offering cheap land, tax preference, credit facilities etc.[283] In addition, as argued by Aili Tian, relevant departments supply these companies with favourable terms concerning tax, industrial and commercial administration and taking out loans outside the companies' registered place.[284]

The preferential terms concerning land are exemplified. For instance, Jiang remarks that many golden commercial sectors are delivered up to FIEs. Indeed, some local authorities even provide flourishing business sections to these firms by removing the shops operated by state-owned commercial enterprises. As a result, the merchandising network plan often stressed by the State Council has been altered completely by local governments. In fact, it becomes a project to crowd out domestic corporations and transfer their blocks and networks to FIEs. Due to the above local fostering care, foreign invested retailers can often be found on the busiest streets of some Chinese cities. It is usually impossible for these big shopping malls with very low profit margin, to afford such prosperous districts, according to some insiders.[285]

Moreover, after meeting the Guiyang government's wish to increase employment and revenues, Wal-Mart China is also treated favourably by the Guiyang municipality. According to the official from this government, this authority offered this city's best parcel of land for Wal-Mart China's first shop in Guiyang. This outlet is also entitled to most favourite policies. In addition, the second shopping center invested by Wal-Mart China in Guiyang can also rent a piece of vacant land from this municipality at an extremely low price.[286]

283 Jiang 2009b.

284 田爱丽，地方政府为沃尔玛等"超国民待遇"开绿灯，第一财经日报，2009年03月06日. Aili Tian, Local Governments Give the Green Light to Super National Treatment for Wal-Mart and other FIEs, China Business News, 6 March 2009.

285 Jiang 2009b.

286 文静，美国销售模式不适合中国国情, 沃尔玛变通开跑, 21世纪经济报道, 2005年4月26日. Jing Wen, The American Selling Model does not Suit Chinese Situation, Wal-Mart Changes its Strategies and Starts to Accelerate its Expansion, 21st Century Business Herald, 26 April 2005.

A senior professional in the real estate field who does not want to be named also reveals some examples. For instance, a city from the middle and west areas grants Wal-Mart China free land for 10 years and the rent is 0.5 RMB per square meter per day for three decades afterwards. The sales tax for the first three years can also be refunded. One Metro China's shop can also use its lots in a central municipality without payment. The local government even commits itself to returning three years' enterprise income tax to this FIE.[287]

Furthermore, both Jiang and Tian hold that the foreign invested retail enterprises are given super national treatment in the process of their expansion in China.[288] Also, according to Aiqun Wang, a manager of a big domestic commercial enterprise, local governments always welcome the establishment by Carrefour and Wal-Mart in any case, after advocating the policy of trade and investment promotion. As attraction measures, they determine to offer favourable conditions at any cost, regardless of the density of commercial network and laws and regulations.[289] Therefore, due to this treatment, it is possible to realize some ambitious plans such as opening 300 shops by Wal-Mart China in 5 years and 80 shopping malls by Carrefour China in 3 years, according to experts within the retail industry.[290]

The reasons why local governments provide the above assistance are the same as those discussed in section 6.2.3. According to Huajun Huang, local authorities expect foreign investment, tax revenues and job chances created by the establishment of new shops by foreign retailers in their regions. In addition, the formation is hoped to promote the business environment and improve the image of those cities. For instance, numerous local municipalities tend to be proud of the presence of the FIEs in their regions. They even want to promote foreign investment at any cost. For their political achievement, the treatment provided by local governments is usually without authorization.[291]

287 田爱丽, 地方政府为沃尔玛等"超国民待遇"开绿灯, 第一财经日报, 2009年03月06日， Aili Tian, Local Governments Give the Green Light to Super National Treatment for Wal-Mart and other FIEs, China Business News, 6 March 2009.

288 *Ibid.*

289 经济观察报, 《商业大店法》背后的纠葛，The Economic Observer, the Conflicts after the Large Stores Law, available at: <www.18108.com/news.asp?nid=780> (last accessed 6 April 2016).

290 厉林、柴莹, 外资结盟地产商, 城市商圈添杀手, 2006年07月15日， 中国经营报, Lin Li and Ying Chai, FIEs are Allied with Real Estate Developers, Creating Competitive Rivals in Urban Commercial Districts, 15 July 2006.

291 田爱丽，地方政府为沃尔玛等"超国民待遇"开绿灯，第一财经日报，2009年03月06日，Aili Tian, Local Governments Give the Green Light to Super National Treatment for Wal-Mart and other FIEs, China Business News, 6 March 2009.

7. Rules Coping with Administrative Monopolies in China

China has introduced laws that are made to deal with administrative monopolies.[292] One example of an administrative monopoly, as Xinzu Zhang and Vanessa Yuanhua Zhang state, is the imposition of restrictions on market access by local authorities. They may restrict or reject the setting up of branches or investment by companies from other areas.[293] Rules dealing with administrative monopolies are expected to ensure the freedom of establishment for companies in different areas.

As demonstrated in the above sections, the interpretation and enforcement of the legal rules on the inter-provincial establishment of companies set up significant obstacles to this establishment in China. This section aims to evaluate whether the rules mentioned in the preceding paragraph can effectively deal with the creation of these barriers. Moreover, the understanding can be deepened as to whether there is freedom in the inter-provincial establishment for companies in China. Also, the application of the rules of this establishment can be examined again.

7.1. *The Provisions of the State Council on Prohibiting Regional Blockades in Market Economic Activities*

To combat administrative monopolies, the Provisions of the State Council on Prohibiting Regional Blockades in Market Economic Activities (revised 2011) was drafted in 2001 (hereinafter the Provisions).[294] It attaches great importance to tackling regional blockades. Pursuant to Article 1, it is intended to break local barriers and ensure a unified market across China. Article 2 provides this responsibility for governments at all levels and their agencies and Article 3 declares the prohibition of all kinds of regional blockades.

Specifically, the Provisions (2011) first lists types of governments' market blockade activities and provides specific remedies. Article 4(7) of the Provisions (2011) reads that local governments are not allowed to treat non-local companies' investment in local areas unequally. Moreover, they shall not restrict or prohibit the setting up of subsidiaries and branches by companies from outside of local regions through imposing unequal treatment. Articles 16 and 18 offer a way to cope with blockade barriers. The provincial governments shall organize their AICs and economic administration departments to investigate and break the blockade and make final decisions to handle this issue. Moreover, the SAIC, the General Administration of Quality Supervision, Inspection and Quarantine (GAQSIQ), the Ministry of Commerce (MOFCOM) and other relevant departments of the State Council may investigate and deal with blockade activities of provincial

292 The notion of administrative monopolies, in the Chinese legal field, means the situation that an administrative agency abuses its administrative power to restrict or eliminate competition. Huang 2008, p. 92.

293 Zhang & Zhang 2007, p. 186.

294 国务院关于禁止在市场经济活动中实行地区封锁的规定（2011年修订). The Provisions of the State Council on Prohibiting Regional Blockades in Market Economic Activities is translated by the author (Revised 2011).

governments when necessary. No local governments or their agencies must interfere with the investigation and handling conducted in accordance with the Provisions (2011) through any means and under any name. Article 19 further provides that if the activities are conducted according to the provisions made by local governments and their departments, they will be changed or revoked besides the remedies of Article 16. Revenue generated from the activities shall be returned or be confiscated when it cannot be returned according to Article 25. Article 21 states that in the case of interference, conniving at and covering up regional blockades by local governments and their agencies, provincial governments will circulate a notice of criticism of them. The State Council will impose the same punishment for the illegal activities of provincial authorities. The responsible person of these organs can also be punished.

Second, the Provisions (2011) prohibit the making of rules with blockade contents and sets up a mechanism for revoking and changing these provisions. Article 5 explicitly prevents the creation of provisions carrying out regional blockade actions or containing regional blockade contents by any region that harms the establishment and development of a national unified market system. Articles 6, 7, 8 and 9 entrust different agencies to implement relevant remedies. According to Article 6, local governments shoulder the responsibility to change or revoke the rules of their agencies. When the governments do not perform this duty, governments at a higher level must fulfil it. Article 7 states that in violation of Article 5 by local governments under the level of province, governments at a higher level will alter or annul these rules. When the governments at a higher level do not carry out this obligation, governments at the level of a province must alter or revoke them. Article 8 reads that the State Council must change or revoke the rules formulated by governments at the level of province. Article 9 asks the central government to change or annul its departments' provisions if they are the legal basis for the illegal rules made by local governments at all levels and their agencies. After mentioning the measures prescribed by the above 4 articles, Article 22 creates administrative sanctions for heads of governments breaking Article 5 and officials validating the illegal rules. They will be demoted or dismissed based on the seriousness of their violation.

Third, the Provisions (2011) encourage individuals and institutions to cope with blockades. According to Article 20, they are entitled to resist regional blocking actions. They can also report them to a provincial government or its economic administration, industrial and commercial administration and quality supervision departments or other ones concerned and even to the State Council, its departments administrating economics, industry and commerce, quality supervision and other related agencies. Within 5 working days after receiving the reports, provincial governments should require relevant local governments to finish the investigation and handling of this issue within 30 working days, or provincial authorities will complete the investigation and handling within 30 working days accordance with the Provisions (2011). The limit of 30 days can be prolonged in special cases, but the extension must not exceed 30 working days. When national authorities receive the reports of regional blocking actions from any citizen or organization, the national governmental agencies must transmit the reporting materials to provincial governments within 5 working days.

To facilitate the implementation of Article 20, sanctions are provided. Article 23 specifies that those who do not fulfil their obligations under Article 20 will be given administrative punishment. According to Article 26, administrative or even criminal sanctions are possible for workers of state organs who retaliate against those reporting blockades.

Fourth, very briefly, Article 27 requires supervisory organizations to supervise blocking activities conducted by administrative authorities and their officials.

Fifth, Article 28 asks for an instant enforcement of the Provisions (2011). Since the time it came into force, any conflicting rules of local governments and their agencies will lose effectiveness and any conflicting local regulations will not be enforced.

These rules are very encouraging. They present a relatively systematic way to tackle the monopolies and shows central government's ambition for a unified market. These provisions gained support of Xingyuan Feng for the list of specific activities and remedies. He also lays emphasis on the importance of the Provisions.[295]

However, he emphasizes that the Provisions should be further improved. Firstly, Feng suggests adding some provisions. They should permit enterprises to bring lawsuits against authorities carrying out those activities and allow victims of regional blockades to seek compensation.[296]

In addition, he shows his concern for an effective system implementing anti-blockade administrative regulations.[297] In Xinyuan Feng's opinion, the combination of this mechanism and these rules are essential for the establishment of a market economic system. However, the Provisions do not have enough authority and operability. Therefore it has not been effectively enforced. Specifically, the cooperation and supervision between superior and inferior local officials cannot successfully cope with protectionism. On the contrary, they usually shield each other. Furthermore, the Chinese central government often stresses the need to build a unified market and takes significant administrative actions to combat protectionism in certain periods. However, state government neglects its duty to make persistent efforts in the long term. In reality, central authority initiates campaigns to execute laws, which are often conducted in a perfunctory way. After

295 冯兴元, 中国的市场整合与地方政府竞争——地方保护与地方市场分割问题及其对策研究, Xingyuan Feng, China's Market Integration and Competitions among Local Governments-Study on the Problem of Local Protectionism and Local Market Segmentation and its Corresponding Resolving Measures, available at: <www.usc.cuhk.edu.hk/PaperCollection/-Details.aspx?id=2354> (last accessed 6 April 2016).

296 冯兴元, 地方保护主义问题与地方政府行为的规则框架，"中央与地方关系的法治化"国际学术研讨会论文集, 2007年1月6日，北京，页113. Xingyuan Feng, Local Protectionism and Skeleton of Rules of Local Governmental Action, essays from International Symposium on the legalization of the relationship between the central and local governments, Beijing, 6 January 2007, p. 113 and 114.

297 *Ibid.*

some 'strike hard' campaigns, no more sufficient measures will be taken by national authorities to rectify the market economic order. This inconsistent practice should be prevented in a society based on the rule of law.[298] For instance, noticeably, numerous authorities issue documents to declare a total prohibition of local blockades and urgently demand powerful measures shortly after the Provisions. They range from central governmental departments e.g., the MOCFOM to various local agencies such as the government of Guangdong Province.[299] However, measures are seldom taken and they certainly do not achieve their potential aims.

In summary, the aims and the implementation effects of the Provisions can be concluded as follows. The Provisions aim to forbid local administrative agencies to impose protectionism barriers, but it is unsure to what degree this prevention has its effect.[300]

7.2. *The Administrative License Law*

As Hui Huang and Yinyin Hu remark, regarding operations of rules and the purpose of legislation, administrative licensing is closely related to resistance against administrative monopolies.[301] Readers may notice that some provisions of the ALL have been interpreted in section 2. That interpretation examines the rules from a theoretical perspective. In other words, the question was addressed to find whether the provision on the licensing regimes for the establishment of a domestic company permits the setting up of entry barriers. The elaboration of the ALL in this section is mainly intended to make sure that in practice obstacles can be created through the actual use of licensing.

The ALL can prohibit administrative monopolies through regulating the application of licensing in six ways; as a result, barriers for the creation of a Chinese domestic company can be avoided. First, which authorities can create licensing systems is prescribed in Articles 14 and 15(1) of the ALL. Only the NPC and its Standing Committee, the State Council, the People's Congress and its Standing Committee at the level of province, the People's Congress and its Standing Committee of relatively large cities and governments at the level of province have the power to establish licenses through making laws, administrative regulations and local regulations. As Zhengkun Yu notes, these provisions are expected to cope with local protectionism. In practice, it is not clear what agencies have the authority to set up licenses. Many administrative departments, social organisations, public

298 *Ibid.*

299 广东省关于认真贯彻执行国务院关于禁止在市场经济活动中实行地区封锁的规定的通知, the Notice from the Province of Guangdong on Implementing the 2011 Provisions Seriously, available at: <http://zwgk.gd.gov.cn/006939748/200909/t20090915_8688.html> (last accessed 6 April 2016). 商务部等关于清理在市场经济活动中实行地区封锁规定的通知, the Notice from MOFCOM and Other Central Governmental Agencies to Review Rules Creating Regional Blockades in Market Economy Activities. One can easily find such documents in official journals of other governmental departments.

300 OECD 2003, p. 183.

301 Huang & Hu 2007, p. 136.

institutions, governments at the levels of county and township and even the internal organisations of some administrative departments establish licenses with an abuse of their power. Moreover, many licensing regimes are established in accordance with normative documents, minutes of meetings and speeches of leaders.[302]

Second, Articles 12 and 13 of the ALL specify for which matters licensing regimes can be created. Licensing is permitted for the activities in Article 12 and for those matters in Article 13 licensing regimes may not be established.[303]

Third, Article 15(2) of the ALL specifies for what matters licensing regimes must not be established by local authorities. This provision states that 'no local regulations or the rules of provincial governments(1) may establish any administrative license for the qualifications of the citizens, legal persons or other institutions that shall be determined by the state and (2)may establish any administrative license and pre-administrative license for the establishment and registration of enterprises or other institutions. The administrative licenses established thereby shall not hinder the individuals or enterprises of other regions from dealing in production and business and providing services in one region, shall not restrict the commodities of other regions from entering into the market of the local region.'[304] What this rule means has been interpreted in section 2.4.3.4 on the approval for licensed operations. This rule intends to prevent the implementation of the market blockade activities by local authorities through licensing, in Aiping Gu's view. Such activities can interfere with the appropriate economic links among different local regions and the exchange relations of these areas in a market, which will affect the formation of the domestic market in China.[305] As demonstrated by Jin Guo and Ning Wu, Article 15(2) of the ALL is an explicit effort to counter administrative monopolies.[306] In Jingming Xiao's opinion, it would certainly assist the development of a unified legal system and market.[307]

Moreover, administrative remedies can be sought where Article 15(2) of the ALL is violated. In terms of the violation by local regulations, Article 90 of the Legislation Law (2000) can be used. The first sentence of Article 90 authorizes the State Council, the Central Military Commission, the Supreme People's Court, the Supreme People's Procuratorate and the Standing Committees of the People's Congresses of provincial governments to take actions. If these authorities consider that local regulations, administrative regulations, autonomous regulations or separate regulations contradict the constitution of the PRC (1982) (hereinafter the Constitution) or laws, they may submit to the Standing Committee of the NPC written requests for examination. As a result, the working offices of the Standing

302 Yu 2006, p. 74.

303 See Section 1.4.3.4 for a theoretical evaluation of Arts. 12 and 13.

304 According to Art. 63 of the Legislation Law, with certain conditions, the People's Congresses and its Standing Committees of provincial regions and of relatively large cities can make local regulations.

305 Gu 2006, p. 23.

306 Guo & Wu 2004, p. 86.

307 Xiao 2004, p. 75.

Committee will refer the requests to its relevant special committees for examination and suggestions.[308]

The second part of Article 90 relates to firms. According to this rule, when other State organs, public organizations, enterprises and institutions or citizens consider that these sorts of legislation contradict the Constitution or laws, they may submit to the Standing Committee of the NPC written suggestions for examination.

However, the views of companies cannot always be accepted for consideration. Article 90 further notes that the working offices of the Standing Committee will study the suggestions and will, when necessary, refer them to the relevant special committees for examination and suggestions.[309]

Regarding the contravention by the rules of provincial governments, ventures can also propose examining these local laws. According to Article 35 of the Rules for the Procedure of Making Regulations (2001), where State organs, public organizations, enterprises and institutions or citizens consider that the rules of local governments and of the departments under the State Council contradict laws or administrative regulations, they may submit to the State Council written requests for examination, and the Legislative Affairs Office of the State Council should study and deal with the suggestions.[310]

Moreover, according to Zhuoming Zhang, such a system of suggestions is also adopted in other legislation of the State Council and of the local people's congresses.[311] For example, Article 9 of the Regulations on the Record Keeping of Rules and Regulations (2002) extends this mechanism to decisions and orders with general binding force formulated and announced by the departments under the State Council and the governments of provincial regions and of relatively large cities. If firms or citizens deem that these decisions and orders contradict administrative regulations or laws, they may propose examining them.[312]

At local levels, for instance, as noted by Article 76 of the Regulation on the Local Legislation of Zhejiang Province (2001), the rules of Zhejiang province can be suggested for examination.[313] Where natural or private persons consider that this kind of legislation contravenes the Constitution, laws, administrative regulations or local regulations of Zhejiang province, they can make suggestions to the Standing Committee of the People's Congress of Zhejiang province. This Committee may

308 As provided in Art. 116 of the Constitution and Art. 66 of the Legislation Law, autonomous regulations and separate regulations are legislation made by the people's congresses of the national autonomous areas. The English text of the Legislation law (2000) basically relies on the document available at: <www.npc.gov.cn/pc/11_4/2007-12/11/content_1617613.htm#> (last accessed 6 April 2016).

309 According to Art. 90, this provision has a broad scope of application. It can be invoked as long as the Constitution or laws are deemed to be contravened. That means it also applies to the situation where unlawful authorities exercise licensing power or licensing regimes are created for illegal matters.

310 规章制定程序条例 (2001).

311 Zhang 2008b, p. 114.

312 法规规章备案条例 (2002).

313 浙江省地方立法条例（2001).

submit their views to relevant special committees for later study. Nevertheless, there is no relevant enforcement mechanism.

Fourth, Article 16 of the ALL puts a limit to the requirements made by administrative regulations, local regulations and rules to implement administrative licenses. These provisions may set conditions for the implementation of administrative licenses within the scope of the matters established by superior laws. But the regulations and rules must not impose specific requirements for this execution set by them, and must not increase administrative licenses; for the specific conditions of administrative licenses, they must not set up any other condition in violation of superior laws.[314] Xianghua Zeng notes that Article 16 aims to cope with the situation that enterprises are already overburdened with administrative license applications.[315]

Fifth, as provided in Article 41 of the ALL, for a licensing regime established by laws and regulations, its license should be of nationwide validity, if no regional limit is imposed on its application scope.

Sixth, as Zhengkun Yu remarks, the ALL asks administrative authorities to create administrative licenses in an unbiased manner.[316] According to Article 5(3) of the ALL, the applicants for administrative licenses are entitled to equal rights under them as long as the applicants meet legal conditions and standards. Moreover, Article 57 of the ALL notes that for a license with quantitative restrictions, where the applications of at least two applicants satisfy the statutory conditions and standards, administrative organs should decide to approve the administrative license according to the priority order of accepting their applications. But if laws and administrative regulations prescribe other methods for approving the administrative license, such provisions should prevail. Therefore, authorities should treat applications for business approvals equally, irrespective of whether the applicants are local companies, or not.

Obviously, the above provisions aim to regulate the setting up of a business licensing system. Mingchen Mao (2005) remarks on the first two points from the perspective of tackling local protectionism. He holds that it is a common practice for local governments to impose local protectionism policies through making local administrative rules arbitrarily. This situation mentioned by him implicitly referred to the time before the ALL was promulgated. In the past, the arbitrary establishment of administrative licenses by local governments was a fundamental reason for the prevalence and unlawfulness of administrative license regimes and local protectionism. Therefore, the ALL grants the authority for creating administrative licensing regimes to local authorities very cautiously. In particular, Article 15 of the ALL sets clear limits on their establishment power by providing that only when dealing with those matters in Article 12 of the ALL can administrative licenses be established. At the same time, only for the purpose of

314 Art. 16(4) of the ALL (2003).
315 Zeng 2006, p. 26.
316 Yu 2006, p. 74.

efficiently managing local affairs, local authorities can have limited licensing authority.[317]

However, according to some empirical studies, the actual use of licensing runs contrary to the provision of the ALL. Three aspects of the problem can be separately identified, relating to who sets up licensing systems, for what matters licensing systems can be established and Article 15(2) of the ALL.

7.2.1. Other than Lawful Authorities Exercising Licensing Authority

With regard to licensing authorities, other than the administrative subjects provided in the ALL, organizations also use licensing power in practice. This can be demonstrated by the following cases and explanations to a certain degree.

First, as argued by Yuchun Zhou and Hongmei Cao, some licensing systems created by certain ministries are still effective; this is recorded in the Document No. 380 of the Jiangsu Administration of Industry and Commerce (2004). Businesses from certain industries are still required to obtain those licenses. Cases in point are the administrative licenses for newly-built city power plants and for the establishment of the appraisal organizations for used motor vehicles.[318] It should be mentioned that according to the ALL, ministries no longer have licensing authority.

Second, in practice, numerous local agencies with no licensing authority establish licensing regimes. For instance, as mentioned in a meeting of the NDRC in 2005, some regional areas and relevant departments exceed their authority to exercise licensing power and to charge fees.[319] In the view of Dalin Sheng (2007), many government departments with no licensing authority do not conform to the provision of the ALL on what authorities can establish administrative licenses. These governmental agencies still establish licensing regimes arbitrarily such as when the ALL was not in place.[320] According to Zhuyi Ye, in real life, to show their administrative achievement and facilitate their administrative work, some officials take advantage of their powerful position, design licensing regimes in their self-interest and establish administrative licenses illegally. The officers also try to legalize these licensing regimes by means of 'red-tape documents'. For instance,

317 Mao 2005, p. 149 and 150.

318 周宇春、曹红梅, 如何规范经营范围前置审批项目，江苏经济报, 2010年11月15日，Yuchun Zhou and Hongmei Cao, How to Standardise the Pre-administrative Licenses for Licensed Operations, Jiangsu Economic Daily, 15 November 2010.

319 发改委: 乱收费问题突出地方部门越权审批收费, the NDRC, the Problem of Unauthorized Collection of Charges is Serious and Regional Departments Exceed Their Authority to Exercise Licensing Power and Charge Fees, available at: <http://news.anhuinews.com/-system/2005/06/20/001287668.shtml> (last accessed 6 April 2016).

320 盛大林：行政审批不降反增源于有法不依, (来源：燕赵都市报)，Dalin Sheng, The Increase in the Number of Administrative Approvals Stems from the Failure to abide by the ALL, Sources: Yanzhao Metropolis Daily, available at: <http://news.qq.com/a/20070316/-000365.htm> (last accessed 6 April 2016).

bureaus of quality and technical supervision at local level exceed their power to create a licensing system.[321]

Moreover, Bill K.P. Chou (2009) notes that all levels of the Chinese governments from province to township had some kinds of power over the establishment of business licenses until that time. Numerous local authorities still use the licensing authority that should be annulled or given to those at higher levels.[322] This situation is certainly contrary to the provision made by Articles 14 and 15 of the ALL. In his opinion, it is extremely difficult for central government to monitor the exercise of licensing authority by the local bureaucrats. According to him, one reason for this is that local bureaucrats account for 93.1 per cent of all government officials in China and the number of central bureaucrats is too small. Another cause can be that central government needs financial support and the human resources of local authorities to implement national policies such as reducing administrative licenses. After the decentralization of administrative and monetary power, national government cannot shoulder the financial burden of local governments including the payment to local officials as before. All these elements allow local officials to have high discretion and even to shape state policies by themselves.[323] It is hard to agree completely with Chou, as his argument lacks sufficient empirical support for the use of licensing power by other institutions. That said, his call for the possibility of other organizations' engagement in licensing in China is convincing.

Furthermore, with a clear case, Yin Zhang, Rusong Sun, Wancheng Zheng and Yongqin Zhang argue that districts and counties can usually decide for what matters a licensing regime is necessary. The types and contents of licensing items in different districts and counties of a certain relatively large city should be no different. This is due to the provision in the ALL that at local levels only authorities of a provincial region and a relatively large city are permitted to create a licensing regime. However, different districts and counties in Suzhou, a relatively large city in Jiangsu Province, have different categories of licensing systems. Specifically, Wujiang, a county administered by that city, has abandoned licensing for some activities according to the ALL. By contrast, other districts and counties in Suzhou still keep some of the licensing systems that have been abolished in Wujiang. This is because these districts and counties have the actual autonomy for licensing.[324]

7.2.2. The Arbitrary Range of Licensing Items

In terms of which matters need licensing, governments can still make a decision arbitrarily. Some authors clearly give a general idea on the extent for application of

321 叶祝颐,"馒头行政许可"背后是权力意志作祟, 来源：河北新闻网, Zhuyi Ye, the Hidden Reason behind 'Administrative Licenses for Steam Bread' is the Will of Administrative Power, Sources: Hebei News Net, available at: <http://comment.hebnews.cn/2012-07/10/-content_2760015.htm> (last accessed 6 April 2016).

322 Chou 2009, p. 162.

323 *Ibid.*

324 Zhang *et al.* 2007, p. 75.

licensing in practice. In Jingbo Wang's view (2011), there is disorder in licensing, which is a major problem. One of the two aspects for this issue is that administrative agencies establish licensing at random. As to for what matters licensing systems can be created, the establishment of licensing systems and the conditions for licensing, there is general confusion.[325] Wang's remark confirms the earlier analysis of Article 12 in section 2.4.3.3: this article is not completely clear about for what matter licensing regimes can be established.

Moreover, in Jinglian Wu's opinion on licensing, governments, on the one hand, take care of many businesses over which they have no jurisdiction and which they cannot manage well. On the other hand, those authorities do not perform their responsibility for the governance over some affairs or they fail to govern them. Measures were announced to be taken to reduce the number of licensing regimes by the State Council in 2001. But currently there are more licensing systems under the name of administrative licenses or with other labels, as reported by entrepreneurs at the 2007 annual sessions of the NPC and the Chinese People's Political Consultative Conference (CPPCC). The key to licensing is to reduce the number of licensing systems and further standardize licensing, as Wu argues.[326]

There have been many cases about the illegal enlargement of the application scope for licensing. As remarked by Zhanqi Shi, some licensing systems are cancelled according to the rules of the ALL. However, very soon new licensing regimes will be created.[327] According to Yan Lin, the 'foolish' use of licenses occurs from time to time.[328] In practice, licensing regimes were established for selling steamed bread in Gansu in 2012 and for selling watermelons in Zhengzhou in 2006.[329]

325 中国网,马怀德、王敬波等院内专家就行政审批改革十年历程接受记者采访 (来源: 法制日报), Zhongguowang, Huaide Ma, Jingbo Wang and other Experts from the Graduate School of the China Univeristy of Political Science and Law are Interviewed for the Ten-year Reform Experience of Administrative Approvals, (sources: Legal daily), available at: <http://law.china.cn/txt/2011-11/25/content_4651071.htm> (last accessed 6 April 2016).

326 吴敬琏、陈清泰:治理腐败关键在减少行政审批, 来源:中国青年报, Jinglian Wu and Qingtai Chen: the Key to Combat Corruption is to Decrease the Use of Administrative Licenses, (Sources: China Youth Daily), available at: <http://news.xinhuanet.com/lianzheng/2007-03/15/content_5850721.htm> (last accessed 6 April 2016).

327 史占旗, 有了好处乱办事 "权大气粗"比"财大气粗"更可怕, 来源：检察日报. Zhanqi Shi, Officials Manage Their Work Irresponsibly After They are Squared; the Ability to Abuse Administrative Power is More Dangerous than the Possibility to be Lavish with Money. Sources: Procuratorate Daily, available at: <http://news.xinhuanet.com/politics/2007-10/09/content_6849830.htm> (last accessed 6 April 2016).

328 林衍, 行政审批改革: 改皮毛更要改骨头, 来源: 中国青年报. Yan Lin, Only Scratching the Surface of the Problems Found in Licensing System Reform is not Enough and Key Issues should be Tackled, Sources: China Youth Daily, available at: <www.qstheory.cn/-zz/ggts/201210/t20121026_189256.htm> (last accessed 6 April 2016).

329 中评社，叫停"馒头许可"，遏制乱设行政许可之风, 来源：工人日报。Zhongpingshe, Stopping Licensing for Steamed Bread and Curbing the establishment of licensing Regimes at Random, Sources: Workers Daily News, available at: <www.zhgpl.com/crn-webapp/spec/ylck/index.jsp?docid=102165235> (last accessed 6 April 2016). 亦菲, "馒头办""西瓜办", 都是"麻烦办", 来源：新华网, Fei Yi, Licensing systems for Steamed →

According to Jing Kang, the establishment of a licensing regime for steamed bread demonstrates the abuse of administrative power for supervision by administrative agencies and departments. Many organizations use administrative methods such as licensing arbitrarily for steamed bread regardless of practical need. Moreover, these agencies are even involved in every field of market exchange and apply administrative means for supervision to very trivial things for economic rents. As a result, adverse effects are felt in all these fields.[330]

Moreover, many licensing items contradicting the ALL operate under other names besides licenses, as argued by Songnian Ying.[331] In the view of Huaide Ma, the vice president of the China University of Political Science and Law, numerous organizations use labels such as 'putting on record' or 'authorizing' for their licensing regimes. Alternatively, they include them in 'approvals of non-administrative licensing', 'inside approvals' or 'approvals regarding civil rights'. Thus, these institutions circumvent the ALL.[332] It is possible for them to go beyond their power to set up licenses.

Licensing items are far beyond the scope of the licensing applicability provided by the ALL and scholars, journalists and critics study the reasons for this problem with their practical experience. According to Shuinan Liao, though the ALL has explicitly restricted the establishment of licensing regimes by administrative agencies at random for a long time, the provision of the ALL has had no effect to curb the random creation of licensing systems.[333] For example, it is necessary to get permission from a town government to harvest corn in its area and the licensing fee is 500 RMB for around 670 square meters. Otherwise there will be severe punishments or even criminal responsibility, as stated by the authority.[334] This unchecked establishment happens in the circumstance that administrative power is used to create economic rents for administrative agencies.[335]

Bread and Watermelons Cause Troubles for Daily Life, Sources: Xinhua Net, available at: <http://news.xinhuanet.com/comments/2006-08/04/content_4914597.htm> (last accessed 6 April 2016).

330 康劲, "馒头的自由"与舌尖上的安全, Jing Kang, 'the Freedom of Steam Bread' and Diet Safety, available at: <http://news.nen.com.cn/jinhushiping/62/4236562.shtml> (last accessed 6 April 2016).

331 应松年，《行政许可法》实施以来所暴露的问题，政府法制半月刊，2005年5月(上), Songnian Ying, Problems Found after the Enforcement of the ALL, Government Legality (bi-monthly), May 2005 (Section I).

332 马怀德, 谁在虚置行政许可法, 新京报, 2005年2月27日, Huaide Ma, Who Makes the ALL Powerless, XinjingBao, 27 February 2005.

333 廖水南, "卖馒头许可证"背后是滥设行政许可, 重庆商报, 2012年7月11日. Shuinan Liao, A Hidden Problem of 'Licensing for Selling Steamed Bread' is that Administrative Licensing Regimes are Set up at Random, Chongqing Economic Times, 11 June 2012.

334 林衍, 行政审批改革: 改皮毛更要改骨头, 来源: 中国青年报, Yan Lin, Only Scratching the Surface of the Problems Found in Licensing System Reform is not Enough and Key Issues should be Tackled, Sources: China Youth Daily, available at: <www.qstheory.cn/zz/ggts/-201210/t20121026_189256.htm> (last accessed 6 April 2016).

335 廖水南, "卖馒头许可证"背后是滥设行政许可, 重庆商报, 2012年7月11日. Shuinan Liao, A Hidden Problem of 'Licensing for Selling Steamed Bread' is that Administrative Licensing Regimes are Set up at Random, Chongqing Economic Times, 11 June 2012.

Shilin Li remarks that governments can still decide for what activities licensing regimes should be established regardless of Articles 12 and 13 of the ALL. His reason is that he cannot decide what matters require the creation of a licensing regime based on the contents of Articles 12 and 13. The first provision uses 'may be' to indicate that for these matters in Article 12 licensing systems can be established. The latter article chooses 'may not be' to demonstrate for what items licensing systems are not necessary. However, 'may be' can be treated as 'may not be' when one considers the meanings of the two terms in Chinese. As a result, Li holds that legislation does not provide for what items licenses shall be established in fact. Moreover, since there is no judicial and administrative interpretation on this problem, what items need licensing could be considered as a legislative gap. He makes his remark, taking into account that local authorities and administrative agencies have some sorts of licensing authority by making administrative regulations, local regulations and rules.[336]

As demonstrated by Dalin Sheng, two causes lead to the additional quantity of licensing regimes. One reason is that new licensing systems are created in the name of administrative licenses. And other, licensing regimes with other titles are also set up, which are administrative licenses in fact. According to Sheng, one can easily understand these phenomena from daily reports. New licensing systems are established almost every day by different departments in different regions, as shown by news reports. Thus, the engagement in various kinds of activities now needs licensing. As pointed out by Sheng further, the violation on the ALL provision on who can be licensing authorities is a fundamental explanation for creating a licensing system in such an easy way. Administrative agencies with no licensing authority can still exercise licensing power as before. That is why many people are completely disappointed about the ALL, though they had high expectations of this law at the moment of its enactment.[337]

Moreover, Yunsheng Zhang proposes to take caution against the establishment of licensing systems for matters not requiring a licensing system by means of local regulations or rules of provincial governments. He holds that whether any matter can be a licensing item should be assessed strictly and reasoned rigorously.[338]

7.2.3. The Violation of Article 15(2)

With regard to Article 15(2) of the ALL, there is a violation of this provision in practice. This provision is designed to cope with local protectionism.

336 Li 2008, p. 69. Other scholars also criticise the choice of 'may be' in Arts. 12 and 13 of the ALL, which is detailed in 1.4.3.4.

337 盛大林：行政审批不降反增源于有法不依, (来源：燕赵都市报)，Dalin Sheng, The Increase in the Number of Administrative Approvals Stems from the Failure to Abide by the ALL, Sources: Yanzhao Metropolis Daily, available at: <http://news.qq.com/a/20070316/-000365.htm> (last accessed 6 April 2016).

338 Zhang 2004, p. 80.

First, Zhou and Cao hold that in accordance with Article 15(2) of the ALL, people's congress at local levels and provincial governments shall not set up pre-administrative licenses for the establishment registration of companies by means of local regulations and rules of provincial governments. However, in practice, local authorities create pre-administrative licenses in Jiangsu Province. The Jiangsu AICs are obliged to take obtaining of these pre-administrative licenses established as a pre-condition for the establishment registration of a new company. As a result, the gap between the provision and the actual situation on the competent authority for pre-administrative licenses has sown serious confusion among the public servants of the AICs.[339] Pre-administrative licenses are licenses a business must obtain before they can apply for the establishment registration of companies, according to the ALL. The AICs will deny the entry of new companies if businesses do not get relevant pre-administrative licenses first.

Moreover, Qinhong Jiang and Wei Chen note that some governments at local levels still require the licenses prohibited by Article 15(2) of the ALL. Other agencies with no licensing authority, under the name of 'putting on record', exercise license powers not permitted by the ALL. They ask companies to submit their materials and determine whether to record them, which plays the same role as licensing in essence.[340] The licenses mentioned by Jiang and Chen are surely pre-administrative licenses since their essay is targeted at the reform of the system about pre-administrative licenses.

Second, the increase of local protectionism by means of licensing remains a problem. As demonstrated by Huaiqing Chen (2008), licensing systems are often used for local protectionism in Huaibei city. The regimes are created through making regulatory documents, which restrict the entry of products from other regions into Huaibei and limit the engagement of individuals and companies of other areas in production and business in the city. For instance, a licensing system is set up to require the use of cement made in Huaibei for construction projects performed in that city. Moreover, construction enterprises from other regions are asked to apply for licenses such as the verification for the qualification as a construction company. All these licensing regimes are created to implement local protectionism. The information on licensing systems in Huaibei is obtained from Chen's practical experience with the legal work of the Huaibei government.[341] Furthermore, according to Min Yang, the government of Guizhou province erects local protectionism barriers by establishing licensing regimes and Article 15(2) is breached. As demonstrated by his example, only design institutes from other provinces are subject to a temporary licensing regime regarding planning and design qualification created by the Guizhou authority.[342]

339 周宇春、曹红梅, 如何规范经营范围前置审批项目,江苏经济报, 2010年11月15日， Yuchun Zhou and Hongmei Cao, How to Standardise the Pre-administrative Licenses for Licensed Operations, Jiangsu Economic Daily, 15 November 2010.

340 Jiang & Chen 2010, p. 65.

341 Chen 2008, p. 25.

342 Yang 2011, p. 30.

The above three points can be considered as reasons to support the restriction on the licensing power of local authorities. However, criticisms were formulated by Liaohui Cao and Taigao Wang in terms of limiting the autonomy of licensing authorities at local levels. Their concern is that local governments' lack of licensing power left themselves simply not knowing how they can cope with challenges in their regions. In some cases, the state has not established any administrative license for those qualifications that must be determined by it in Article 15(2). In other cases, new problems arise in some regions because of the unbalanced development between different regions. Moreover, the centralisation of administrative license power impedes competition between different local governments. In more economically developed areas, it is already possible to raise the standards on market access, safety and environment. This could be achieved by establishing administrative licenses in different ways, according to the different regions.[343]

All the above empirical studies reveal a paradox between the provision and the implementation on licensing. From the relevant legal provisions, it follows that central government constrains the autonomy of licensing power owned by local authorities, so that local administrative agencies cannot implement local protectionism measures. This is the goal of the ALL. According to this law, at local levels, only the people's congress and its standing committee at provincial level and the people's congress and its standing committee of relatively large cities may create administrative licenses. Moreover, a licensing regime can be established for the activities in Article 12 and for those matters in Article 13 licensing systems may not be set up. Furthermore, the administrative licenses established by the local authorities should not obstruct the engagement of any company in business in the areas governed by the regional governments in accordance with Article 15(2).

However, according to practical experience, the actual use of licensing significantly departs from the regulation of the ALL. More specifically, other governmental agencies than the statutory licensing authorities set up licensing regimes and the matters which can be licensing items are decided at random. Moreover, pre-administrative licenses for the establishment registration of companies are created by provincial authorities and local protectionism obstacles are erected by means of licensing. The real application of licensing can lead to considerable entry barriers for companies. Some cases in this section have demonstrated that the establishment of businesses is obscured by the abuse of licensing.

The paradoxical situation of licensing raises the question of why enormous entry barriers can be created, though the ALL explicitly constrains licensing authority. The causes may be based on the lack of judicial review or the power structure between the central government and local authorities. The potential reasons will be examined here by empirical research on the inter-provincial establishment of companies in China.

343 Cao & Wang 2012, p. 130-133.

7.3. *The Anti-Monopoly Law*

The prohibition of administrative monopolies, in Giacomo Di Federico's opinion, is recognised as the most noticeable characteristic of the AML.[344] Article 8 of the AML reads that administrative departments and organisations authorised by laws and regulations to perform the function of administering public affairs should not abuse their administrative power to eliminate or restrict competition. Moreover, according to Article 35 of the AML, they should not abuse their administrative power to exclude or limit non-local undertakings' investment in their regions or restrict their establishment of branches and subsidiaries there by such means as not giving equal treatment to that which local undertakings receive. This provision recalls Article 49 of the Treaty on the Functioning of the European Union (TFEU) to a certain extent.[345] They, in accordance with Article 37 of the AML, are also warned against abusing their administrative powers to make regulations with contents eliminating or restricting competition.

In addition, according to the AML, sanctions can be imposed if there is abuse of administrative power. One effective remedy is that the superior authority of the administrative organisations orders them to rectify the situation. Moreover, the anti-monopoly enforcement agencies can propose suggestions to the authority at a higher level on how to deal with the matter.[346]

Rules on how to put forward the proposal can be found in legal documents facilitating the enforcement of the AML. In accordance with the Rules on the SAIC's Main Mandates, Internal Bodies and Officials (2008), the SAIC shoulders the responsibility of enforcing the relevant AML rules for dealing with the abuse of administrative power to eliminate or restrict competition.[347] Specifically, the Anti-monopoly and Anti-unfair Competition Enforcement Bureau of the SAIC is charged with the enforcement of these rules and with making specific measures.[348] Moreover, according to the provisions made by the SAIC, it can make suggestions to the State Council for handling the mentioned abuse of the departments under the State Council and provincial governments.[349] Its departments at provincial level can make such suggestions when the departments under the governments at provincial level, the governments at county levels and their departments abuse administrative power resulting in the restriction and limitation of competition.[350] Such provision is also made in the Provisions for the Industry and Commerce Administrations to Stop

344 Di Federico 2009, p. 261.
345 *Ibid.*, p. 262.
346 Art. 51 of the AML (2007).
347 国家工商行政管理总局主要职责内设机构和人员编制规定 (2008).
348 *Ibid.*
349 《工商行政管理机关制止滥用行政权力排除、限制竞争行为程序规定》(2009)第3条. Art. 3 of Provisions on the Procedure for the Industrial and Commercial Administrations to Stop Acts of Abusing Administrative Power for Excluding or Limiting Competition (2009).
350 *Ibid.*, Art. 4.

Acts of Abusing Administrative Power for the Purpose of Eliminating or Limiting Competition (2010).[351]

In reality, based on available reports, it can be found that the proposal right has been successfully used for one time. In 2010, one local government in Guangdong province told all the companies for navigation technology services in that city to use the satellite positioning platform provided by the New Horizon Navigation Technology Co., Ltd. In return they needed to pay a certain sum of money to this company. Otherwise, the vehicles owned by them could not pass an annual inspection by this government. The AIC of Guangdong province put forward its suggestion to the Guangdong government that the abuse of administrative power and the restriction of competition by that city needed to be rectified according to laws. Finally, this suggestion was followed in 2011. Yong Huang and Jieming Sheng highly estimate this case.[352] Learning from the case, one could assume that if a local government in Guangdong province abuses its power to restrict the investment by companies from other regions, the AIC of Guangdong province can raise its proposal to the Guangdong government, but it still needs the Guangdong authority's approval.

Moreover, the administrative remedies provided in other laws, as discussed in section 7.2, can also be applied to a violation of Articles 8, 35 or 37 of the AML. Where restrictions are imposed on the establishment by non-local businesses through local legislation, firms can convey their concerns to relevant departments.

However, doubts on the enforcement of the above provisions of the AML exist. There is particularly widespread strong criticism about the effectiveness of Article 51. The punishment for the risk of abusing administrative power, in Jinglian Wu's opinion (China's leading economist), is completely inadequate. He holds that the rectification by administrative authorities at a higher level is almost impossible.[353] Many legal scholars such as Yan Gao also share this view.[354] Among them, Xiaoye Wang draws a lesson from the enforcement experience of the Anti-Unfair Competition Law (AUCL). In her opinion, this correction mechanism has its equivalence in Article 30 of the AUCL, and it has seldom been used according to the execution history of the AUCL for more than 10 years. However, almost every one learns that administrative monopolies cause the most severe harm in practice.[355]

Various researchers have tried to explain the ineffectiveness further. First, some consider that the relationship between the higher and lower administrative

351 《工商行政管理机关制止滥用行政权力排除、限制竞争行为的规定》（2010）第6条. Art. 6 of Provisions for the Industry and Commerce Administrations to Stop Acts of Abusing Administrative Power for the Purpose of Eliminating or Limiting Competition (2010).

352 《工商机关首次行成功使反行政垄断建议权》，来源：2011年7月27日中国工商报，the AICs Successfully Uses the Proposal Right against Administrative monopolies for the First Time, China Industry and Business News, 27 July 2011.

353 《财经》杂志，吴敬琏：我国经济社会矛盾几乎到了临界点，Caijing Magazine, Jinglian Wu: China's Economic and Social Conflicts almost Reach a Critical Point, available at: <http://finance.sina.com.cn/review/hgds/20120903/091613027382.shtml> (last accessed 6 April 2016).

354 Gao 2009, p. 114.

355 Wang 2009, p. 57.

departments causes this problem. For example, Xiaoye Wang, a member of the Expert Advisory Board for the Anti-Monopoly Committee of the State Council, is highly sceptical of the effectiveness as the tolerance of the abuse of administrative power, especially local protectionism, by the departments at a lower level would create considerable economic rents for the higher agency. Local enterprises are often major sources of revenue for local governments.[356] This opinion is also expressed in her earlier essay in the Anti-trust Law Journal.[357] In the third article, she remarks that governments at higher levels are not expected to execute this article with justice and in a neutral way. They even have no willingness to enforce it. The reason is that administrative monopolies often share in the profits of the SOEs and companies owned by local governments. The protection for them can bring benefits to the lower agencies and also to the higher ones.[358] The situation mentioned by Wang can be exemplified as follows. If a government at county level can receive tax revenues, increase employment and bring other benefits by protecting local business, it could be argued that it benefits a provincial region as a whole. Very likely, the local enterprises will also pay some tax directly to the provincial authority. It should be pointed out that all these advantages created by local protectionism are considered from an industrial policy perspective rather than from a competition policy view. Moreover, if they are companies owned by the provincial government, it will certainly permit the protectionism activities conducted by its county agencies. According to Wang, besides the economic relations, personnel relations can make fair and independent correction almost impossible since leaders of these agencies are often friends or acquaintances.[359]

Second, some show their worry about the status of the higher agencies. Xiaoye Wang notes that who become the institutions at a higher level depends on the specific context of different cases. Also, one could not expect that administrative departments for execution will play this part. Therefore, in most cases, officials of the possible higher authorities do not have a sense to cope with monopolies and do not take anti-monopolies as their main responsibilities.[360]

Third, the administrative agencies may lack the ability to cope with administrative monopolies.[361] According to Yong Huang, one of the drafters of the AML, the higher authority may not take the suggestions either because of its special relationship with its lower agencies or its lack of expertise in coping with administrative monopolies. Even in case of approving the proposal, the instruction to rectify the problems is not severe enough to deter administrative agencies from

356 南方都市报（记者: 杜强、杨章怀、李召），2012年1月3日，反垄断委员会专家：反垄断法对行政垄断无奈, Southern Metropolis Daily (Journalists: Qiang Du, Zhanghuai Yang and Zhao Li), 3 January 2012, an Expert from the Expert Advisory Board for the Anti-Monopoly Committee: the AML Can Not Have an Effect on Administrative Monopolies, 3 January 2012.

357 Wang 2008, p. 149.

358 Wang 2009, p. 57.

359 *Ibid.*

360 *Ibid.*

361 Wang 2008, p. 149.

abusing its power.[362] Xinzu Zhang and Vanessa Yuanhua Zhang remark that this restriction prohibits the enforcement agencies from applying the AML to administrative monopolies effectively.[363] Wang, Harris and Zhang hold that it has no practical effect against administrative authorities for the lack of direct sanctions against such a monopoly.[364]

Furthermore, some negative evaluations arise from the right of proposal and its successful use. Firstly, as remarked by Yong Huang, the AICs cannot cope with administrative monopolies if local governments refuse to follow their suggestion.[365] Wang criticizes the right for its lack of enforceability. Some people even take it as a problematic feature of the ALL. This law puts too much emphasis on creating impractical, but good sounding measures.[366] Secondly, Shanming Jin argues that it is necessary to deepen our thinking on the current enforcement system of the AML. The only case for enforcement after the adaptation of the AML contradicts the reality that administrative monopolies are still widespread in practice.[367] Thirdly, the single example cannot demonstrate that the AICs can tackle the monopolies independently. As early as 2001, Feng doubted whether they could fulfil the obligation of anti-monopoly agencies successfully. The AICs are led by governments and rely on their monetary support. Moreover, the AICs are directly or indirectly involved in administrative monopoly activities and local protectionism.[368] This problem may become more severe when considering today's relationship between local authorities and the AICs.

7.4. *Limits of Dealing with Administrative Monopolies through Legislation in China*

Undoubtedly, administrative monopolies could be challenged to a certain extent through the mentioned laws. However, after the AML became effective, some scholars have shown their concern that merely making and enforcing legislation cannot effectively cope with this problem in China. Wang admitted that she has written many articles on administrative monopolies and sometimes is not sure how

362 Huang 2008, p. 93.

363 Zhang & Zhang 2007, p. 188.

364 Weishaar 2011, p. 120.

365 《工商机关首次行成功使反行政垄断建议权》, 来源: 2011年7月27日中国工商报, the AICs Successfully Uses the Proposal Right against Administrative monopolies for the First Time, China Industry and Business News, 27 July 2011.

366 Wang 2009, p. 57.

367 金善明,《<反垄断法>能根除行政垄断吗》，来源：学习时报，人民网，2012 年10 月29 日，Shanming Jin, 'Can the AML Eliminate Administrative monopolies?', (Sources: Study Times), People's Daily Online, available at: <http://theory.people.com.cn/n/2012/-1029/c49153-19423542.html> 29 October 2012 (last accessed 6 April 2016).

368 冯兴元, 地方保护主义问题与地方政府行为的规则框架, "中央与地方关系的法治化", 国际学术研讨会 论文集, 2007年1月6日, 北京, 页113. Xingyuan Feng, 'Local Protectionism and Skeleton of Rules of Local Governmental Action', essays from International Symposium on the legalization of the relationship between the central and local governments, Beijing, 6 January 2007, p. 114.

this problem could be tackled. She directly points out that the presence of administrative monopolies relates to the structure of the Chinese state, which cannot be solved only through the AML. According to this law, no strong measures could be taken to combat administrative monopolies. Fundamentally, it is advisable to deepen economic structural reforms with the aim of developing a market economy.[369] She expects the deepening of economic structure reform and the coming of political structure reform.[370] Likewise, Wu mentions that besides the ineffectiveness of the AML, a significant defect of the current structure is another reason why administrative monopolies are common.[371] According to Stefan Weishaar, similarly, some Chinese experts also note that the fundamental changing of China's political and administrative mechanism plays a crucial part in solving the administrative monopoly problem. This transformation could not be easily triggered by the introduction of the AML.[372] More recently, an article in the Study Times suggests some fundamental solutions. The writer thinks that it is not very beneficial to make slight improvements following the model in the current legislation. Instead, some steps could be taken to improve the overall environment for the enforcement of existing legislation. They include further political and economic reforms, strengthening the sense to develop a market economy and the idea of the rule of law. Moreover, the following measures could be considered for specific implementation, i.e. promoting law-based administration, improving accountability mechanism and judicial system and strengthening judicial ability.[373]

8. Causes for the Widespread Occurrence of Barriers to Inter-provincial Establishment

Previous sections have shown that from time to time firms encounter obstacles concerning their inter-provincial establishment of branches and subsidiaries. Moreover, the enforcement of the rules tackling administrative monopolies is far from satisfactory. This section therefore examines the reasons for these barriers. One explanation is that there are deficiencies in relevant laws. Another cause is that these laws cannot be enforced well.

369 南方都市报（记者：杜强、杨章怀、李召）, 2012年1月3日，反垄断委员会专家：反垄断法对行政垄断无奈, Southern Metropolis Daily (Journalists: Qiang Du, Zhanghuai Yang and Zhao Li), 3 January 2012, an Expert from the Expert Advisory Board for the Anti-Monopoly Committee: the AML Can Not Have an Effect on Administrative monopolies.

370 Wang 2009, p. 57.

371 《财经》杂志，吴敬琏：我国经济社会矛盾几乎到了临界点, Caijing Magazine, Jinglian Wu: China's Economic and Social Conflicts almost Reach a Critical Point, available at: <http://finance.sina.com.cn/review/hgds/20120903/091613027382.shtml> (last accessed 6 April 2016).

372 Weishaar 2011, p. 101.

373 金善明，《<反垄断法>能根除行政垄断吗》，来源： 学习时报，人民网，2012 年10 月29 日，Shanming Jin, 'Can the AML Eliminate Administrative Monopolies?', (Sources: Study Times), the People's Daily Online, available at: <http://theory.people.com.cn/n/2012/-1029/c49153-19423542.html> (last accessed 6 April 2016).

It should be mentioned that the contents of these laws have been discussed in detail previously and their problems have also been discussed. Thus, section 8.1 only sums up these flaws. All the previous remarks can certainly support the demonstration of the deficiencies.

8.1. Deficient Contents of National Law

According to Shoulong Mao, numerous administrative laws and regulations have been enacted. Nevertheless, the drawbacks of these rules are prevalent. This prevalence can be identified as the greatest weakness of China's administrative law system.[374] The ALL and the AML also have their own problems and the deficiencies in these two laws are concluded as follows.

To establish licensing regimes at random appears possible due to the loopholes and limitation of Articles 12 and 13 of the ALL. The two provisions regulate for what matters such systems can be created, which are full of significance to firms. However, some terms of these rules are hard to define, such as national security and the situation for the preference of alternatives over licensing is not clarified. Moreover, the licensing items can be extended to all matters according to Article 12(6). As a result, it is likely for companies to experience troubles with the abuse of these articles. Readers can find the assessment of these provisions in depth in section 2.4.3.4.

With regard to the AML, section 7.3 has pointed out that the sanction provided by Article 51 for administrative monopolies is of little practical value. In the case of the abuse of administrative authority by lower administrative departments, higher authorities can ask for rectification according to this rule. Moreover, the anti-monopoly enforcement agencies can convey their views on solving monopolies to these authorities at higher levels. Such regulations appear too simple. The provision even does not entrust the administrative departments for execution to punish the abuse of administrative power.

8.2. Undesirable Implementation of National Law

Compared to the problematic contents of the ALL and the AML, the defects in the relevant implementation systems are more likely to undermine these two laws. Based on the previous discussion, three enforcement systems to cope with the licensing barriers inhibiting companies' expansion can be recognized.

First, AICs are empowered to fight against the abuse of administrative authority limiting competition, according to the argument in section 7.3. They are authorised to propose suggestions to relevant administrative agencies.

374 《中国经济周刊》， 毛寿龙：行政许可法的缺憾——访中国人民大学行政管理学系主任毛寿龙教授, China Economic Weekly, Soulong Mao: the Defects of the ALL-an Interview with Prof. Mao, the Head of Administrative Management Department of Renmin University of China, available at: <http://theory.people.com.cn/GB/40764/55938/55941/3939671.html> (last accessed 6 April 2016).

In addition, as touched upon in section 7.2, firms and citizens are entitled to request the Standing Committee of the NPC to examine local regulations deemed to contradict the Constitution or laws. However, it is not clear whether their requests can be considered. Moreover, they can also ask to check the rules of local governments and of the departments under this council and certain decisions and orders where laws or administrative regulations may be contravened.[375]

Considerable importance can be attached to this right theoretically. This is because private persons can only rely on such administrative remedies where illegal licensing regimes are established through local regulations, the rules of local governments or these decisions and orders.

The following passages point out the reasons for AICs' ineffectiveness in coping with administrative monopolies first. Moreover, the suggestion mechanism for firms to deal with illegal licensing systems themselves is evaluated next. Finally, the impossibility of seeking a remedy for illegal licensing systems is examined. The first two points of the weaknesses of administrative remedies are discussed in section 8.2.1.

8.2.1. The Problems of Administrative Remedies

First, the AICs lack both authority and independence to deal with administrative monopolies. In 1998, Xiaoye Wang expressed worries that local governments can affect the executing of laws by them. It could lead to regional separation, which can damage the seriousness of laws. The reason is that these agencies shoulder the responsibility to implement legislation dealing with monopolies, but they also perform functions as governmental departments at the same time. They are subject to government influence because of their reliance on the authorities' financial, human and material resources.[376] Moreover, such deficiencies in AICs' status have also been demonstrated in section 7.3.

However, scholars often value the position of the AML enforcement institutions. Wang argues that the legislators' determination and the creation of an effective implementation institution play an essential role to stop administrative monopolies rather than some superficial problems, e.g., which piece of legislation should govern this issue. Without a competent and authoritative agency, the AML can only be a toothless tiger, having no effect on stopping administrative monopolies.[377] Moreover, only an independent and authoritative agency with all necessary power can fulfil the obligation to cope with the monopolies.[378] According to Lin Sang, an official of the SAIC responsible for anti-monopolies, these qualities turn out to be crucial when one considers the complexity of monopoly activities, the

375 According to section 2, other institutions can also challenge such contradiction through the same way. The only difference is that the opinions of certain state organs are asked to be accepted for consideration.

376 Wang 1998, p. 8.

377 Wang 2009, p. 51.

378 *Ibid.*, p. 57.

nature of governmental agencies violating the AML and their special status and influence.[379]

Besides administrative authorities, people should also pay enough attention to the functions of courts, in Wang's opinion. They should be entrusted to monitor the power of governments and the legitimacy of rules made by them. Enterprises or consumers should be allowed to seek judicial remedies in the case of damage to their benefits by administrative monopoly activities.[380]

Second, the right to make suggestions laid down in the Legislation Law has not once initiated the examination of any law, regulation or local rules according to Qinguo Shen (2013). Indeed, the Standing Committee has not responded to any suggestions ever made, let alone reviewing legislation.[381]

However, as demonstrated by Wangsheng Zhou, there are numerous administrative regulations conflicting with the Legislation Law in his field. Zhou is a professor at Beijing University and his research interests focus on law making.[382]

Therefore, an immediate necessity is to create a procedural obligation according to Bin Chen. Relevant authorities should be asked to react to the requests made by average citizens and private institutions.[383]

Moreover, as argued by Jianmiao Hu and Chengdong Jin, the public ought to be allowed to litigate where any rules are deemed to be unlawful, apart from the mentioned responding system. This right is the key to the relief function, legislation oversight and citizens' role in societies.[384]

8.2.2. Absence of Judicial Review of the Establishment of Illegal Licensing Regimes

Section 8.2.1 has pointed out that scholars pay much attention to the role of courts in dealing with illegal rules or administrative monopolies. However, where unlawful

379 桑林, 反垄断立法需要权威执法者, Lin Sang, The Legislation for Anti-monopolies Requires law Enforcement Officials with Authority, available at: <http://finance.sina.com.cn/-review/20060124/14532302831.shtml> (last accessed 6 April 2016).

380 Wang 2009, p. 57.

381 汪红, 公民可诉"红头文件"违宪, 法制晚报，2013年4月17日，Hong Wang, Citizens can Sue for the contravention of the Constitution by Red Tape, Legal Newspapers, 17 April 2013. It seems unlikely citizens and firms have triggered other reviewing mechanisms regulated by other regulations. First, these systems are the same as the way provided in the Legislation law. Moreover, there is no report on their operation in practice. In addition, according to Shen, the five national authorities provided in Art. 90(1) of the Legislation Law have not suggested to examine any law or regulation. The main reason is that such suggestions can conflict with their own interests. For example, the State Council is not likely to challenge its own regulations. Moreover, possibly, the considerations for their relations with each other keep them from asking for examinations.

382 闵家桥, 立法法语焉不详？, Jiaqiao Yan, the Legislation Law is unclearly defined?, available at: <www.politicalchina.org/printnews.asp?newsid=84439> (last accessed 6 April 2016).

383 陈斌, 激活法规审查, 助力依宪治国, 南方周末, Bin Chen, to Make the Reviewing System for Regulations Effective and Promote the Running of the Country by the Constitution, available at: < www.infzm.com/content/89434> (last accessed 6 April 2016).

384 Hu & Jin 2005, p. 139.

licensing regimes are established through local legislation, decisions or orders, such cases cannot be brought before courts. This provision is made in the APL and its judicial interpretation.

According to Article 12(2) of the APL, the people's courts should not accept suits brought by citizens, legal persons or other organizations against administrative regulations, the rules of local governments, the rules of the departments under the State Council or decisions and orders with general binding force formulated and announced by administrative organs.

The concept of decisions and orders in Article 12(2) is defined in Article 3 of the Judicial Interpretation for the APL (2000).[385] They refer to administrative normative documents promulgated by administrative agencies that target unspecified objects of regulation and can be applied repeatedly.

A conclusion can be drawn from the wording of Article 12(2) and the relevant explanations that general rules cannot be challenged for their legality and constitutionality in China. Nevertheless, individual administrative acts can be challenged in courts, as was explained in section 2.4.3.5.

It should be noted that the Provisions on the Application of Laws in the Trial of Civil Disputes arising from Monopolistic Practices (2012) (hereinafter the SPC Provisions) does not cover the establishment of an illegal licensing system.[386] According to Article 1, the SPC Provisions only govern the civil litigation regarding disputes over the damages caused by monopolistic practices and over the violation of the AML by industry association charters or contract articles. Monopolistic practices, as laid down in Article 2 of the AML, include (1) the establishment of monopoly agreements between operators, (2) the abuse of a dominant market position by operators and (3) operator consolidation which has or may have the effect of eliminating or restricting market competition.

Challenges to rules of general application are impossible on the bases of the APL. Therefore, there are numerous adverse consequences in practice, according to Xingde Liu and Jiquan Huang (2000). Due to the lack of jurisdiction over local legislation, the interests of the public and firms governed by them cannot be effectively protected. Administrative goals cannot be achieved either. Moreover, the tendency of some administrative agencies to legislate in their own interests is de facto encouraged.[387]

As identified by Wenzhao Xiong and Wei Zhang (2006), such a trend is mainly shown in the following aspects. First, when making macro-economic policies, some administrative departments use administrative power to erect unnecessary market entry barriers, expand the extent of their licensing authority and make duplicate and multiple licensing requirements. These agencies even designate operators for certain industries, set market prices and define operation scope. Thus, they can interfere in certain trades in terms of personnel, distribution and management to

385 最高人民法院关于执行《中华人民共和国行政诉讼法》若干问题的解释 (2000).

386 关于审理因垄断行为引发的民事纠纷案件应用法律若干问题的规定 (2012).

387 Liu & Huang 2000, p. 57.

some extent. As a result, it becomes difficult to introduce the competition mechanism.

Second, some other administrative agencies seek the maximizing of sector authority and sector interests deliberately. In addition, these gains are legalized through making laws and regulations, department rules and state policies. These organs even form the strongest administrative monopoly with government-owned corporations or policy corporations e.g. administrative restriction for entry, sector protectionism, planned resource allocation, government monopoly etc.

With regard to monopolies, they also help make department rules with the feature of pursuing sector interests and sector power. This is because these firms usually rely on state administrative industrial regulators. Thus, these companies struggle for more authority and benefits for them where such ventures assist the state in preparing policies and draft laws.[388]

Moreover, the problem that laws can be instituted for the administrative departments' own profits is also pointed out in the 1997 government legislative affairs seminar. As argued by some participants, attention should be paid to the serious interference of local protectionism and sector protectionism with law making and law enforcement. These organs strive mainly for the power of licensing, certificate issuing, charges and sanctions through strengthening and broadening their authority excessively. Some officials take administrative legislation as ways to advance the interests of and increase the extent of their departments. As a result, these civil servants manage to create various sorts of administrative authority for their organs through administrative legislation.[389]

In addition, according to one official from MOFCOM (2013), the trend to misuse administrative power has not been curbed after many years. Legislative authority is still exercised to make local rules and orders to protect local enterprises. Ze Song, a research director from the Chinese Academy of Social Sciences, also notes that local protectionism has evolved into market entry restrictions on non-local products and firms.[390]

As concluded by Xiong and Zhang, some administrative agencies give too much consideration to their power and benefits in the process of administrative rule making. Therefore, they tend to develop policies, establish licensing regimes, raise licensing barriers, obtain more authority for themselves and perform other functions in a way that can profit themselves.[391] All these administrative activities,

388 熊文钊、张伟, 防止国家政策部门化, 来源: 瞭望新闻周刊, Wenzhao Xiong and Wei Zhang, Protecting State Policies from being Used for Sector Interests, Sources: Liaowang News Weekly, available at: <http://news.sohu.com/20060521/n243333237.shtml> (last accessed 6 April 2016).

389 Liu & Huang 2000, p. 57.

390 张斌，国务院三破地区封锁行业垄断时间表年内完成， 经济观察报, Bin Zhang, the State Council will Break Local Protectionism for the third Time, the Schedule will be finished within 2013, Economic Observers, available at: <www.eeo.com.cn/2013/0523/244356.shtml> (last accessed 6 April 2016).

391 熊文钊、张伟, 防止国家政策部门化, 来源: 瞭望新闻周刊, Wenzhao Xiong and Wei Zhang, Protecting State Policies from being Used for Sector Interests, Sources: Liaowang News →

as shown in the previous sections, constitute obstacles for the inter-provincial establishment of companies to a certain degree.

According to Xiong and Zhang, together the above phenomena and the widespread local protectionism cause the differentiation of state policies, making their execution far from satisfactory. Furthermore, various organs have their desire for self-interest and power. As a result, there are gaps, policy conflicts, even criticism and shirking of responsibility between them. State interests and social welfare are thus undermined.[392]

As demonstrated by Liu and Huang, Article 12 of the APL leads to adverse effects in practice. In addition, it is also unreasonable from the view of jurisprudence to exclude local and ministerial legislation from judicial review. As a result, courts should have jurisdiction over these laws.[393]

Courts' supervision over administrative legislation is far superior to other examination ways in China, as demonstrated by Junxiang Liu. The reason is that the people's congresses cannot examine administrative regulations effectively. Moreover, the oversight by higher administrative organs has its limitations due to its internal characteristics.[394]

However, as argued by Hu and Jin, to create the right to institute suits against unlawful regulations would be a historic leap that cannot easily be made in China. This is because the establishment of such a right means the creation of constitutional litigation. The latter result relates to the various aspects of constitutionalism and can only be realized through reform over a long time.[395]

9. Important Changes in the Regulation of Establishment Following the Reform Measures 2013

9.1. *The 2013 Reform Concerning the Regulation of Establishment*

9.1.1. Business Deregulation as Main Changes

The State Council unveiled its Framework Plan for a China (Shanghai) Pilot Free Trade Zone on Sep. 18th 2013.[396] Meanwhile, other laws have already been issued. Moreover, other laws will be promulgated in future. Concerning the establishment of companies, the most important legislations are (1) the Regulations on the Administration of Company Registration in the China (Shanghai) Pilot Free Trade Zone (2013) (hereinafter the RARC in the CPFTZ) and (2) the Special Administrative

Weekly, available at: <http://news.sohu.com/20060521/n243333237.shtml> (last accessed 6 April 2016).

392 *Ibid.*

393 Liu & Huang 2000, p. 57.

394 Liu 1999, p. 72.

395 Hu & Jin 2005, p. 139.

396 国务院关于印发中国（上海）自由贸易试验区总体方案的通知 (2013).

Measures (Negative List) on Foreign Investment Access to the China (Shanghai) Pilot Free Trade Zone (2013) (hereinafter the SAM on FIA).[397]

The most significant rules in the above documents in sections 9.1.1.1 and 9.1.1.2 are presented separately concerning the set-up process of domestic companies and FIEs. It should be remembered that the project to create the pilot zone will be refined constantly and the concrete contents of most rules are still to be issued, as Yao (2013) holds.[398] The contents described below primarily aim to show a tendency to deregulate the establishment. The reform is expected to considerably increase the efficiency and certainty concerning the set-up process of businesses in China, according to Covington & Burling LLP.[399]

9.1.1.1. *Removing the Requirements of Capital and Licensing for the Establishment of Domestic Companies*

According to Article 6 of the RARC in the CPFTZ, minimum capital requirements of domestic companies are removed.[400] Restrictions on the amount of initial capital, capital forms and the period for paying off capital contributions are also eliminated, as prescribed in Articles 4 and 5. Shareholders may decide all these issues in the companies' articles of association and ensure that capital is contributed as they agree. However, if laws and regulations stipulate different requirements, such provisions will apply.

Due to the above elimination of minimum capital requirements, paid-in capital is no longer subject to registration. Relevant laws of the pilot zone also lift the current requirement for companies to verify their capital payment.

Moreover, approval for licensed operations is not required for the establishment. After completing establishment registration with AICs, the set-up process of domestic companies is finished. These businesses legally established are allowed to engage in general operations, according to Article 7 of the RARC in the CPFTZ. If these firms want to carry out licensed operations, they need to obtain the relevant licenses after they are established. This is different from the licensing requirements discussed in previous sections. Under the Company Law (2005), if the proposed business is governed by a licensing regime, entrepreneurs are asked to obtain the license first, before applying for establishment registration.

397 关于中国（上海）自由贸易试验区内企业登记管理的规定(2013), 中国（上海）自由贸易试验区外商投资准入特别管理措施（负面清单）（2013年）. Art. 21 of the RARC in the CPFTZ notes that 'this law will be enforced from 1 October 2013 to 1 October 2016.' Moreover, the SAM on FIA states that 'according to the progress that will be made in the pilot zone and the changes that will be made to laws on FDI, the SAM on FIA will be modified timely.' Therefore, dynamic flexibility has been introduced for the pilot reform.

398 Louise Watt and Kelvin Chan, China's 1st Pilot Free Trade Zone Opens, available at: <www.philstar.com/world/2013/09/30/1239848/china-pilot-free-trade-zone-opens-reform-push> (last accessed 6 April 2016).

399 Timothy Stratford and Scott Livingston, The Third Wave?, available at: <https://www.amcham-shanghai.org/NR/rdonlyres/89B7633D-3682-4EBF-AC3F-F64D40151D1A/20363/1Cover1.pdf> (last accessed 6 April 2016).

400 关于中国（上海）自由贸易试验区内企业登记管理的规定 (2013).

9.1.1.2. Creating a Record-filing System for the Establishment of FIEs

The pilot adopts a 'negative list' method towards foreign investment management, according to the SAM on FIA. This approach means that foreign investors are permitted to invest in all fields other than those provided in the 'negative list'.

The formation of FIEs in fields outside the 'negative list' only needs to go through establishment registration by AICs and record-filing by commercial departments, according to Article 8 of the RARC in the CPFTZ. Previously, foreign investment sectors were divided into encouraged, restricted and prohibited categories by the Catalogue, as discussed in section 3. Compared to the previous provision, foreign investment in many sectors will not be subject to the approval of commercial authorities.

9.1.2. To Sustain Economic Growth through Deregulation

According to Yao, Chinese leaders want to deregulate the corporate sector and to liberalize the finance industry nationwide through the Shanghai test. Thus, a boost can be generated for economic development. Deregulation and liberalization are valued as new pulses for growth in the short term.[401]

Looking at the changes described in section 9.1.1, one can understand that the test aims to explore the way for deepening business deregulation in China, as summarized by MOFCOM.[402] Since the goal of the pilot reform is to move the test to the rest of the nation, business regulation is expected to be lightened nationwide, as section 9.1.3.3 will explain.

In the deregulation reform, the center of administrative management should shift from ex ante approval to ex post supervision through replacing licensing with record-filing systems, according to the State Council.[403] The shift would remove governmental control on economic activities that can be managed well by the market or society.[404]

Moreover, the replacement is also an attempt to explore the reform of the administrative system through controlling abuse of regulatory power by

401 Yao Wei, Business Deregulation, Finance Liberalization are Pluses for Growth, 30 September 2013, Shanghai Daily.

402 *Ibid.*

403 中国（上海）自由贸易试验区总体方案 (2013). Framework Plan for China (Shanghai) Pilot Free Trade Zone (2013).

404 韩正: 上海自贸区改革是剥夺政府部分权力, Zheng Han, available at: <http://news.ifeng.com/mainland/special/2014difanglianghui/content3/detail_2014_01/20/33184193_0.shtml > (last accessed 6 April 2016).

authorities.[405] Thus, administrative power can be checked and its operation can be standardized.[406]

Among the expected benefits of the business deregulation, encouraging investment stands out as being most relevant to economic development. According to Deloitte China, the pilot reform offers investment opportunities worth serious consideration.[407] Capital, either international or domestic, can be provided with easier investment access, as Bryan Cave LLP explains.[408] A more investor-friendly regulatory environment for business activities can be created in the whole of China, as PWC predicts.[409]

China's economy has already benefited from new investment made after the deregulation. After the pilot zone and some other regions adopt the measures described in section 9.1.1, the number of start-ups nationwide is promoted to grow at a relatively rapid speed, according to national authorities. This increase plays an important role in ensuring that in the 3rd quarter of 2013, the economy continued to improve, with a steady growth rate.[410]

9.1.3. Social Background of the Business Deregulation

To grasp the significance of restricting business licensing authority in the pilot zone, one needs to consider the background after President Xi Jingping and Premier Li Keqiang took office. This section explains five aspects of the social context.

9.1.3.1. Curbing the Abuse of Licensing Power to Provide Economic Impetus

As soon as he was appointed China's premier, Li started to strongly advocate the deepening of reform, focusing on cutting and decentralizing government licenses for investment and companies. As a result, the market can be stimulated, as

405 中国新闻网，聚焦上海自贸区: 新思维试验田以开放倒逼改革，China News, Focusing on the Shanghai Pilot, a Testing Ground for New Thoughts and Generating Pressures for Reform through Openness, available at: <http://news.xinhuanet.com/fortune/2013-09/29/-c_125469161.htm> (last accessed 6 April 2016).

406 韩正：上海自贸区改革是剥夺政府部分权力，Zheng Han, the Power of Governments are Aimed to be Diminished in the Pilot Reform, available at: <http://news.ifeng.com/-mainland/special/2014difanglianghui/content-3/detail_2014_01/20/33184193_0.shtml> (last accessed 6 April 2016).

407 Timothy Stratford and Scott Livingston, The Third Wave?, available at: <https://www.amcham-shanghai.org/NR/rdonlyres/89B7633D-3682-4EBF-AC3F-F64D40151D1A/20363/1Cover1.pdf> (last accessed 6 April 2016).

408 Bryan Cave LLP, New Milestone: China (Shanghai) Pilot Free Trade Zone Opens, available at: <www.lexology.com/library/detail.aspx?g=a3593c95-c47f-4f56-b03f-ca4724186066> (last accessed 6 April 2016).

409 PWC, China (Shanghai) Pilot Free Trade Zone, a New Era of Opening up and Reform in China, available at: <www.pwccn.com/webmedia/doc/635205395205529503_sh_pftz_-paper_nov2013.pdf> (last accessed 6 April 2016).

410 上海自贸区注册公司数量激增5倍成绩喜人. Startups in the Pilot Zone Increases Manifold – a Gratifying Situation, available at: <www.chinanews.com/gn/2013/11-07/5473885.shtml> (last accessed 6 April 2016).

reported by the Southern Metropolis Daily. Indeed, streamlining administration and delegating authority to governments at lower levels was the first priority of the Chinese central government in 2013.[411] According to Li's article in the Financial Times (2013), 'government will leave to the market and society what they can do well while concentrating on those matters within its purview.'[412]

The premier strives to constrain licensing authority, because there is a tendency to abuse this power, influencing economic development. Until now, licensing systems have been established for almost everything in the name of effective macro-control, as argued by Wang (2013), a participant in the pilot reform. As a result, licensing has created tremendous difficulties for China in upgrading its economy.[413] The previous discussion in section 7 can already be considered a demonstration of Wang's point. Specifically, there seems to be no restriction on who can use licensing power and on which matters can be licensing items. As a result, companies have difficulties in their investment.

At a press conference after the closing meeting of China's 12th NPC (2014), Premier Li demonstrated that streamlining administration and delegating power had been proven powerful to drive economic growth and stimulate social creativity. In 2013, the State Council nullified or delegated to governments at lower levels 416 items subject to the approval of the Cabinet. As a result, economic impetus had been provided. As the premier pointed out, the amount of companies newly registered in 2013 maintained a rapid growth at 27.6 per cent, among which newly established privately-hold enterprises grew at 30 per cent. These growth rates were the highest in more than ten years.[414]

In 2014, the central government would further the streamlining and delegating, in order to encourage Chinese citizens' to start their own business, as the premier revealed. As a result, fresh energy would be injected to the economy.[415]

411 Premier Li: China to Better Handle Relations between Government and Market, available at: <http://news.xinhuanet.com/english/special/2014-03/13/c_133183261.htm> (last accessed 6 April 2016).

412 Li Keqiang, China Will Stay the Course on Sustainable Growth, the Financial Times (UK), available at: <www.china.org.cn/chinese/2013-09/09/content_29968353.htm> (last accessed 6 April 2016).

413 辛省志，专家称上海自贸区以开放倒逼改革欲终结审批制，南方都市报，Shengzhi Xin, According to experts, the Shanghai Pilot Generates Pressure for Reforms and Tries to End License System, the Southern Metropolis Daily, available at: <http://news.qq.com/a/-20130928/000961.htm> (last accessed 6 April 2016).

414 Premier Li: China to better handle relations between government, market, available at: <http://news.xinhuanet.com/english/special/2014-03/13/c_133183261.htm> (last accessed 6 April 2016).

415 李克强：简政放权是铲除腐败釜底抽薪之术，新华网，Li Keqiang, streamlining Administration and Delegating Power are Fundamental Ways to Stamp out Corruption, Xinhua Net, available at: <http://news.163.com/14/0313/11/9N7B3LGB0001124J.htm> (last accessed 6 April 2016).

9.1.3.2. Launching Pilot Business Registration Reforms in a Number of Regions

In 2012, Shenzhen launched a pilot reform to enforce new business-registration provisions, aiming to cut the red tape for companies to finish establishment registration.[416] As a result, investment could be encouraged, according to an official for business registration in Shenzhen.[417] A few other areas such as Zhuhai also have implemented the same reform measures as Shenzhen.

The changes in establishment regulation in Shenzhen are basically not different from the reform measures presented in section 9.1.1. Nevertheless, as explicitly provided by the Regulation on Commercial Registration in Shenzhen (2012), fees are not charged on establishment registration. Moreover, AICs should complete the registration process for qualified firms in three working days.[418]

Due to the reforms, the number of start-ups in Shenzhen and other pilot regions increased significantly. For example, in Shenzhen, 108,504 enterprises have finished establishment registration from March to September, 2013, up 96 per cent over the same period of 2012.[419] People in this city have shown a stronger entrepreneurial spirit than those in any other region in China, since the launching of the pilot reform.[420]

9.1.3.3. Extending the Deregulation of Establishment to the Entire Nation

As explained by Han, opening the Shanghai pilot is a national strategy. One purpose of the central government is to experiment with reforms of administrative management and to extend the test to all China.[421] According to the State Council, the experience obtained from the Shanghai reform should be adopted in the rest of the nation.[422] History shows that it is useful to stimulate local policy experiments and then feed the local experiences into state policymaking.[423]

416 Benjamin Kessler, Shenzhen and Zhuhai Roll out Business Registration Reforms, available at: <www.fcpablog.com/blog/2013/3/8/shenzhen-and-zhuhai-roll-out-business-registrationreforms.html#sthash.52pBAQ2M.dpuf> (last accessed 6 April 2016).

417 米燕，商事登记制度改革深圳已先走一步，Yan Mi, Shenzhen Pioneers in Commercial Registration Reform, available at: <http://paper.oeeee.com/nis/201310/29/130509.html> (last accessed 6 April 2016).

418 深圳经济特区商事登记若干规定 (2012).

419 米燕，商事登记制度改革深圳已先走一步，Yan Mi, Shenzhen Pioneers in Commercial Registration Reform, available at: <http://paper.oeeee.com/nis/201310/29/130509.html> (last accessed 6 April 2016).

420 何泳，深圳一年新增商事主体41万户，Yong He, over 410,000 Commercial Subjects Have Been Registered in Shenzhen in one Year, available at: <http://sztqb.sznews.com/html/2014-03/07/content_2798155.htm> (last accessed 6 April 2016).

421 Han Zheng: How Shanghai's Free Trade Zone Works, available at: <http://english.caixin.com/2013-11-14/100604877.html?p2> (last accessed 6 April 2016).

422 何欣荣，上海自贸区提出98项改革措施，探索可复制可推广改革模式，新华网，Xinrong He, the Shanghai Pilot Proposes 98 Initiatives, Tracing a Reform Model Applicable to the Whole Country, Xinhua Net, available at: <http://news.xinhuanet.com/fortune/2013-12/12/c_118536558.htm> (last accessed 6 April 2016).

423 Fewsmith & Gao 2014, p. 171.

Therefore, all of China would introduce the changes concerning the establishment of companies that are described in section 9.1.1. This could lead to the deregulation of the corporate sector nationwide. In terms of the formation of domestic companies, capital restrictions and licensing requirements would be lifted. Regarding the establishment of FIEs, the 'negative list' approach would be used nationwide.[424] This means if the incorporation of FIEs falls in sectors other than those mentioned in this list, there is no necessity to obtain the approval of commercial authorities.

9.1.3.4. Fighting Corruption

One important aspect of Xi Jinping's policy for governing is combating corruption, according to Prof. Pei.[425] Until 2013, almost a dozen vice-ministerial level officers have been removed, a fairly large number of which are regulators.[426] For example, Liu Tienan, a former deputy head of NDRC, was convicted of severe corruption through abusing licensing power for investment.[427]

Licensing has been a major reason for many recent corruption scandals, as the China Business Focus points out (2013).[428] This is because, in certain circumstances, only through providing bribes can companies obtain licenses, as the CEO of the Wahaha Group (2014) demonstrated.[429] For instance, Liu Tienan who was mentioned before, refused to deal with applications for foreign invested auto plans, prior to being offered bribes.[430]

In fact, there is always a possibility to seek rents, as long as licensing systems are established, according to a lawyer in the foreign investment field. As early as in 2008, concerning some major national authorities for licensing the operation of foreign companies, a chain of corruption events occurred. Some senior officials in

424 孙韶华, 外资三法修订正式启动, 最核心内容是适应"负面清单"全面推广, 经济参考报, 2014年1月10日. Shaohua Sun, Initiating to Revise Foreign Investment Laws Soon and Extending the 'Negative List' to the Whole Nation, Jinjicankaobao, 10 January 2014.

425 Minxin Pei, How Xi Jinping Can Sustain His Anti-Corruption Drive, available at: <www.chinausfocus.com/political-social-development/how-xi-jinping-can-sustain-his-anti-corruption-drive/> (last accessed 6 April 2016).

426 Edward Schwarck, Xi Jinping's Anti-Corruption Campaign, available at: <https://www.rusi.org/analysis/commentary/ref:C526E43690AD78/> (last accessed 6 April 2016).

427 滕朝阳，刘铁男惊人腐败警示审批改革刻不容缓, 羊城晚报, 2013年08月13日. Chaoyang Teng, the Corruption of Liu Tienan Serves as a Reminder to Reform Licensing with no Delay, Yangcheng Evening News, 13 August 2013.

428 郁风, 刘铁男案重创发改委, 中国经贸聚焦, Feng Yu, the Case of Liu Tienan Brings a Heavy Blow to NDRC, China Business Focus, <www.zcom.com/article/108748/> (last accessed 6 April 2016).

429 张林、孙晶、孙朝方，行政审批难，易造成腐败，羊城晚报，Lin Zhang, Jin Sun and Chaofang Nan, Corruption can Easily Occur, Since to Obtain Licenses is too Difficult, Yangcheng Evening News, available at: <http://news.163.com/13/0303/13/8P20P81A00014AED.html> (last accessed 6 April 2016).

430 滕朝阳，刘铁男惊人腐败警示审批改革刻不容缓, 羊城晚报, 2013年08月13日. Chaoyang Teng, the Corruption of Liu Tienan Serves as a Reminder to Reform Licensing with no Delay, Yangcheng Evening News, 13 August 2013.

MOFCOM and SAIC were found guilty of taking huge amounts of bribes; they were key officials in granting business licenses to foreign companies. According to the Southern Weekly, to prevent corruption cases like those in 2008, the current administrative approval system should be reformed drastically.[431]

The case of Liu Tienan, the high-ranking official of NDRC, serves as a reminder to reform licensing without delay, according to the Yangcheng Evening News. To combat corruption through using licensing authority, licensing power should be diminished, decentralized or supervised closely. There would certainly be opposition from licensing authorities to the first two approaches.[432]

At the press conference mentioned in section 9.1.3.1, Premier Li pointed out that streamlining administration and delegating power were fundamental ways to rule out corruption. They not only stimulated the economy in 2013, but also curbed rent seeking through power.[433]

9.1.3.5. Leading to Inter-jurisdictional Competition to Ease Control on Market Access

It is anticipated that if one provincial area e.g. Shanghai, deregulates its corporate sector, other provinces may follow. In other words, all provinces may start to compete with each other to provide investor-friendly rules. This is because companies may compare the governance of different regions and they may choose to establish in areas with simpler regulations. Other jurisdictions offering complex laws may not be able to attract capital, as a result, they have to change. This assumption can be backed by empirical evidence. Section 9.1.4.3 will show that more and more firms prefer to invest in Shanghai rather than in other provinces, after the business deregulation in Shanghai. This generates pressure for other provincial areas to learn from Shanghai. Here I present how commentators view the pilot test from a perspective of competition among governments at municipal or provincial levels.

According to the Securities Times, compared to the creation of free trade zones, it is more important for local governments to see the adverse effects of overusing administrative power on economic growth. Though not all local regions are selected as the zones, local jurisdictions can still copy the Shanghai pilot's administrative model in their own areas, streamline the administration and loosen

431 南方周末，外资审批腐败窝案调查逐步扩大化，Southern Weekly, More and More Licensing Officials in the Foreign Investment Field are under Investigation, available at: <www.dsblog.net/article/view/id/13034> (last accessed 6 April 2016).

432 滕朝阳，刘铁男惊人腐败警示审批改革刻不容缓, 羊城晚报, 2013年08月13日. Chaoyang Teng, the Corruption of Liu Tienan Serves as a Reminder to Reform Licensing with no Delay, Yangcheng Evening News, 13 August 2013.

433 李克强：简政放权是铲除腐败釜底抽薪之术，新华网，Li Keqiang, streamlining Administration and Delegating Power are Fundamental Ways to Stamp out Corruption, Xinhua Net, available at: <http://news.163.com/14/0313/11/9N7B3LGB0001124J.htm> (last accessed 6 April 2016).

control over market entry. More capital would be attracted in places where more restrictions on investment are released.[434]

As argued by Xu, the first priority of the test in Shanghai is a reform of local governments. Through expediting the functional transformation of governments, the basic aim of the reform is to create new rules for competition among local governments. Currently, local jurisdictions increasingly intervene in the market, holding back economic growth. After this transformation, each region would compete to provide more effective services, create a more open market environment and make rules more in line with international standards. More importantly, regional entities would compete with each other to deal with the relation between the market and governments more scientifically.[435]

9.1.3.6. Summary

Considering the above, one can find that business deregulation has become a primary task of the new central government. Chinese leaders mainly aim to provide economic impetus and encourage investment through relaxing regulation. Section 9.1.2 has already shown that the goal of business deregulation is to sustain economic development.

Through curbing licensing power, the side effects of abusing this authority are also expected to be reduced. One important consequence is that corruption can be combated. Moreover, the deregulation can also contribute to curtail local governments' tendency to erect entry barriers through licensing.

It should be remembered that the deregulation is only one aspect of the Shanghai reform. After taking into account all reform measures in Shanghai and their future use nationwide, it appears reasonable for many commentators to highly value this test.[436] According to one essay from the Wall Street Journal, the prospect of China, the world's second biggest economy, to some extent, relies on the success of the Shanghai pilot.[437] The Economist reports that this experiment can end the

434 周俊生，建自贸区重要，政府放权更重要，证券时报，Junsheng Zhou, Easing Grip is More Significant than Opening Free Trade Zones, the Securities Times, the Securities Times, available at: <http://epaper.stcn.com/paper/zqsb/html/epaper/index/content_517073.-htm> (last accessed 6 April 2016).

435 徐瑾，以开放倒逼改革的自贸区，Jin Xu, In the Shanghai Test Ground: Generating Pressures for Reforms through Openness, available at: <www.ftchinese.com/story/001052723> (last accessed 6 April 2016).

436 As summarized by PWC, the Shanghai reform centers on four fields totally: (1) financial reform, (2) upgrading of customs supervision framework, (3) simplification of administrative systems supporting the further opening up of the services sector, and (4) creation of a competitive regulatory and tax environment for businesses. See PWC, China (Shanghai) Pilot Free Trade Zone, a New Era of Opening up and Reform in China, available at: <www.pwccn.com/webmedia/doc/635205395205529503_sh_pftz_paper_nov2013.pdf> (last accessed 6 April 2016).

437 Andrew Browne, 中国政府有多重视上海自贸区？，华尔街日报中文网络版，How Much Importance is Attached to the Shanghai Pilot by Chinese Government?, the Wall Street Journal Website (Chinese), available at: <http://finance.sina.com/gb/wsj-ftchinese/wsj/su/20131008/0119874849.html> (last accessed 6 April 2016).

strong desire of officials and of regulators to control market access, as the most beneficial result of the test. According to the chairman of American Chamber of Commerce in Shanghai, this biggest progress may play a decisive role in China's further development.[438]

9.1.4. Possible Reasons for Shanghai to Agree to Initiate Business Deregulation

On several occasions, Premier Li Keqiang has stressed that the pilot experiment mainly aims to test reforms of administrative management rather than offer preferential policies.[439] Therefore, as described in section 9.1.1, the pilot reform replaces licensing with record-filing systems for establishment. Li's statement is also the reason why he does not grant favourable conditions for establishment in the pilot zone. Before launching the reform, to encourage the development of enterprises, the municipality of Shanghai expected to lower Enterprise Income Tax to 15 per cent in the zone, as one insider reveals.[440]

The premier's decision can be understood easily. Section 9.1.2 has shown that further economic growth requires business deregulation. In contrast, it appears difficult to grasp why the Shanghai government agreed to launch the deregulation. This is because the current establishment regulations can allow local authorities to gain their own benefits. As revealed in section 5, to increase taxation, bureaucrats either lower or create barriers to entry, in some cases. Reducing business regulation certainly can prevent the municipality of Shanghai from abusing these rules to seek rents.

Still, due to its consideration for its own advantages, the city of Shanghai may accept to give more establishment freedom. Possible benefits can be listed as follows.

First, the Shanghai government may want to lift business licensing burdens imposed by national authorities, since these licensing systems may impede investment promotion. If local governments want to launch investment projects on a large scale, such as those in the industries of oil, coal etc., they are asked to obtain the approval of NDRC first, according to China Newsweek. These investment plans are particularly important to these governments.[441] Nevertheless, to obtain licenses from national authorities, including NDRC, may be extremely difficult or may take

438 The Economist, Shanghai Free Trade Zone, the Next Shenzhen?, available at: <www.economist.com/news/china/21587237-new-enterprise-zone-could-spark-wider-market-reforms but-only-if-bureaucrats-ease-their-grip> (last accessed 6 April 2016).

439 张颖，李克强曾再三追问上海市长: 要政策，还是要改革，Ying Zhang, Li Keqiang Asks the Mayor of Shanghai for Several Times whether Shanghai Aims to Promote Reforms, available at: <http://finance.ifeng.com/a/20130812/10405091_0.shtml> (last accessed 6 April 2016).

440 兰格钢铁，上海自贸区迎四重利好，江苏如何"分红"？，Lange Steel, the Shanghai Pilot Has four Sorts of Benefits and How Jiangsu can Profit from the Reform, available at: <http://info.lgmi.com/html/201307/05/6979.htm> (last accessed 6 April 2016).

441 曾建中、刘蔚，国家发改委的"权力清单"，中国新闻周刊，Jianzhong Zeng and Wei Liu, How Much Power NDRC Has, China Newsweek, available at: <http://news.qq.com/a/20130426/000832.htm> (last accessed 6 April 2016).

too long, according to a national newspaper.[442] For instance, when Liu (whom is referred to in section 9.1.3.4) directed NDRC, the licensing authority of this national agency created tremendous barriers for investment to both enterprises and local governments, as the Southern Weekly reports. Only when Liu, the former deputy head of NDRC, could profit from approving an investment plan, would he start to process the relevant licensing application.[443]Due to this delay, provincial governments cannot obtain the investment approval for the energy industry, according to the China Business Focus. As a result, there is much animosity between NDRC and these local governments. Indeed, this conflict has intensified.[444]

Before the pilot reform, although Shanghai intended to remove certain national licensing regimes sometimes, it had no way to realize this aim, as an official from this city revealed. This is because, as a provincial region, Shanghai is not allowed to challenge central licensing agencies.[445] By contrast, in this test, licensing regimes created by national regulators can be cut.

Second, the Shanghai government is not very concerned about whether the test can promote the GDP growth of Shanghai, as the mayor of Shanghai demonstrates. Instead, this municipality mainly aims to build Shanghai into a world financial, trade, shipping and economic center through the pilot reform.[446] Since economic growth is not the government's priority, this authority may not be reluctant to relax establishment regulation. As demonstrated in section 5, the chief aim of local authorities is to accelerate economic development, by means of lowering or erecting barriers to entry.

Moreover, making Shanghai the global center fully depends on the support of the State Council.[447] In fact, the premier strongly supports financial reform in the pilot zone.[448] Therefore, the city may be willing to accept the central government's plan of business deregulation.

442 上海自贸试验区启动，江浙等周边地区忧虹吸效应，国际商报，2013年10月11日，After Launching the Shanghai Pilot Reform, Shanghai's Surrounding Regions Worry about their Difficulties to Attract Businesses, GuojiShangbao, 11 October 2013, available at: <http://wx.fzg360.com/archive.php?aid=43011> (last accessed 6 April 2016).

443 南方周末，外资审批腐败窝案调查逐步扩大化，Southern Weekly, More and More Licensing Officials in the Foreign Investment Field are under Investigation, available at: <www.dsblog.net/article/view/id/13034> (last accessed 6 April 2016).

444 郁风，刘铁男案重创发改委，中国经贸聚焦，Feng Yu, the Case of Liu Tienan Brings a Heavy Blow to NDRC, China Business Focus, 2013, available at: <www.zcom.com/article/108748/> (last accessed 6 April 2016).

445 翁海华、魏洪磊、叶锋，上海转型密码，财经国家周刊，2012年06月25日，Haihua Wen, Honglei Wei and Feng Ye, the Key Path of Economic Transition for Shanghai, Economy News Weekly, 25 June 2012.

446 杨雄答记者提问实录，解放日报，2014年1月24日，the Mayor of Shanghai Meets the Press, Jiefang Daily, 24 January 2014.

447 翁海华、魏洪磊、叶锋，上海转型密码，财经国家周刊，2012年06月25日，Haihua Wen, Honglei Wei and Feng Ye, the Key Path of Economic Transition for Shanghai, Economy News Weekly, 25 June 2012.

448 陈澍，上海是展示李克强经济学的橱窗，南华早报，2013年7月15日，Peng Chen, Shanghai Provides a Window on Likonomics, South China Morning Post, 15 July, 2013.

Third, there was some positive anticipation over the business deregulation in Shanghai, prior to launching the reform. As shown in section 9.1.3.3, some commentators point out that easing the grip on market entry could be profitable for Shanghai's development. A possible result could be the attraction of more capital, after loosening the control.

Thus, it can be argued that the Shanghai government may agree to initiate the business deregulation, since deregulation appeared unlikely to harm its advantages. The above reasons seem not to contradict the fact that the current establishment regulation can permit rent seeking; therefore, local authorities may want to maintain these provisions.

9.1.5. Prospects for the Business Deregulation Test

The future of the Shanghai reform remains unsure, even if the president and the premier support the test.[449] Apart from the two highest ranking officials, central licensing authorities and local governments, including the Shanghai municipality, can influence the progress of the business deregulation experiment. This section discusses the attitudes of the three groups towards the test, namely, the top leaders, central regulators and local governments.

9.1.5.1. Driving Forces from the President and the Premier to Sustain Economic Growth

President Xi and Premier Li firmly backed the business deregulation. The key issue to China's economic development is that market reform is urgently required to sustain the growth.[450] As shown in section 9.1.2, business deregulation is of great importance to China's further development. The launching of the test in Shanghai, China's economic and financial centre, clearly shows their intention to push forward and to accelerate nationwide reform in the corporate sector.[451]

Almost immediately after taking office, President Xi Jingping engineered an economic reform, according to one report of Covington & Burling LLP. To implement the test, Premier Li Keqiang offers assistance to Xi. The premier is widely recognized as an engine for the creation of the Shanghai pilot zone.[452]

Probably due to two reasons, the president and the premier have introduced reforms only in the Shanghai pilot rather than in the entire nation at once. First, resistance from national licensing authorities appears very powerful, thus, it turned out to be too difficult to launch a reform nationwide. Second, the business

449 Timothy Stratford and Scott Livingston, The Third Wave?, available at: <https://www.amcham-shanghai.org/NR/rdonlyres/89B7633D-3682-4EBF-AC3F-F64D40151D1A/20363/1Cover1.pdf> (last accessed 6 April 2016).

450 *Ibid.*

451 Yao Wei, Business Deregulation, Finance Liberalization are Pluses for Growth, Shanghai Daily, 30 September 2013.

452 Timothy Stratford and Scott Livingston, The Third Wave?, available at: <https://www.amcham-shanghai.org/NR/rdonlyres/89B7633D-3682-4EBF-AC3F-F64D40151D1A/20363/1Cover1.pdf> (last accessed 6 April 2016).

deregulation in the test zone alone can give other parts of China incentives to deregulate the corporate sector. The two causes are interpreted separately as follows.

9.1.5.2. Opposition from Central Regulators for Department Interests

Central licensing agencies are bitterly opposed to the Shanghai pilot reform, according to many experts.[453] Some authors think SOEs are another opposing force.[454] Nevertheless, since SOEs in monopoly positions are under the jurisdiction of central governmental agencies,[455] it can be argued that all opposition to change is coming from central regulators. The following passages discuss why they oppose the changes and describe how these agencies resist the reforms.

National licensing authorities are against the reform, because the change can prevent them from benefiting from licensing power. They have several sorts of interests in preserving this authority, as argued by Prof. Zhan.[456]

Firstly, the interests of licensing departments depend on licensing authority, according to Zhan. For example, these agencies are entitled to receive license fee revenues. Abolishing licensing power can even mean that these agencies are to be dissolved.[457]

Secondly, the interests of SOEs can be preserved through erecting entry barriers. SOEs share fundamental common interests with governmental agencies, thus, these organizations open the door to these enterprises in market access.[458] At the same time, state regulators make various kinds of industrial rules and create many licensing regimes for investment, hindering private-owned capital from entering into fields dominated by these SOEs.[459]

453 刘玉海，上海自贸区：另一种突破还是某一种困境，21世纪经济报道，the Shanghai Pilot: Another Breakthrough or Difficult Situation, 21st Century Economic Report, available at: <www.dongshihui.com.cn/Writter/ArticleDetail/1203> (last accessed 25 January 2014).

454 Timothy Stratford and Scott Livingston, The Third Wave?, available at: <https://www.amcham-shanghai.org/NR/rdonlyres/89B7633D-3682-4EBF-AC3F-F64D40-151D1A/20363/1Cover1.pdf> (last accessed 6 April 2016).

455 黄少卿，南方都市报，从国企手中拯救社会主义，2012年3月25日. Shaoqing Huang, Saving Socialism from SOEs, the Southern Metropolis Daily, 25 March 2012.

456 人民日报，深水区，水有多"深"？People's Daily, Tackling Difficult Tasks in China's Reform, How difficult They are?, available at: <http://news.xinhuanet.com/theory/2007-05/11/-content_6084473.htm> (last accessed 6 April 2016).

457 *Ibid.*

458 天则经济研究所，国企改革分报告之一，Unirule Institute of Economics, Report 1 on Reforming SOEs, available at: <http://www.unirule.org.cn/index.php?c=article&id=1447> (last accessed 6 April 2016).

459 黄少卿，南方都市报，从国企手中拯救社会主义，2012年3月25日. Shaoqing Huang, Saving Socialism from SOEs, the Southern Metropolis Daily, 25 March 2012.

Thirdly, it is considered that officials can manage industries easily through licensing. As Zhan explains, a fair number of officials get used to rely on licensing and take this regulatory control as the only way of administrative management.[460]

Fourthly, licensing officials tend to take advantage of their positions and take bribes.[461] This problem has been demonstrated in section 9.1.3.4.

In short, in case of enforcing reform, the problem that should be solved first is that licensing authorities profit from the existing structure.[462] Due to their vested interests, in terms of restructuring, a reform of licensing procedures is very difficult.[463]

Naturally, the experiment in the zone, according to Ma, a research director from MOFCOM, poses a significant challenge to national regulators' authority. The Shanghai test aims to achieve improved market access and realize the liberation and facilitation of trade and investment. This purpose fundamentally relies on reforming the current administrative systems and loosening control on market entry. In other words, various governmental agencies are asked to ease their grip on market access.[464]

A case in point is the 'negative list' approach, as Ma points out. This method curbs the establishment of licensing regimes at random. The regulators are deeply concerned about this method, since they cannot abuse their regulatory power and seek rents.[465] Obviously, this is because national regulators can only establish licensing regimes for the sectors mentioned in the list.

Moreover, bureaucrats can no longer use power to their own benefit under the name of safeguarding public interests, according to Ma. The possible result of the reform would be that without excessive administrative restrictions, the economy develops better, but the regulators' alarmist market failures do not emerge. Thus, the regulatory bodies fear that in the progress of the test in Shanghai, their ideas to justify regulation on public interest grounds would collapse. Their fear deepens, since the experiment in Shanghai would move to the rest of the nation.[466]

460 人民日报，深水区，水有多"深"？People's Daily, Tackling Difficult Tasks in China's Reform, How difficult They are?, available at: <http://news.xinhuanet.com/theory/2007-05/11/-content_6084473.htm> (last accessed 6 April 2016).

461 史晨、张翔、翁海华，国家改革试验区启航，财经国家周刊，2013年08月30日，Chen Shi, Xiang Zhang and Haihua Wen, Launching China (Shanghai) Free Trade Zone, Economy News Weekly, 30 August 2013.

462 刘玉海，上海自贸区：另一种突破还是某一种困境，21世纪经济报道，Yuhai Liu, the Shanghai Pilot: Another Breakthrough or Difficult Situation, 21st Century Economic Report, available at: <www.dongshihui.com.cn/Writter/ArticleDetail/1203> (last accessed 6 April 2016).

463 辛省志，专家称上海自贸区以开放倒逼改革欲终结审批制，南方都市报，Shengzhi Xin, Experts Hold That Pressures Would be Generated for Reform in the Pilot, Pushing an End to Administrative Approval System, the Southern Metropolis Daily, available at: <http://news.163.com/13/0928/04/99R665780001124J.html> (last accessed 6 April 2016).

464 马宇，管制之手最好从上海自贸区收回去，中国经营报，2014年1月20日. Yu Ma, Bureaucrats Should be Asked to Ease Their Grip in the Shanghai Pilot, China Business, 20 February 2014.

465 *Ibid.*

466 *Ibid.*

There has been regulatory resistance, since making the first attempt to establish the Shanghai test bed. The premier's program to open the pilot met with fierce opposition. After the pilot zone was launched, central regulators seemed unwilling to diminish their authority.

First, before initiating the Shanghai testing ground, many governmental agencies strongly opposed such a pilot plan.[467] In the end, central administrative departments unwillingly agreed to the Shanghai reform program, under great pressure from Premier Li, as reported by the South China Morning Post.[468]

According to one expert, it is highly possible that national departments oppose reform under the name of implementing pilot experiment initiatives. They intend to obstruct a nationwide reform by preferring a local test. After the course of several years of the Shanghai experiment, national regulatory bodies can still find a good reason to avoid moving the reform to the rest of China. A possible excuse can be that the successful experience gained from the test cannot serve nationwide without any problem, since the zone is too small. As a result, the Shanghai pilot cannot be considered as a model for future reforms.[469]

Second, the Shanghai test's progress is not desirable and related reform initiatives cannot be implemented after a long period of time, as argued by Ma (2014). The underlying reason is that industrial regulatory bodies do not want to diminish their power.[470] They delay the implementation of the pilot reform, according to an essay published on the website of the Financial Times.[471]

If these departments are unwilling to give up their licensing power, the reform is unlikely to go smoothly. This is because, according to Ma, the decision making of Premier Li cannot directly influence the operation of the pilot. It is state administrative agencies, such as NDRC and MOFCOM, which can affect the implementation of reforms, since they manage industries through policies and regulations.[472]

The formulation process of the negative list (the 2013 version) can well demonstrate that it is very difficult to cut back on licensing systems of the national

467 刘玉海，上海自贸区：另一种突破还是某一种困境，21世纪经济报道，the Shanghai Pilot: Another Breakthrough or Difficult Situation, 21st Century Economic Report, available at: <www.dongshihui.com.cn/Writter/ArticleDetail/1203> (last accessed 6 April 2016).

468 李克强拍桌动怒后，上海自贸区才成形，中国时报，After Premier Li Got Angry, the Shanghai Pilot Plan Took Form Finally, China Times, available at: <www.boxun.com/-news/gb/finance/2013/07/201307180242.shtml> (last accessed 6 April 2016).

469 刘玉海，上海自贸区：另一种突破还是某一种困境，21世纪经济报道，the Shanghai Pilot: Another Breakthrough or Difficult Situation, 21st Century Economic Report, available at: <www.dongshihui.com.cn/Writter/ArticleDetail/1203> (last accessed 6 April 2016).

470 马宇，管制之手最好从上海自贸区收回去，中国经营报，2014年1月20日. Yu Ma, Bureaucrats Should be Asked to Ease Their Grip in the Shanghai Pilot, China Business, 20 February 2014.

471 刘胜军，中国改革如何破除既得利益藩篱？《金融时报》中文网，Shengjun Liu, How China's Reforms can Break Barriers Erected by Interest Groups, Financial Times Chinese Website, available at: <http://m.ftchinese.com/story/001054006> (last accessed 6 April 2016).

472 马宇，管制之手最好从上海自贸区收回去，中国经营报，2014年1月20日. Yu Ma, Bureaucrats Should be Asked to Ease Their Grip in the Shanghai Pilot, China Business, 20 February 2014.

regulators.[473] These authorities seem reluctant to lose power. As a result, companies are still not allowed to invest in numerous sectors.

The negative list was made by the city of Shanghai, MOFCOM and NDRC together, as Chen points out. Among them, the national authorities gave guidance on the formulation of this legislation.[474] MOFCOM and NDRC wanted to categorize many industries as allowed only with government approval.[475] Very likely, these central regulators were guided by department interests, as remarked by one researcher.[476]

As a result, the negative list (the 2013 version) contains numerous prohibited fields for investment, as Ma reveals. Nevertheless, MOFCOM and NRDC are still not satisfied with the 2013 version and hold that this list fails to include many justified licensing regimes.[477]

In conclusion, as demonstrated by Ye, the key to the success of the Shanghai test is whether central licensing authorities would ease their grip on market entry. The reform would be stalled, if central regulators fight against the change and support the plan publicly.[478]

Since currently interest groups in China appear powerful, Chinese leaders have to adopt a strategy to launch nationwide reform through the pilot program.[479] President Xi and Premier Li have an uphill battle against old-established regulatory bodies and SOEs to support the test.[480]

473 *Ibid.*

474 东方聊天室，"负面清单"带来了什么？——专家解读上海自贸区，Eastday, What Results a Negative List can Lead to, Interpreting the Pilot Zone by Experts, available at: <http://chat.eastday.com/eastday/node3521/node144492/chat/zxft/u1a7824032_4.html> (last accessed 6 April 2016).

475 马宇，管制之手最好从上海自贸区收回去，中国经营报，2014.01.20, Yu Ma, Bureaucrats Should be Asked to Ease Their Grip in the Shanghai Pilot, China Business, 20 February 2014.

476 刘玉海，上海自贸区：另一种突破还是某一种困境，21世纪经济报道，the Shanghai Pilot: Another Breakthrough or Difficult Situation, 21st Century Economic Report, available at: <www.dongshihui.com.cn/Writter/ArticleDetail/1203> ((last accessed 25 January 2014).

477 马宇，管制之手最好从上海自贸区收回去，中国经营报，2014年1月20日. Yu Ma, Bureaucrats Should be Asked to Ease Their Grip in the Shanghai Pilot, China Business, 20 February 2014.

478 叶檀，上海自贸区的最大风险是权力与金融，Tan Ye, the Biggest Risks for the Shanghai Pilot are Power and Finance, available at: <www.caogen.com/blog/Infor_detail.aspx?id=0-&articleId=52275> (last accessed 6 April 2016).

479 中金在线，何为倒逼式改革？China Finance Online, What is 'Forced Reform'? available at: <http://news.cnfol.com/131011/101,1277,16125863,00.shtml> (last accessed 6 April 2016).

480 Timothy Stratford and Scott Livingston, The Third Wave?, available at: <https://www.amcham-shanghai.org/NR/rdonlyres/89B7633D-3682-4EBF-AC3F-F64D40151D1A/20363/1Cover1.pdf> (last accessed 6 April 2016).

9.1.5.3. Support from Local Areas to Win Investment

After launching the pilot reform, the leaders of Shanghai strongly support the progress of the business deregulation.[481] Experiencing the pilot zone's success in attracting more investment, numerous other local governments, either at municipal or provincial levels, show support for deregulating the corporate sector in their own areas.

The progress of the Shanghai pilot zone demonstrates that this test bed won much more investment after the deregulation. Within the first month of initiating the pilot reform, the zone attracted much business establishment, 5 times more than in the corresponding period of 2012.[482] Within three months of its launch, more than 3,600 firms had been registered in the pilot test zone, with registered capital of more than RMB 75 billion.[483] By contrast, before deregulating the corporate sector, only 778 enterprises were established in this zone in the whole year of 2012.[484]

According to Business Daily, the overwhelming interest in investing in the test bed is solely due to lightening business regulation. Instead of offering preferential policies such as tax reduction, the pilot program has reformed business licensing regimes as a main measure.[485]

At the same time, other regions apart from Shanghai begin to face difficulties in promoting investment. According to many local governments, either provincial or municipal, the reason lies in the fact that the business deregulation is attracting capital to Shanghai.

For example, as one commercial official from the city of Suzhou reveals, the operation of the pilot, in short terms, creates far more challenges than opportunities to Suzhou, especially in attracting capital. Many local officials in Suzhou feel that pressure to promote investment has increased enormously. Immediately after launching the pilot program, Suzhou has lost its advantages in terms of promoting business.[486]

481 韩正：上海自贸区改革是剥夺政府部分权力，Zheng Han, available at: <http://news.ifeng.com/mainland/special/2014difanglianghui/content-3/detail_2014_01/20/33184193_0.shtml> (last accessed 6 April 2016).

482 上海自贸区注册公司数量激增5倍成绩喜人，Startups in the Pilot Zone Increases Manifold- a Gratifying Situation, available at: <www.zhuce51.com/news/510.html> (last accessed 6 April 2016).

483 杭州如何接轨上海自贸区？争取成为第二批试验区，每日商报，2014年2月10日，How to Bring Hangzhou more in Line with the Shanghai Pilot Zone, Striving to be Another Pilot Test Bed, Business Daily, 10 February 2014.

484 季明，改革高地何以成为投资热土？——上海"自贸热"的冷思考，Ming Ji, Thoughts on why the Pilot Zone Becomes a real Hotspot of Investment, available at: <www.yicai.com/-webapp/news.php?nid=3374341> (last accessed 6 April 2016).

485 杭州如何接轨上海自贸区？争取成为第二批试验区，每日商报，2014年2月10日，How to Bring Hangzhou more in Line with the Shanghai Pilot Zone, Striving to be Another Pilot Test Bed, Business Daily, 10 February 2014.

486 上海自贸试验区启动，江浙等周边地区忧虹吸效应，国际商报，2013年10月11日，After Launching the Shanghai Pilot Reform, Shanghai's Surrounding Regions Worry about their Difficulties to Attract Businesses, GuojiShangbao, 11 October 2013.

Moreover, according to the commercial authority of Jiangsu, the most significant impact of the pilot reform on Jiangsu is that more investment would be made in Shanghai, due to the business deregulation in Shanghai. Competition among these two provincial areas to promote investment would become much fiercer.[487]

It becomes increasingly difficult to win investment, since the business deregulation has significantly facilitated investment in Shanghai, according to the Jiangsu authority.[488] In other regions apart from the pilot zone, investing in certain sectors is still subject to strict licensing requirements, as the officer from Suzhou demonstrates. Usually, it takes too long time to obtain these licenses or these permits are too hard to get. By contrast, due to the 'negative list' approach, investment projects in these industries are only required to file for registration in the test bed. Therefore, the pilot zone rather than other areas would be chosen as an investment destination, in the case of investing in these fields.[489]

Due to the difficulties in promoting investment, these local governments show their intention to loosen control of market access. This is because without reforming business regulations, they cannot attract establishment as successfully as Shanghai.

Since the opening of the Shanghai test bed, there have been wishes from provincial officials to establish free trade zones in their own regions.[490] Other local areas, including Guangdong and Tianjin, just cannot wait to follow Shanghai's model. Instead, they want to operate their own test grounds instantly.[491] Some regions have already sent in their applications for their own zones.[492]

Very soon after publicizing the program for the Shanghai pilot, high-ranking officers from Guangdong and Tianjin had aggressively attempted to influence their important connections in the central government, according to official sources. To establish their own free trade zones similar to Shanghai's, they went to lobby statesmen such as leaders in MOFCOM and the State Council. A dozen more local

487 刘金松、姜鑫，"邻居"的喜与忧，经济观察报，2013年10月19日，Jinsong Liu and Xin Jiang, the Hopes and Fears of the Provinces Neighboring Shanghai, the Economic Observer, 19 October 2013.

488 *Ibid*.

489 上海自贸试验区启动，江浙等周边地区忧虹吸效应，国际商报，2013年10月11日，After Launching the Shanghai Pilot Reform, Shanghai's Surrounding Regions Worry about their Difficulties to Attract Businesses, GuojiShangbao, 11 October 2013.

490 Gordon G. Chang, China's Currency Will Be Fully Convertible in Months, available at: <www.forbes.com/sites/gordonchang/2013/09/15/chinas-currency-will-be-fully-convertible-in-months/> (last accessed 6 April 2016).

491 George Chen, Have Trade Zones Become a Victim of Power Struggle?, The South China Morning Post, available at: <www.scmp.com/business/economy/article/1414376/have-trade-zones-become-victim-power-struggle> (last accessed 6 April 2016).

492 China Briefing, China's MOFCOM Denies Having Approved 12 New Regional Free Trade Zones, available at: <www.china-briefing.com/news/2014/01/27/chinas-mofcom-denies-having-approved-12-new-regional-free-trade-zones.html#sthash.hGoCxuqT.dpuf> (last accessed 6 April 2016).

areas, including the small Zhoushan Island, also used their contacts in the cabinet and made their pitches for becoming another pilot.[493]

Nevertheless, regions other than Shanghai can still learn from the pilot reform, regardless of approving new pilot zones or not, according to Prof. Wu. For example, measures can be taken to promote the reform of licensing systems and open the door to privately owned firms in market entry.[494]

Many local governments have also recognized the importance to relax establishment regulation, apart from preparing to become another pilot zone. Responding to the pressure from Shanghai to promote investment, the Hangzhou government is advised to adopt the 'negative list' approach and reduce business licensing systems, according to the Business Daily. Only through business deregulation can Hangzhou attract the establishment by non-local firms.[495]

As the commercial agency of Jiangsu points out, if Jiangsu does not change the current business licensing systems, many firms would establish companies in Shanghai rather than in Jiangsu. In particular, this department warns about the danger of lagging behind Shanghai in terms of reforming the management system for foreign investment. Confronted with the advantages of Shanghai, the commercial authority of Anhui also suggests accelerating and simplifying the approval procedure for foreign investment, including the establishment of companies.[496]

It should be pointed out that other advantages in the test bed may also attract establishment, apart from reducing establishment regulation. Certain companies tend to be headquartered in the pilot zone, due to trade facilitation, finance liberalization and other measures beneficial to international operation.[497] Likewise, the above applicants for trade zones not only want to loosen control on market entry, but also promote reforms of finance, trade administration, etc.

In sum, Shanghai provides support for deregulating the corporate sector, since the deregulation enormously helps this city to win investment. Concerning other local governments, either provincial or municipal, there is a growing recognition that relaxing business regulation is needed to attract establishment, after initiating the deregulation in Shanghai.

493 George Chen, Have Trade Zones Become a Victim of Power Struggle?, The South China Morning Post, available at: <www.scmp.com/business/economy/article/1414376/have-trade-zones-become-victim-power-struggle> (last accessed 6 April 2016).

494 武汉或将成下一个经济自贸区，继重庆后也在申报，21世纪经济报，2013年10月15日，Following Chongqing, Wuhan is Applying to Become another Pilot Zone, 21st Century Business Herald, 15 October 2013.

495 杭州如何接轨上海自贸区？争取成为第二批试验区, 每日商报, 2014年2月10日，How to Bring Hangzhou more in Line with the Shanghai Pilot Zone, Striving to be Another Pilot Test Bed, Business Daily, 10 February 2014.

496 刘金松、姜鑫，"邻居"的喜与忧, 经济观察报, 2013年10月19日，Jinsong Liu and Xin Jiang, the Hopes and Fears of the Provinces Neighboring Shanghai, the Economic Observer, 19 October 2013.

497 上海升级自贸区对浙江是利好还是利空，Can Zhejiang Profit from the Creation of the Shanghai Pilot Zone?, available at: <www.021zhaoshang.com/xinwenzhongxin/meitibaodao/20130412/45.htm> (last accessed 6 April 2016).

Because of the above attitudes of local authorities, the establishment of a single free trade zone is likely, in practice, to reduce regulation in the entire nation. It can be expected that various local areas will compete to provide simpler establishment regulations.

9.1.5.4. *Summary*

Whether the business deregulation can succeed depends on the top policy makers, national regulators and local authorities. The leaders drive to reform the administrative licensing system for national interests, since deregulating the corporate sector is considered as a new engine for China's economic growth.

The greatest opposition to the reform comes from central governmental agencies.[498] This is because they have entrenched interests in keeping the current business licensing systems. By contrast, regional governments tend to support the deregulation. The reason is that promoting capital attraction will become much more difficult, if they do not follow Shanghai in deregulating their business sector.

9.2. *An Amendment to Company Law on the Basis of the 2013 Initiatives*

A few months after opening the China (Shanghai) Pilot Free Trade Zone, the 2013 revision of the Company Law (2005) adopted all the reform measures presented in section 9.111. Since the 2013 amendment came into force on March 1, 2014, domestic companies can be established more freely in China.

Prof. Qiao (2013) states that more people can be encouraged to start their own business and a dynamic market can emerge only through accelerating a reform of China's incorporation process. Market entry control turns out to be too tight under the Company Law (2005), curbing investment significantly.[499] The earlier sections of chapter 2 have shown that businesses face barriers to expand nationwide, since governments abuse the regulations of the establishment of companies.

10. Conclusion

Chapter 2 revealed that in some circumstances, companies in China encounter difficulties when they try to establish firms across provinces. These difficulties are partly caused by the contents of national law governing this establishment. Furthermore, the unsatisfactory implementation of these rules should be given special attention. Moreover, the lack of judicial review over the abuse of licensing authorities can be a key reason for barriers to cross-provincial establishment.

498 刘玉海，刘玉海，上海自贸区：另一种突破还是某一种困境，21世纪经济报道，Yuhai Liu, the Shanghai Pilot: Another Breakthrough or Difficult Situation, 21st Century Economic Report, available at: <www.dongshihui.com.cn/Writter/ArticleDetail/1203> (last accessed 6 April 2016).

499 乔新生，自贸区设立昭示公司法修改方向，法制日报，2013年10月8日，Xinsheng Qiao, the Establishment of China (Shanghai) Pilot Free Trade Zone Shows the Direction the Modification of the Company Law will Take, Legal Daily, 8 October 2013.

This chapter began by presenting the provisions on how to establish domestic companies and FIEs in China. Section 4 explained the rules on the inter-provincial establishment by domestic companies and by FIEs. It can be concluded there are mainly requirements on capital and licensing, which are imposed in the entire incorporation context.

According to the rules on the establishment of companies, there is a possibility that legal barriers can be erected. First, the abuse of Article 12(6) of the ALL can pose an obstacle to the formation of domestic ventures and FIEs. According to Article 12(6), licensing systems can be established for every other matter except for those governed by the first five items of Article 12, as long as such establishment is permitted by laws and regulations. Second, being too broad and providing few checks on authority discretion, the criteria for the approval by both DRCs and commerce departments can create barriers for forming FIEs.

As demonstrated by the provisions on inter-provincial establishment of companies, legal barriers are also likely to be created. To begin with, relying on Article 12(6) of the ALL, regulators can hinder this formation. Second, the cross-provincial establishment can be impeded by the same criteria mentioned in the last paragraph and their problems.

The actual practice of the cross-provincial establishment by both FIEs and domestic businesses was studied next. Such practice demonstrates that the actual use of the rules for this formation is a cause for entry barriers to companies. First, domestic firms in some fields face obstacles, mainly due to the exercise of licensing power by local authorities. Second, the licensing authority of both national and local agencies is used to erect obstacles for FIEs to establish in different regions. Nevertheless, in some other cases, FIEs rather *receive* support from government departments for their cross-provincial establishment.

The difficulties for firms to establish ventures across provincial borders raised the question whether administrative monopolies can be effectively tackled by existing laws. Unfortunately, the ALL cannot cope with the disorder in terms of who can create licensing regimes and for what matters the systems can be established in practice. Furthermore, there are abundant examples violating Article 15(2) of the ALL, the purpose of which is to deal with local protectionism.

The sanctions proposed by the AML are deemed to be unable to tackle administrative monopolies effectively. One explanation for this ineffectiveness is that higher organs are unlikely to order lower departments to rectify the abuse of administrative power. The status of higher agencies and their inability to deal with administrative monopolies are pointed out as the other two reasons.

Potential causes for the occurrence of barriers to the inter-provincial establishment of companies were offered in section 8. In terms of law in the books, Article 12(6) of the ALL makes the abuse of licensing authority possible and sanctions provided by Article 51 of the AML lack effectiveness. In addition, existing administrative remedies fighting licensing barriers prove to be of no practical value. Moreover, the absence of judicial control over the establishment of licensing systems at random constitutes the third vital explanation.

Finally, section 9 briefly presented the attempts in the Shanghai pilot to make the establishment of companies easier. The goal of the reform was to erase licensing for business that can be managed well by the market, with a focus on changing administrative management. This change has been confined to the Shanghai test zone, probably because central licensing authorities oppose nationwide reform strongly. Nevertheless, launching the pilot reform is likely to lead to the ease of regulatory control over market access in the rest of the nation.

Chapter 3

THE EU REGULATION OF CROSS-BORDER ESTABLISHMENT OF COMPANIES

1. Introduction

Chapter 3 considers the regulation of the cross-border establishment of companies in the EU. In section 2 of this chapter, the evolution of the EU internal market is analysed. This shows the role of the Commission and the Court of Justice of the European Union (CJEU) in promoting market integration in the EU.[1] Section 3 presents how the EU regulates the cross-border establishment of companies. It first elaborates on the EU Treaty provisions on freedom of the establishment of companies. Thereafter, Section 3 considers leading cases in which the CJEU has applied these provisions to national obstacles to the freedom of establishment, in order to assess the extent of this freedom. At the end of section 3, a description is provided of the relevant provisions of the Services Directive 2006/123 that codify the case law on establishment of service providers. To reflect on the practice of the freedom of establishment, section 4 discusses remaining barriers to this freedom and ways to tackle the barriers. Section 5 provides conclusions.

2. The Evolution of the Internal Market

Section 2 shows the evolution of the internal market of the EU since the Treaty of Rome. The development of the internal market has gone through a number of phases: from the Treaty of Rome to the Single European Act (SEA), from the SEA to the Maastricht Treaty, and from the Maastricht Treaty to the Lisbon Treaty. In chronological order, this section examines the evolution at these stages, with a particular focus on important Treaty provisions on promoting market integration. Also, specific attention is given to the contributions of the CJEU and the European

[1] After the entry into force of the Treaty on European Union, the judicial system of the Union is now called the Court of Justice of the European Union (CJEU), which consists of the following separate courts: 'Court of Justice', 'General Court' and 'Specialized Courts'. The term CJEU will be used throughout this thesis rather than the informal term ECJ.

Commission to the establishment of an internal market. According to Craig, apparently, the CJEU and EU institutions (especially the Commission) have interacted with each other, playing an important role in promoting economic integration. The institutions have drawn on principles of EU law developed by the CJEU in the area of the internal market, in order to shape legislative and administrative priorities. The court has been cognizant of legislative and administrative troubles with the internal market and legal doctrines have emerged from the case law to alleviate these problems.[2]

2.1. *From the Treaty of Rome to the Single European Act*

2.1.1. The Treaty of Rome: Providing for Negative Integration and Positive Integration

The Treaty of Rome, officially the Treaty Establishing the European Economic Community (TEEC) (1957) set a target for the European Community to build a common market.[3] Most provisions of this treaty on the creation of the common market were regarded as examples of negative integration i.e. the prohibition of discrimination against goods, workers etc. from other Member States.[4] Free movement of goods is one of the essential elements of the common market.[5] Articles 48-51 of the Treaty of Rome dealt with the free movement of goods, which prohibited Member States from imposing quantitative restrictions on the flow of goods. The treaty also provided for the free movement of workers, freedom of establishment and the provision of services.

According to Craig, some of other articles took the form of positive integration aiming at harmonizing the legislations of the Member States, which was necessary to guarantee the proper functioning of the common market. There were two ways of providing positive integration in the treaty of Rome. Some articles related strictly to a particular field. For example, Article 57 of the treaty of Rome allowed the Council to issue directives for the mutual recognition of professional diplomas with an aim to benefit freedom of establishment. Also, a general enabling rule was provided by Article 100 that is now Article 115 of TFEU. This provision empowered the enacting of directives to harmonize the legislations of Member States that directly influenced the operations of the common market.[6]

2 Craig 2002, p. 40. The SEA introduced the term 'internal market' to replace 'common market'.

3 Frankel 2010, p. 38.

4 Craig 2002, p. 3.

5 Frankel 2010, p. 38.

6 Craig 2002, p. 3. The Council or the Council of Ministers is an institution established by the Treaty of Rome and the task of this institution is to promote the economic and trade cooperation of Member States. The general information of the Council is available at: <http://europa.eu/about-eu/institutions-bodies/council-eu/index_en.htm> (last accessed 30 April 2015).

2.1.2. The CJEU: Introducing Mutual Recognition

As noted by Craig (2002), during the period from the Treaty of Rome to the SEA, mutual recognition emerging out of the Cassis de Dijon case was recognized as the strongest boost to the common market given by the court. In this case, the CJEU held that the article on the free movement of goods applied to indistinctly applicable measures. These measures were national provisions that did not impose discriminative restrictions on imported goods, but that hindered trade nonetheless due to the rules' differences from the trade requirements applicable in the exporting countries.[7] As a result of this ruling, a Member State was asked to open its market for products lawfully manufactured in another Member State, unless the importing Member State could justify a prohibition of these products on the grounds of mandatory requirements e.g. the protection of public health and safety.[8] Hence, harmonized national regulatory standards, according to the CJEU, were not necessary to ensure the free movement of goods, which brought important changes to the governance of the common market.[9]

As demonstrated by Craig, the CJEU also made judicial contributions to the integration through purposive interpretation of the Treaty of Rome, apart from introducing the mutual recognition principle. For instance, concerning the provision on the free movement of goods, the Cassis de Dijon judgment interpreted that indistinctly applicable measures fell into the scope of this rule· Moreover, the court functioned as legislative catalyst in the integration process; a case in point is the Reyners case.[10] According to this ruling, individuals can invoke the provision on freedom of establishment before courts, thereby challenging instances of discrimination on grounds of nationality. This case demonstrates that the CJEU accords direct effect to the provision on the freedom of establishment, in order to make compensation for not enough action taken by the community legislators.[11]

2.1.3. The Commission: Bringing in Legislation Based on Negative Integration and Positive Integration Measures

According to Craig, in the area of negative integration, the Commission promoted the enactment of regulations and directives. Such passage was designed to support the Treaty of Rome, which was aimed at eliminating obstacles to the freedom enriched in the treaty, e.g. regarding the freedom of establishment. A typical example was Directive 64/221 that defined the scope of derogations from the free

7 Craig 2002, p. 7. Case 120/78, *Rewe-Zentrale AG v. Bundesmonopolverwaltung für Branntwein*, [1979] ECR 649.

8 Pelkmans 2005, p. 87.

9 Wagner 2011b.

10 Craig 2002, p. 6 and 8. Case 2/74, *Reyners v. Belgium*, [1974] ECR 631.

11 Craig & de Búrca 2011, p. 188.

movement. As the Treaty of Rome provided, Member States were permitted to limit the freedom on the grounds of public interests, e.g. public health.[12]

Relying on Article 100 of the treaty of Rome, the Commission also harmonizes the legislations of Member States (positive integration). However, there are problems with this law making method.[13] As McGee and Weatherill hold, this legislative mechanism replaces diverse national systems with fully harmonized Community standards. One of the difficulties arising from the single and mandatory rules is that national legal traditions have to be scrapped and manufacturers become less active in innovations. The harmonization also requires arduous negotiating processes to produce detailed measures.[14]

2.2. *From the Single European Act to the Maastricht Treaty*

2.2.1. The Single European Act: Institutionalizing Minimum Harmonization

The Single European Act (SEA) significantly modified the Treaty of Rome for the first time in 1987.[15] The SEA incorporated the 1985 Commission White Paper, which had as its aim to establish 'an area without internal frontiers in which the free movement of goods, services, persons and capital is ensured' by 1992.[16] Numerous scholars consider the internal market introduced by the White Paper as a deepening of the common market.[17] To achieve the aim of constructing the internal market, European politicians showed their determination to deal with issues never solved in a multinational forum, e.g. erasing non-tariff barriers created by domestic regulations and liberalizing trade in services.[18]

The SEA institutionalized minimum harmonization within the Treaty.[19] According to Moravcsik, the previous integration process employed harmonization and set out detailed and uniform requirements for domestic regulators, but that strategy took time and failed to function. Considering this downside, the White Paper proposed a 'new approach' on the basis of 'mutual recognition' that sets down minimum standards for the laws of Member States and turns out to be less invasive.[20] Section 2.2.3 takes into account the new approach to harmonization in more details.

12 Craig 2002, p. 5. Council Directive 64/221/EEC of 25 February 1964 on the Coordination of Special Measures concerning the Movement and Residence of Foreign nationals which are Justified on Grounds of Public Policy, Public Security or Public Health, *OJ* 56, 4.4.1964.

13 Craig 2002, p. 5.

14 McGee & Weatherill 1990, p. 582. The point held by McGee and Weatherill can be understood from a perspective of the economics of federalism. Chapter 4 discusses pros and cons of centralization of regulation.

15 Thieffry *et al.* 1989, p. 357.

16 The Commission of the European Community 1992, p. 5.

17 Biermeyer 2015, p. 51.

18 Moravcsik 1991, p. 20.

19 Dougan 2000, p. 853.

20 Moravcsik 1991, p. 20.

2.2.2. The CJEU: Delimiting the Scope of the Free Movement of Goods and Taking a Purposive Approach to Treaty Interpretation

During the period from the SEA to the Maastricht Treaty, one dominant strand in the CJEU case law defines the scope of the provision on the free movement of goods, according to Craig. After the Cassis de Dijon judgment, there was a fear that all provisions regarding trade, directly or indirectly, could be taken as elements that can influence the free movement of goods somehow.[21] Craig and de Búrca study the case law development. According to some post-Cassis judgments, if provisions have nothing to do with the characteristics of the products and do not place an additional burden on the importing companies, but are only about the sale conditions for all goods, these rules cannot be caught by the provision on prohibiting quantitative restrictions. Nevertheless, in other post-Cassis cases, the CJEU has demonstrated that Article 34 extends to national provisions that are quite similar to those national requirements mentioned.[22]

Moreover, another strand within the jurisprudence continues to take a purposive approach to Treaty interpretation, which can be easily noticed in the cases about the freedom of establishment. In these rulings, the court employed the principle of direct effect to erase obstacles to free movement and has promoted the development of the internal market. These rulings are an expansion of the Reyners judgment.[23] For example, in the Heylens (Case 222/86) and Vlassopoulou (Case C-340/89) rulings, the CJEU asks Member States to take into account the equivalence of qualifications acquired in other EU states, regardless of the lack of secondary legislation.[24]

2.2.3. The Commission: Introducing Legislation Based on Minimum Harmonization

During the period between the SEA and the Maastricht Treaty, the Commission's law making was in line with the principle of minimum harmonization.[25] Based on this principle, the Commission only considers harmonizing the laws of Member States that survive the direct application of the Treaty provisions.[26] Craig takes the free movement of goods as an example. Due to the mutual recognition principle provided for in the Cassis de Dijon case, national rules are obliged to offer market access opportunities to products lawfully marketed in any Member State. These national measures are not subject to harmonization.[27] Only when Member States are able to justify their refusal to import these goods e.g. on grounds of public safety

21 Craig 2002, p. 22.
22 Craig & de Búrca 2011, p. 651 and 652.
23 Craig 2002, p. 25.
24 Craig & de Búrca 2011, p. 777. Claessens 2008, p. 20.
25 Craig 2002, p. 20.
26 Snell 2014, p. 310.
27 Craig 2002, p. 24.

and health, is there a need for harmonizing national legislations on these standards. As a result, such barriers to trade can be eliminated.[28]

Moreover, legislative harmonization in the EU only focuses on essential health, safety and other standards, as Snell demonstrates. Private standardization organizations such as the European Committee for Standardization (CEN), instead of the Commission, take the responsibility for formulating detailed requirements.[29] Member States are obliged to open their doors to products complying with the standards of the organs.[30]

According to Craig, minimum harmonization has many benefits. As one advantage to this approach to harmonization, the Commission can propose directives more easily, since it does not need to regulate details.[31] Moreover, Member States are permitted to lay down more stringent requirements than those made by directives, as long as these requirements do not violate the Treaty.[32]

At the same time, negative integration still plays a role in promoting the development of the internal market, according to Craig. After the passage of the SEA, the Commission attempted to solve many particular problems relating to customs duties, in order to break down barriers to trade.[33]

2.3. *From the Maastricht Treaty to the Lisbon Treaty*

2.3.1. Treaty Amendments: Creating an Economic and Monetary Union and Assigning the Internal Market to Shared Competence

The Maastricht Treaty (formally, the Treaty on European Union or TEU) entered into force in 1993, which led to the creation of the European Union (EU).[34] Under the Maastricht Treaty, the European Economic Community (EEC) becomes one of the three pillars of the EU, the European Community.[35] After the Maastricht Treaty entered into force, the TEEC was renamed the Treaty Establishing the European Community (TEC). The Maastricht Treaty has been amended by the treaties of Amsterdam, Nice and Lisbon. The following passages present the most significant impact of these provisions on the internal market.

In substantive terms, the establishment of the Economic and Monetary Union (EMU) is regarded as the main innovative measure introduced by the Maastricht Treaty.[36] Some EU countries reached an agreement to strengthen the coordination of

28 Craig 2002, p. 20.
29 Snell 2014, p. 310.
30 Craig 2002, p. 24.
31 *Ibid.*
32 Dougan 2000, p. 853 and 855.
33 Craig 2002, p. 20 and 21.
34 Feldstein 2012, p. 105.
35 Delors 1994, p. 46.
36 Craig 2002, p. 28.

their economic and financial policies and create the single currency, the euro.[37] According to Bovenberg and De Jong, the most significant reason to support the EMU is to stabilize the internal market by combining this market with prudent financial and budgetary policies. Particularly, the EMU prevents the economic fluctuation and political tensions arising from large exchange-rate movements among Member States.[38] However, the introduction of the euro could promote price stability, but may have had an adverse impact on productivity growth and employment.[39]

The most significant change of the Lisbon Treaty (2007) is to set rules on categories and areas of Union competences.[40] After the Lisbon Treaty came into force, the TEC was renamed as the Treaty on the Functioning of the European Union (TFEU). According to the Lisbon Treaty, the EU will have exclusive competence to establish 'the competition rules necessary for the functioning of the internal market'. Moreover, the internal market, whose definition is based on the free movement rules, falls into the category of shared competences between the EU and EU countries.[41] Shared competence means that Member States cannot act to the extent that the EU has decided to.[42] Classifying the internal market as a shared competence would allow EU states to take action that is 'ahead' of Union action.[43]

2.3.2. The CJEU: Refining the Scope of the Union's Competence and Ensuring Effective Use of Power

According to Craig, the case law concerning the internal market in the 1990s had one dominant strand: defining the scope of the Union's competence more clearly and limiting the boundaries to some extent. The Tobacco case (Case C-376/98) is particularly important to show the limits of the competence.[44] As Craig and de Búrca note, for the first time, a harmonized directive based on Article 95 of the TEC is declared invalid. The court rules that legislative practice on the basis of this article 'must genuinely have as its object the improvement of the conditions for the establishment and functioning of the internal market'.[45] As the CJEU holds, the regulatory authority granted by Article 95 must be controlled. Otherwise, any

37 Kristin Archick, the European Union: Questions and Answers, Congressional Research Service, 15 January 2014, Washington, p. 4, avalaible at: <www.fas.org/sgp/crs/row/-RS21372.pdf> (last accessed 6 April 2016).

38 Bovenberg & De Jong 1997, p. 85 and 86.

39 Nello 2005, p. 252.

40 Tosiek 2008, p. 10.

41 Brisimi 2014, p. 51.

42 Craig 2010, p. 171.

43 Craig 2004, p. 328.

44 Craig 2002, p. 31 and 32.

45 Craig & de Búrca 2011, p. 847. Art. 95 of the TEC provides that 'The European Parliament and the Council shall, ..., adopt the measures for the approximation of the provisions laid down by law, regulation or administrative action in Member States which have as their object the establishment and functioning of the internal market.' This article is the predecessor of Art. 114 of the TFEU.

diversity among national legislations would be a justification for harmonization, meaning that the Union would gain unlimited positive regulatory competence.[46]

In recent years, the CJEU has continued to refine the boundaries of the EU's competence. However, unlike the Tobacco judgment, almost no directives or regulations are annulled.[47] Even in cases where the objective of a harmonized directive is not really relevant to the functioning of the internal market, the court still considers the legislation to be aimed at benefiting the functioning through interpretations.[48] As a result, judicial interpretations give the EU legislative bodies significant autonomy.[49]

In the 1990s, another more significant strand was to make sure that the Union's authority could be exercised effectively.[50] As Craig and de Búrca note, initiatives taken by the CJEU have helped the Union legislature to ensure the freedom of movement and the principle of mutual recognition. More particularly, the responsibility to include mutual recognition provisions in legislation provides such assistance and this obligation is introduced by the Foie Gras case (Case C184/96 Commission v France). According to this ruling, as long as a Member State provides for requirements about product characteristics and the like in a legal instrument, this instrument is required to contain a mutual recognition clause.[51]

2.3.3. The Commission: Turning to Maximum Harmonization

According to Weatherill (2011), the Commission's legislation practice concerning the internal market is shifting from minimum harmonization to maximum harmonization. Maximum harmonization means that Member States must implement rules set out in EU legislation and they must apply only these provisions.[52] In some fields, the Commission rejected the idea of diverse but coordinated domestic law regimes and preferred a way to harmonize national law more completely.[53] A case in point is the Consumer Rights Directive 2011 (Directive 2011/83/EU). This legislation provides standard measures for 'consumer information and the right of withdrawal in distance and off-premises contracts' (full harmonization).[54] Due to different consumer protection provisions of Member States, the internal market cannot offer the greatest potential benefits to firms in the

46 Craig 2002, p. 33 and 34.
47 Saydé 2014, p. 262.
48 Weatherill 2011, p. 836, 837 and 843.
49 Saydé 2014, p. 262.
50 Craig 2002, p. 31.
51 Craig & de Búrca 2011, p. 687.
52 Weatherill 2012, p. 178 and 188.
53 Snell 2014, p. 310.
54 Recitals 2 and 5 of Directive 2011/83/EU. Directive 2011/83/EU of the European Parliament and of the Council of 25 October 2011 on consumer rights, amending Council Directive 93/13/EEC and Directive 1999/44/EC of the European Parliament and of the Council and repealing Council Directive 85/577/EEC and Directive 97/7/EC of the European Parliament and of the Council, *OJ* L304, 22.11.2011.

direct-selling sector.[55] Adopting a full harmonization approach to the consumer protection issues would significantly decrease compliance costs for these companies and would benefit the functioning of the internal market.[56]

Nevertheless, taking into account the above shift, Weatherill holds that there may be some disadvantages to seeking uniformity of the legislation of Member States. At least, it cannot be denied that pursuing the uniformity will possibly cause costs.[57] As Smits demonstrates, even if more cross-border commercial activities occur due to maximum harmonization of consumer law, this result alone cannot decide the adoption of a maximum harmonization approach. Economic theory has pointed out the importance to consider both this element and other factors, e.g. the potential cost caused by harmonization. Particularly, maximum harmonization will create considerable costs for implementation practice. One reason is that without various sorts of judicial intervention, uniformity in interpretation of the European provisions would be almost impossible. It should also be noticed that because of full harmonization, national law cannot reflect citizens' preferences regarding consumer interest protection.[58]

3. The EU Regulation of Cross-Border Establishment of Companies

3.1. *Treaty Provision on Freedom of Establishment of Companies*

3.1.1. Freedom of Establishment of Companies

The Treaty on the Functioning of the European Union (TFEU) prohibits restrictions on the freedom of establishment of companies. Article 49 TFEU is aimed at guaranteeing the freedom of establishment of individuals. This article provides that 'Within the framework of the provisions set out below, restrictions on the freedom of establishment of nationals of a Member State in the territory of another Member State shall be prohibited. Such prohibition shall also apply to restrictions on the setting-up of agencies, branches or subsidiaries by nationals of any Member State established in the territory of any Member State.' Article 54 TFEU extends the freedom of establishment to companies. This article reads that 'Companies or firms formed in accordance with the law of a Member State and having their registered office, central administration or principal place of business within the Union shall, for the purposes of this Chapter, be treated in the same way as natural persons who are nationals of Member States. 'Companies or firms' means companies or firms constituted under civil or commercial law, including cooperative societies, and other legal persons governed by public or private law, but excluding those which are non-profit-making.'

A combined reading of Articles 49 and 54 shows that nationals or legal persons of a Member State enjoy the right to establish and manage undertakings, in

55 *Ibid.*, Recital 5.
56 *Ibid.*, Recitals 5 and 6.
57 Weatherill 2012, p. 188.
58 Smits 2010, p. 9.

particular companies or firms, in other Member States (primary establishment). Moreover, nationals or legal persons of a Member State are given the right to set up agencies, branches or subsidiaries in another Member State (secondary establishment).

3.1.2. Derogation from the Freedom of Establishment of Companies

The treaty contains two derogations that allow Member States to restrict the freedom of establishment of companies. Article 52(1) TFEU provides for the public policy, security and health derogation and Article 51 permits Member States to derogate from Articles 49 and 56 on the grounds of the exercise of official authority.

Article 52(1) TFEU notes that 'the provisions of this Chapter (Chapter 3 Right of Establishment) and measures taken in pursuance thereof should not prejudice the applicability of provisions laid down by law, regulation or administrative action providing for special treatment for foreign nationals on grounds of public policy, public security or public health.' According to Weiss and Kaupa, the European Court of Justice defines the scope of this exception narrowly. However, the court generally agrees that Article 52(1) leaves considerable discretion to Member States in interpreting the requirements of public policy, public security and public health.[59]

Article 51(1) TFEU states that 'the provisions of this Chapter (Chapter 3 Right of Establishment) shall not apply, so far as any given Member State is concerned, to activities which in that State are connected, even occasionally, with the exercise of official authority.' It seems that the derogation clauses provided for in Article 52(1) must be confined to activities which, in themselves, are directly and specifically associated with the use of official authority.[60]

3.2. *Judicial Interpretation on the Freedom of Establishment of Companies*

According to Weiss and Kaupa, the right to establish companies was limited by the considerable differences between the national legal systems. Since handing down its decision in the case Centros, the court had effectively dealt with these constraints, which significantly facilitated the free movement of companies.[61] This section seeks to analyse the leading cases in this context, i.e. Daily Mail, Centros, Überseering, Inspire Art and Cartesio, thereby showing how the court interprets the freedom of establishment of companies.

3.2.1. C-81/87 The Queen v Treasury and Commissioners of Inland Revenue, ex parte Daily Mail and General Trust PLC, [1988]ECR 5483

In this case, the court holds that Articles 49 and 54 do not permit firms to move their central management from one Member State to another while still being subject to

59 Weiss & Kaupa 2014, p. 209.

60 Barnard & Snell 2014, p. 421.

61 Weiss & Kaupa 2014, p. 197.

the company legislation of the first nation.[62] In other words, the state of incorporation has the regulatory autonomy to restrict the companies' right to retain legal capacity when these firms transfer their registered office or center of administration from this state to other Member States.

The court starts its analysis by demonstrating that Articles 49 and 54 grant firms or citizens the right to establish in other Member States. As a result, companies formed according to the law of one Member State are allowed to leave this country and establish themselves in other Member States.[63]

However, the court points out that in the current state of Community legislation, firms, unlike natural persons, are created under the law of Member States. Their existence depends on the differing national law which decides their formation and functioning.[64] Since the provisions on incorporation have not been harmonized, a Member State has the authority to define what it means to be a company subject to the company law of this country.[65]

3.2.2. C-212/97 Centros Ltd v Erhvervs-og Selskabsstyrelsen , [1999] ECR I-1495

In this case, the CJEU took a liberal approach to explain the freedom of the secondary establishment of companies granted by Articles 49 and 54 TFEU.[66] According to these two provisions, investors are allowed to first form a company in a Member State with lenient minimum capital requirements and then establish branches in Member States with stringent capitalization rules, even if the aim of this strategy is to circumvent the strict minimum capital requirements. The shareholders are also allowed to conduct the entire business of the company in the country where the branches are established. The refusal to recognize such branches, as the court points out, constitutes an obstacle to the freedom of establishment of companies.[67]

First, Articles 49 and 56, as the court confirms, guarantee the freedom of secondary establishment of companies. A company formed in accordance with the law of a Member State can establish a branch in another Member State, no matter whether the company is commercially active only in the second Member State.[68] Moreover, whether the establishment of the branch is to circumvent minimum capital requirements in the second Member State does not influence the exercise of the freedom of secondary establishment of companies.[69]

Second, nationals of a Member State can take advantage of Articles 49 and 56 to benefit the establishment of companies, which cannot be treated as abuse of the freedom of establishment of companies. Citizens from a Member State, according to

62 C-81/87, *The Queen v. Treasury and Commissioners of Inland Revenue, ex parte Daily Mail and General Trust PLC*, [1988] ECR 5483, paras. 24-25.

63 *Ibid.*, para. 16.

64 *Ibid.*, para. 19.

65 *Ibid.*, para. 23.

66 Kaczorowska 2013, p. 701.

67 Case C-212/97 *Centros Ltd v. Erhvervs-og Selskabsstyrelsen*, [1999] ECR I-1495, the judgment.

68 *Ibid.*, para. 17.

69 *Ibid.*, para. 18.

these provisions, enjoy the right to set up a company in a Member State whose establishment regulations appear most lenient to them.[70] After primary establishment of companies, as the court holds, the nationals can form branches in other Member States. Moreover, the fact that the natural persons pursue the entire business activities in the Member State in which the branches are located does not constitute abuse of the freedom of establishment of companies.[71]

Third, where a national of a Member State sets up a branch in the way mentioned above, Member States cannot refuse to register the branch on the ground of creditor protection. In the case that Member States impose restrictions on the freedoms granted by the treaties of the EU, the restrictions must meet four conditions: "(1) they must be applied in a non-discriminatory manner; (2) they must be justified by imperative requirements in the general interests; (3) they must be suitable for securing the attainment of the objective which they pursue; and (4) they must not go beyond what is necessary in order to attain it."[72] Nevertheless, in this case, the refusal to register a Danish branch of a business incorporated under the law of the UK fails to meet the requirements: (1) the fact that the parent company had not conducted business in the UK, the incorporation place of the parent corporation, is irrelevant to the protection for Danish creditors, so this fact cannot be used to justify Denmark's refusal to register the branch;[73] （2） the creditors of the branch company could seek protection by referring to some EU directives, since they noticed that the branch was established by a UK company;[74] (3) Denmark could rely on less restrictive measures to offer creditor protection;[75] and (4) in case of registering the branch, Denmark and the UK may still take action against (potential) fraud.[76]

3.2.3. C-208/00 Überseering BV v Nordic Construction Company Baumanagement GmbH, [2002] ECR I-9919

This case concerns the fact that a company is first incorporated in a Member State and then this firm moves its centre of administration to another Member State. According to the judgment in this case, the second Member State is asked to recognize the legal capacity of this venture. Consequently, this venture has legal standing in the courts of this EU country. If the second Member State refuses to recognize the legal personality, such action violates the freedom of establishment.

The court holds that Articles 49 and 54 apply to a company formed in one Member State which relocates its centre of administration to another EU country.[77]

70 *Ibid.*, para. 27.
71 *Ibid.*, para. 29.
72 *Ibid.*, para. 34.
73 *Ibid.*, para. 35.
74 *Ibid.*, para. 36.
75 *Ibid.*, para. 37.
76 *Ibid.*, para. 38.
77 C-208/00 *Überseering BV v Nordic Construction Company Baumanagement GmbH*, [2002] ECR I-9919, para. 52.

First, though Member States have not adopted a convention on the mutual recognition of companies according to Article 293 of the EC treaty, this fact does not affect the right of companies to exercise the freedom of establishment.[78] As the court points out, according to Article 293, Member States can open negotiation in order to, inter alia, help resolve problems caused by the discrepancies between the legislation concerning the mutual recognition of firms and the retention of legal capacity in case of relocating their seats within the European Community.[79] Taking into account the 'so far as is necessary' clause in Article 293, the court holds that this provision cannot be interpreted as reserving to Member States legislative competence.[80] As a result, Member States cannot justify restrictions on the freedom of establishment for the fact that no convention on the mutual recognition of companies has been signed in accordance with Article 293.[81]

Second, in the Daily Mail case, the court noted that freedom of establishment does not cover the transfer of a company's seat,[82] but this judgment has no relevance in Überseering.[83] As the court states, Überseering is different from Daily Mail. The first case is about relations between a firm and the EU country under whose laws this company was formed. The second case is about the recognition by one EU nation of an operation established under the law of another EU country.[84] Moreover, Daily Mail does not concern the loss of a firm's legal capacity, but the denial of a company's legal personality is the dispute in Überseering.[85] Therefore, the ruling in Daily Mail is not applicable in cases where an industry is first organized in one Member State and later moves its center of administration to another Member State.[86]

The court further demonstrates that the denial of a company's legal personality cannot be justified on the grounds mentioned by the German government.[87] The German government argues that the justifications for such restriction on the freedom of establishment are to protect creditors and to improve legal certainty.[88] In the court's opinion, these overriding requirements relating to the general interest, under some conditions, may justify restrictions on this freedom.[89]

78 Art. 293 of the EC Treaty provides that 'Member States shall, so far as is necessary, enter into negotiations with each other with a view to securing for the benefit of their nationals: ... the mutual recognition of companies or firms within the meaning of the second paragraph of Article 48, the retention of legal personality in the event of transfer of their seat from one country to another...'.

79 *Ibid.*, para. 54.

80 *Ibid.*

81 *Ibid.*, para. 60.

82 *Ibid.*, para. 24.

83 *Ibid.*, para. 75.

84 *Ibid.*, para. 62.

85 *Ibid.*, para. 65.

86 *Ibid.*, para. 73.

87 *Ibid.*, para. 93.

88 *Ibid.*, para. 87.

89 *Ibid.*, para. 92.

Nevertheless, denying the legal personality and as a consequence dismissing a suit by the firm would entirely negate the freedom of establishment.[90]

3.2.4. C-167/01 Kamer van Koophandel en Fabrieken voor Amsterdam v Inspire Art Ltd, [2003] ECR I-10155

According to the judgment in this case, Member States are prohibited from requiring firms exercising the freedom of secondary establishment to meet company formation conditions of their own legal systems on capital requirements and directors' liability. The freedom of establishment allows operations to be formed in one Member State for whatever reason and conduct all their business (almost) only in another Member State, save where abusive practices are recognized on a case-by-case basis.[91]

First, the court confirms that Articles 49 and 56 TFEU give companies formed in one Member State the right to open up a secondary establishment in another Member State. Nevertheless, a restriction on secondary establishment can be identified in this case.[92] Adhering to its ruling in Centros, the court holds that Articles 49 and 56 allow a company established in one Member State to set up a branch in another Member State and carry on all its business through the branch.[93] Even though the secondary establishment is to circumvent minimum capital requirements in the second EU nation, this purpose does not affect the exercise of the freedom of secondary establishment.[94] Therefore, as the court notes, the situation is permitted in this case where a firm formed in a Member State conducts its activities (almost) exclusively in another Member State through a branch. When this company registers its branch in the second nation, this country's requirement for the firm to fulfil obligations on capital and directors' liability constitutes restrictions on the freedom of establishment.[95]

Second, the court demonstrates that no argument can be made for justifying the restriction on the freedom of establishment of companies in this case i.e. the requirements on capital and directors' liability.[96] If Member States try to restrict the freedoms guaranteed by the treaties of the EU, the restrictive measures are asked to satisfy four conditions: '(1) they must be applied in a non-discriminatory manner; (2) they must be justified by imperative requirements in the public interest; (3) they must be suitable for securing the attainment of the objective which they pursue; and (4) they must not go beyond what is necessary in order to attain it.'[97] Applying these criteria in this case, the court holds that creditor protection cannot be invoked, since

90 *Ibid.*, para. 93.
91 C-167/01 *Kamer van Koophandel en Fabrieken voor Amsterdam v. Inspire Art Ltd*, [2003] ECR I-10155, the judgment.
92 *Ibid.*, para. 104.
93 *Ibid.*, para. 97.
94 *Ibid.*, para. 98.
95 *Ibid.*, para. 104.
96 *Ibid.*, para. 142.
97 *Ibid.*, para. 133.

the industry opening up secondary establishment in the Netherlands had done enough to inform potential creditors of its register place. This company held itself out as a legal person incorporated under the law of England and Wales.[98] In addition, the court cannot conclude that this firm had improper recourse to freedom of establishment. As the court has already pointed out in Centros, Articles 49 and 54 permit citizens from a Member State to establish an operation in the Member State with the lax entry controls and then open up secondary establishment in other EU countries.[99] The nationals are also permitted to carry on all the activities of the company in the nation where its branch is located.[100] Lastly, the requirements on capital and directors' liability cannot be justified on the grounds of protection of fairness in business dealing and efficiency of tax inspection either.[101]

3.2.5. C-210/06 CARTESIO Oktató és Szolgáltató bt, [2008] ECR I-09641

This case confirms the decision made in C-81/87. In this case, as the court holds, according to Articles 49 and 54, Member States are allowed to impose restrictions on retaining legal personality by companies subject to the law of these countries in the event of relocating their seats to other EU countries.[102] In such cases, the companies are governed by the law of the Member State where they are incorporated.[103]

Following the reasoning in case C-81/87, the court demonstrated that firms are created according to national law. Moreover, the existence of firms is decided by the national law which regulates their formation and functioning.[104] Consequently, the question whether a company is protected by Article 49 depends on the applicable national law. In other words, the freedom of establishment only applies to a firm which is validly established according to the law of a Member State.[105] A Member State is free to make a requirement for a company subject to the law of this Member State to move its seat.[106]

The court also addresses the situation where a company moves its seat from one Member State to another with the change of applicable law. If the change of applicable law is allowed by the law of the second country, the first state is not permitted to prohibit the company from converting into a firm regulated by the second Member State.[107]

98 *Ibid.*, para. 135.
99 *Ibid.*, para. 138.
100 *Ibid.*, para. 139.
101 *Ibid.*, para. 140.
102 C-210/06 Cartesio Oktató és Szolgáltató bt, [2008] ECR I-09641, the judgment.
103 *Ibid.*, para. 111.
104 *Ibid.*, para. 104.
105 *Ibid.*, para. 109.
106 *Ibid.*, para. 110.
107 *Ibid.*, paras. 112 and 113.

3.2.6. Main Trends in the Case Law on the Freedom of Establishment

According to Čiočys, case law study on the freedom of establishment and particularly corporate mobility in the EU can be classified into emigration situations and immigration situations. In both cases, companies incorporated in one country transfer their administrative seats or registered offices into another. Immigration situations e.g. Centros, Inspire Art, Überseering mean the country of arrival imposes restrictions on this transfer. Emigration situations e.g. Daily Mail and Cartesio mean the country of departure places limits on this transfer.[108] It has been demonstrated that the CJEU deals with immigration cases and emigration cases differently.[109]

Centros, Inspire Art, Überseering and some other cases on the freedom of establishment are considered a powerful form of harmonization induced by the court.[110] Rather than waiting for the EU legislators to harmonize incorporation rules, the CJEU has asked host states to allow companies legally incorporated in another country to form businesses in these states, as noted by Craig and de Burca. The Court also prohibited the host states from imposing undue regulatory burdens on the parent firms, e.g. asking these companies to meet the company formation conditions of these states. These rights of secondary establishment still need to be protected, even though the home country and the host states have very different incorporation regulations.[111] A case in point is Centros. This case shows a judicial willingness to eliminate the remaining barriers to the freedom of the establishment of companies in the EU.[112] According to De Waele, on the basis of the freedom of establishment, the support provided by the Centros judgment to the circumventing company turns out to be quite generous. He holds that the CJEU should have adopted a slightly narrower interpretation of the freedom of establishment.[113]

Daily Mail and Cartesio show that certain restrictions on emigrating companies are allowed by the CJEU. As demonstrated by Wymeersch (2003), without further judicial decisions or EU legislation, one may analyse the Daily Mail case as permitting the EU countries to place significant restrictions on emigrating firms. This regulatory power of Member States would allow these countries to significantly impede or even annihilate free movement of companies.[114] As noted by Valk, however, the Cartesio judgment shows an increase in the freedom of establishment. In emigration situations, if the transfer of companies' administrative seats results in changing applicable national law, emigrating companies can rely on this freedom.[115]

108 Čiočys 2010, p. 146.
109 Valk 2010, p. 158.
110 Barnard & Snell 2014, p. 440.
111 Craig & de Búrca 2011, p. 813.
112 Cabral & Cunha 2000, p. 163.
113 De Waele 2010, p. 6 and 7.
114 Wymeersch 2003, p. 677.
115 Valk 2010, p. 160.

3.3. *The Provision of the Services Directive on Establishment of Service Providers*

According to Barnard, the application of the treaty provisions governing the freedom of establishment creates a large body of case law. The codification of this case law forms Chapter 3 of Services Directive 2006/123.[116] The law was passed to fully tap the potential of the market in services, which covers almost 70 per cent of EU's GDP.[117] The Commission proposed this legislation, since barriers in the internal market for services seriously affected companies engaging in cross-border business.[118]

This legislation contains some powerful articles.[119] In Chapter 3, this directive deals with three types of national provisions concerning the establishment of service providers, which are presented respectively in this section: authorization schemes, prohibited requirements and suspect requirements. According to Article 4(5), "'establishment' means the actual pursuit of an economic activity, as referred to in Article 49 of the Treaty, by the provider for an indefinite period and through a stable infrastructure from where the business of providing services is actually carried out". As Barnard explains, the directive thus regulates both primary establishment and secondary establishment. In the first case, service providers try to establish themselves in a Member State where they offer services through this new company. In the second case, a firm opened up under the law of a Member State wishes to form a new business i.e. a branch, agency or subsidiary.[120]

3.3.1. Authorization Schemes

Section 1 of Chapter 3 regulates authorization schemes, defined as rules which provide that a person is not allowed to establish or start their activities with no authorization.[121] Article 9 provides that such schemes are not allowed unless '(a) the authorisation scheme does not discriminate against the provider in question; (b) the need for an authorisation scheme is justified by an over-riding reason relating to the public interest; and (c) the objective pursued cannot be attained by means of a less restrictive measure, in particular because an a posteriori inspection would take place too late to be genuinely effective.' Less restrictive measures refer to notifications or prior declarations. Notifications or prior declarations allow service providers to exercise their activities after notifying authorities.[122]

The meaning of 'an over-riding reason relating to the public interest' is provided in Article 4(8). According to Article 4(8), this phrase means: 'reasons

116 Barnard 2010, p. 348. Directive 2006/123/EC of the European Parliament and of the Council of 12 December 2006 on services in the internal market, *OJ* L376, 27.12.2006.
117 Barnard 2008, p. 326.
118 Kowalsky 2006, p. 233.
119 Davies 2007, p. 232.
120 Barnard 2010, p. 349.
121 Chalmers *et al.* 2014, p. 890.
122 Franch & Torrelles 2012, p. 580.

recognised as such in the case law of the Court of Justice, including the following grounds: public policy; public security; public safety; public health; preserving the financial equilibrium of the social security system; the protection of consumers, recipients of services and workers; fairness of trade transactions; combating fraud; the protection of the environment and the urban environment; the health of animals; intellectual property; the conservation of the national historic and artistic heritage; social policy objectives and cultural policy objectives.' Thus, this provision contains an indicative, but not exhaustive, list of over-riding reasons relating to the public interest.[123]

Article 10 provides for the criteria for granting authorization. According to Article 10(2), the criteria must be: '(a) non-discriminatory; (b) justified by an overriding reason relating to the public interest; (c) proportionate to that public interest objective; (d) clear and unambiguous; (e) objective; (f) made public in advance; (g) transparent and accessible.' Moreover, as Article 10(3) notes, 'the conditions for granting authorisation for a new establishment shall not duplicate requirements and controls which are equivalent or essentially comparable as regards their purpose to which the provider is already subject in another Member State or in the same Member State.'

Article 10(4) of the Directive states that the authorization shall be effective nationwide unless there are good reasons why not. According to Article 10(4), 'the authorisation shall enable the provider to have access to the service activity, or to exercise that activity, throughout the national territory, including by means of setting up agencies, subsidiaries, branches or offices, except where an authorisation for each individual establishment or a limitation of the authorisation to a certain part of the territory is justified by an overriding reason relating to the public interest.'

3.3.2. Prohibited Requirements

Article 14 prohibits some types of measures concerning establishment. The first group of rules, as Article 14(1) notes, concerns 'discriminatory requirements based directly or indirectly on nationality or, in the case of companies, the location of the registered office.' Article 14(2) prohibits rules preventing providers from having an establishment or, being registered in more than one Member State. Article 14(3) forbids a provision which restricts the type of establishment (for example requiring a principal establishment rather than secondary establishment or requiring a specific form of secondary establishment, such as an agency). Member States are also prohibited from entering into conditions of reciprocity with the Member State where the service supplier already has an establishment (Article 14(4)). Article 14(5) does not allow an economic test that asks applicants for authorization to prove the existence of an economic or market need. According to Article 14(6), competing operators are not allowed to engage in decision making of granting individual authorization. Article 14(7) prohibits the EU country from obliging operators to

123 Hatzopoulos 2012, p. 152.

obtain financial guarantees or insurances from operators established in the same state. Lastly, Article 14(8) prevents Member States from requiring the providers to have been previously registered or to have conducted their business for a certain period in that state.

3.3.3. Suspect Requirements

In addition to the prohibited requirements listed in Article 14, Article 15(1) contains eight obstacles to the freedom of establishment that are subject to evaluation. These measures include: 'quantitative or territorial restrictions'; 'an obligation on a provider to take a specific legal form'; 'requirements relating to shareholding in a company'; requirements relating to reserved functions; 'a ban on having more than one establishment in the territory of the same State'; 'requirements fixing a minimum number of employees'; 'fixed minimum and/or maximum tariffs with which the provider must comply' and 'an obligation on the provider to supply other specific services jointly with his service'.

Article 15(2) asks the EU countries to review the mentioned requirements. The legislation of Member States is only permissible if they are non-discriminatory, necessary and proportionate. In this regard, as demonstrated in Article 15(3)(a), a requirement is discriminating, if it directly or indirectly discriminates according to nationality or, with regard to companies, according to the location of the registered office. As Article 15(3)(b) notes, a requirement is necessary, if it can be justified by an over-riding reason relating to the public interest. According to Article 15(3)(c), a requirement is proportional, if this requirement is suitable for securing the attainment of the objective pursued, does not go beyond what is necessary to attain that objective and cannot be replaced by other less restrictive measures which obtain the same result.

3.3.4. The Actual Effect of the Directive Provision on Cross-border Establishment

According to Mustilli and Pelkmans (2013), from a business perspective, it was at first considered that the expected economic benefits of the Services Directive mainly came from the provision of the establishment chapter. With regard to the actual effect of this law, by 2011, the Services Directive had successfully dealt with the prohibited requirements provided by Article 14. Erasing these barriers is deemed to significantly facilitate cross-border investment in the internal services market in the long term. However, certain barriers to cross-border establishment regulated by the directive remain, such as quantitative restrictions. Due to these remaining obstacles, it might be too expensive and time consuming for firms to engage in cross-border business. Thus, though the Services Directive plays a useful role in opening up certain services bastions of Member States and reducing transaction costs by administrative simplification, the remaining barriers could discourage more companies from establishing businesses across borders in other markets.[124]

4. Removing Remaining Barriers to Cross-border Establishment

4.1. *Remaining Barriers to Cross-border Establishment*

According to Pelkmans and De Brito (2012), even in the ideal scenario of the single market, one cannot rule out the possibility for industry to complain about 'barriers'. The first reason is the 'incompleteness' of the single market. For instance, although financial services regulation is of noticeable influence, the regulation does not apply to mortgages in such a manner as to promote integration of the mortgage sector at European level. The second factor is that EU countries enjoy regulatory autonomy in certain matters and they often opt for the protection of this autonomy due to national political legitimacy considerations.[125]

With specific reference to cross-border business establishment, the existence of national regulatory autonomy in some matters appears to be the main causes of remaining barriers. As demonstrated by Hertig and McCahery, company taxes, employees' protection and other social constraints constitute important obstacles to the free movement of companies.[126] Member States exercise taxing power in the EU.[127] Co-determination and labor standards also fall in the core scope of national production and welfare systems.[128] Below, this section looks at two areas that are within the scope of Member States' regulatory competence: taxation and employee participation.

With regard to corporate taxation, according to the OECD (2012), conforming to different national tax systems and dealing with different national tax departments in the EU can impose extra administration costs on businesses. Given the lack of a consolidated tax base, there can be differences in tax treatment between conducting new business in the same state and doing so outside this country. For instance, a parent company based in one Member State cannot always deduct the losses of its subsidiary in another EU state from the overall tax costs of this group. This difficulty could create disincentives for establishing firms across borders in the EU.[129] Moreover, as demonstrated by Ilzkovitz and others, firms setting up subsidiaries or permanent establishments in another EU state face higher compliance costs than enterprises with only domestic subsidiaries. This indicates tax obstacles to conducting business activities in different EU countries. For

124 Mustilli & Pelkmans 2013, p. 26.
125 Jacques Pelkmans and Anabela Correia De Brito, Enforcement in the EU single market, Centre for European Policy Studies, Brussels, 2012, p. 6, available at: <http://ec.europa.eu/internal_market/scoreboard/_docs/2014/07/solvit/enforcement-in-the-eu-single-market.pdf> (last accessed 6 April 2016).
126 Hertig & McCahery 2007, p. 228.
127 Genschel & Jachtenfuchs 2011, p. 293.
128 Höpner & Schäfer 2015, p. 726.
129 OECD 2012, p. 19.

example, engaging in cross-border business entails considerable additional tax costs coming to at least one or two millions of euros for medium-sized European multinational companies.[130]

In terms of worker participation, rules relating to employee participation within the framework of the formation and operation of a European Company (Societas Europaea, SE) are considered to be restrictions on the freedom of establishment.[131] A SE mainly serves to provide businesses with the possibility to ease business across national borders.[132] The worker participation regime in a SE is a political compromise agreed upon by Member States allowing them to preserve their respective industrial relations models.[133] It should be noted that reaching agreement on employee participation in a SE is lengthy and complex, which is often mentioned as the major shortcoming of this company form.[134] The research of Ernst & Young commissioned by the Commission (2009) identifies the worker involvement system as a factor hindering the creation of SE in some EU countries.[135]

4.2. *Tackling the Remaining Barriers through Intergovernmental Negotiations and Judicial Integration*

Section 2 shows the different roles of negative integration and positive integration in promoting market integration in the EU. This has also been translated into political literature as the difference between judicial integration and political integration. Political integration and judicial integration are two forms of integration that can address the barriers to cross-border establishment. According to Höpner and Schäfer, Weiler and Scharpf analytically differentiate between two different types of integration in the EU: political integration and judicial integration. The first form is based on intergovernmental negotiations among Member States, while the second type derives from how the Commission and the CJEU interpret EU law. With growing diverse production and welfare regimes of Member States, the interpretation seems more likely to promote integration.[136]

Harmonization of regulatory standards or reaching agreements on redistribution across heterogeneous EU will be difficult. Enlargement has added to the diversity of national social support systems and institutions. In fields central to the production and welfare regimes of EU countries e.g. company taxation and co-determination, intergovernmental bargains have often taken too long and reached

130 Fabienne Ilzkovitz, Adriaan Dierx, Viktoria Kovacs and Nuno Sousa, Steps towards a Deeper Economic Integration: the Internal Market in the 21st century, available at: <http://ec.europa.eu/economy_finance/publications/publication784_en.pdf> (last accessed 10 April 2015).

131 Storm 2006, p. 134.

132 Pellé 2008, p. 8.

133 Callaghan 2011, p. 6.

134 Pellé 2008, p. 8.

135 Ernst & Young, Study on the Operation and the Impacts of the Statute for a European Company (SE) (Final Report), available at: <http://ec.europa.eu/internal_market/-consultations/docs/2010/se/study_SE_9122009_en.pdf> (last accessed 13 April 2015).

136 Höpner & Schäfer 2015, p. 726.

deadlock. Moreover, the negotiations have not brought about consensus on harmonization, but the protection of national sovereignty.[137]

Meanwhile, the political-economic heterogeneity of EU countries has made judicial integration more possible, as the ability of Member States to correct CJEU rulings is based on political negotiations. Usually, the decision to change the judgments is required to be unanimous. A super-majority system for political decision making and different varieties of national production and welfare systems give the CJEU significant room to maneuvre. Thanks to this room for maneuvre, the court has expanded the scope of its authority and EU provisions.[138]

With specific reference to cross-border establishment, judicial integration rather than political integration seems more likely to cope with the remaining barriers. To demonstrate this point, this section discusses the taxation case where political integration has given way to the protection of national autonomy. At the same time, in this case, CJEU judgments remove some tax obstacles to cross-border establishment that have not been erased through political bargains.

With regard to political integration, according to the OECD (2012), the Commission has developed a proposal for a Common Consolidated Corporate Tax Base (CCCTB) (2011), in order to tackle the taxation barriers. This would provide a single system for calculating the tax base of companies doing business in the EU. Despite some negative economic effects in the short term, the proposal, as the Commission evaluates, would significantly lower tax-related compliance expenditure for enterprises engaging in different national markets. This would particularly profit cross-border establishment. Also, the common system proposed would benefit half of multinational firms in all industries apart from finance through consolidating their cross-border losses. As held by the OECD, reducing set-up costs would translate into increased cross-border establishment in the EU.[139]

However, according to Panayi (2012), adopting the draft CCCTB Directive remains subject to unanimity voting and the adoption is becoming more and more unlikely.[140] In practice, Member States have been unable to agree upon introducing a CCCTB in the EU.[141] Take the year 2008 as an example. At that time, Ireland, Poland, Latvia and Slovakia opposed the idea of a CCCTB.[142]

Since Member States have different corporate tax systems, if an EU legislative measure on a CCCTB is adopted, some MS will gain, while some will lose.[143] Ireland and some other EU countries are concerned that participation in a CCCTB would

137 *Ibid.*

138 *Ibid.*

139 OECD 2012, p. 50. European Commission, 11 March 2011, Proposal for a Council Directive on a Common Consolidated Corporate Tax Base (CCCTB), COM(2011) 121/4; IP/11/319.

140 Panayi 2012, p. 257.

141 Bellingwout 2014, p. 175.

142 Charles Gnaedinger, News Analysis: CCCTB Opponents Stake out Different Positions, available at: <www.tlegal.eu/publikacje/international_bar_association/21122008_ccctb.pdf> (last accessed 11 May 2015).

143 Ernest & Young, Study on the Economic and Budgetary Impact of the Introduction of a Common Consolidated Corporate Tax Base in the European Union, available at: <http://taxinstitute.ie/portals/0/CCCTBrepjan2011.pdf> p. 61 (last accessed 12 May 2015).

undermine their competitiveness and lead to decreased foreign direct investment.[144] Ireland's tax regime has played an important role in attracting foreign investment.[145] Due to the nature of a CCCTB, there would be no possibility for EU countries to offer tax incentives to businesses.[146] Moreover, Member States of Eastern Europe with flat tax rates are concerned that the harmonization could decrease their tax base, resulting in the deterioration of the governmental financial situation.[147] After the EU's enlargement to the East, added heterogeneous preferences for tax results in increased opposition to tax harmonization.[148]

With regard to judicial integration, relying on the freedom of establishment, some CJEU rulings in 2003 and 2004 tackled a fair number of tax obstacles to cross-border establishment.[149] According to Garbarino, in Bosal (C-168/01) and Keller (C-471/04), the court permitted parent companies resident in one Member State to deduct costs incurred by their subsidiaries established in another. Moreover, the CJEU judgment in Rewe Zentralfinanz (C-347/04) allowed a controlling firm incorporated in one EU country to deduct losses stemming from write-downs on its participations in subsidiaries resident in other EU countries.[150] These rulings have dealt with some fiscal impediments the CCCTB proposal (2011) aims to address. The rules proposed by the Commission confirm the recognition of write-downs allowed by the Rewe Zentralfinanz case. Moreover, the proposal offers a single set of rules for controlling companies to calculate costs attributable to controlled firms.[151]

The application of the freedom of establishment to national tax provisions appears to show the court's willingness to achieve integration of national tax systems.[152] A case in point is the Bosal case. According to Weber, EU countries enjoy regulatory autonomy in defining the criteria for taxation. The criteria can be an economic link between the participation costs of a parent company relating to a subsidiary and the subsidiary's profits taxable in Member States. In case of defining the criteria for taxation on the basis of this link, Member States may allow the parent company to allocate the costs to the profits. Nevertheless, the CJEU did not permit this allocation, because the allocation would impose restrictions on the freedom of establishment. The author holds that the prohibition has undermined Member States' sovereignty.[153] This case shows the great determination of the CJEU to take

144 Munin 2011, p. 125.
145 Morisset & Pirnia 1999, p. 8.
146 Lamotte 2012, p. 278.
147 Munin 2011, p. 125.
148 Wasserfallen 2013, p. 11.
149 Vanistendael 2006, p. 416.
150 Garbarino 2012, p. 255. Case C-168/01 *Bosal* [2003] ECR I-9409; Case C-471/04 *Keller Holding* [2006] ECR I-2107; Case C-347/04 *Rewe Zentralfinanz* [2007] ECR I-2647
151 Garbarino 2012, p. 260.
152 Vanistendael 2006, p. 416.
153 Dennis Weber, 'Is the limitation of tax jurisdiction a restriction of the freedom of movement?', Paper for the Annual Conference of the European Association of Tax Law Professors in Helsinki 7-9 June 2007.

steps towards further integration of the internal market with fair and equal conditions for businesses.[154]

5. Conclusion

Chapter 3 showed that a major effort has been undertaken in the EU to achieve market integration. Today companies have much more freedom to establish businesses across borders. However, some barriers to the cross-border establishment of companies still exist.

This chapter began with analyzing the evolution of the internal market. Section 2 presented the important Treaty provisions on the development of the internal market. Also, a discussion was provided of the role of the CJEU and the Commission in promoting the market integration. It can be concluded that both negative integration and positive integration significantly contribute to the establishment of the internal market.

Chapter 3 then presented the EU provision on the cross-border establishment of companies. Section 3 discussed the relevant Treaty provisions, the important case law and the Services Directive, respectively. The case law revealed that the court significantly restricts the power of the country of arrival to impose restrictions on the freedom of establishment, while some obstacles to emigrating companies are permitted. Authorization schemes, prohibited requirements and suspect requirements are dealt with by the Services Directive, in order to facilitate cross-border establishment. Among these sorts of national provisions, prohibited requirements have been removed, while some barriers of the third category remain.

Thereafter, section 4 discussed the remaining barriers to cross-border establishment and potential ways to cope with these obstacles. It was recognized that the remaining barriers mainly arise from the existence of national regulatory autonomy in some matters such as company taxation. CJEU rulings seem better able to cope with these obstacles than inter-governmental bargains among Member States.

154 Vanistendael 2003, p. 193.

PART II

THEORETICAL FRAMEWORK

Part II

Part II turns the focus of this dissertation to economic theory. Chapter 4 addresses two views of regulation (the public interest approach and the private interest approach) and investigates whether there is an economic rationale to regulate business establishment.

Chapter 5 analyses regulatory intervention in the cross-border establishment of companies in a multi-level jurisdiction. Chapter 5 first illustrates the necessity of regulating the cross-border establishment of companies and then discusses the pros and cons of providing such regulation at the federal level.

Chapter 4

AN ECONOMIC ANALYSIS OF THE REGULATION OF THE ESTABLISHMENT OF COMPANIES

1. Introduction

The aim of Chapter 4 is to explain government intervention in the establishment process in a single-level jurisdiction in the light of the economic theory of regulation. Chapter 4 discusses whether government intervention in the formation of companies is necessary at all. Moreover, the question will be addressed whether a certain type of regulation is an appropriate remedy to the problems that it aims to tackle.

This chapter looks at two particular ways of regulating establishment: licensing and minimum capital requirements. Licensing as a legal control on entry is widely accepted.[1] Nevertheless, whether licensing is a proportional instrument to tackle market failure also needs to be considered.

Another way of regulating market entry can be to introduce minimum capital requirements. Minimum capital requirements can increase the costs of capital; as a result, business entry may decrease.[2]

The rest of this chapter is structured as follows. Section 2 presents two different approaches concerning regulation as discussed in the law and economics literature: the public interest approach and the private interest approach. It also addresses the main kinds of regulatory controls in the process of business establishment. Section 3 elaborates on whether regulatory intervention in the form of registration, certification and licensing is warranted in the establishment. From a public interest perspective, section 4 looks at the pros and cons of these instruments to tackle market failure in the set-up process, respectively. Having discussed public interest arguments for licensing in the set-up process, section 5 takes into account private interest considerations for employing licensing in the establishment process. Section 6 turns the focus of this chapter to minimum capital requirements. The aim

1 Demsetz, 1982, p. 48.

2 OECD, Barriers to Entry, available at: <www.OECD.org/regreform/sectors/36344429.pdf.> p. 31 (last accessed 6 April 2016).

of this section is to see whether minimum capital requirements can be justified on public interest grounds or rather explained on private interest grounds. Section 7 provides conclusions.

Some examples relating to China are treated in chapter 4, but it is not until Part III that this thesis will look into the regulation of the cross-border establishment of companies in China in detail.

2. Theory of Regulation

2.1. *The Public Interest Approach*

A public interest approach to regulation starts from the assumption that regulation is always aimed at increasing social welfare. Applying this (optimistic) view to the regulation of market entry, this approach demonstrates that entry regulation of new ventures can cut inferior products from unreliable providers out of the market, therefore increasing the average quality of products. As a result, entry regulation has the potential to increase consumer welfare. However, whether excluding certain products from the market increases social welfare, depends crucially on (the heterogeneity of) actual consumer preferences.[3]

Theoretically, if there is a market failure in the form of externalities, information problems, market power or public goods, regulation may be justified on the ground of public interest. However, this of course does not imply that *licensing* needs to be introduced. Public interest theory suggests that a proportional cure for the market failure at hand needs to be chosen, and the less a particular regulatory instrument intervenes in a market, the better. Rules on mandatory information provision, labelling, certification or performance standards may be (better) alternatives for licensing, depending on the seriousness of the market failure and the specific context.[4]

The first market failure that may justify regulation on public interest grounds is the existence of externalities.[5] Externalities arise if the effects of the actions performed by subject A partially influence subject B. In many developing countries, licensing systems have been introduced in relation to construction safety, waste disposal and other areas. Some goods and services subject to these regimes can potentially cause externalities. For instance, the use of nuclear materials can have a significant adverse impact on third parties. If left unregulated, badly designed buildings may collapse (calling for licensing of architects and engineers); food and medicines can have a negative health impact, etc. Nevertheless, it follows from the economic literature that negative externalities may explain operation licensing, but do not necessarily justify entry licensing.[6]

3 See more particularly Shapiro 1986.

4 For further details on instrument choice, see Ogus 1994 and Philipsen 2003.

5 Of course, government intervention is only necessary when transaction costs prevent efficient bargaining from taking place, according to the well-known Coase theorem.

6 Ogus & Zhang 2005, p. 139. The failure to obtain an entry license results in companies not being able to conduct business in any sector. However, the failure to acquire an operation →

The presence of information asymmetry can be another public interest reason for regulation. These problems can be caused when experience goods and trust goods are provided.[7] The quality of experience goods cannot be properly evaluated before purchasing.[8] Trust goods have the features that consumers cannot judge their qualities even after consumption.[9] In the case of offering trust goods or experience goods, the providers have information that is not available to the purchasers.

Akerlof argues that in an unregulated market, asymmetric information between buyers and sellers will lead to the reduction of the quality of the goods offered in the market. Adverse selection is the reason for the quality deterioration. It is demonstrated that consumers cannot observe the quality of used cars, while sellers know all the information about the quality. Buyers cannot judge whether used cars are good or defective and they therefore suppose that a given car is of average quality. Accordingly, buyers are only willing to pay the price of a car of average quality. As a result, sellers of good used cars will not sell their cars in the market. If the information asymmetry is not solved, low quality used cars will chase good used cars out of the market. In the end, the whole market may be destroyed.[10] An adverse selection problem often arises in the field of liberal professions whose services are usually experience goods or trust goods. The public interest theory holds that regulatory intervention may be able to deal with quality deterioration and decrease in price that are caused by information asymmetry between professionals and consumers.[11]

In addition to adverse selection, asymmetric information may also cause a moral hazard problem. Moral hazard arises where the agent has different individual goals from the principal's and the principal has difficulties in deciding if the agent reports and acts to achieve the principal's objectives or the agent's self-interest.[12] This problem has been widely discussed in the literature on the regulation of professionals. For example, a moral hazard problem occurs when architects and their clients possess different objectives and the consumers cannot easily evaluate the necessity and the usefulness of the professionals' actions.[13] A typical example of a moral hazard problem is demand generation, meaning that professionals provide more services or over-supply quality than is necessary. If fully informed, clients will

license, does not prevent a company from being formed, nor does it prevent a company from operating in unregulated fields, as long as it does not engage in the industries governed by the operation licensing regime (Ogus & Zhang 2005, p. 126).

7 Den Hertog 2003, p. 13 and 14.

8 Nelson 1970, p. 312.

9 Darby & Karni 1973, p. 68 and 69.

10 Akerlof 1970.

11 Philipsen 2003, p. 16.

12 Milgrom & Roberts 1992, p. 170. Moral harzard refers to 'the form of post-contractual opportunism that arises because actions that have efficiency consequences are not freely observable and so the person taking them may choose to pursue his or her private interests at others' expenses.' The concept was first used in the insurance sector, meaning that individuals with insurance tend to act in a risker way as they can claim on their insurance (Milgrom & Roberts 1992, p. 167).

13 Milgrom & Roberts 1992, p. 170.

refuse to purchase these services. The selling of such services produces a welfare loss to society. Regulation of professional services can improve the market equilibrium e.g. supplying more available information about the quality of such services.[14]

Apart from externalities and information problems, market power can also lead to the failure of markets. A monopolist can set the price of its product at the level that is significantly higher than the marginal costs of manufacturing this product. In a perfectly competitive market, the price of a product that a firm will set is equal to the marginal costs of producing this product.[15] Therefore, monopolists earn profits that are higher than those that can be found in a competitive industry. Moreover, firms can also be involved in a cartel. Regulation in the form of competition law may be warranted to tackle this problem, which is not the focus of this thesis.

It should be pointed out that in some cases caused by economics of scale, one or a small number of firms maybe can supply the market better than numerous small companies. This is the situation where one or a few companies provide certain products at a lower cost than many smaller manufacturers. Such monopolies are named natural monopolies. Natural monopolies should be permitted to prevail.[16]

The fourth public interest justification for regulation is the presence of public goods. These sorts of goods are those that people cannot be excluded from consuming, due to either impossibility or huge costs. The second characteristic of public goods is that consumption of the goods does not affect their utility. In short, being non-rivalrous and non-excludable are the two qualities of public goods.[17] The market does not always have incentives to produce public goods.

It seems unlikely that a 'free-rider problem' can occur concerning the services and products provided by companies. A 'free-rider problem' means that people usually have no willingness to pay for services or goods, if they can benefit from these goods or services paid by others. As a result, in a free market, there will be a short supply of such services or goods.[18]

It is important to note that the existence of market failure does not necessarily require regulation.[19] In case of tackling externalities, market based instruments (tradable pollution permits etc.), liability rules and a Pigouvian tax can also be chosen, if the transaction costs are prohibitive.[20] Section 2.4 will present these alternative legal instruments.

14 Garoupa 2004, p. 6.
15 Philipsen 2003, p. 12.
16 Ogus 1994, p. 30.
17 Den Hertog 2000, p. 230.
18 Bjørn Volkerink, Patrick de Bas, Nicolai van Gorp and Niels Philipsen, *Study of Regulatory Restrictions in the Field of Pharmacies, study for the European Commission*, Rotterdam: ECORYS Nederland B.V. in co-operation with Metro, Maastricht University. Availale at: <http://ec.europa.eu/internal_market/services/docs/pharmacy/report_en.pdf> (last accessed 15 March 2014).
19 Den Hertog 2003, p. 42.
20 Coase argues that the internalization of externalities can be realized through a bargaining between the parties, in the absence of transaction costs (Coase 1960).

Moreover, regulatory failures and market failures have to be compared in any case. If added transaction costs or mis-allocations in other economic sectors outweigh the increased value in efficiency arising from regulation, this may result in regulatory failures.[21]

2.2. *The Private Interest Approach*

The private interest approach to regulation stresses the influence of interest groups (such as industry lobby groups and professional associations) in the formation of regulation. The basic assumption is that there is a demand and supply for regulation; and interest groups (the demand side) try to influence the political decision-making process with the aim of seeking rents for themselves. The fact that resources are used to capture wealth transfers from the general public to specific interest groups is unproductive from a social welfare point of view.[22] Interest groups, such as industry lobby groups, are more likely to be successful in their lobbying activities if they are relatively small, well organized and focused on a clear common goal; especially when there are high information costs for the public at large of finding out that regulation is not in the public interest.[23]

According to Stigler's 'theory of economic regulation' (1971), regulation originates where the benefits are concentrated (the industry) and the costs can be divided over a large group. Industry lobbies for restrictive entry regulation, for example in the form of licensing, as this restricts competition and increases profits of the insiders in the market.[24] *Legal* entry barriers (i.e. in the form of protective regulation) according to Stigler are more effective against competitive pressure than 'traditional' entry barriers discussed in economic literature, such as limit pricing strategies, collusion, vertical integration and product differentiation. Peltzman,[25] who extended Stigler's model, Posner[26] and Becker[27] all later pointed to the fact that different interest groups are often in competition with each other for political favours.[28] The political outcome will reflect concessions to all interest groups, and depends on the respective strengths and efficiency (in lobbying) of each interest group in the lobbying process. In Becker's model, the view that governments correct

21 Ogus 1994, p. 30.
22 Philipsen 2007, p. 116.
23 Olson 1965, Chapters 1-3. The concept of 'rent seeking', introduced by Anne Krueger in the Political Economy of the Rent-Seeking Society, refers to the political activity of citizens and groups using scarce resources to pursue monopoly rights granted by authorities (Den Hertog 2000, p. 243).
24 Stigler 1971, p. 3-4. He famously stated that; "as a rule, regulation is acquired by the industry and is designed and operated primarily for its benefits." It should be emphasized that Stigler's work has a strong empirical basis.
25 Peltzman 1976.
26 Posner 1974.
27 Becker 1983.
28 Together these contributions are usually referred to as the 'Chicago theory of regulation'. See e.g. Philipsen 2003, p. 25-26 and Boehm 2007, p. 4-7.

market failures (public interest approach) and the view that governments favour the politically powerful (private interest approach) are to some extent unified.[29]

In contrast to the Chicago theory of regulation, the Virginia (Public Choice) school emphasizes the costs of the lobbying process - a process famously termed 'rent seeking' by Krueger (1974). The fact that resources are only used to obtain or maintain legal protection or other political favours, is a clear cost to society.[30] A starting point of any Public Choice analysis, as found e.g. in Buchanan and Tullock (1962), is that in essence there is no difference between the behaviour of politicians and the behaviour of market actors; both groups are pursuing the maximization of utility.[31] Politicians may want to be re-elected, or they may want to increase the size of their bureaucracy or power, and in the process they are likely to provide inefficient regulation (serving particular lobbying groups) in exchange for obtaining votes.[32] Due to the 'vote motive' for being re-elected, politicians will especially have incentives to meet the needs of small and tightly organized groups.[33]

In the Chicago and Public Choice theories described above, public agents play a relatively passive role as a broker between the different interest groups. Boehm (2007) explains that the so-called 'tollbooth theory' goes one step further, as it claims that public agents play a much more active role. Scholars such as De Soto (1989) and Shleifer and Vishny (1994) have pointed out that politicians and bureaucrats enjoying a monopolistic position are able to formulate inefficient regulations (red tape), which enable them to obtain rents through bribes and campaign contributions.[34] The regulatory control that politicians have over firms provides opportunities for officials to seek rents through corruption.[35] Shleifer and Vishny (1994) refer in that respect to the situation in Italy and the Philippines.[36] The authors hold that an important reason for the existence of many permits and regulations is that it allows officials to take bribes, since they are entitled to decide whether or not permits will be granted.[37] The creation of more extensive regulation in their view is connected with producing socially inferior results.[38]

29 Becker 1983, p. 383.
30 See also the work by Bhagwati 1982.
31 Buchanan & Tullock 1962, p. 17-39.
32 Philipsen 2003, p. 24. See also Buchanan *et al.* 1980 and Boehm 2007, p. 7-8.
33 Shughart II 2008.
34 Boehm 2007, p. 9.
35 For a brief overview of the economic literature on corruption, see Boehm 2007, p. 11-15. Corruption differs from lobbying in that it is illegal, secret and non transparent and reflects narrow interests (e.g. of one firm), whereas lobbying is legal, relatively transparent and reflects broader interests (e.g. of one industry). The main forms in which corruption presents itself are defined by Boehm as bribery, embezzlement, fraud, extortion, favouritism and nepotism. See also Andvig *et al.* 2000.
36 Shleifer & Vishny 1994, p. 1007.
37 Shleifer & Vishny 1993, p. 601.
38 Djankov *et al.* 2002, p. 3.

2.3. *Regulatory Instruments in the Set-up Process*

Registration and licensing are two main forms of government intervention in the process of establishing companies. In some cases, notification is alternatively used which has the same meaning as registration.[39] Registration mainly intends to obtain data as the basis for future regulatory intervention. By contrast, licensing can be taken as ex ante regulatory action, setting the precondition for conducting a business that prior approval should be obtained and minimum criteria should be met.[40]

It should be pointed out that certification is a third regulatory instrument in the set-up process. Like licensing, certification is also an ex ante regulatory measure and granting certification means complying with minimum standards. The difference between licensing and certification is that certification is not mandatory. Without obtaining certification, companies can still engage in the regulated business activities.[41]

2.3.1. Registration

Registration only requires businesses to provide detailed data to authorities; after this step, engagement in business activities is permitted. The acceptance of this information is automatic and it is not necessary for officers to evaluate whether market entry conditions are met.[42] Authorities' task is to ensure that all required information is supplied by companies.[43] The consequent permission is also automatically given, which does not depend on administrative discretion.[44]

Notification may be adopted, with the aim to cut the costs of recognizing and locating businesses mainly.[45] The only purpose of registration is to decrease information costs, thus the locations of firms can be easily found.[46]

Nevertheless, based on the information offered by companies, authorities can also know a whole list of potential triggers for externalities and information failures in their areas. With this benefit, agencies can allocate audit resources and give better guidance to inspections. For instance, the data about firms' location and business can indicate risks, which may assist agencies in strengthening enforcement against

39 Ogus & Zhang 2005, p. 125 and 126.

40 Roy Kelly and Nick Devas, Regulation or Revenue? Implementing Local Government Business License Reform in Kenya, available at: <www.cid.harvard.edu/hiid/723.pdf> (last accessed 6 April 2016).

41 The Bureau of Industrial Economics (Australia) 1996a, p. 7.

42 Zhang & Ogus 2005, p. 1092.

43 The United Nations Economic and Social Commission for Asia and the Pacific (ESCAP), Guidelines for Minimum Standards and Codes of Professional Conduct for Freight Forwarders, Non-Vessel Operating Common Carriers and Multimodal Transport, available at: <www.unescap.org/sites/default/files/FF-standard-fulltext.pdf> (last accessed 26 December 2015).

44 Ogus & Zhang 2005, p. 126.

45 The Bureau of Industrial Economics (Australia) 1996b, p. 11.

46 Ogus 1994, p. 215.

more dangerous companies and activities.[47] Therefore, notification is especially effective when it is significant to identify the cause of possible externalities for carrying out future inspections or audits.[48]

Notification is also adopted in incorporation regimes with a purpose to avoid duplication of firm names. This regulatory measure can supply average citizens with information of a new venture in terms of directors, capital and goals too. Tax administration and government acquisition of data can also profit from notification.[49] Naturally, the public's access to companies' facts can be useful to tackle information problems.

If the same social goal can be achieved by registration and licensing, the first type of regulatory control is preferable.[50] Notification alone, instead of licensing, may be enough in some cases.[51] The possible reasons maybe relate to the properties of registration. As demonstrated above, registration can function as an indicator. Moreover, registration does not involve officials' determination power and does not set a minimum standard for approval. This means that administrative costs are rather low and entry barriers can hardly be erected.

Nevertheless, policing and monitoring turn out to be more important when registration rather than licensing is used. This is because there is still a necessity to conduct inspections in a few limited situations, in case of using registration. Either documented reviews or site inspections should be carried out, if businessmen are suspected of being involved in illegal activities or may break minimum criteria concerning health, environment and society. Thus, authorities have to monitor whether companies operate legally.[52]

2.3.2. Licensing

In the set-up process, licensing is aimed at checking and at showing whether applicants or their conditions satisfy substantive requirements. Sometimes checks can be conducted on both the conditions and the applicants. Compared to registration, licensing officials have certain discretion to reject licensing applications.[53]

The public interest justification for licensing is that the quality of goods and services in a market will increase, since unqualified companies are not allowed to enter into the market. As a result, some externalities may be prevented. Some information problems between consumers and producers may be thereby alleviated too.

47 The Bureau of Industrial Economics (Australia) 1996b, p. 18.

48 *Ibid.*, summary.

49 *Ibid.*

50 Roy Kelly and Nick Devas, Regulation or Revenue? Implementing Local Government Business License Reform in Kenya, available at: <www.cid.harvard.edu/hiid/723.pdf> (last accessed 6 April 2016).

51 The Bureau of Industrial Economics (Australia) 1996b, p. 18.

52 OECD 2005, p. 17.

53 Ogus & Zhang 2005, p. 126.

Nevertheless, there is a doubt whether licensing will improve the overall quality level of services and goods. This is because a Pareto improvement will not result from licensing. Some buyers would rather have purchased goods or services of inferior quality that are cheaper.[54] These low quality goods or services will be used as a substitute for the licensed services or goods with relatively higher prices.

Licensing as a step for establishment can be divided into GSL (general set-up licensing) and SSL (sectoral set-up licensing).[55] GSL means a licensing regime established for any investor that wants to set up any sort of business and SSL is a licensing system only imposed on businessmen that expect to form companies in certain sectors.[56]

2.3.2.1. GSL (General Set-up Licensing)

It is not possible to justify most GSL requirements, since Zhang and Ogus cannot identify a licensing regime suitable for all companies, all industries and all activities. They examine some widely used GSL regimes and demonstrate that these GSL systems are not appropriate for all sectors, all enterprises and all business activities.[57]

A case in point is capitalization requirements that aim to prevent the opportunism of firm owners through exploiting limited liability. Nevertheless, shareholders can circumvent this requirement and, as the practice in China shows, one available way is to counterfeit capital verification reports. Therefore, it is not clear whether this requirement can avoid this opportunism.[58]

Moreover, not all commercial practice involves significant potential losses. In fact, at least some possible losses can be better dealt with by regulation that is applied ex-post (i.e. after firms are established), e.g. information regulation (mandatory disclosure) and/or performance standards. These ex-post regulatory methods do not control entry.[59]

The OECD (1999) also holds that general permits should be eliminated. In the context of the research paper by the OECD, general permits have the same meaning as GSL. General permits are usually relicts of previous red tape that are applied to impose confusing minimum requirements for conducting business. A primary example is how high an office should be in former communist countries of Southeast Europe such as Albania. Such general licenses have provided big chances for officials to seek rents through examining premises on the spot. Such checks have

54 Shapiro 1986, p. 856.

55 Zhang & Ogus 2005, p. 1092.

56 *Ibid.*

57 *Ibid.*, p. 1096.

58 *Ibid.*

59 *Ibid.*, p. 1105. Information regulation supervises the flow of information that the provision of goods or services is based on. Mandatory disclosure asks suppliers to offer information about price, identity, composition, quantity or quality. Performance standards prescribe quality standard for goods or service at the moment of supply, but disregard how providers achieve the conditions. Licensing is the most interventionist regulatory instrument, followed by standards and information regulation. See Ogus 1994, p. 121 and 151.

no relation to whether local communities and the public can be protected. This is because the engagement in a particular hazardous activity still needs to be inspected separately, to obtain a separate license and to undergo a process for accreditation.[60]

2.3.2.2. SSL (Sectoral Set-up Licensing)

It is hard to justify SSL as one set-up step, according to Zhang and Ogus. Most importantly, if registration, 'independent licensing' (IL) and some necessary actions are adopted together, regulatory compliance under SSL can also be achieved, but potential costs may be lower.[61] IL refers to licensing requirements not integrated in the establishment procedure. IL only controls whether the engagement in certain business is permitted. The failure to meet the requirement of IL has no impact on the formation of firms and companies' involvement in other activities.[62]

If IL, registration and other measures are used together, regulatory compliance can be generated in a number of ways; as a result, these regulatory measures can meet their regulatory aims. For instance, registration authorities can inform licensing authorities about unlicensed commercial activities, as one measure. Licensing authorities can also fine unlicensed operations heavily. Moreover, consumers can be notified that under registration, the mere completion of registration does not allow companies to engage in licensed business. Thus, the purchases from unlicensed firms can be decreased.[63]

Of course, all these policies would impose more administrative costs on registration and licensing agencies and more information costs on consumers (receiving information from officers). Nevertheless, the authors remark that these expenses can sometimes be less than the costs under the SSL regime.[64]

The costs under the SSL system are listed as follows. Ventures have costs of compliance and other expenses under this system. Consumers also incur indirect welfare losses, since there would be fewer competitors, if SSL rather than registration was used.[65]

Moreover, in the case of introducing SSL rather than registration, IL and other interventions together, entrepreneurs perhaps cannot save compliance costs on other set-up steps apart from acquiring licenses.[66] It seems that the monitoring costs of authorities cannot be saved either.[67]

Furthermore, the use of SSL may lead entrepreneurs to enter the informal economy. In other words, businessmen do not complete any official procedure for conducting certain economic activities and they engage in these activities directly.

60 OECD 2005, p. 19.
61 Zhang & Ogus 2005, p. 1100 and 1105.
62 *Ibid.*, p. 1092.
63 *Ibid.*, p. 1100 and 1105.
64 *Ibid.*, p. 1100.
65 *Ibid.*
66 *Ibid.*, p. 1100-1102.
67 *Ibid.*, p. 1101.

The expansion of the informal economy is due to the high compliance costs for businessmen to go through a SSL regime. Entrepreneurs need to spend money on making applications and meeting capital requirements. There are also potential profit losses, since during the application process, they cannot enter the market.[68] The existence of SSL systems was considered as an important reason why in 2002, 8,000 business proprietors conducted business in the informal economy in the municipality of Shenzhen, China.[69]

In addition to the above costs, private interest arguments for SSL need to be taken into account, when deciding to choose SSL or not in the set-up process. The private interest approach already points out that existing companies will ask for licensing requirements to create entry barriers and politicians will provide this regulation to seek re-election. Section 4.3 will discuss the private interest considerations for licensing in the establishment of businesses.

From a practical perspective, many SSL regimes could be used after incorporation registration, and at the point companies start to operate in particular sectors. Moreover, these sectors should only include business activities that can pose a hazard or ought to be monitored. A case in point is the military industry. It is not reasonable to require firms to mention all possible business they may engage in at the moment of set-up registration and obtain individual licenses for all these activities. Ventures may not even conduct these possible business activities in future.[70]

In short, usually, a justification can hardly be offered for SSL as one step in the establishment, as demonstrated above. However, it is possible that costs arising from applying SSL can be less than those caused by using registration, IL and other measures together. On this assumption, one question concerning the adoption of SSL or not is whether the matters regulated by licensing can lead to substantial market failure.[71] Section 3.2 elaborates on the public interest reasons for using SSL in the establishment process.

In fact, there are in total three conditions for socially beneficial licensing. The first one is that the matters governed by licensing regimes can result in substantial market failure, as mentioned above. The other two are that (1) regulation does more good than harm and (2) licensing is more effective than other regulatory instruments.[72] It seems that the above discussion of Ogus and Zhang on choosing SSL or other alternatives focuses on the latter two conditions.

68 *Ibid.*, p. 1095 and 1100-1102.

69 *Ibid.*, p. 1097.

70 OECD 2005, p. 19.

71 Roy Kelly and Nick Devas, Regulation or Revenue? Implementing Local Government Business License Reform in Kenya, available at: <www.cid.harvard.edu/hiid/723.pdf> (last accessed 6 April 2016).

72 *Ibid.*

2.3.3. Certification

Certification is an alternative to licensing. Certification can overcome the information deficit as well as licensing.[73] As section 3.1.2 shows, since some services or goods provided by companies are experience goods or trust goods, consumers cannot evaluate quality before consumption. Certification with a management standard may serve as signals of good quality on a market.[74] If a company wants to acquire a certificate, the firm will need to meet certain requirements.

When certification is used, every company may do business in the regulated industries.[75] By contrast, licensing is a barrier to entry. Compared to licensing, certification has an additional advantage that consumers are still free to choose uncertified services or certified services. The quality of uncertified services is poorer, but their prices are lower.[76] However, a disadvantage of certification to consumers is that they need to be able to understand and use information provided by certification, thereby making the right choice between certified and non-certified service providers.[77]

Nevertheless, there are not always very obvious differences between licensing and certification in practice. Without being certified, potential entrants will have great difficulties in entering the market if (almost) all incumbents have been certified or market demand for goods or services provided by companies without certification is insufficient.

2.3.4. Minimum Capital Requirements

Minimum capital requirements are aimed at protecting creditors, since some opportunist shareholders might abuse limited liability.[78] However, employing such entry regulation can also limit the flow of entrant firms into markets. In section 6, minimum capital requirements will be discussed in detail.

2.4. *Other Legal Instruments to Internalize Externalities in Establishment*

2.4.1. Coase Theorem

Another possible solution for private parties to internalize externalities is through bargaining, where transaction costs are low enough to allow negotiation.[79] In this way, private parties trade externalities through a contract. Coase reminds us that

73 Ogus 1994, p. 217.
74 Terlaaka & King 2006, p. 581.
75 The Bureau of Industrial Economics (Australia) 1996b, p. 7.
76 Ogus 1994, p. 217.
77 Philipsen 2011, p. 208.
78 Pistor *et al.* 2002.
79 Transaction costs consist of search and information costs, bargaining costs and policing and enforcement costs. Dahlman 1979, p. 148.

harm has a reciprocal nature.[80] In this particular case this refers to the fact that pollution is not only caused by firms that discharge pollutants, but also by the presence of victims. In these situations, a conflicting use of property rights arises. The question is whose right (i.e. the companies' or the victims') should be limited. From an efficiency perspective, the answer will depend on which party can take precautionary measures to reduce or prevent the harm.[81] According to the Coase theorem, if transaction costs are sufficiently low or zero, negotiation will lead to an economically efficient outcome, regardless of the initial allocation of property rights. This is because private parties will decide how to maximize their utility and social welfare through negotiation, thereby curing externalities.[82] In the above situation of dealing with pollution, the company and the victim can bargain and correct the externality by means of installing a filter.[83] Therefore, the Coase theorem may be useful to internalize externalities caused by the activities of companies. Also, the Coase theorem may have its relevance in the market of goods or services offered by companies. For instance, manufacturers and purchasers can reach an agreement that will ask the producers to manufacture a safe product with a higher price. Through bargaining, the extra money included in the price will be equal to the costs that the users can save due to the reduction in accidents.[84]

However, in the case of high transaction costs, Coasian bargaining will not take place and some legal intervention will be needed. In terms of tackling pollution, massive pollution damages, the health of numerous people and transaction costs will be prohibitive. Moreover, the victims and the polluting companies do not have full information about the harm and the effective pollution-prevention measures.[85] Since information is one aspect of transaction costs,[86] in markets for goods and services supplied by companies, the transaction costs can also be high. The goods offered can be experience goods and the services can be experience goods or trust goods. Thus, consumers cannot be fully informed of the information associated with some goods and services provided by firms.

2.4.2. Pigouvian Tax

Another way to correct negative externalities is to impose a Pigouvian tax on activities that generate negative externalities. Levying such a tax can give companies incentives not to engage in these activities. This tax should have the same value as the external costs. If a sand-excavating firm causes damage to water environment by dumping in the waters, the government may take action to curb the pollution. In this case, a Pigouvian tax might be levied to raise funds for paying for

80 Coase 1960, p. 2.
81 Faure 2012, p. 278.
82 Coase 1960.
83 Faure 2012, p. 277.
84 Miceli 2009, p. 67.
85 Faure 2012, p. 278.
86 *Ibid.*

these measures. As a result, the tax might increase the incentive of the operation to avoid the dumping.

A commonly raised objection to a Pigouvian tax is that it is usually difficult to precisely calculate negative externalities. People find it relatively straightforward to evaluate the amount of taxation to tackle activities that influence marketable products directly e.g. emitting smoke by factories that does damage to a nearby laundry. However, there will be more difficulties to decide social costs in cases where the physical extent of the externality is indefinite and the damage caused by a particular extent of the externality is hard to measure. For instance, though it is widely accepted that social costs arising from the current emissions of CO_2 deserve concern, people have much less agreement about the magnitude of these social costs. One reason is that the influence of the emissions on climate is uncertain and another explanation is that the cost of global climate change is indefinite.[87] Hence, a Pigouvian tax alone cannot always effectively deal with the problem of externalities in the set-up process. Regulation or liability rules may still need to be adopted sometimes.

2.4.3. Market Based Instruments

Market based instruments provide economic incentives for people and firms to change their behaviour.[88] For example, in the field of environmental law, market mechanisms e.g. tradable pollution permits have been valued for their efficiency advantages. Market based instruments can decrease the total cost of meeting emission reduction targets due to the flexibility of the mechanisms.[89] Social welfare could be promoted if pollution rights were given to firms that could decrease pollution with the lowest prices.[90]

Market based instruments have been widely adopted to tackle environmental problems and resource administration issues. Other fields where these mechanisms have been used include dividing up resources e.g. radio frequency spectrum.[91] However, it does not always seem sensible to take market based instrument approaches. This problem can be noticed even in the area of the environment where these mechanisms have received frequent usage. If the information necessary to adopt this approach cannot be acquired, it may still be reasonable to use command and control approaches (i.e. regulation) as an initial way to tackle the relevant environmental problem.[92]

87 Tideman & Plassmann 2010, p. 176.

88 OECD 2002, p. 5.

89 Christiansen & Smith 2012, p. 359.

90 Faure *et al.* 2006, p. 218.

91 OECD 2002, p. 5.

92 Kevin Guerin, Property Rights and Environmental Policy: A New Zealand Perspective, available at: <www.treasury.govt.nz/publications/research-policy/wp/2003/03-02/09.htm> (last accessed 6 April 2016).

2.4.4. Liability Rules

Private law in the form of liability rules may also remedy market failures. By attributing the costs of actions to those that take these actions, the total social costs of accidents will be decreased, because the costs of damage and prevention will be minimized by the level of care.[93]

Nevertheless, in some cases, liability rules may not be optimal to offer incentives to parties to conduct careful behaviour.[94] Liability rules cannot always remedy externalities and regulatory intervention is still needed. According to Shavell's theoretical model, regulatory intervention should be used instead of or in conjunction with liability rules, if (1) the government possesses better (channels to obtain) information than courts to set the optimum level of care that must be taken to avoid negative externalities; (2) there is a possibility that the potential defendant will go bankrupt and become unable to pay compensation for the losses caused by the externality; and (3) the damage is widespread or no clear causal link can be found.[95] In the above cases, liability rules will not suffice to prevent negative externalities. Regulation is warranted to set pre-determined standards, by means of e.g. licensing or certification. For example, in a case where the test report for plane components given to carriers is not correct, the plane may crash, which obviously affects passengers as the third party. It may be too difficult to find out the cause of the accident; thus, private law in the form of liability rules cannot remedy these externalities. Moreover, significant externalities can be potentially caused. In the example of preventing the air accident, entry licensing may be needed.

3. Market Failure Justifications for Regulation in the Set-up Process

Having presented theories of regulation in section 2, this chapter continues to apply these theories to the establishment of companies. Section 3 elaborates on whether regulatory intervention in the form of registration, certification and licensing is warranted in the establishment process. Licensing here refers to SSL, since section 2.3.2 has demonstrated that almost no GSL system can be appropriate for all sectors, all firms and all activities. If the intervention can be supported, section 4 will discuss the adoption of these regulatory instruments according to the degree of intervention into markets. Minimum capital requirements, as the fourth regulatory tool in the set-up process, will be separately assessed in section 6.

According to the public interest approach, regulation of the establishment process e.g. registration, certification or licensing can increase social welfare. Entry regulation of new ventures can cut inferior products provided by unreliable providers from the market; therefore, only products of qualified manufacturers will be purchased. As a result, such regulation can increase the welfare of consumers.[96]

93 Faure 2008, p. 78.
94 Faure 2009.
95 Shavell 1984, p. 359-363.
96 Djankov *et al.* 2002, p. 2.

There should be a link between the stricter entry regulation, as indicated by more procedures particularly, and socially improved results.[97]

3.1. *Externalities*

Goods supplied by companies can lead to externalities. For example, if sound-deadening insulation is ineffective, the users of this sound-deadening material can generate serious environmental noise pollution, potentially disturbing neighbouring residents. Externalities can also arise from services offered by firms. For instance, network downtime caused by the mistakes of Internet service providers may keep authors from sending their papers to editors promptly, as a result, the editors cannot publish the book on time.

Moreover, the operation of unregulated companies may cause negative externalities such as pollution and potential safety hazards. Chemicals released by firms can harm the health of neighbouring inhabitants, and affect agricultural protection etc. The building activity of companies in the construction industry may cause life-threatening accidents. Such negative externality problems resulting from the business of ventures can hence be easily exemplified.

As described in section 2.4.1, the criteria presented by Shavell should be taken into account when deciding whether regulation or liability is required to deal with externalities. Applying Shavell's criteria seems to support the idea that regulation should also be used to cure externalities in the establishment of companies.

With regard to the first criterion, the government maybe can better acquire the information that is necessary to deal with industrial risks. The government often has the advantage of economies of scale in research and development.[98]

In terms of the second argument, companies may be unable to pay damages caused by the presence of externalities as a result of business activities. For example, an oil spill caused by the collision of oil tankers can result in great damage to the marine environment and clean-up and recovery from the spill may cause huge costs. Moreover, bad quality services can also lead to catastrophic damage that may be more than the service providers can afford. For instance, in the case of providing a wrong component test report to aircraft companies, aviation accidents may occur, potentially resulting in disastrous effects to people both on board and on the ground. Thus, it turns out to be obvious that some regulation is necessary in the set-up process; as a result, companies will be obliged to take optimal care.

Shavell's third determinant also seems to favour regulation. Liability rules cannot always achieve a deterrent effect.[99] In some cases, it is difficult to determine a causal relationship between the purchase of services and goods and the externalities resulting from this consumption. For instance, in case of the earlier example of the air crash, one cannot easily decide whether the faulty test report of plane components is the exact cause of the accident. In other cases, goods and

97 *Ibid.*
98 Faure 2014a, p. 702.
99 *Ibid.*

services of poor quality may cause widespread damages. For example, if nuclear disasters occur due to low-quality technologies and equipment, the effect of these catastrophes on the environment, the economy etc. can last for many years.

Even though the above criteria indicate that regulation rather than liability is preferable to cure externalities associated with the establishment, liability rules can still be used jointly to correct these externalities. Liability under tort can back up weak spots in regulation. First, regulation cannot always prevent externalities effectively, as this depends on enforcement. Second, regulatory capture may result in setting standards that are far from being optimal. Third, safety regulation cannot easily adapt to ever-changing reality. In cases where regulation cannot effectively solve externalities due to these weaknesses, liability rules should intervene.[100]

It is important to note that the above preference for regulation cannot provide an argument in favour of licensing in the establishment of companies. What type of regulatory instrument should be applied in the set-up process depends on the extent of a particular externality. Chapter 2 has provided a list of regulatory instruments, i.e. registration, certification and licensing. The issue of how regulators should choose these instruments for dealing with externalities in the establishment will be later discussed in Section 4.1.

3.2. *Information Asymmetry*

Information asymmetry arises particularly in situations where people are dealing with experience goods or trust goods. Products generated by companies can be experience goods e.g. tinned food, bottles of wine and motor cars. It is difficult or even impossible for consumers to evaluate the quality of these products before purchasing.

Services rendered by firms can be experience goods such as investment advice. Certain services, e.g. life assurance may be more appropriate to fit into the category of trust goods. These services cannot be assessed by the experience based on buying.

Therefore, in some cases, information asymmetry exists between consumers and companies. Purchasers do not possess all the information about the quality of some goods or services provided by firms, while businesses have such information. According to the theory presented in section 2, problems of adverse selection and moral hazard will arise. As a result of adverse selection, the quality of these goods and services would decline, finally being lower than the socially efficient level. Moreover, firms may not always take actions for the benefit of consumers, which may make companies supply these services and goods more than is necessary.

100 *Ibid.*

4. Choosing Regulatory Instruments to Tackle Market Failure in the Set-up Process

4.1. *Opting for Regulatory Instruments to Tackle Externalities*

In cases where externalities occur and ex-ante regulation is required according to Shavell's criteria, registration, certification and licensing can be adopted to tackle this market failure. From a public interest perspective, section 4.1 looks at the pros and cons of these instruments, respectively.

Registration seems to be preferable to the other instruments, if the operation of companies does not give rise to high costs and the third party can grasp the data publicized. In this case, it is probably efficient for the third party to have access to the relevant information and to adopt proper measures to avoid the potential damage. In the US, information disclosure has been widely used as a regulatory instrument to prevent externalities and a case in point is the release of the Toxics Release Inventory (TRI) by the EPA (the US Environmental Protection Agency). Under the requirement of TRI, when manufacturing firms employ more than 10 workers, they are required to notify the discharge of around 650 hazardous substances. The EPA then transmits the data to the general public. Entrepreneurs and those who have concern about the environmental impact of companies can identify ventures discharging considerable volumes of waste and change investment plans accordingly. Moreover, relying on the available information, people can more easily avoid contaminated areas.[101] Of course, information disclosure will not work, if average citizens do not read the information publicized. In the area of consumer protection, the empirical investigation by behavioural economists points out that consumers are likely to ignore the information provided by contracts.[102] Therefore, it is better not to be too optimistic about the role of registration in dealing with externalities.

It seems also appropriate to use registration to tackle the externalities of goods and services in some cases. If companies disclose the information about the danger of their products, this activity can potentially benefit society. The disclosure may enable purchasers to make better decisions about buying these goods and using these products.[103] However, consumers may fail to have a correct understanding of the information released.[104] Moreover, consumers, as demonstrated above, might not read the relevant data. As a result, registration cannot always cure externalities caused by goods and services.

Certification rather than registration may remedy negative externalities, when consumers cannot well understand the risks from products, services and the activities of companies. Certification can effectively inform buyers about the impacts of various products and their purchasing decisions. However, the possibility should be considered that consumers cannot always believe certification

101 Oberholzer-Gee & Mitsunari 2006, p. 142.
102 Luth 2010, p. 177.
103 Polinsky & Shavell 2012, p. 360.
104 Dranove & Jin 2010, p. 939 and 959.

shown by firms. A case in point is eco-labelling. Eco-labels are one of the most commonly used instruments for companies to disclose to consumers information about their products. In particular, eco-labels mainly aim to allow customers to identify the impact that products have on the environment.[105] However, green washing is a common problem when employing eco-labels. This problem arises in part from that fact that eco-labelling is a voluntary system, so companies can easily avoid punishment.[106]

Licensing would be better than certification, if the losses generated by low-quality services or goods and the operation of companies are heavy or widespread. Licensing prevents companies which do not meet certain criteria from penetrating a market. If licensing can actually improve the quality of services and goods, this regulatory instrument can be a cure for externalities. However, there is a possibility that some consumers would purchase low-quality goods or services at lower prices to substitute goods or services offered by licensed firms, where licensing is adopted in the establishment of companies.

It should be noted that licensing is a suitable tool only in cases of severe externalities. It is not efficient to adopt licensing to control the entry of ordinary companies whose activities do not lead to significant negative externalities.[107] As section 2.3.2 demonstrates, licensing enables authorities to create entry barriers. When using licensing, services and products can only be supplied by the companies that have a license granted by the regulating authority. In this way, the regulator controls the entry into a market. Without acquiring a license, firms cannot do business in a market. Moreover, licensing may incite some investors to enter the informal economy. The firms established by these entrepreneurs may provide low quality products or services. The operation of these companies may also result in potential safety hazards and pollution. In these cases, licensing may lead to a decrease in social welfare.

Apart from the above regulatory instruments, to some extent other solutions may suffice to solve certain forms of negative externalities in the set-up process. As section 2.4 has shown, alternatives include Coasian bargaining, a Pigouvian tax, market based instruments and liability rules.

4.2. *Choosing Regulatory Instruments to Remedy Information Asymmetry*

In the case of the existence of information asymmetry, registration, certification and licensing can be adopted to tackle this market failure. From a public interest perspective, section 4.2 analyses the strengths and the weaknesses of these instruments, respectively.

The least restrictive of competition would be registration that simply provides the information of products and services. A case in point is product labels. However, offering information on quality is not always an easy matter, since the

105 Martinez 2013, p. 24.
106 *Ibid.*
107 Ogus 2007, p. 157.

products and services concerned can be experience goods or trust goods. Also, the data provided cannot always be well grasped by consumers.[108] Moreover, a more severe problem may be that average citizens are likely to ignore the information publicized. Luth criticizes information economics from the perspective of behavioural economics: consumers are unlikely to read contract terms.[109]

Certification maybe can tackle information asymmetry better than registration, if purchasers can recognize the value of a certain certificate.[110] Disclosure of information may incentivize buyers to select good quality products and perhaps only high-quality producers can survive eventually. Quality disclosure has helped purchasers to choose sellers that best satisfy their needs, for example in the catering industry. However, disclosure has its own weaknesses such as consumer misunderstanding. There is no evidence that quality disclosure in some important industries has unambiguously benefited purchasers. A case in point is the financial sector.[111] Another example is the insurance industry where most of insurance holders do not know the most basic elements of their insurance plans, as shown by empirical evidence.[112] Consumers have difficulties to observe the quality attributes of companies, since such attributes are usually complicated and hard to evaluate. Therefore, it is usually difficult for purchasers to choose (ex-ante) providers whose goods or services are of consistently good quality.[113]

Licensing rather than certification seems to be suitable in case where serious information asymmetry exists between consumers and firms. Licensing may be preferable to certification when evidence shows that consumers underestimate the risk associated with low quality products and the variation in quality is considerable; or when buyers are unable to be in contact with suppliers.[114] If licensing can actually improve the quality of services or goods, licensing can alleviate the information asymmetry between companies and customers. However, licensing is more restrictive than certification and registration.

108 Bjørn Volkerink, Patrick de Bas, Nicolai van Gorp and Niels Philipsen, *Study of Regulatory Restrictions in the Field of Pharmacies, study for the European Commission*, Rotterdam: ECORYS Nederland B.V. in co-operation with Metro, Maastricht University. Available at: <http://ec.europa.eu/internal_market/services/docs/pharmacy/report_en.pdf> (last accessed 6 April 2016).

109 Luth 2010, p. 177.

110 Bjørn Volkerink, Patrick de Bas, Nicolai van Gorp and Niels Philipsen (2007), *Study of Regulatory Restrictions in the Field of Pharmacies, study for the European Commission*, Rotterdam: ECORYS Nederland B.V. in co-operation with Metro, Maastricht University. Available at: <http://ec.europa.eu/internal_market/services/docs/pharmacy/report_en.pdf> (last accessed 15 March 2014).

111 David & Jin 2010, p. 939 and 959.

112 Loewenstein *et al.* 2013, p. 851.

113 Terlaaka & King 2006, p. 581.

114 The Bureau of Industrial Economics (Australia) 1996b, p. 30.

4.3. *Summary*

An important factor in choosing the form of regulation to cure market failure in business establishment is the extent of the market failure problems. Moreover, regulation should not go beyond (in controlling market entry) what is necessary to remedy the existing market failure.[115] Licensing seems to be a suitable instrument in case of severe externalities and information asymmetry. In other cases, registration and certification can also work.

It is also significant that the costs arising from using regulation to remedy market failure should be less than the benefits of the regulation.[116] One effect of licensing is limiting market entry and incentivizing investors to enter the informal economy. By contrast, the use of registration and certification still permits all companies to enter a market. Consumers can still decide to purchase low quality services or goods whose prices are cheaper. The fact should be considered that licensing restricts market entry more than other regulatory instruments.

5. Private Interest Considerations for Licensing in the Set-up Process

The discussion above demonstrates that from a public interest perspective, licensing may be warranted in the case of the presence of severe externality and information asymmetry problems. This section takes into account private interest considerations for employing licensing in the set-up process. As section 2 points out, interest groups may abuse public interest arguments for licensing and adopt business licensing to their advantage.

The private interest approach warns against the problem that incumbents will lobby politicians to create entry barriers. Existing companies tend to lobby for high entry barriers, while entrants are likely to lobby for policies that make entry easy.[117] As a result, incumbents and potential entrants may compete with each other to gain policies that meet their interests. If incumbents win the competition, high entry barriers can be created. Licenses may be used as an entry barrier. It is obvious that existing firms profit from a quantitative limitation of potential entrants. Therefore, there is a possibility that incumbents actively promote licensing. The stricter licensing requirements which potential entrants need to meet, the higher the entry costs.[118] If competition is restricted, incumbents could charge higher prices. Public choice theory already predicts that regulators may give into the above lobbying by incumbent companies, in order to seek votes and re-election.

Politicians and public officials are also self-interested and they can benefit themselves by creating business establishment licensing systems. Obviously, political decision makers may receive support from incumbents in exchange for providing these regulations. Moreover, these entry controls may offer opportunities that allow officials to take bribes. According to the rent-seeking theory, government

115 Philipsen 2011, p. 216.
116 *Ibid.*
117 Mukoyama & Popov 2014, p. 383.
118 Svorny 2000, p. 300.

intervention in economic activities is a principal cause of corruption.[119] An important reason to create licensing obligations is that licensing officials are empowered to deny licensing applications, so they can have opportunities to collect bribes.[120]

Below, this section explores the above hypothesis through ascertaining what interests politicians, public officials and incumbents may have in imposing establishment licensing requirements on companies. How they can profit from these entry controls provides support that the establishment licensing can be explained on private interest grounds.

First, the interests of incumbent companies are addressed. Incumbents may view business establishment licensing obligations as a protecting measure that can deter the entry of new firms. Existing companies may use regulations to form a barrier to entry. Specifically, incumbent firms could encourage authorities to adopt regulatory measures to inhibit entry by domestic companies in a specific industry. A possible strategy is to lobby for strict safety and pollution standards.[121] It is demonstrated that industry influences the draft of environmental regulation to its advantage. Incumbent firms introduce grandfather clauses when the regulation is drafted, which are used to restrict market entry.[122] Increased difficulties to obtain approval caused by environmental legislation can confer an advantage to incumbents, since entrant companies may face more difficulties in trying to enter a new market.[123]

In China, SOEs may lobby for business establishment licensing requirements to inhibit the entry of privately-owned entrant companies. In developing countries, a group of monopolies, including SOEs may control the market and their status can win government support in making licensing requirements for their own benefits.[124] In China, numerous licensing systems have been established to control entry into the industries that are dominated by SOEs. As a result, these entry controls have protected SOEs' monopolies in the market, almost excluding potential privately-owned entrants completely. Due to the special relationship between SOEs and the Chinese government, it is SOEs that promote the erection of these licensing barriers through abusing administrative power.[125]

Second, the interests of politicians are investigated. The creation of business licensing systems in the set-up process may benefit politicians who want to enhance their power or seek re-election to office. Evidence is found that the general public's level of acceptance of power inequality or power distance should have a significant positive effect on the regulatory measures of new firm entry, and vice versa.[126] In countries like China, where power inequality between the public and the

119 Buchanan *et al.* 1980, p. 3-15.
120 Shleifer & Vishny 1994, p. 1007.
121 Porter 1980, p.7.
122 Maloney & McCormick 1982, p. 100.
123 Dean & Brown 1995, p. 292.
124 Ogus & Zhang 2005, p. 139.
125 Wang 2014a, p. 10.
126 Baptista 2007, p. 787.

government may be more socially acceptable, the society may prefer strict entry controls. By imposing licensing restrictions on newly established companies, politicians may win support from the general public, potentially facilitating their governing power or increasing their chances for re-election.

Third, public choice analysis is applied to public officials involved in the entry controls. Officials' decision-making power to grant business establishment licenses creates opportunities for them to extract bribes. In China, governmental intervention in economic activities, e.g. licenses, has a substantial positive impact on companies' bribery of officials, when the intervention creates benefits (perceived by companies). This finding is supported by the responses from 132 CEOs and vice CEOs of Chinese companies.[127] For example, Wal-Mart Kunming Supermarket bribed a licensing official from the city of Kunming to get approval for the opening of this company.[128] In Ghana, Mozambique, Namibia, Tanzania and Uganda, administrative constraints on the business establishment such as licensing facilitate corruption. The wider the scope of the entry controls, the more the chances to take bribes.[129] In a survey in which 96 Polish start-ups participated, 29 per cent of these firms responded that in Poland, bribes are commonly used to accelerate the registration procedure including acquiring activity-specific approval.[130]

Moreover, licensing officials may use business establishment licensing systems to pocket the relevant licensing fees. In China, public officials seek to increase licensing systems, in order to raise incomes. The exercise of licensing power allows officers to charge all sorts of fees, which are used to improve their salaries in the form of bonuses.[131] For instance, a company registration announcement would be issued after company registration application is approved. According to laws and regulations, this issuing is free of charge, but the AICs in the city of Guangzhou charge fees for this service.[132] A significant part of the expenses of acquiring licenses can be divided among licensing officials through numerous ways.[133] Scholars point out that one of the root causes of pocketing the payment is the low income of licensing officers.[134] In many African countries like Nigeria where the payment of

127 Gao 2011, p. 179 and 181.

128 从亚平，新华社高级记者: 中国要严惩“洋腐败”，A Senior Journalist from the Xinhua News Agency: China Should Severely Punish Corruption by Foreign Invested Companies, available at: <www.peacehall.com/news/gb/china/2006/02/200602120716.shtml> (last accessed 6 April 2016).

129 Emery *et al.* 2000, p. 45.

130 Balcerowicz *et al.* 1998, p. 20.

131 Yang 2003b, p. 29.

132 广州日报，广州市工商收取企业登记公告费属于乱收费，Guangzhou Daily, Charging Fees for Issuing Enterprise Registration Announcement by Guangzhou AICs is Illegal, available at: <http://news.sohu.com/40/36/news213793640.shtml> (last accessed 6 April 2016).

133 Zhuo 2011, p. 106.

134 王战、周汉民，探索“收放”背后的机理性问题，Zhan Wang and Hanming Zhou, Searching for the Underlying Reason of Limiting the Use of Approval Systems, available at: <www.shdrc.gov.cn/main?main_colid=427&top_id=314&main_artid=22442> (last accessed 21 August 2014).

civil servant salaries is often delayed,[135] the problem of stealing licensing fees may be more severe.

6. An Economic Approach to Minimum Capital Requirements in the Set-up Process

This section applies theories of regulation presented in section 2 to minimum capital requirements in the set-up process. The focus of this section is to see whether minimum capital requirements can be justified on public interest grounds or rather explained on private interest grounds.

6.1. *Market Failure Justifications for Minimum Capital Requirements in the Set-up Process*

The following passages discuss public interest reasons to impose minimum capital requirements on start-ups. A possible public interest justification for the requirements in the set-up process is that capitalization rules can be used to tackle information problems and externalities. This section also takes into account alternatives that may be superior to minimum capital requirements.

6.1.1. Information Problems

One of the agency problems in company law is conflicts between shareholders and companies' other constituencies such as creditors. Creditor protection, due to limited liability, turns out to be of more significance in company law than in partnership rules.[136]

It is argued in this section that to study whether capitalization rules are still necessary to protect creditors, one needs to classify the categories of creditors. The following passages distinguish voluntary creditors from other creditors (e.g. tort victims) and discuss voluntary creditors first.

Voluntary creditors do not need to rely on capitalization rules for protection.[137] As pointed out by Mulbert and Birke, due to voluntary creditors' contractual relationship with companies, they can freely decide on credit extension to companies. Whenever corporations are likely to default, they can refuse to grant credits to firms or, optionally, to increase the interest rate to reflect this risk financially. Therefore, voluntary creditors' interests can only be harmed through change to contractual relations made by company owners unilaterally that is beyond the creditors' ex ante control. This means voluntary creditors have to take the risk caused by shareholders' opportunistic activities.[138]

135 Friday Olokor and Ifeanyi Onuba, Civil Servants Threaten Strike over Delayed Salary, available at: <www.punchng.com/business/business-economy/civil-servants-threaten-strike-over-delayed-salary/> (last accessed 21 August 2014).

136 Armour *et al.* 2009b, p. 2 and 3. Armour *et al.* 2009a, p. 36.

137 Schoen 2004, p. 437.

138 Mulbert & Birke 2002, p. 708 and 709.

Armour also argues that some creditors voluntarily provide considerable financial support and are willing to pay transaction costs. The expenses arise from the creditors' activities enabling them to adjust the terms of their loans rationally, e.g. collecting information and negotiation. Thus, these lenders can receive appropriate compensation based on the risk they take.[139] This means they can rely on themselves and reach protection agreements on the ideal amount of capitalization. There is not a necessity to safeguard these creditors by adopting minimum capital requirements.[140] Typical examples of these creditors are banks having economies of scale to carry out the above activities.[141]

With regard to the second type of creditors, minimum capital requirements are an effective means to protect tort victims, though some academics do not agree on this point. These scholars argue that capitalization rules do not effectively protect creditors other than voluntary creditors. Below, are their arguments against capitalization rules first and then point out weaknesses in the arguments.

Capitalization rules do not provide useful protection to creditors that do not adjust their loan terms to reflect the riskiness of their debtors.[142] These creditors such as employees, consumers and trade creditors cannot change their terms easily according to the specific situation of a borrower.[143] Because the conditions for credit extension cannot be adjusted, it is possible for shareholders to seek self-interest at the creditors' costs by way of under-capitalization.[144] Armour examines some types of these creditors and concludes that no group of these creditors receives real protection under minimum capital requirements.[145]

Regarding the protection of tort victims, capitalization rules are a very haphazard way to internalize the costs of risky business.[146] It is impossible for legislators to control the amount of initial capital in a dependable way that can compensate potential tort victims. Neither do registration agencies for establishment.[147] Only the features of the activities can decide how much capital is necessary for firms to realize this internalization.[148] For instance, it is unjustifiable to ask low leveraged software firms to pay the same capital as radioactive waste transportation companies with a high debt ratio.[149] Therefore, the statutory capital is only of symbolic significance.[150]

139 Armour 2006, p. 9. Armour defines these creditors as adjusting creditors. According to Armour, the term 'non-adjusting creditors' is coined by Bebchuk and Freid, see Armour 2006, p. 9.
140 Armour 2006, p. 11.
141 *Ibid.*, p. 9.
142 *Ibid.*, p. 9 and 15.
143 *Ibid.*, p. 9.
144 Armour 2000, p. 363.
145 Armour 2006, p. 15.
146 *Ibid.*, p. 14.
147 Schoen 2004, p. 438.
148 Armour 2006, p. 15.
149 Enriques & Macey 2001, p. 1186.
150 Armour 2000, p. 377.

Moreover, to safeguard the interests of tort victims, other more accurate ways can also internalize the risk such as company insurance tailored to firms' individual situation.[151] Insurers can establish positive correlations between premium and risk. Thus, as the residual claimants in companies, company owners would be compelled to bear the costs of investment decisions.[152] Lifting the corporate veil is also one of the less expensive measures to protect tort victims and the state as tax creditors.[153]

Through collecting information on a worldwide basis, Elkind offers a summary concerning alternatives to capitalization rules. Based on the company, bankruptcy and/or creditor protection legislation, a number of other instruments have been developed in various nations. For example, within the insolvency law framework in some jurisdictions, creditors should be allowed to file claims and take part in the procedure by the end of which any liquidation plan would be approved. Elkind holds that as a practical issue, creditors always prefer these alternatives to minimum capital requirements for protection.[154]

Regarding safeguarding the interests of the state as a tax collector, minimum capital requirements are not appropriate, as remarked by Armour. Legal capital cannot ensure that companies can pay tax after they are established. If firms try to shirk tax responsibility in the process of business operation, they usually use unpaid tax monies to continue operation. In this case, it is very likely that companies have used up their initial capital.[155]

Moreover, the state with valid tax claims can adjust its position to reflect the riskiness of tax evasion to some extent. Through relying on its position for checks and enforcement, the State can strengthen enforcement, based on companies' creditworthiness.[156]

In terms of protecting trade creditors, granting them access to data maintained by credit data authorities would be more beneficial than minimum capital requirements. Due to a short-term horizon since these creditors' debt is usually less than three months, statutory capital is basically of no relevance.[157]

Moreover, empirical evidence suggests trade creditors adjust their positions through varying the amount of loans they make, though the terms provided by them are the same.[158] The number depends on the credit worthiness of loan takers

151 Armour 2006, p. 15.
152 Mulbert & Birke 2002, p. 725.
153 Enriques & Macey 2001, p. 1185 and 1172.
154 Geoffrey M. Elkind, ESQ., Minimum Capital Requirements, a Comparative Analysis, United States Agency for International Development, March, 2007, available at: <http://pdf.usaid.gov/pdf_docs/pnadm740.pdf> (last accessed 12 January 2014).
155 Armour 2006, p. 10.
156 *Ibid.*
157 Geoffrey M. Elkind, ESQ., Minimum Capital Requirements, a Comparative Analysis, United States Agency for International Development, March, 2007, available at: <http://pdf.usaid.gov/pdf_docs/pnadm740.pdf> (last accessed 12 January 2014).
158 Armour 2006, p. 11.

and the range of borrowers' misconduct.[159] Trade creditors have a list of tools e.g. credit rating to alleviate risks caused by companies' hazardous business.[160]

The above arguments against using capitalization rules to protect involuntary creditors, especially those concerning the protection of tort victims, have some weak spots. On the one hand, the experts above do not carefully assess the alternatives to capitalization rules in terms of creditor protection. Therefore, whether these alternative instruments can protect creditors effectively is still a question. The instruments that can prevent an agent from engaging in risky activities e.g. mandatory liability insurance, all have their disadvantages and all come at a price.[161] For instance, lifting the veil of incorporation can only be initiated in exceptional cases in most jurisdictions. On the other hand, some scholars ignore the fact that minimum capital requirements have some advantages in safeguarding the interests of tort victims. The text below shows that in some cases, minimum capital requirements may be still useful to provide protection to tort victims.

First, minimum capital requirements can be an option, in cases where firms are not able to get insurance for tort damages. According to Fares and Abou-Bakr, insurers are not willing to cover risks caused by natural catastrophes.[162] Some insurance companies refuse to include coverage for property damage resulting from (natural) disasters and argue that such risks cannot be insured.[163] A case in point is the oil transport industry. Insurance companies are reluctant to sell insurance against risks in this industry, since insurance claims for environmental damages can be infinite.[164]

Second, compared to insurance, minimum capital requirements may be relatively less expensive to companies. When purchasing insurance, businesses cannot get back their insurance premium, regardless of whether accidents occur. The premium paid by firms can even be higher than the expected harm resulting from participating in risky actives. By contrast, with minimum asset requirements, companies compensate victims only when accidents happen.

Third, Shavell argues that if insurers cannot observe levels of care, asset requirements may be better than mandatory liability insurance to provide incentives for companies to reduce risks. Due to moral hazard, mandatory liability insurance tends to dilute firms' incentives to avoid harmful activities. Shavell reaches his conclusion through studying his economic model.[165]

Fourth, theoretically, there is a possibility to differentiate between the amounts of legal capital for different types of companies. Thus, minimum capital requirements maybe can have a flexible response to a real risk of firms in a particular industry.

159 Petersen & Rajan 1997, p. 678 and 679.
160 Mulbert & Birke 2002, p. 714.
161 Wagner 2009, p. 398.
162 Fares & Abou-Bakr 2013, p. 100.
163 Faure & Bruggeman 2008, p. 27 and 28.
164 Faure & Wang 2003, p. 249 and 250.
165 Shavell 2005, p. 74.

In sum, it is not necessary to protect voluntary creditors through minimum capital requirements. Nevertheless, the interests of involuntary creditors still need to be safeguarded. Capitalization rules are an alternative means to protect these creditors, even though some scholars deny that asset requirements can offer effective protection. Having compared insurance with minimum capital requirements, this section shows some advantages the second instrument has for tort victim protection.

6.1.2. Externalities

A company with lower capitalization is more likely to carry out hazardous business.[166] The issue discussed here can also be understood as moral hazard in a corporate governance context.

Section 6.1.1 has demonstrated that there is no necessity to adopt minimum capital requirements for voluntary creditor protection. Below, the passages analyse whether capitalization rules can effectively internalize the externalities caused by companies' risky activities, thereby protecting involuntary creditors.

Legally required capital requirements are one way to internalize the costs arising from the incentive to take risks.[167] Minimum capital rules can curb the potential risk takings of undercapitalized firms. If capitalization rules are combined with the restrictions on returning capital to shareholders, firms will have more difficulties if they conduct risky business.[168]

Nevertheless, the argument seems weak that minimum capital requirements make it difficult for companies to conduct risky activities. Armour argues that minimum capital cannot prevent a decrease in firms' assets in future.[169] According to Schoen, the provision on capital contribution and maintenance is irrelevant to whether firms go bankrupt or not. These rules only govern the activity that shareholders transfer properties to companies.[170] In the case of filing for insolvency, ventures' initial capital has already been exhausted possibly.[171] The future reduction in capital inevitably undermines the minimum capital requirements' function in curbing companies' tendency to conduct hazardous business. Thus, it seems that minimum capital requirements cannot effectively deal with the externalities stemming from companies' hazardous activities; therefore, involuntary creditors cannot be well protected.

166 Easterbrook & Fischel 1996, p. 60.
167 *Ibid.*
168 Armour 2006, p. 11.
169 Armour 2000, p. 378.
170 Schoen 2004, p. 437.
171 Armour 2009c, p. 131.

6.2. *Private Interest Explanations for Minimum Capital Requirements in the Set-up Process*

The private interest economists warn of the danger that incumbents are able to support the imposition of minimum capital requirements on newly established companies. Obviously, minimum capital requirements may be used as an entry barrier. It is clear that the financial resources invested by new entrants form an entry cost. Moreover, the more significant the amount of capitalization rules, the more difficult entering a market will be. Thus, incumbents tend to compete with entrant firms to win the favour of politicians and lobby for the creation of minimum capital requirements. Due to the motive to maximize votes, those who make the regulation may succumb to the lobbying of incumbents to impose minimum capital requirements on new entrants.

Empirical studies have demonstrated that minimum capital requirements place obstacles in the ways of forming companies. Relying on the database and the survey results of the Word Bank, Doing Business shows that a strong negative correlation exists between capitalization rules and the amount of new registered companies globally. This provides clear evidence that the requirements obstruct entrepreneurial activity, thus, barriers to business growth are erected.[172] A research of 5 EU Member States also indicates that abolishing capitalization rules makes the establishment of small and medium-sized firms easier.[173] Based on these empirics, one can learn that minimum capital requirements give rise to costs, though as section 6.1 demonstrates, these requirements can increase social welfare.

The following passages demonstrate that some interest groups can benefit from imposing minimum capital requirements on entrants. The role of these interest groups in the formation of the regulation supports the idea that capitalization rules, in some circumstances, can be explained on private interest grounds.

First, incumbent companies can benefit from capitalization rules. If companies are burdened with strict capital requirements, entry barriers will be created and existing ventures will be allowed to ask high prices.[174] Enriques and Macey (2001) demonstrate that legal capital rules provided by the Second Directive profit incumbent producers in the EU, and particularly incumbents in the most mature markets. The reason is that it becomes harder to start companies in the relevant markets due to these provisions.[175]

Many legal professionals hold that minimum capital requirements lead to unnecessary regulatory burdens and deter the establishment of companies.[176] Mandatory initial capital functions as entry fees for potential entrepreneurs. Even if the amount of such costs may be small in most cases, small companies may have

172 Doing Business 2014, p. 45.

173 *Ibid*., p. 43.

174 Easterbrook & Fischel 1996, p. 60.

175 Enriques & Macey 2001, p. 1203.

176 Geoffrey M. Elkind, ESQ., Minimum Capital Requirements, a Comparative Analysis, United States Agency for International Development, March, 2007, available at: <http://pdf.usaid.gov/pdf_docs/pnadm740.pdf> (last accessed 12 January 2014).

difficulties to pay the 'entry fee'. Shareholders' capital contribution responsibility prior to registration or conducting business postpones or limits their competence to establish firms.[177] Start-up capital can impose financial burdens especially to potential entrepreneurs with innovative technology and college graduates that lack initial finances.

Apart from capitalization, there may be other expenses caused by minimum capital requirements, e.g. legal expenses in most cases. For example, the legal capital rules of the EU unreasonably impose burdens on firms through ways like requiring companies to afford meaningless expert reports and lawyers' advice.[178]

Moreover, if legally required capital accounts for the lion's share of investors' finances, future shareholders may not be able to cover other costs in the set-up process and may give up their investment plans. Initial capital legally required, especially if its amount is fairly large, could constrain companies' expenditure on other issues, e.g. employing or purchasing equipment.[179]

Second, minimum capital requirements can serve the interests of certain professionals, usually lawyers and accountants, which assist companies in fulfilling the responsibility arising from the requirements. In Europe, accountants and lawyers noticeably benefit from the legal capital doctrine of the Second Directive, according to Enriques and Macey (2001).[180]

As remarked by McCahery and others (2006), lawyers and other legal practitioners that profit from current laws arguably have motives to resist creative rules. Thus, the complete change from existing laws to innovative provisions constitutes a tough task that reform-minded legislators have to face. For example, German law makers decreased legally required capital to 10,000 EUR, rather than eliminating capitalization rules. The reason is that the legislators faced pressure from legal professionals.[181]

Enriques and Macey (2001) argue that companies have to rely on lawyers' guidance on the maze of the provisions in the EU, so lawyers in particular defend the capital provisions of the Second Directive. Due to lawyers' lack of financial and economic expertise, they may honestly but erroneously hold that the capital rules are effective to safeguard creditors' interests. In addition, it is common that company lawyers have spent considerable human resources on understanding the capital provisions. If these rules are abolished, they cannot profit from the human capital any more.[182]

In certain jurisdictions, accountants can significantly profit from minimum capital requirements. In these countries, capital contributed by shareholders has to be checked by accountants before incorporation can be registered. When capital

177 Machado 2010, p. 685.

178 Enriques & Macey 2001, p. 1203.

179 Doing Business 2014, p. 43.

180 Enriques & Macey 2001, p. 1202 and 1203. The doctrine includes minimum capital rules and restrictions on dividend payment, share repurchase and other issues. See Enriques & Macey 2001, p. 1171-1184.

181 McCahery *et al.* 2007, p. 13.

182 Enriques & Macey 2001, p. 1202 and 1203.

contributions are made in non-currency properties, capital verification professionals also play a role in assessing the value of such assets. In China, capital verification is one of the two most important revenue sources for small and medium-sized capital verification institutions.[183] Companies have to pay asset assessment services provided by accountants in the EU, due to the legal capital doctrine.[184]

Therefore, accountants tend to block the abolishing of minimum capital requirements. In China, nationwide reform measures to abandon capitalization rules and capital verification responsibility have encountered much opposition from the accountant association, according to a partner from one Chinese law firm (2014). This is because accountants cannot make a profit by providing accountancy services after the elimination.[185]

When implementing pilot projects to eliminate minimum capital requirements in some cities, there has also been much opposition from accountants. For example, Huang (2013) reports that the Shenzhen Institute of Certified Public Accountants opposed the abolishing in Shenzhen most strongly. After removing the requirements, there would be no need to verify initial capital, accounting for one third of accountancy services. This would constitute a hard blow to the whole accountancy industry in Shenzhen and almost 10,000 accountants would lose their jobs, as complained one insider.[186] Similar reform steps in Guangzhou also worried local accountants deeply since there would be no market for accountancy services and their interests would be harmed.[187]

Third, if incorporation registration authorities are authorized to verify that minimum capital requirements are satisfied before registration, they may have chances to seek rents. The agencies are likely to acquire power or bribes, because the delay in verifying leads to the failure of establishment. This can cause substantial losses to investors, especially if they have invested significantly in formation. All the entrepreneurs' time and effort will be wasted, in the case of stating that they do not comply with capitalization rules. Therefore, entrepreneurs may be willing to provide bribes in order to receive approval from the registration authorities.

183 李少鹏，烟台中小会计所面临生存困境，部分人员另找出路，Shaopeng Li, Small and Medium-sized Capital Verification Institutions may Close Down, Some Employees Find Other Jobs, available at: <http://news.shm.com.cn/2013-11/25/content_4179985.htm> (last accessed 14 January 2014).

184 Enriques & Macey 2001, p. 1202 and 1203.

185 中国青年报，公司法大修： 门槛降低实惠与风险一起进门，The China Youth Daily, The Revision of Company Law can Lower Entry Barriers and Bring Risks at the Same Time, available at: <www.chinacapitallaw.com/article/default.asp?id=12504> (last accessed 12 January 2014).

186 黄金萍：深圳：公司如何自由出生，"阻力很大，跟各路人马PK"，南方周末，Jinping Huang, Shenzhen: how can Ensure Free Incorporation, 'Facing too Much Opposition and Dealing with Different Interest Groups', Southern Weekly, available at: <www.infzm.com/content/88780> (last accessed 12 January 2014).

187 广州商事改革如何体现"宽进严管"？，南方周末，How to Follow the Principle of Lowering Entry Barriers but Strengthening Supervision Afterward in Guangzhou's Commercial Registration Reform, Southern Weekly, available at: <http://blog.soufun.com/22324976/-16754780/articledetail.htm> (last accessed 12 January 2014).

According to empirical evidence, higher minimum capital requirements robustly deter firms' entry into the market, but corruption significantly increases the number of start-ups in the presence of such barriers to entry.[188]

Fourth, banks can profit from capitalization rules. Any meaningful start-up capitalization rules would cause unreasonable financial burdens to companies that want to enter the securities markets.[189] According to Downs, if minimum capital requirements exceed the amount of equity that achieves a sufficient return rate for any firms' share-holders, such rules have simply hindered the utilization of these markets by these companies. Such hindrance can still be caused even in the case that public offering is likely to be the cheapest source to raise capital.[190] In Europe, banks benefit significantly from the legal capital rules in the Second Directive e.g. minimum capital requirements and want to keep them, as argued by Enriques and Macey (2001). This is because these provisions have a negative effect on the equity market. Thus, banks' market power in the European financial markets is preserved.[191]

7. Conclusion

Both public and private interest reasons can explain government intervention in business establishment. According to the public interest approach, licensing in the set-up process can be justified on the grounds of externalities and information problems. Licensing seems to be a suitable regulatory measure in the case of significant externalities and serious information problems. In other cases, alternatives i.e. registration and certification should be considered, since licensing restricts market entry more than these alternative instruments.

Externalities and information problems are also a potential justification for imposing minimum capital requirements on newly established companies. The interests of some creditors, e.g. tort victims, need to be protected and capitalization rules may provide better protection than other instruments such as insurance. Minimum capital requirements can be used to internalize the costs caused by companies' incentives to carry out hazardous activities, but this function appears weak due to a potential decrease in companies' assets.

From a public choice perspective, this section has identified some interest groups that can benefit from imposing licensing requirements on start-ups. Licensing in the set-up process can protect existing companies against competition from new entrants. The creation of business establishment licensing regimes can also help politicians to be re-elected or facilitate their ruling power and allow officials to take bribes and pocket licensing fees.

Incumbent companies, some professionals (e.g. accountants), incorporation registration agencies and banks can all obtain benefits from minimum capital requirements. In particular, there are many studies which demonstrate that

188 Dreher & Gassebner 2013, p. 415.
189 Enriques & Macey 2001, p. 1200.
190 *Ibid.*
191 *Ibid.*, p. 1203.

capitalization rules can benefit the first two types of interest groups. Learning from these studies, one can argue that minimum capital requirements can be used to restrict entry into the market, serving the interest of existing companies. The creation of minimum capital requirements may lead to other legal obligations, for example if they require newly established companies to purchase services from lawyers and accountants.

Taking into account both the private and public explanations, one should be careful about adopting licensing requirements and minimum capital requirements in the set-up process. On the one hand, there may be public interest reasons in favour of some licensing and minimum capital requirements concerning new business establishment. On the other hand, the reality shows that interest groups sometimes abuse the public interest arguments and introduce licensing regimes to benefit themselves, thereby pursuing private interests. Moreover, even in the case of serious information asymmetry or significant externalities, licensing will not always have to be employed in the establishment procedure. The same problem may arise with the protection of creditors. The protection of creditors is often used as an argument in favour of employing minimum capital requirements in the establishment process. However, other instruments, e.g. insurance, could equally protect creditors as well as minimum capital requirements.

Chapter 5

A LAW AND ECONOMICS VIEW ON CENTRALIZATION OF THE REGULATION OF THE CROSS-BORDER ESTABLISHMENT OF COMPANIES

1. Introduction

Chapter 4 offered the public and private interest reasons for national authorities to regulate the establishment of companies. Licensing and minimum capital requirements were discussed in Chapter 4 as two ways to regulate business establishment. Chapter 5 studies the cross-border establishment of companies in a multi-level jurisdiction and provides economic explanations for the regulation of cross-border establishment. The discussion in this chapter covers conditions of licensing for business establishment such as environmental standards and labour and safety requirements, since these conditions are of particular importance for the set-up process.

The study in Chapter 5 raises two questions. In section 2, the question is addressed whether cross-border business establishment should be regulated by rules different from the regulations of the establishment of companies. After that, sections 3 to 7 treat the issue whether the existence of the cross-border establishment is a reason to shift the regulatory competence to a higher level. More specifically, section 3 briefly introduces competitive federalism and fiscal federalism, followed by section 4 that discusses the criteria for centralization. Section 5 applies the arguments from section 4 to cross-border business establishment. Section 6 considers whether it is necessary to regulate cross-border establishment at central level, in order to deal with local protectionism. In section 7, attention is shifted to the implications of public choice theory for the centralization of the regulation of cross-border establishment. Section 8 contains a conclusion.

2. An Economic Analysis of the Regulation of the Cross-border Establishment of Companies

2.1. *Public Interest Reasons for Regulating the Cross-border Establishment of Companies*

When companies establish businesses across borders, the investment destination may impose stricter establishment requirements on these non-local companies than local enterprises. The public interest reason for greater regulation of the cross-border establishment of companies can be information asymmetry. Compared to businesses funded by local enterprises, consumers may have more difficulties to find information about companies formed by investors from other states, for example in relation to the reputation of a company. As Jeng asserts, company reputation is a signal of quality when considering buying new products or services. Nevertheless, he points out that the reputations influence customers' assessment of the quality only before the goods or services are used.[1] Due to the difficulty of knowing the reputations of subsidiaries established by non-local companies, local consumers cannot rely on this attribute to judge whether these subsidiaries' new products and services are good. Hence, governmental intervention may be more necessary to alleviate the information asymmetry problem associated with the products and services of these subsidiaries.

2.2. *Private Interest Explanations for Regulating the Cross-border Establishment of Companies*

Incumbents and local entrants may try to make companies establishing businesses across borders subject to strict establishment regulation. Chapter 3 has demonstrated that usually different interest groups compete with each other to win favourable regulation. Regulators favour the pressure groups that win the competition. In situations of cross-border establishment of companies, three competing interest groups can be recognized: existing companies, local entrants and non-local entrants. Moreover, the following assumption can be proposed. Incumbents usually lobby for stringent establishment rules for the two sorts of entrants, since regulation, as entry barriers, can profit incumbent companies. Local entrant firms often want lenient requirements to benefit their establishment, but strict requirements to deter market entry by potential entrant companies from other states. By contrast, non-local entrant firms usually lobby for rules that allow them to enter easily, but make entry by local entrants more difficult. Possibly, one consequence of the competition could be that business formation provisions would be made for all entrants, regardless of their registration places. Moreover, companies from other jurisdictions would face stricter entry restrictions than local competitors. In this case, entry barriers would be created, potentially profiting existing companies. As another benefiting party, local entrants can benefit from the stringent cross-border establishment regulation for non-local companies.

Furthermore, politicians may make strict requirements for the cross-border establishment of companies. There are always incentives for state political rulers in decentralized regimes to impede the movement of goods, workers and capital over state borders.[2] Local governments could deny the right of capital, services and

1 Jeng 2011, p. 854.
2 Rodden & Rose-Ackerman 1997, p. 1547.

workers from other jurisdictions to enter their territories.[3] In some cases, they erect regulatory barriers for non-residents through various ways, including offering preferential treatment to local capital.[4] As chapter 3 has pointed out, politicians offer regulation to meet the interests of the interest group that has the strongest influence on them. In return, the pressure group provides political leaders with votes and other things beneficial to re-election. In the case that local companies win the above competition, the wish of these companies would be fulfilled. More stringent establishment rules would be imposed on non-local companies than on local enterprises.

Moreover, providing strict establishment regulation for non-local firms allows officials to take bribes. As discussed in chapter 3, if business licensing systems are established, corruption opportunities for officials can be created. This is because public officials are entitled to decide whether or not permits will be granted.

3. The Economics of Federalism

The economics of federalism, in the context of the US, can be classified into two branches: competitive federalism and fiscal federalism. Competitive federalism studies competition between states. Fiscal federalism focuses on the division of regulatory competences between the federal and state governments.[5]

3.1. *Competitive Federalism*

The Tiebout model is the starting point for the traditional analysis of inter-jurisdictional competition.[6] Tiebout argues that citizens can influence the provision of public goods at local levels by votes or by moving.[7] Residents can use votes to influence decision makers to provide local services satisfying their preferences. People can also vote with their feet to choose communities according to their personal preferences. Residents with similar preferences clustering together leads to an efficient provision of local public goods.[8] For example, people who want jobs could move to communities that offer abundant job opportunities, even if living conditions in these communities may be poor. In accord with these citizens' demands, some jurisdictions will probably construct factories to expand employment opportunities.

3 Deakin 2006, p. 442.

4 Anwar Shah, Interregional Competition and Federal Cooperation - To Compete or to Cooperate? That's Not the Question in Anwar Shah (ed.), Macrofederalism and Local Finances (Washington DC: World Bank, 2007), available at: <http://info.worldbank.org/etools/docs/library/207227/InterregionalCompetitionandFederal.pdf> p. 8 (last accessed 10 July 2014).

5 Kobayashi & Ribstein 2007, p. xiii.

6 Heremans 2012, p. 91.

7 Faure 2003, p. 40.

8 Tiebout 1956, p. 416.

Tiebout's model is also applicable to legal rules. Regulations in a given local community will correspond with the preferences of companies and residents in this jurisdiction. Firms and citizens will move to communities whose laws best reflect their preferences.[9] Competition between law makers leads to some benefits: different legal rules can satisfy various preferences better and make different experiences possible.[10] In the ideal world of Tiebout, residents will sort themselves into jurisdictions whose laws best reflect their preferences. When citizens with full information are not satisfied with the legal rules provided, they can move to states that best satisfy their preferences.[11]

Competition between legal orders is assumed to realize an efficient provision of legal rules and some conditions should be fulfilled to achieve this competition.[12] The conditions include a sufficiently large number of legislators, full information about alternative legal rules that are available and mobility of residents or production factors.[13] Moreover, the decisions in one legal system should not impose external effects on other legal orders.[14]

As held by Van den Bergh, competition between legal orders initiates a learning process. One state might change its legislation due to amendments to codes in other states. Otherwise, there is a risk that companies from this state will relocate in the places that are most responsive to their preferences for legal rules.[15]

3.2. *Fiscal Federalism*

Taking Tiebout's model as a starting point, reasons can be found to support a 'bottom up federalism'. In principle the local level is always better at providing public goods, because the local level is better at knowing local problems and matching citizens' preferences. Only when some criteria are satisfied should decisions be made at a higher level.[16] Section 3.1 has demonstrated that Tiebout's model can be extended to law making. Therefore, as a principle, legal rules should be provided at local levels, e.g. national governments in the EU or provincial governments in China. Only in some circumstances, the provision of legal rules should be moved to a higher level.

Economists have provided efficiency criteria for shifting law-making power to the central, federal or transnational level. Reasons for centralization are to internalize trans-boundary externalities, to avoid a 'race to the bottom', to achieve economies of scale and to reduce transaction costs.[17] The arguments in favour of

9 Van den Bergh 1994, p. 340.
10 Van den Bergh 2000, p. 437.
11 Faure 2003, p. 40.
12 Faure 2001, p. 266.
13 Van den Bergh 2000, p. 438.
14 Faure 2001, p. 267.
15 Van den Bergh 1994, p. 345.
16 Faure 1998, p. 171.
17 Van den Bergh 2000, p. 436.

centralization will be presented in section 4. It should be noted that these arguments still need to be evaluated on the basis of empirical evidence.

4. Economic Arguments in Favour of Centralization

4.1. *Internalizing Trans-boundary Externalities*

Trans-boundary externalities may be an argument in favour of centralization. In the case of interstate externalities, decentralized entities lack motives to enact strict rules applying to their own residents if the adverse effects of activities only materialize in third states. Therefore, without centralized rulemaking, trans-boundary externalities might lead to inefficiencies.[18] Visscher provides an example. If the air pollution originated in state A mainly affects the air quality of state B, state A would make lenient regulations for environmental protection. If state A makes rules for its own interests, this obviously decreases the joint welfare of state A and B.[19] In case that negotiations between countries cannot deal with the trans-boundary problem due to the countries' strategic behaviour, trans-boundary externalities may be a powerful argument for centralization.[20]

It should be noted that only if countries are able to externalize negative effects, interstate externalities may justify centralized rulemaking or multilateral agreements among Member States in the EU. Moreover, as Van den Bergh points out, trans-boundary externalities can provide justifications for centralized rulemaking only when national law cannot effectively cope with trans-boundary problems. Only in some cases, national laws are not able to deal with the relevant externalities arising from the private laws of another decentralized entity. For example, national legislation generally does not address tort damages caused by its own citizens in another state.[21]

4.2. *Avoiding a 'Race to the Bottom'*

A 'race to the bottom' means that states, as the providers of regulations, may try to attract mobile factors by providing regulations attractive to them. States may lower the standards for the protection of the environment, labour etc., in order to pursue their own interests e.g. to attract capital. There is a fear that states may compete with each other to offer more attractive regulations to companies. As a result, their laws for the protection will be lowered to a sub-optimal level. A 'race to the bottom' may be an argument in favour of centralization.[22]

It should be noted that not all researchers believe that, in theory, regulatory competition will lead to a 'race to the bottom'. William Fischel studies the competition among jurisdictions for industrial locations and holds that this

18 Faure 2003, p. 42.
19 Visscher 2012, p. 80.
20 Van den Bergh 2008, p. 80-95.
21 Van den Bergh 2000, p. 446.
22 Visscher 2012, p. 81.

competition results in socially beneficial results rather than in a 'race to the bottom'. In the model of Fischel, jurisdictions allow business establishment in their zones, only when companies compensate the damages caused by the investment. Jurisdictions that attach great importance to environmental protection will permit fewer firms to be established and get less compensation. If there are any citizens who want higher payment, they can move to a state that does not highly value environmental quality.[23]

Since theoretically it is uncertain whether regulatory competition leads to a 'race to the bottom', the question ultimately needs to be answered by empirical evidence.[24] The empirical evidence for the race to the bottom argument is weak.[25] Referring to some empirical studies, Drezner demonstrates that in some cases, companies move manufacturing to countries with lax labour standards. Nevertheless, in other cases, these standards are irrelevant to the decision making of investment destinations.[26]After reviewing an extensive literature, Faure shows that in the field of environmental law, low environmental standards are a trivial factor in choosing production locations.[27]

The above analysis shows that regulatory competition may cause the problem of a 'race to the bottom'. The principle of mutual recognition is often thought of as a way to ensure regulatory competition, while at the same time avoiding a 'race to the bottom'. This principle asks two or more states to recognize one another's regulations that provide equal protection.[28]

However, Kerber and Van den Bergh (2008) hold that the rule of mutual recognition cannot enable regulatory competition. Under the principle of mutual recognition, regulators of one state can make mandatory rules for domestic producers, but not for non-local companies that sell products in this state. As a result, this jurisdiction no longer has regulatory autonomy over its market and cannot enact laws to reflect the preferences of citizens from this jurisdiction.[29]

Moreover, according to the two academics, the EU experience shows that the main rationale for applying mutual recognition is to initiate a process of reallocating regulatory authority in a two-level system of regulations. This application can be used as a test for breaking up an old structure of regulatory powers in the EU (national regulatory autonomy plus the country of destination principle).The practice in the EU also demonstrates that mutual recognition is very likely to trigger off a process towards (de facto) harmonization. For example, since the Cassis de Dijon ruling, the CJEU has introduced the principle of mutual recognition in some cases, which gives the European Commission and the EU Member States two choices. They are urged either to reallocate regulatory powers as the court decides

23 Revesz 1992, p. 1237 and 1238.
24 Van den Bergh 2000, p. 445.
25 Visscher 2012, p. 81.
26 Drezner 2006, p. 7.
27 Faure 2003, p. 58 and 59.
28 Pelkmans 2005, p. 90.
29 Kerber & Van den Bergh 2008, p. 453 and 454.

or to bring forward their own plans for the reallocation. In some fields, directives are approved that choose (partial) harmonization as solutions.[30]

4.3. *Reducing Transaction Costs and Profiting from Scale Economies*

If important scale economies exist, centralized rulemaking may be necessary.[31] Centralization can exploit scale economies, in the case where it is less expensive to have one regulator at the central level rather than several regulators at the local level.[32] For example, since the establishment of a law making organ costs a fixed amount of money, it would be more economical if the enacted rules apply to more citizens. Moreover, legislation may have other costs, such as the legal knowledge and the production of information needed to make legal rules, which may also involve economies of scale to some degree.[33]

There may also be an economic argument for centralization, if centralization can save substantial transaction costs.[34] The essence of the transaction cost argument is that the existing differences in legal systems cause legal uncertainty and increase the costs of international transactions. Such legal diversity leads to several types of costs. For instance, participants in transactions have to spend on costs about getting to know the laws of different countries and drafting different contracts for different states.[35]

However, the reduction of transaction costs is a valid argument in favour of centralization only when the transaction cost savings of uniform law outweighs the advantages of differentiated legislation.[36] A variety of laws provides substantial advantages that different legal rules can be made to meet the preferences of citizens.[37]As Wagner points out, diversity in laws also means regulatory competition, which leads to an efficient result including a learning process of different law makers etc. Moreover, competition is the most efficient way to control the rent seeking behaviour of politicians such as increasing their budget by all means.[38]

According to Wagner, the impact of harmonization on transaction cost savings should not be over-estimated. Much evidence can be found that full harmonization would cause considerable costs of restructuring old bureaucracies.[39] Moreover, as Van den Bergh and Visscher hold, transaction costs saved by uniform laws may not be substantial. The harmonization of laws may require translation, which may generate language differences. As a result, the same provision may be given several

30 *Ibid.*, p. 461 and 462.
31 Van den Bergh 1994, p. 343.
32 Visscher 2012, p. 82.
33 Heremans 2012, p. 107.
34 Van den Bergh 1994, p. 343.
35 Visscher 2012, p. 82.
36 Faure 2003, p. 42.
37 Faure 1998, p. 173.
38 Wagner 2011a, p. 56 and 57.
39 *Ibid.*

interpretations. If different interpretations of the law exist, harmonized rules cannot increase legal certainty.[40]

5. Centralization of the Regulation of the Cross-border Establishment of Companies from an Economic Perspective

5.1. *Trans-boundary Externalities*

As demonstrated by Rodden and Rose-Ackerman, apart from local protectionism, inefficiency from inter-jurisdictional competition can be another problem associated with decentralization. This competition can encourage states to generate externalities favouring local firms and people, at a cost to other states. For instance, firms are perhaps permitted to be situated on state borders, thus, these companies can be a source of pollution to bordering states.[41]

Naturally, regulating at a higher level (e.g. transnational, federal) is one method of approaching the inefficiency from inter-jurisdictional competition for business formation. For instance, Centralization can effectively react to trans-boundary pollution. Leaders in a decentralized unit will lack motives to impose strict environmental requirements on polluters that may have the ability to transport the pollution to another jurisdiction. Obviously, the polluting business operation could bring benefits such as tax revenues to this unit, while the pollution will materialize in the neighbouring country. States would have incentives to internalize the externality, but only if they enact legislation that can be effectively enforced.[42]

As Bowman argues, effective interstate cooperation may provide an alternative solution. The relevant empirical information demonstrates that in the 1990s, the states of the US cooperated with each other to seek common goals or address common issues. Even when unbridled competition exists, a multi-state cooperation mechanism may also be created, since 'loosing states' choose to make collective efforts that are deemed to improve the chances for success. For instance, there had been much competition among five states to attract new companies. In 1989, these five jurisdictions established the Pacific Northwest Economic Region that functions as a multistate cooperation program to promote investment in the region.[43]

Nevertheless, according to Bowman, one cannot jump to conclusions that interstate agreements can be used as an alternative to federal laws without any problem. The actions of states are motivated by self-interest, so the probability of coordination and cooperation between fifty states in the US is always problematic. On a particular affair, states will show different willingness to participate in interstate accords.[44]

40 Van den Bergh & Visscher 2006, p. 521.
41 Rodden & Rose-Ackerman, p. 1547.
42 Faure 2014b, p. 237.
43 Bowman 2004, p. 544.
44 *Ibid.*, p. 545.

Another problem of interstate cooperation is that it proves hard to implement interstate agreements. As Ruhl points out, cooperative interstate agreements, without powerful interstate enforcement agencies, are unlikely to effectively control interstate pollution and plan resource development that may have trans-boundary effects. The interstate authorities should have at least as much authority as the federal organizations responsible for enforcing federal regulations.[45]

An alternative to centralized governance in the EU is multilateral agreements between the Member States concerned. If the influence of an externality problem is relevant only in a few countries and the risk of strategic behaviour is likely to be alleviated, bargaining between states on the basis of well-defined property rights may produce efficient results. In this regard, attention should be paid to organizing the bargaining and enforcing the agreements reached.[46]

In sum, centralization and interstate cooperation (or multilateral agreements between Member States of the EU) are two approaches to deal with the inefficiency arising from inter-jurisdictional competition for business establishment. The downside to cooperation among states is that there are no strong enforcement authorities. Moreover, not all states are willing to join in such cooperation due to their self-interest.

5.2. *A Race to the Bottom*

A race to the bottom in the business establishment field means that states are induced to lower e.g. environmental, public health and safety standards in order to attract investment. In a response, firms will set up businesses in the state with the laxest regulation of business establishment.[47]

Simply put, the concern is that, if a race to the bottom in case of business establishment regulation occurs, social welfare cannot be maximized without federal or transnational regulation. All states will offer more lenient legislation in terms of environmental protection, public safety etc. than those they would enact where there is no competition for mobile factors, especially firms.[48] As a result, there would be less environmental protection, greater risks of safety hazards and a race to the bottom in the domain of other standards.

According to Klevorick, the engagement of decentralized units in a race to the bottom is decided by how states compete with each other. Therefore, we need to collect the information of the market concerned, in order to understand the existence of a race to the bottom. Empirical studies are needed to know how competing states impose the requirements of environmental protection, labour

45 Ruhl 1988, p. 314.

46 Van den Bergh 2000, p. 446.

47 The race to the bottom to attract businesses has been frequently discussed. For example, Stone explains the race to the bottom in labor standards (Stone 2007, p. 565 and 566). Revesz discusses the race to the bottom in environmental standards (Revesz 1992, p. 1210-1255).

48 Klevorick 1996, p. 178.

safety and product safety on companies. Empirical data is further required to consider how lenient environmental standards influence firm locations.[49]

Previous evidence seems to suggest that a race to the bottom does not exist, at least in the domain of environmental protection. As Faure points out, a significant body of literature shows that there is no strong empirical evidence to support the 'pollution haven' hypnosis. Environmental regulation is only a trivial influence in the relocation decisions made by businesses.[50] However, according to the recent empirical literature on competition between American states, such regulation is statistically important to affect companies' decision of where to establish.[51]

It should be noted that scholars have different opinions about whether the race to the bottom in the domain of environmental protection justifies environmental regulatory centralization. According to Faure and Johnston, 3 different views have been conveyed on this issue. There is ongoing debate among legal academics over whether the race to the bottom rationale offers justification for environmental regulatory federalization. Law and economics academics tend to attach importance to the benefits arising from competition between local governments. Other legal scholars have a tendency to conclude that the race to the bottom rationale for centralization is valid.[52]

As far as other standards that can influence site choosing are concerned, there seem to be few empirical studies. Braun (1998) lists all the factors that have an impact on the cross-border relocation of small and medium German manufacturers and assesses their importance to the relocation. The top 6 elements (in descending order) are lower labour costs, access to new markets, penetration of existing markets, reaction to moves by competitors, differences in costs for supplies and shortage of production capacities. Among all the other factors, demands of major customers ranks No. 7, followed by lower environmental standards, enlargement of the range of products, lower level of taxation, currency-related advantages, import restrictions and trade barriers and other motives.[53]

In short, the question whether states are involved in a race to the bottom to attract business establishment cannot be answered without empirical evidence. Without referring to the evidence of the market concerned, one cannot suppose this problem exists among decentralized jurisdictions. The reality is that, as Vadlamannati (2011) points out, there is scant information on the potential effects of competition to promote investment within a nation.[54]

49 *Ibid.*, p. 180.

50 Faure 2003, p. 58 and 59.

51 Faure 2011, p. 398.

52 Faure & Johnston 2009, p. 246.

53 Braun 1998, p. 257.

54 Krishna Chaitanya Vadlamannati, A Race to Compete for Investment among Indian States? – An Empirical Investigation, p. 4, available at: <www.uni-heidelberg.de/md/awi/-professuren/intwipol/regional.pdf> (last accessed 16 July 2014).

5.3. *Economies of Scale and Transaction Costs*

Scale economies may be significant for the production of rules of public law. Scale economies arise if the information collected by a single legislator is relevant at national level.[55]

Nevertheless, centralization of business establishment regulation cannot always profit from scale economies in information. In some cases, information necessary for the regulation in one jurisdiction is not relevant for another. For example, carbon monoxide emissions regulation that passes cost-benefit analysis in health protection in Denver's business district may be seriously wasteful in a mountain state.[56] Moreover, similar to Tiebout, Aubert and Laffont hold that the local level has better information about managing natural material e.g. forest. This is the reason why there is a tendency for the local authorities to make regulation for the management.[57]

Scale economies could not provide a strong argument in favour of a far-reaching centralization in the field of business establishment, but transaction cost saving seems to be even weaker. Clearly, it cannot be denied that a single set of business establishment rules may lead to reduction of transaction costs. This is because lawyers and entrepreneurs do not need to learn different legal systems. If firms want to expand in other Member States and this expansion is governed by the host state provision, persistent differences in state company law can be a hindrance to the freedom of establishment.[58] Harmonization of company law may decrease the transaction costs of incorporation and facilitate capital movement across borders.[59]

However, it is vital to note that the potential decrease in transaction costs of harmonization should be balanced against the advantages of differentiated legislation.[60] Section 3 already points out the advantages of decentralization. This section shows that differentiation of business establishment regulation can deliver some benefits that cannot be obtained when centralizing the regulation. It remains a matter of empirical evidence to see if the costs outweigh the gains.

First, Enriques argues that harmonization of law creates more difficulties for states to experiment in their search for new regulatory solutions, even prevents such experimentation. There is also less possibility for the monopolist legislators to promote legal innovation. As Woolock points out, just as monopolist markets lack the ability to respond on the market, a single legal system cannot react to changes as promptly as different legal orders that compete with each other.[61]

With specific reference to business establishment regulation, chapter 2 has shown that China's central regulators delayed the experimentation of business deregulation in the Shanghai pilot zone. These agencies created numerous business

55 Van den Bergh 1998, p. 145.
56 Hahn *et al.* 2003, p. 47.
57 Aubert & Laffont 2003, p. 20.
58 Enriques & Gatti 2006, p. 960.
59 Barnard & Deakin 2002, p. 219.
60 Faure 1998, p. 173.
61 Enriques 2006b, p. 77.

licensing regimes through laws and regulations and had entrenched interests in keeping these licensing systems. Therefore, they became the greatest opposition to the deregulation innovation. It was even anticipated that the regulators would stall the pilot reform.

Second, a decentralized system for cross-border establishment allows for regulatory competition, which can generate certain advantages. One main benefit for decentralization of regulation could be that regulatory competition guarantees efficiency in the provision of local public goods.[62] With increasing levels of capital mobility in the future, people begin to accept that governments have to pursue economic policies more efficiently, according to Geradin and McCahery. This is because governments with the most efficient level of public good provision are most likely to win competition among jurisdictions for mobile resources. The purpose to attract the production factors has significantly influenced the area of public policy formulation and has been a decisive factor of establishment locations.[63] Obviously, decentralization allows firms to identify the regulation most suitable to the preferences of firms in both formal and substantial terms.[64]

As Vadlamannati notes, because of ending controls of the central government of India over company formation and expansion, states are forced to enter competition to absorb investment. In 1991, India removed the 'license and permit raj' that asked businesses to acquire licenses from the federal government in the case of establishment and expansion. An empirical investigation confirms that the withdrawal of the controls indeed leads to competition, though how states compete with each other depends on their development levels. The interstate competition would increase bureaucratic efficiency, curb corruption, improve investment legislation and investment climate etc. The driving force behind the interstate competition to attract investment is the state governments' wishes to create jobs, promote economic development and seek re-election.[65] Moreover, according to a survey by Kuncoro, in Indonesia, the immediate effect of licensing decentralization on firm locations was that companies began to show their willingness to establish in areas with less corruption.[66]

Third, regulating cross-border establishment at local levels maybe can meet the different needs of different regions. In line with the starting point of Tiebout, Van den Bergh holds that a single set of rules cannot reflect citizens' preferences or adapt to different economic situations as well as a decentralized system where numerous regulatory solutions are possible.[67] Decentralization allows decision makers to make full use of localized data about policy issues and measures to

62 Trachtman 1993, p. 65.

63 Geradin & McCahery 2004, p. 90.

64 Vihanto 1992, p. 411 and 415.

65 Krishna Chaitanya Vadlamannati, A Race to Compete for Investment among Indian States? – An Empirical Investigation, p. 25, available at: <www.uni-heidelberg.de/md/awi/-professuren/intwipol/regional.pdf> (last accessed 16 July 2014).

66 Arji Kuncoro, The Impact of Licensing Decentralization on Firm Location Choice: the Case of Indonesia, available at: <http://siteresources.worldbank.org/DEC/Resources/84797-1251813753820/6415739-1251814020192/kuncoro.pdf> p. 11 (last accessed 17 July 2014).

67 Van den Bergh 1998, p. 130-134.

address these problems.[68] Through tailoring regulatory requirements and solutions to suit societal desires, more efficient regulations can be formulated and social welfare can be increased.[69]

6. Centralization and Internal Market

It is assumed that in a federation, the internal market is the same thing as a single market. Nevertheless, decentralization allows local authorities to make their own rules, which may result in a de facto fragmentation of the national market.[70] It has been indicated in Chapter 3 that although the freedom of establishment has been developed for many years, companies in the EU still face some barriers in their expansion across the borders of Member States. Moreover, Chapter 2 has shown that local licensing authorities in China abuse regulatory power; as a result, companies from one province cannot freely establish branches and subsidiaries in other provinces. Hence, there may be a fear that in case of decentralizing the regulatory authority for the cross-border establishment of companies, local regulatory power may lead to the fragmentation of a single market.

However, according to Trillas, decentralization and the establishment of a unified internal market are obviously not mutually exclusive. Historically, the US is the biggest and most dynamic internal market, but this country adopts great political and administrative decentralization.[71] For example, each US state has its own incorporation rules with slight differences.[72] Although cases about market disintegration can be found in the US, these examples rarely constitute major concern.[73]

It should be noted that according to Montinola, Qian and Weingast, there is almost no possibility to preserve a unified domestic market without explicit protection from federal authorities. For example, without enabling the US Supreme Court to police the domestic market in the US, this common market could not have been sustained during the first half of the nineteenth century. The American experience demonstrates that the states used various kinds of ways to create barriers for interstate commerce. Relying on the American constitution, the US Supreme Court placed significant restraints on these states that encroached upon the free movement of factors.[74]

Apart from judicial bodies, also federal governments can play a role in preserving a unified market. The central government should shoulder the responsibility of ensuring the free flow of the factors of production.[75] If local legislation is designed to shield local business rather than genuinely reflect the

68 Adler 2012, p. 95.
69 Esty & Geradin 2000, p. 239.
70 Tanzil 2000, p. 52.
71 Trillas 2011, p. 33.
72 Klein & Coffee 2004, p. 137-140.
73 Pelkmans 2008, p. 40.
74 Montinala *et al.* 1995, p. 59.
75 Deakin 2006, p. 442.

different preferences of citizens in various states, the central authority should seriously consider deciding on potential intervention with interstate commerce.[76] In some mature federations, e.g. Canada, the US and Australia, the constitutions empower the federal governments to regulate interstate commerce, in order to prohibit states from impeding the free movement of factors.[77]

7. A Public Choice Analysis of the Centralization of the Regulation of the Cross-border Establishment of Companies

Different kinds of interest groups may profit from centralization and therefore support centralization.[78] It is possible to enlarge competences or create entry barriers by asking for the regulation of the cross-border establishment of companies at the central level. The following text identifies some groups that may be interested in shifting the regulation of cross-border business establishment to the central level.

First, politicians and bureaucrats of the central government may favour the centralization of the cross-border establishment regulation. According to Vaubel, policy makers and officials have an interest in (too) much centralization. It is clear that they expect an increase in the financial and human resources and functions of the central authority, in order to enhance their prestige and authority.[79] Due to the promotion motive, the bureaucrats may also seek to enhance the interests of their organization.[80] Obviously, the power and influence of the central government can be broadened by shifting the cross-border establishment regulation to the central level.

Also, central governmental agencies may want to bear the responsibility to regulate cross-border establishment, since this regulatory power allows corruption to occur. Licensing officers, through deciding whether to grant business licenses, can have chances to accept bribes.[81] According to a global survey, stricter entry regulation is generally linked to more serious corruption.[82]

Second, incumbents may require centralized regulations in the field of cross-border business establishment. It has been discussed in chapter 3 that existing companies have an incentive to ask for business establishment regulation as a barrier to new firm entry. Moreover, it is possible that the requirements to form a company differ in different states. Thus, companies from states with high market entry barriers may have an interest in making federal or transnational laws that adopt these strict requirements on business establishment. This adoption may

76 Rose-Ackerman 1993, p. 173.

77 Anwar Shah, Interregional Competition and Federal Cooperation - To Compete or to Cooperate? That's Not the Question in Anwar Shah (ed.), Macrofederalism and Local Finances (Washington DC: World Bank, 2007), available at: <http://info.worldbank.org/-etools/docs/library/207227/InterregionalCompetitionandFederal.pdf> p. 8 ((last accessed 10 July 2014).

78 Van den Bergh 2000, p. 436.

79 Vaubel 1994, p. 153.

80 Schafer 2014, p. 913.

81 Shleifer & Vishny 1994, p. 1007.

82 Djankov *et al.* 2002, p. 26-27.

benefit these firms, since companies from the states with low entry barriers would face stricter market access conditions.

There are examples of incumbents asking for the centralized market entry regulations to restrict the conditions of entry. Oksanen and Valimani hold that the harmonized business legislation of the EU only safeguards the interests of existing firms, prior to providing equal chances for start-ups. This tendency is strongest in the regulation of the rapidly developing information industry. To demonstrate their point, the authors study the most related EU directives on the property rights of software. It has been shown that the relevant legislative procedure has favoured existing companies that can rely on their resources and have an effective way to lobby the national and the EU lawmakers. These directives form entry barriers to new entrants most of which are situated in the new Member States.[83]

Third, the state policy makers and bureaucrats in a federal system may be in favour of the centralization of cross-border establishment regulation. As mentioned above, business establishment requirements may vary in different states. As a result, incumbent companies may have an interest in making the federal regulation on the basis of the state law that imposes the strictest requirements on expansion. The private interest view of policymaking holds that incumbents would lobby their government to design policies benefiting themselves.[84] Because of the vote motive, leaders from the states with more restrictive access conditions would favour their national interest groups i.e. existing firms and ask for the regulation at the central level. According to Potters and Sloof, empirical models also demonstrate that the national pressure groups and other relevant players assess the utility of a legislative draft and try to prompt their government to negotiate from the position towards their own ideal points.[85]

The previous experience demonstrates that centralization is sometimes used as a way to limit competition. According to Canoy, Liddle and Smith, the early lawmakers in the EU tended to utilize the existing laws of member states to form the basis of harmonizing EU regulations. When harmonizing these regulations, the legislators also sought the help of trade associations protecting the interests of existing companies. As a result, EU legislation created entry barriers, which undermined innovation and restricted competition as a consequence.[86]

Moreover, empirical evidence can be found that the national leaders may have an interest in favouring the centralized business regulations. As Enriques points out, the national leaders may choose to harmonize corporate law in the EU, as long as conducting commercial activities in the union may become as costly as in their home state. As a result of raising the costs, the interests of the relevant national

83 Oksanen & Välimäki 2003, p. 3.

84 Chari & Gupta 2008, p. 634.

85 Potters & Sloof 1996, p. 403.

86 Marcel Canoy, Roger Liddle and Peter Smith, The Single Market: Yesterday and Tomorrow, Bureau of European Policy Advisers (BEPA), European Commission, available at: <http://ec.europa.eu/dgs/policy_advisers/publications/docs/single_market_yesterday_and_tmorrow_en.pdf> (last accessed 6 August 2014).

pressure groups can be safeguarded.[87] A typical example is that those Member States that already asked their firms to disclose annual accounts most actively lobbied for a creation of the same duty in the EU.[88]

8. Conclusion

One finding of this chapter is that both public and private interest reasons can explain the creation of tougher conditions for cross-border establishment compared to those for regular establishment. On the one hand, a public interest justification to make stricter requirements for the former can be information asymmetry between companies established by non-local investors and local customers. It is possible that consumers have more difficulties finding information about companies formed by non-local firms than those established by local enterprises, such as company reputations. The difficulty of knowing the reputations of subsidiaries funded by non-local firms can influence consumers' perception of the quality of these subsidiaries' new products and services. On the other hand, raising entry barriers to companies from jurisdictions with lower standards may be in the private interest of incumbents, local entrants and politicians and officials from states with higher standards.

This chapter also finds that there do not seem to be many reasons to provide the regulation of the cross-border establishment of companies at the central level. However, the centralization of the regulation rather than interstate cooperation may effectively cope with any inefficiency caused by inter-jurisdictional competition for business establishment. It is also possible to benefit from certain scale economies in information in case of centralization. Moreover, formulating regulation at the federal or transnational level can prohibit states from implementing local protectionism measures, but in a decentralized system, the federal authorities can also ensure the freedom of the cross-border establishment of companies.

It is difficult to answer the question whether a race to the bottom and transaction cost savings are arguments in favour of the centralization of the regulation of the cross-border establishment of businesses. The answer depends on the availability of empirical evidence. In particular, when evaluating the argument of transaction cost savings, it is important to take into account the benefits generated by the differentiation of the regulation.

Moreover, one should be aware of the fact that some interest groups may require the centralization of the regulation for private interests. The desire to make the regulation at the federal level may serve the interests of the politicians and officials of the central government to increase influence and power. Incumbents may also undertake strong lobbying exercises in favour of the cross-border establishment regulation at the central level, since barriers to entry can be created. The national policy makers and bureaucrats, as the third type of pressure groups,

[87] Enriques 2006a, p. 59.
[88] Ommeslaghe 1969, p. 233.

may favour their national interest groups and support the centralization of the regulation.

PART III

ECONOMIC EVALUATION

Part III

This part contains two chapters. Based on Part I (Legal Analysis) and Part II (Theoretical Framework), Chapter 6 uses the theoretical framework to examine the regulation of inter-provincial establishment in China. Chapter 7 then approaches the question of whether lessons can be drawn for China from the European experience in facilitating cross-border establishment.

Chapter 6

AN ECONOMIC ANALYSIS OF REGULATION OF THE INTER-PROVINCIAL ESTABLISHMENT OF COMPANIES IN CHINA

1. Introduction

Chapter 2 of this thesis considered the regulation of cross-provincial establishment of companies in China, concluding that in some circumstances, businesses in China encounter difficulties when trying to establish firms across provinces. Moreover, the existing regulatory framework cannot effectively deal with these obstacles.

Part II of this book provided the theoretical framework to study cross-border business establishment. As shown by the theory, there are some public interest justifications to impose different requirements on cross-border establishment on the one hand and regular establishment on the other hand. Nevertheless, regulating cross-border establishment can profit certain interest groups. Another issue treated by Part II was whether cross-border business establishment should be regulated at central level or at local level. The theory demonstrates that some public interest grounds can be used to justify regulating cross-border establishment at central level. However, some interest groups can benefit from centralization of the regulation of cross-border establishment.

In this chapter, the framework developed in Part II will be employed to examine regulation of the inter-provincial establishment of companies in China. Section 2 summarizes the rules concerning inter-provincial establishment and points out that regulators at central level shoulder the responsibility of governing this activity. Section 3 provides a public interest analysis of the regulation of the inter-provincial establishment of companies. More specifically, section 3.1 examines public interest grounds to differentiate requirements for inter-provincial and general establishment. Public interest arguments in favour of empowering central regulators to govern the inter-provincial establishment of companies are explored in section 3.2. Section 4 analyses the regulation of the inter-provincial establishment of companies from a private interest perspective. Section 4 starts with the discussion of private interest justifications for having different rules for inter-provincial establishment and general establishment in section 4.1. Thereafter, private interest reasons to regulate the inter-provincial establishment of companies at central level are discussed in section 4.2. Section 5 contains a conclusion.

2. Regulation of the Inter-provincial Establishment of Companies in China

As discussed in Chapter 2, minimum capital requirements and licensing are essential requirements to expand across provincial borders in China. Firms from one province seeking to establish operations in another can choose between subsidiaries and branches. Minimum capital requirements apply for subsidiaries, but not for branches. Apart from the capitalization rules, obtaining an establishment registration license is a necessary step to open subsidiaries and branches in China. Moreover, firms engaging in inter-provincial establishment may be required to go through a system of other approvals, depending on the scope of the investment project and the sources of the investment.

Central regulators have the exclusive power to issue rules setting out the capital requirements and the licensing obligations. The Company Law (2005) lays down the capitalization rules, as adopted by the Standing Committee of National People's Congress (NPC). Concerning the licensing obligations, NPC including its standing committee and the State Council are empowered to create licensing systems for inter-provincial establishment through national law and administrative regulations respectively. According to the Administrative License Law (ALL) (2003), only national law and administrative regulations may be enacted in respect of establishing the licensing regimes. Specifically, Articles 12(5) and 14 of the ALL note that 'as to the establishment of the enterprises or other institutions that need to determine a subject qualification,' administrative licenses may be created by means of national law;[1] 'Where there is no governing law, administrative licenses may be established by means of administrative regulations.' As Article 15(2) of the ALL states, no local regulation or governmental rule of provincial regions may establish any licensing system for the establishment and registration of enterprises.

In practice, the national regulators have established numerous licensing systems for doing business in various sectors.[2]

3. A Public Interest Analysis of Regulation of Inter-Provincial Establishment in China

Section 3.1 first addresses the question of to what extent having different requirements for the inter-provincial establishment of companies and the establishment of companies can serve a public interest goal. Then section 3.2 explores public interest arguments for regulating the inter-provincial establishment of companies at central level.

1 The English translation is adopted from: <www.fdi.gov.cn/1800000121_39_1797_0_7.html> ((last accessed 17 April 2016).

2 Wang 2014a, p. 10.

3.1. *Public Interest Reasons for Having Different Requirements for Inter-Provincial Establishment and General Establishment*

Some regions in China impose more stringent requirements on both local and non-local firms seeking to establish businesses there than those required by national law. For instance, in 2014, Beijing increased entry barriers for inter-provincial establishment in some sectors compared to those required in the rest of China, in order to tackle its air pollution problem.[3]

The tougher entry conditions for inter-provincial establishment, while aimed at tackling externalities, can also seek to protect local firms. As a result, Beijing can justify the introduction of higher entry barriers for the new establishment on the ground of coping with the pollution, as long as it does not abuse the justification to protect local firms. Apparently, Beijing did not abuse this justification, since this city announced plans to close companies with severe pollution, rather than only increasing entry barriers for the new establishment.[4]

3.2. *Public Interest Reasons for Regulating the Inter-Provincial Establishment of Companies at Central Level*

3.2.1. Disadvantages of Centralization

The disadvantages of regulating the inter-provincial establishment of companies at central level are the mirror image of the advantages of regulating this activity at local level. Two benefits can arise from empowering local authorities to regulate inter-provincial establishment. First, as discussed in chapter 5, regulating cross-border establishment at local level allows for regulatory competition among local authorities.[5] The deregulation of business formation initiated in Shanghai shows that in the case of regulating inter-provincial establishment at local level, local governments may compete with (and learn from) each other to relax rules on business establishment. After Shanghai erased licensing barriers to company formation, many other regions followed. In other words, these local authorities, either at provincial or city level, began to compete with each other to offer easier rules for establishment. This is because firms started to compare local provisions for business formation and some companies preferred expanding business in regions where overly restrictive licensing barriers have been removed. The following

3 京华时报, 北京将建工业准入负面清单拒绝高耗能高污染企业, 2013年11月12日, Jinghuashibao, the Construction Industry will be Added to the Negative list and High-energy Consuming and Heavy-polluting Industries will Move out of Beijing, 12 November 2013.

4 京津冀拟推市场准入负面清单，北京疏解非首都功能. 经济参考报，2015年6月16日. Beijing, Tianjin and Hebei will Introduce the Negative List, Jinjicankaobao, 16 June 2015.

5 Regulatory competition may lead to both positive effects and negative effects. As a starting point, this section discusses the positive outcomes of regulatory competition in the business establishment field in China. The negative effects of the competition will be investigated in the following sections.

passages elaborate on how the reform of business licensing systems in Shanghai lead to regulatory competition.

The China (Shanghai) Pilot Free-Trade Zone introduced the first innovation in China to deregulate business establishment in 2013. As discussed in chapter 2, concerning the formation of domestic firms, minimum capital requirements were removed. Moreover, acquiring licenses for licensed operations is no longer necessary for business establishment in many sectors. Regarding the establishment of FIEs, foreign investment in many sectors does not need to obtain permission from commercial agencies.

After deregulating the set-up process, more and more companies decided to locate to Shanghai rather than in other regions. In the first month of launching the pilot program, businesses set up in the zone grew by 5 times over the same period of 2012.[6] Within the first year of establishing the pilot zone, many FIEs were registered within the zone, ten times more than in the previous year.[7] The measures reforming business licensing systems are a main driving force for the investment, according to Business Daily.[8]

Meanwhile, other areas apart from Shanghai started to face pressure in attracting business establishment. They realized that the difficulties arise from the fact that they do not relax regulation on company formation as Shanghai does.

For instance, a commercial officer from the municipality of Suzhou has stated that after the creation of the pilot zone, in the short run, the city would face more challenges than opportunities to promote investment. The operation of the pilot has put intense pressure on many officials in the city who are responsible for attracting capital. The officer noticed that many companies have left Suzhou and moved to Shanghai. According to many other local officials, shortly after the pilot program was initiated, the municipality no longer had advantages in terms of attracting business.[9] The reason why Suzhou became less attractive to investors was that it, unlike Shanghai, still imposed unnecessary licensing requirements on business establishment, as shown by the following.

Moreover, as the commercial agency of Jiangsu Province reveals, the most important influence of the test reform on Jiangsu is that Shanghai would show

6 上海自贸区注册公司数量激增5倍成绩喜人, Startups in the Pilot Zone Increases manifold – a Gratifying Situation, available at: <www.zhuce51.com/news/510.html> (last accessed 7 March 2014).

7 澎湃新闻, 上海自贸区一年成绩单: 新设外资企业数同比增10倍， the Paper, the Achievement of Shanghai Pilot Zone in 2014: a Ten Time Newly Registered FIEs more than the Last Year, available at: <www.thepaper.cn/newsDetail_forward_1268733_1> (last accessed 17 February 2015).

8 杭州如何接轨上海自贸区？争取成为第二批试验区，每日商报，2014年2月10日， How to Bring Hangzhou more in Line with the Shanghai Pilot Zone, Striving to be Another Pilot Test Bed, Business Daily, 10 February 2014, available at: <http://hz.house.sina.com.cn/news/2014-02-10/09243912722.shtml> (last accessed 6 March 2014).

9 上海自贸试验区启动，江浙等周边地区忧虹吸效应，国际商报，2013年10月11日， After Launching the Shanghai Pilot Reform, Shanghai's Surrounding Regions Worry about their Difficulties to Attract Businesses, GuojiShangbao, 11 October 2013, available at: <http://wx.fzg360.com/archive.php?aid=43011> (last accessed 6 March 2014).

stronger investment inflows, because of lightening regulation on business in Shanghai. There would be much fiercer competition among these two regions to become a key investment area.[10]

The difficulty of promoting investment has increased enormously, since the deregulation has enabled Shanghai to significantly facilitate capital inflow, as the Jiangsu authority holds.[11] Other areas apart from the pilot zone still impose stringent licensing requirements on investment in certain industries and acquiring these licenses is often too time consuming or too difficult, according to the Suzhou official. In contrast, the 'negative list' approach makes investment projects in these industries in the test zone only subject to record-filing. Therefore, it is anticipated that investing in these fields will be made in the pilot zone rather than in other regions.[12]

Because of the difficulties in attracting capital, other local areas tend to loosen control on business establishment. Reforming administrative systems following the pilot reform would be the most efficient way for local governments to keep abreast of the development in Shanghai, as one public officer from Jiangsu states. Many reform plans publicized by local authorities such as Suzhou and Hangzhou give a top priority to the reform of administrative systems.[13] Facing the pressure from Shanghai to promote business, the government of Hangzhou is given the advice to employ the 'negative list' method and decrease business licensing regimes, as the Business Daily reports. The establishment by non-local firms can only be attracted through lightening regulation on business in Hangzhou.[14] As officers from Suzhou demonstrate, the hope and the requirements of the government of Suzhou are that its agencies can adopt the reform measures in Shanghai through every means. These departments have reformed their licensing regimes swiftly, abolishing 150 licensing items. Also, it now takes less time for these authorities to process certain licensing applications than for their Shanghai counterparts. For instance, the time for FIEs to start up decreased from 9-11 weekdays to 6-8 weekdays.[15]

10 刘金松、姜鑫，"邻居"的喜与忧, 经济观察报, 2013年10月19日，Jinsong Liu and Xin Jiang, the Hopes and Fears of the Provinces Neighboring Shanghai, the Economic Observer, 19 October 2013, available at: <www.p5w.net/news/gncj/201310/t20131019_341883.htm> (last accessed 6 March 2014).

11 *Ibid.*

12 上海自贸试验区启动，江浙等周边地区忧虹吸效应，国际商报，2013年10月11日，After Launching the Shanghai Pilot Reform, Shanghai's Surrounding Regions Worry about their Difficulties to Attract Businesses, GuojiShangbao, 11 October 2013.

13 21世纪经济报道, 上海自贸区: "制度高地"延伸方法论, 21st Century Business Herald, Shanghai Pilot Zone: Reforming Administrative Systems and Gaining Experience for Other Local Areas, 12 August 2014.

14 杭州如何接轨上海自贸区？争取成为第二批试验区, 每日商报, 2014年2月10日，Business Daily, How to Bring Hangzhou more in Line with the Shanghai Pilot Zone, Striving to be Another Pilot Test Bed, 10 February 2014.

15 上海自贸区虹吸效应渐显， 苏州便利化政策跟进， 21世纪经济报道，2014年9月24日，the Shanghai Pilot Reform Creates Difficulties for Shanghai's Surrounding Regions to Attract Businesses, Suzhou Learns from Shanghai and Provides Facilitation Measures, 21st Century Economic Report, 24 September 2014.

Second, as demonstrated in Chapter 5, empowering local authorities to regulate cross-border establishment allows them to adopt policies suitable for local needs. Since local governments in China have different preferences for company formation, decentralizing regulatory power on inter-provincial establishment may be beneficial to respond to the various preferences for investment.

Provinces at different stages of economic growth vary in their preferences for inbound investment. Regional disparity in economic development in China appears very large and the gap has widened.[16] On the basis of their own development situations, ten provinces and municipalities set out their different principles to promulgate investment guidelines, according to the Beijing Business Daily (2014). These instructions would list specific sectors where business establishment is not allowed. For instance, considering the current development situation of Beijing, this city's priorities are likely to restrict the investment in high-energy consuming and heavy-polluting industries.[17] One officer from this municipality reveals that new establishment in some sectors in Beijing would face stricter entry requirements than those provided by national authorities. It would be impossible to enter these domains, unless the local requirements are satisfied. Ensuring the higher standard is expected to tackle air pollution in this city.[18]

Beijing's guidelines on establishment entered into force in October, 2014. Authorities for investment plan approvals and company registration agencies are asked to approve company formation according to these instructions.[19] Auto manufacturing and the pharmaceutical industry are now restricted and some companies in these fields have relocated factories to Tianjin and Hebei. More and more industries affected by the new policy would shift investment from Beijing to these neighbouring regions, according to Gui Zhang, a scholar of regional studies at Hebei University of Technology. One official from Hebei holds that companies relocated here from Beijing would promote the development of the relevant industries in local areas of Hebei, becoming an engine of local economic growth. At the same time, leaders of some industrial associations in Beijing regard the relocation as an important opportunity to upgrade industries. The industry transfer, hence, would bring benefits to all the three regions, as demonstrated by Zhang.[20]

As shown above, if local authorities have been given the power to regulate inter-provincial establishment, they may remove unnecessary licensing barriers to

16 Yao & Zhang 2008, p. 47.

17 孙丽朝，各地集体瞄准负面清单模式， 北京商报，2014年2月12日，Lichao Sun, Numerous Regions are Planning their Negative Lists, Beijing Business Daily, 12 February 2014.

18 京华时报， 北京将建工业准入负面清单拒绝高耗能高污染企业， 2013年11月12日，JinghuaShibao, the Construction Industry will be Added to the Negative list and High-energy Consuming and Heavy-polluting Industries will Move out of Beijing, 12 November 2013.

19 新京报，北京推出"负面清单"全市禁止新建高尔夫球场，2014年07月26日，the Beijing News, Beijing Prohibits Some Industries including Building Golf Courses, 26 July, 2014.

20 新华网，北京：两份"清单"做减法疏解协同见真章，2015年1月25日，Xinhuanet, the Restriction of Some Industries in Beijing Benefits readjusting the locations of industries, 25 January 2015, available at: <http://finance.sina.com.cn/china/dfjj/20150125/171121392144.shtml> (last accessed 12 February 2015).

business establishment and create business licensing systems adapted to local conditions. However, regulatory competition may create negative outcomes rather than beneficial effects. Chapter 5 has pointed out that regulating cross-border establishment at local level may also lead to a race to the bottom. There may be other arguments in favour of centralization of regulation of cross-border establishment: trans-boundary externalities, scale economies and transaction cost savings. These arguments are applied to inter-provincial establishment in China in the following sections.

3.2.2. Trans-boundary Externalities

As noted in Chapter 5, trans-boundary externalities are an important reason for the centralization of regulation of cross-border establishment. Duvivier and Xiong (2013) argue that trans-boundary pollution problems exist in China by showing that polluting enterprises have higher possibilities of being situated in counties near provincial borders than those located within provinces. Moreover, such an effect seems to have increased in the course of time.[21] The authors also explain the cause of China's trans-boundary pollution problems. One proposed explanation is given that national environmental standards are implemented by provincial regulators in China. Moreover, it is assumed that they may impose less strict environmental regulation on business establishment in border regions than in interior areas. One of the two factors for adopting such a strategy is the benefits that can be brought to the authorities. On the one hand, some of the polluting activities of firms established near the border materialize in neighbouring provinces. On the other hand, the company formation generates economic advantages to the province where the industry is located, e.g. tax revenues and employment.[22] Following this hypothesis, the authors conduct research on the decisions of polluting enterprises' about where to locate in Hebei province from 2002 to 2008.[23] As their study demonstrates, border cities of Hebei are more likely to be chosen as locations. In the same way, the more distant counties are from the border, the lower the possibility of firms establishing polluting businesses there.[24]

Empowering central regulators to establish environmental licensing systems for inter-provincial establishment does not seem to be appropriate to tackle the trans-boundary pollution problems. It should be noted that while in China it is the State Council that establishes environmental standards, they are (supposed to be) enforced by local governments.[25] One explanation for the existence of China's trans-boundary pollution problems is that provincial regulators do not respect these national standards.[26] Therefore, the key to the solution of the environmental problems is to ensure local authorities' compliance with the national standards.

21 Duvivier & Xiong 2013, p. 479.
22 *Ibid.*, p. 463.
23 *Ibid.*, p. 460.
24 *Ibid.*, p. 473.
25 *Ibid.*, p. 460.
26 *Ibid.*, p. 463.

The six regional supervision centers established by the Ministry of Environmental Protection (MEP) could be an approach to curb the trans-boundary pollution.[27] Each of the six centers governs a few provincial areas and supervises the enforcement of the national environmental standards in these regions. The six institutions also take the responsibility of coordinating inter-provincial environmental conflicts.[28] Currently, mainly because MEP does not grant enough power to these centers, they cannot cope well with major problems e.g. cross-provincial water pollution accidents.[29] To enable these institutions to fulfil their tasks better, it is most desirable but radical to improve the capacity building of these centers as subordinate agencies of MEP.[30]

3.2.3. A Race to the Bottom

As analysed in Chapter 5, the risk of a race to the bottom is an important argument in favour of centralization of regulation of cross-border establishment. We need to know how local authorities in China compete with each other to attract business establishment, in order to test whether Chinese authorities engage in a race to the bottom. According to Prof. Ran Tao from Renmin University of China, local governments usually adopt three ways to attract investment within development zones: (1) keeping land prices down, (2) providing weak labour protection and paying social insurance premiums in inadequate amounts and (3) weakening environmental regulation on market entry.[31] Development zones are regions designated by authorities for industrial and commercial growth and the export and GDP of these areas accounted for 68 per cent and 87 per cent of the national total respectively in 2006.[32] Among the three measures introduced in development zones, the first measure to attract investment is governed by laws on land transfers and the second by laws on labour. As a result, one should concentrate on how lenient environmental regulation may influence firm locations, in order to understand the existence of a race to the bottom in the business establishment field in China.

According to some Chinese scholars whose views are stated in the following paragraphs, less developed provinces are involved in a race to the bottom and relax environmental regulation on business establishment to attract plants relocating from Eastern China to Western China and Central China. As a response, these firms tend to choose their establishment locations based on lenient environmental rules.

According to Wei and Bi (2011), Western China and Central China provide a pollution haven to the polluters incorporated in Eastern China. They chose 19 economic sectors where the production processes have been relocated from the advanced regions to the developing areas and conduct research on the number of

27 *Ibid.*, p. 479 and 480.
28 *Ibid.*, p. 462.
29 Huan 2011, p. 154 and 157.
30 *Ibid.*, p. 157.
31 财经，竞次式招商引资纵容污染，2013年01月02日，Caijing, Competition for Investment and Capital Causing Pollution, 2 January 2013.
32 Zhang 2011, p. 145.

start-ups in these industries from 2004 to 2008. Their paper indicates that companies have a tendency to move their plants to regions with weaker environmental regulation in the process of the relocation. It is also reasonable to assume that local authorities in Western China and Central China have strong incentives to create a race to the bottom in environmental requirements on business establishment, because of this tendency.[33]

As held by Zhang (2013), the under-developed regions are becoming a pollution haven for polluting companies registered in Eastern China. He studies the cross-provincial establishment of Chinese listed companies in high-polluting industries between 2009 and 2011 and the parent companies and the newly established branches amount to 11951. It is demonstrated that the listed companies with registered places in Eastern China moved around half of their branches from this rich area to Western China and Central China. Moreover, some local governments in the poor regions tend to promote investment at the expense of the environment.[34]

Other empirical studies here offer some examples demonstrating the existence of the race to the bottom. For instance, one official from a poor province in Western China asked Z, an officer from Shandong (a developed province in Eastern China) to help him attract companies to invest in the poor region. The first official notes that his region welcomes all investments, regardless of the pollution the investments may contribute to.[35]

Considering the race to the bottom rationale being valid, one could ask whether giving central regulators the power to create environmental licensing regimes for inter-provincial firm formation would be suitable to manage this risk. As discussed in chapter 5, scholars have different opinions about whether the race to the bottom in the domain of environmental protection justifies environmental regulatory centralization. Therefore, we may need to consider the practical situation in China to decide whether empowering central regulators to establish these licensing systems would be a suitable solution.

Literature shows that improving the capacity building of the regional centers for environmental protection could be a way to tackle the race to the bottom in China. As Huan demonstrates, giving more power to these institutions can tighten the state supervision of environmental protection over regional authorities. After gaining more authority, these organizations will be upgraded to the top local-level governmental departments for environmental protection, thereby holding fully authorized power to enforce environmental laws within their jurisdictions. As a result, the environmental agencies and other functional departments of local governments will take these centers more seriously. Specifically, local economic authorities will have to create a balance between economic decision-making and environmental protection. Moreover, local environmental departments will receive

33 Wei & Bi 2011, p. 73 and 74.
34 Zhang 2013, p. 100.
35 Interview with Z, August 2013. With 17 years of experience, Z leads the work in a local department for company registration.

strong support from these centers, when implementing environmental legislation.[36] Thus, with more power, these organizations can manage the risk of the race to the bottom arising from empowering local authorities to create environmental licensing systems for inter-provincial establishment.

3.2.4. Scale Economies and Transaction Cost Savings

Scale economies in information are sometimes absent, in the context of centralizing business establishment regulation. It should be pointed out that information for formulating company formation rules in one province may be not always be relevant to another. A case in point is environmental regulation for business establishment. Due to environmental variations and economic development differences between regions, local authorities should be empowered to make regulation for environmental management.[37] As legal experts demonstrate, the variations have led to different approaches to tackle environmental issues. Concrete environmental protection measures should be proposed by local authorities on the basis of local conditions.[38] Therefore, each province maybe needs to collect its own information to make efficient environmental regulation for company establishment.

Transaction cost savings seem to be a weak argument justifying regulating inter-provincial establishment at central level too. Due to the enactment of national law, the legal environment for Chinese companies in different regions should be almost the same, but there are marked inter-regional differences in the environment arising from some other factors.[39]

However, a careful study shows that the regulation for inter-provincial establishment in China seems unable to create much legal certainty. This view is based on the relevant provision of the ALL. As Article 16 of this law notes, provinces, autonomous regions, municipalities directly under the central government and relatively large cities 'may, within the scope of the matters of administrative license established by the laws and administrative regulations, make specific requirements for the implementation of the administrative license.' This provision can create costs for expansion across provincial borders. Obviously, companies have to stay on top of the specific requirements made by potential investment destinations, in order to fulfil licensing obligations imposed by the national regulation.

Take the provision on company domiciles as an example. As Article 7 of the Company Law (2005) provides, the business license of a company should state the domicile (the place where the main executive office is located). Moreover, company domiciles should meet certain conditions. According to a recent document, provincial regions are empowered to either prescribe these requirements

36 Huan 2011, p. 155.

37 Ren 1987, p. 22.

38 霍桃，地方立法权将扩至全国282个设区市，环境立法率先示范，中国环境报，Tao Huo, 282 Cities Divided into Districts are Given Legislative Power to Make Environmental Regulation, 17 December 2014.

39 Fan *et al*. 2007, p. 383.

themselves or authorize municipal governments to stipulate these conditions.[40] Some provinces have dispatched documents providing that municipal governments should set out these conditions for business establishment within their administrative regions.[41] As a result, participants in inter-provincial establishment have to spend time learning the provision made by these cities.

4. A Private Interest Analysis of the Regulation of the Inter-Provincial Establishment of Companies in China

This section first addresses the question of to what extent regulating inter-provincial establishment by rules different from the regulation of general establishment can be considered as serving a private interest goal. Then it will investigate which private interests may be pursued through regulating inter-provincial establishment at central level.

4.1. *Interests of the Actors Involved in Having Different Requirements for Inter-provincial Establishment and General Establishment*

This section demonstrates that the interests of local officials, local firms, and other companies may be served by having different requirements for the inter-provincial establishment of companies and the establishment of companies. Moreover, this section provides an analysis of a qualitative empirical analysis of the formation of companies across provinces, in order to back the private interest approach.

4.1.1. Local Officials

As noted in chapter 5, according to 'traditional' public choice theory, the goal of being re-elected drives politicians to meet the needs of incumbents, i.e. imposing strict requirements on the cross-border establishment of companies. Obviously, the incentive device for local officials in China to provide stringent regulation for the inter-provincial establishment of companies may differ to some extent from the vote incentive. Therefore, the focus of this section is on how the 'traditional' private interest approach may need to be adapted to better fit the more specific (legal, cultural and political) context of China.

As stated by Mehra and Meng (2008), "barriers to external competition that bolster the income of local enterprises translate into higher levels of employment for the local population and more tax revenues for local government."[42] Local governments therefore clearly face incentives to protect local industry in order to generate market demand for local products and labour. Moreover, from a private

40 国务院关于印发注册资本登记制度改革方案的通知, the Notice of the State Council on Issuing the Plan for Reforming the Capital Registration System (2014).

41 例如，《江苏省政府关于推进注册资本登记制度改革的实施意见》. For example, see the Implementation Opinion of the Government of Jiangsu Province on Promoting the Reform of the Capital Registration System (2014).

42 Mehra & Meng 2008, p. 399 and 400.

interest perspective, local officials have additional reasons to protect local industry. In the following there will be a focus on two of these reasons: the quest for promotion and the problem of corruption.

This section concentrates on local officials' incentives to protect local industry, but this does not mean that they always create entry barriers to non-local firms. There remain many situations where investment by non-local industries is welcomed, since it enhances local economic growth and employment, as shown in previous chapters. Hence, whether local public officials welcome non-local firms or not depends on the specific context, e.g. whether the market concerned is competitive or profitable.

4.1.1.1. Promotion

One explanation for local protectionist practices in China may be that local officers are striving for promotion within the Communist Party of China (CPC).[43] When entry barriers are created for companies from other jurisdictions, this can serve as a shield that protects local economies. Moreover, local protectionism may negatively affect the economic development of other regions. As a result, local officials are more likely to receive promotion. To grasp this causal relationship, one needs to consider how local governors can obtain career advancement in China.

According to Li-An Zhou (2004), the growth rate of GDP is the most important criterion for promoting officials in China. Local officials from different regions not only compete with each other in terms of GDP growth and taxation; they also compete for advancement in their official careers.[44] In reality, getting a promotion is likely to be more important to officers.[45] If a region outpaces others in economic growth, the leader of the area will have better chances at getting a promotion.[46] Pi (2008) demonstrates that, currently, local officeholders attach high importance to winning the competition for advancement.[47] Moreover, only a limited number of local officers can obtain a promotion.[48] This results in a situation in which local governors are motivated to promote the economic development of their own areas at the expense of other regions, as pointed out by Zhou.[49]

Local protectionism can boost local economic development in the short term, according to Pan (2009).[50] Moreover, since a local governor's term of office is usually short, welcoming the investment of non-local firms may not be helpful in the search for promotion. Due to the rotation of local governors across regions, they serve

43 Zhou 2004, p. 37.
44 *Ibid.*, p. 34.
45 Zhou 2007, p. 38.
46 Xu 2011, p. 1079.
47 Pi 2008, p. 122.
48 Zhou 2004, p. 34.
49 *Ibid.*
50 潘勇，"保增长"别纵容了地方保护主义，齐鲁晚报，Yong Pan, 'Do Not Allow Local Protectionism under the Name of Increasing Economic Growth', Qiluwanbao, available at: <http://news.sohu.com/20090217/n262287832.shtml> (last accessed 6 February 2014).

short terms in one locality.[51] In practice, more than half of all local officeholders serve for only 2 years, as reported by the 21st Century Business Herald (2014). The average tenure in office for governors at county level is 3 years.[52] According to the Legal Daily (2013), it can be learnt from press reports that the term of a local public servant in a particular job is often very short.[53] If the actual term of office is only 2 or 3 years, start-ups funded by businesses from other regions would not generate much tax revenue in this period of time.

Creating barriers to market access can be profitable for local economies. The development of locally important industries is immediately connected with the revenue of local governments.[54] Moreover, State-owned enterprises (SOEs) pay taxes according to their administrative subordination, as pointed out by Mao. For example, SOEs administrated by a provincial government have tax obligations to this particular provincial authority.[55] Furthermore, it is common for local governments to take profits from township and village enterprises and use them to invest in other enterprises.[56] If administrative power is used to shield local enterprises, local enterprises can squeeze out any competition, make more profits and pay more taxes.[57]

According to Hu and Guo (2002), if locally owned companies are not competitive and suffer from shrinking profits, local agencies usually exercise their administrative powers to restrict or prohibit the entry of non-local firms rather than increasing the local companies' competitive abilities. This type of behaviour may result in the presence of administrative monopolies.[58]

Furthermore, obstructing the establishment of non-local firms can harm the economy of other regions. If companies headquartered in province A open branches

51 O'Brien & Li 1999, p. 175 and 176.

52 21世纪经济报道，地方债治本之道：地方官员向当地百姓负责，2014年1月3日， 21st Century Business Herald, 'A Fundamental Way to Solve Local-government Debt: Local Officials Should Be Responsible to Local Inhabitants', 3 January 2014, available at: <http://henan.sina.com.cn/news/finance/2014-01-03/0759-118650.html> (last accessed 6 April 2014).

53 法制日报，严格任期制，避免官员成"临时工"，2013年7月15日， Legal Daily, 'The Provision on the Term of Office Should be Implemented Strictly', 15 July 2013, available at: <http://epaper.legaldaily.com.cn/fzrb/content/20130715/Articel07002GN.htm> (last accessed 6 April 2014).

54 Yong Guo and Angang Hu (2002), 'Administrative Monopoly in Economy Transition in China'. Availabe at: <www.chinareform.org/publications/reports/200206/-t20020618_111297.htm> (last accessed 5 January 2014).

55 Zhongguowang, Regional Protectionism Weakening State Capacity, available at: <www.china.org.cn/english/2001/Mar/9673.htm> (last accessed 7 February 2014).

56 Oi 1995, p. 1140.

57 潘勇，"保增长"别纵容了地方保护主义，齐鲁晚报，Yong Pan (2009), 'Do Not Allow Local Protectionism in the Name of Increasing Economic Growth', Qiluwanbao, available at: <http://news.sohu.com/20090217/n262287832.shtml> (last accessed 6 February 2014).

58 Yong Guo and Angang Hu(2002), 'Administrative Monopoly in Economy Transition in China', available at: <www.chinareform.org/publications/reports/200206/-t20020618_111297.htm> (last accessed 5 January 2014). The notion of administrative monopolies refers to a situation in which an administrative agency abuses its administrative power to restrict or eliminate competition. See Yong 2008, p. 92.

in another region B, these branches pay the bulk of their enterprise income tax to province A.[59] The enterprise income tax, the consumption tax and the VAT are the main taxes imposed on enterprises; together accounting for the lion's share of tax revenues.[60] Entry barriers may also cause additional negative effects on the economic growth of other areas: for example, firms from other jurisdictions may not be able to provide services in regions outside their headquarters without establishing branches in these regions. Pan (2009) concludes that local officials can take protectionist measures in the name of promoting economic development, benefiting the public, etc., and rather than being punished for this, they gain prestige and wealth.[61]

A conclusion that we can draw from this is that in China, local office-holders' incentives to seek promotion seem to differ to some extent from the incentives discussed in 'traditional' public choice theory. Promotion rather than the 'vote motive' drives local officials to introduce entry barriers.

4.1.1.2. Corruption

As demonstrated in chapter 5, imposing stringent requirements on the cross-border establishment of companies makes it easy for public officials to take bribes. In the context of the inter-provincial establishment of companies, rent seeking by officials through the creation of market entry barriers can be understood from two perspectives.

First, local officeholders may erect entry barriers in exchange for personal gains provided to them by market incumbents. Existing producers may try to exclude competitors from other jurisdictions from the market; entry barriers, such as licensing, serve that purpose well. As demonstrated by Xin, there is a tendency to impose additional licensing requirements on non-local firms in order to protect local industries.[62] Also, a study by Deng reports that local protectionist measures often result from 'an improper use of administrative power', i.e. corruption.[63]

According to Jun Hu and Feng Guo (2013), corruption by local officers and rent seeking by local companies have caused severe regional market disintegration in China. The authors back up this statement with convincing empirical evidence: on the basis of panel data concerning 28 provinces in the period 1988-2010, they conclude that the more corrupt local public officials are, the greater the regional market fragmentation, and vice versa. Creating entry barriers for non-local ventures

59 This information is obtained from two civil servants of tax authorities in Beijing and Chengdu.

60 Deng 2003, p. 16.

61 潘勇，"保增长"别纵容了地方保护主义，齐鲁晚报，Yong Pan, Do Not Allow Local Protectionism under the Name of Increasing Economic Growth, Qiluwanbao, available at: <http://news.sohu.com/20090217/n262287832.shtml> (last accessed 6 January 2014).

62 新望，"地方保护主义"该收场了, Wang Xin, Local Protectionism should be Stopped, available at: <www.china-review.com/sao.asp?id=5707> (last accessed 15 October 2014).

63 Deng 2003, p. 15.

allows local officials to take bribes from local enterprises and increase tax revenues. These incentives drive officeholders to implement local protectionist measures.[64]

Second, local officials may want to create entry barriers, as this provides them with the opportunity to take bribes from non-local firms. If businesses from other jurisdictions want to enter local markets, they may have to offer bribes to local officers. For example, in Jilin province some officials in charge of the establishment by non-local firms "used every opportunity to make personal gains", and were strongly criticized for their behaviour by the CPC provincial chief of Jilin. These officials were seeking rents, whenever non-local businesses applied for approval of their investment plans or had to complete other procedures necessary for establishment in Jilin. The officeholders concerned even claimed that it is "the custom of Jilin officers to gain benefits in the process of non-local firms' investment".[65]

4.1.2. Local Industries

According to Zhang, Wang and Liu (2013), firms tend to rely on local governments in regions where local protectionism is severe. When encountering difficulties, local firms often seek help from local governments.[66] For example, when faced with the expansion plans of non-local rivals, local leading supermarkets have repeatedly used their influence over regional governments, creating numerous difficulties to retailers from other areas.[67]

Guo and Hu (2004) state that favoured firms and industries can develop cosy relationships with local officeholders. This provides tremendous opportunities for rent seeking, since administrative authorities are able to use their administrative power to reward local business.[68]

According to the empirical research of Jun Hu and Feng Guo mentioned above, companies tend to bribe local officials to exercise protectionism in the regions in which they are headquartered. Local enterprises prompt authorities to create impediments for market entry, thus avoiding competition with ventures from other regions. Rent seeking by local firms leads to market fragmentation.[69]

64 Hu & Guo 2013, p. 45.

65 常旭，吉林省委书记批少数部门对外来企业雁过拔毛，城市晚报，2008年04月17日，Xu Chang, 'The Jilin Provincial CPC Chief Criticizes Some Departments for Making Personal Gains Through Governing Non-Local Companies', Chenshiwanbao, 17 April 2008, available at: <http://news.sina.com.cn/c/2008-04-17/005315370056.shtml> (last accessed 20 February 2014).

66 Zhang *et al*. 2013, p. 85.

67 潘沩，本土超市卖场为何难出苏宁国美，21世纪经济报道，Wei Pan (2011), 'Why Domestic Supermarkets Cannot Grow to Giants like Gome and Suning', 21st Century Business Herald, available at: <http://finance.sina.com.cn/leadership/20111009/033210584730.shtml> (last accessed 2 February 2014).

68 Guo & Hu 2004, p. 265 and 279; Mehra & Meng 2008, p. 400.

69 Hu & Guo 2013, p. 45.

4.1.3. Other Industries

Also other industries are likely to cater to local authorities that are responsible for managing entry into local markets. As pointed out in a workshop organized by the American Chamber of Commerce in China (hereinafter AmCham China), it is necessary for FIEs to show their definite contribution to the market and industry sites they want to operate in. Drawing support from regional governments can accelerate the granting of licenses due to their ability to facilitate the application procedure. Local authorities are often willing to provide such assistance since they might want to increase employment and attract capital, whereas the central government might not.[70]

For instance, foreign invested retailers, including Carrefour China and Wal-Mart China, make use of public media to show that they contribute substantially to the Chinese (local) economy, e.g. by increasing local tax revenues or creating jobs. A senior PR officer from a renowned FIE once made the humorous remark that his venture could easily win more government favours if it would advertise the company's contribution to administrative achievement.[71]

Moreover, since officers can arbitrarily decide to implement local protectionist measures, firms may have to bribe officials when entering into regional markets.[72] The 21st Century Business Herald reports that rent seeking is more likely when there is local protectionism. The cost of PR increases if non-local companies want to enter into local markets or provide market access opportunities for their products.[73] The China Business (2013) reveals that Wal-Mart China might have offered bribes to acquire licenses for new shops, to finish establishment procedures and deal with government inquiries. However, Wal-Mart could not comment on these statements, as an investigation was being conducted under the Foreign Corrupt Practices Act (US).[74]

70 AmCham China, License to Expand – A 2012 Business Climate Survey Event 25 April 2012, available at: <www.amchamchina.org/article/9560> (last accessed 8 October 2014). AmCham China points out that some of the key problems for FIEs in obtaining licenses include the inconsistency of Chinese licensing requirements, the uneven enforcement of licensing rules, lengthy procedures, and the fact that licenses are not granted equally to Chinese and foreign firms.

71 黄霞，洋零售的"讨好"术, 羊城晚报, Xia Huang, Yangcheng Evening News, 'Foreign Invested Retailers' Ways to Win Favours', available at: <www.ycwb.com/gb/content/2002-08/21/-content_408528.htm> (last accessed 2 February 2014).

72 Deng 2003, p. 15.

73 21世纪经济报导, 警惕国内地方保护主义复苏, 21st Century Business Herald, 'Being Aware of a Revival of Local Protectionism', available at: <http://news.sohu.com/20090217/-n262288107.shtml> (last accessed 6 February 2014).

74 中国经营报,沃尔玛反腐调查波及中国，或关闭100家亏损门店，China Business (2012), 'Wal-Mart's Anti-Corruption Inquiry Spreads to China, 100 Shops at Loss Position may be Closed', available at: <http://finance.qq.com/a/20121124/001799.htm?pgv_ref=aio2012&ptlang-=2052> (last accessed 22 September 2013).

4.1.4. Interview Results

A number of interviews have been conducted to provide further insights into the reality of the inter-provincial establishment of companies. The information obtained from these interviews offers some support for the assumption that promotion is a significant incentive (as presented in Section 3.1.1.1 above), although hard conclusions could not be reached. All interviews were held on a semi-structured basis, i.e. interviewees conveyed their opinions on specific issues of establishment on the basis of a questionnaire.

4.1.4.1. Access Barriers Erected by Local Licensing Authorities

Strict licensing requirements are imposed to create market entry barriers in certain fields, according to Z, a local licensing official. In these industries, monopolies or SOEs have occupied a significant market share and have gained huge profits. To impose obstacles for potential competitors, authorities usually set very harsh terms for businesses to obtain licenses. The establishment of these licensing systems can block the expansion of non-local companies.[75]

Z provides an example concerning the difficulties of entering the market for public transport. Currently, mainly local SOEs provide public transportation services and they make good profits doing so. In order to prevent (or restrict) competition, local authorities have established licensing regimes that regulate market access. Ordinary individuals or businesses can hardly form companies for passenger transport, because of the strict requirements that need to be fulfilled in order to obtain a license.[76]

According to N, a local licensing officer, it is likely that local protectionism is the norm in the café industry. The same is true of the coal mining, highway construction, and town and village bank establishment industries. Local ventures are more likely to obtain licenses and to do business in these industries than companies that have been incorporated in other regions.[77]

According to a recent report, in the logistics industry, when non-local companies try to form branches, local Administrations of Industry and Commerce (AICs) in some cases refuse to deal with business license applications. These authorities have given various reasons for their refusal. In other cases, additional licensing requirements have been defined for non-local entrepreneurs that need to be carried out before a company can be registered.[78]

75 Interview with Z, a local licensing official, 20 August 2013 (interview transcript on file with the authors). With more than 17 years of experience, Z is a licensing official of a local Administration of Industry and Commerce in Shandong Province.

76 Interview with Z, a local licensing official, 20 August 2013 (interview transcript on file with the authors).

77 Interview with N, a local licensing official, 6 August 2013 (interview transcript on file with the authors).

78 中国物流与采购联合会, 物流业消除地区封锁、打破行业垄断的政策建议（内部资料）, 页1. China Federation of Logistics and Purchasing (CFLP), Policy Suggestions for the Logistics Industry to Erase Regional Blockades and Break Industrial Monopolies (unpublished), p. 1. In →

The expansion of café chains is hindered significantly by local cultural authorities, as C, a national café chain manager, demonstrated. Although C's company has a permit for opening cafés nationwide, as a result of the behaviour of local cultural agencies, it still encounters tremendous difficulties in the process of establishing branches. These licensing authorities require C's firm to obtain their permission prior to opening shops in their regions. Local protectionism can be noticed here in the approval process. In some cases, enterprises meeting certain conditions have been granted licenses, whereas non-local firms meeting the same conditions were not.[79]

C provided us with several examples demonstrating the difficulties in the expansion of his company. For example, one requirement made in a particular district provides that a license for an additional cyber café will be given only if a firm can open five such branches in this area. This provision most certainly benefits local companies only. This is because these businesses have already established numerous internet cafés and therefore can easily obtain a new permission. By contrast, most non-local enterprises are only starting their business in this region and hence are by no means able to meet these requirements.[80]

4.1.4.2. *Interests of Officials in Creating Entry Barriers*

4.1.4.2.1. Promotion

According to X, apart from legal restrictions on business scope, other elements that can influence the inter-provincial establishment of companies include tax revenues, employment and social stability. Governments usually expect that benefits in the form of taxation, employment and stability can be derived from the establishment of companies in their local areas.[81]

First, with respect to taxation, when new factories are opened, local governments always consider the ability of such factories to make profits and generate tax revenues, as pointed out by X. For tax reasons, local governments usually prefer the establishment of subsidiaries to the establishment of branches. As mentioned before, subsidiaries pay a large share of their taxes in local regions, whereas branches do not. In order to attract subsidiaries, local authorities often apply favourable conditions to this business form.[82]

our interview with a senior researcher from the CFLP, the interviewee indicated that AICs and local governments make it difficult for logistics companies to set up businesses.

79 Interview with C, a national café chain's manager, July 2013, (interview transcript on file with the authors).

80 *Ibid.*

81 Interview with X, an enterprise manager, 13 August 2013 (interview transcript on file with the authors). Mr X works on company registration and investment in the logistics industry. His employer is a Fortune 500 enterprise in a coastal province, which has opened hundreds of subsidiaries across China.

82 Interview with X, an enterprise manager, 13 August 2013 (interview transcript on file with the authors).

A case in point is X's own corporate group. Most businesses established by this group are subsidiaries rather than branches, because the conditions attached to this particular business form are more favourable. For example, governments are usually willing to provide land so that subsidiaries can be formed in the logistics industry. In addition, attractive terms can be given in terms of land prices and locations, and land is highly valuable to the establishment in the logistics trade. Moreover, subsidiaries can get tax refunds. In contrast, it is very uncommon for branches to receive such advantageous treatment.[83] Recent empirical research has indicated that, for tax reasons, only the establishment of subsidiaries is allowed in the logistics industry.[84]

Some firms establish branches rather than subsidiaries, but it is noted that this business form is used in special situations only. For instance, enterprises owned by the central government sometimes choose to establish branches in the Zhejiang province. These SOEs are usually large firms in monopolistic industries, such as petrochemicals, telecoms and banking. In addition, they own advanced technology in these fields that local authorities do not have. As a result, it is difficult for local governments to influence the investment intentions of these firms.[85] There may also be other cases in which branches are opened rather than subsidiaries. However, this may be possible only when tax agreements are reached. Such contracts are signed between local governments and enterprises, requiring the latter to pay a certain amount of taxes.[86]

Local licensing official N notes that in some cases both subsidiaries and branches can be opened. In other cases, the establishment can only be in the form of subsidiaries. A case in point is the formation of project ventures in the real estate/property industry. When real estate businesses bid for a vacant lot in areas other than their places of incorporation, they are usually asked to establish subsidiaries rather than branches. This is because companies formed for land development projects often need to pay up to 30 per cent of their investment as tax. Moreover, such investments often have an enormous scale amounting to billions of RMB. This means that the tax contributions of such plans can be considerable. Therefore, for tax reasons local governments usually require the incorporation of subsidiaries in that trade.[87]

Local protectionism in the café industry can also be explained by tax reasons. According to C, local firms usually share common benefits with local authorities via tax payments. Moreover, some local cafés are funded by regional cultural

83 Interview with X, an enterprise manager, 13 August 2013 (interview transcript on file with the authors).

84 中国物流与采购联合会， 物流业消除地区封锁、打破行业垄断的政策建议（内部资料）， 页1. CFLP, Policy Suggestions for the Logistics Industry to Erase Regional Blockades and Break Industrial Monopolies (unpublished), p. 1.

85 Interview with X, an enterprise manager, 13 August 2013 (interview transcript on file with the authors).

86 *Ibid.*

87 Interview with N, a local licensing official, 6 August 2013 (interview transcript on file with the authors).

companies, which in turn are funded by local authorities governing the café industry.[88]

Second, local authorities usually hope that the establishment of non-local firms can benefit existing local firms that are in financial difficulties. For example, local governments may require non-local firms to explore new markets for local ventures.[89]

Corporations that can bring these advantages are more likely to (be allowed to) form businesses in local markets. SOEs tend to accept the local governments' terms because of their social commitment. Thus, these enterprises do not experience any difficulties when establishing across provincial borders, although their operating costs may be high.[90] Because of the SOE's contribution to local welfare, local governments often offer attractive conditions to the incorporation of SOEs in their areas. For example, as mentioned above, they can supply land with high economic value to these companies, which is essential to the formation in certain fields.[91]

As for Mr X's business, it usually employs local workers. Moreover, it can promote the sales of local products in other provinces. For example, his company assists in the marketing of steel produced in the province where his business opened a steel plant. In return, the corporation receives generous treatment in terms of land use.[92]

Also the foreign invested giants such as Wal-Mart China can establish their companies in different provinces rather easily. The explanation provided by Mr X is that they can ensure a high employment rate because of their commercial strength. Being competitive and dynamic corporations, they are better able to deal with certain business risks, and to grow rapidly and stably. This reduces the risk that their employees are laid off.[93] In contrast, private holding companies tend to downsize their staff. With an aim of pursuing economic efficiency, they are usually reluctant to recruit and maintain a large work force. Moreover, they lack the motivation to promote the development of related industries and local economies. Thus, it is likely that local authorities do not applaud the establishment by private enterprises.[94]

4.1.4.2.2. Corruption

Not surprisingly, it is difficult to obtain hard evidence of corruption from interviews. Nevertheless, it has been found that licensing agencies sometimes deal

88 Interview with C, a national café chain's manager, July 2013 (interview transcript on file with the authors).

89 Interview with X, an enterprise manager, 13 August 2013 (interview transcript on file with the authors).

90 *Ibid.*

91 *Ibid.*

92 *Ibid.*

93 *Ibid.*

94 *Ibid.*

with licensing applications 'with strings attached'. Furthermore, it is rather common that personal connections are used in license applications.

According to N, some licenses with high market values are hard to obtain, such as licenses for the opening of cafés. As a result, elements other than those provided for in law play a role in the license approval procedure. For example, enterprises affiliated with governments are more likely to obtain approval. Also, personal connections are sought. It is not uncommon for companies to ask their acquaintances in licensing authorities for help. Furthermore, companies may offer bribes to licensing officials with the profits they can earn from their investment projects. However, such practices take place only in highly profitable or competitive markets. In other markets, license applications are likely to be approved according to the law.[95]

To acquire licenses in backward regions, businesses usually have to pay additional fees to licensing authorities, as H remarks. License applications that appear to satisfy all requirements can still be denied by licensing officials in these areas who deliberately create difficulties for applicants. For example, private holding companies from Wenzhou, a city renowned for its private economy, first had to establish connections with licensing officers before they could invest in certain under-developed areas. Only after having established such connections could they obtain the necessary licenses. It should be noted that these licensing barriers do not necessarily imply that there is a prevalence of local protectionism in these places; local officials usually want to attract investment.[96]

As demonstrated by C, in a northern province, local cultural agencies set a precondition for his firm to obtain licenses. The authorities asked his business to fund them by contributing 0.8 million RMB, to support local cultural activities.[97]

4.2. *Interests of the Actors Involved in Centralization of the Regulation of Inter-provincial Establishment*

This section demonstrates that the private interests and objectives of the regulators of inter-provincial establishment and incumbent firms under the jurisdiction of these regulators may be sought through governing inter-provincial establishment at central level.

95 Interview with N, a local licensing official, 6 August 2013 (interview transcript on file with the authors). Mr N is a licensing official of a local Administration of Industry and Commerce in a province in Eastern China.

96 Interview with H, a corporation lawyer, 26 August 2013 (interview transcript on file with the authors). Mr H works at the legal department of an SOE and has also dealt with the legal affairs of other private companies. One of his duties is to complete registration procedures and obtain licenses for the expansion of these businesses.

97 Interview with C, a national café chain's manager, July 2013 (interview transcript on file with the authors).

4.2.1. Regulators of Inter-provincial Establishment

Reality in China shows that making the regulation of inter-provincial establishment at central level can bring economic benefits to the central regulators. An important reason for governmental agencies to oppose delegating and giving up licensing power in China is that licensing applicants usually have to pay licensing fees.[98] As the China Business News reports, apart from this payment, it is also necessary to purchase services from firms affiliated to the regulators, otherwise the applications will not be accepted. A case in point is the licensing system for enterprise investment created by the National Development and Reform Commission (NDRC). NDRC will start to consider approving investment projects, only if research associations of NDRC have assessed the feasibility of these plans.[99] In certain industries, acquiring the NDRC project approval is necessary, if the establishment of new branches by foreign invested enterprises reaches a certain amount of investment.[100]

According to the Vice Minister of Industry and Information Technology (IIT) Weiming Mao (2014), some fee items of licensing authorities charge enterprises too much without authorization, significantly increasing the burdens of companies.[101] Findings of one IIT's research center (2014) demonstrate that paying the institutes under the jurisdiction of licensing agencies for their work gives heavy financial burdens to firms. Since enterprises have to buy the services from these organizations, these institutes impose substantial charges on their service items and the costs take various forms.[102] A report of NDRC (2015) shows that institutions affiliated to regulators responsible for approving enterprise investment projects offer services at unauthorized charges.[103]

As Lixin Zheng, a spokesman of IIT, holds, streamlining administration and delegating power to lower levels is regarded as a fundamental way to solve the high

98 Wang 2014a, p. 18.

99 张旭东， 中编办理出600余项审批权部委"割肉"讨价还价， 第一财经日报， Xudong Zhang, Central Licensing Agencies Bargain over the Plan to Cancel 600 Licensing Regimes, China Business News, available at: <www.yicai.com/news/2013/04/2608824.html> (last accessed 8 August 2014).

100 The US Chamber of Commerce, China's Approval Process for Inbound Foreign Direct Investment: Impact on Market Access, National Treatment and Transparency, available at: <www.uschamber.com/sites/default/files/reports/020021_China_InvestmentPaper_hires.pdf> (last accessed 1 January 2016).

101 人民日报, 涉企收费: 说不清的"费"， 何时能杜绝, 2014年12月15日. People's Daily, When can Rampant Charges upon the Enterprises be Stopped, 15 December 2014.

102 定军， 审计发现乱收费300多亿， 将建收费清单制度， 21世纪经济报道， 2014年11月19日， Jun Ding, Audit Reports: Arbitrary Collection of Charges on Enterprise Amount More than 300 Billion and List of charges Will be Drawn up, 21st Century Business Herald, 19 November 2014.

103 周素雅、夏晓伦, 发改委: 行政审批存前置手续繁杂、中介收费不合理等问题, Yasu Zhou and Xiaolun Xia, National Development and Reform Commission: Licensing Applications Have Some Problems, e.g. involving a great deal of red tape, available at: <http://finance.people.com.cn/n/2015/0108/c1004-26349183.html> (last accessed 22 May 2014).

cost problem mentioned by Weiming Mao, Vice Minister of IIT. In 2013, the State Council cancelled and delegated 416 administrative licensing items and introduced two other kinds of measures, thereby reducing the burdens on industries by more than 150 billion RMB each year.[104] The background of the business deregulation was discussed in chapter 2.

Moreover, empirical evidence demonstrates that companies engaging in cross-provincial business sometimes offer bribes to central licensing officials. In recent years, many licensing officials have been investigated for abusing licensing authority, as reported by the 21st Century Business Herald.[105] Take the licensing regime for enterprise investment plans established by NDRC as an example again. Courts find Liu Tienan, a former deputy head of NDRC and some other key officials of NDRC guilty of corruption tied to the project approvals.[106] Court rulings show that Liu Tienan took advantage of his office and illegally received 10 million RMB in exchange for allowing the Guangzhou Automobile Industry Group to open a new plant and operate another project.[107]

In the current corruption crackdown targeting licensing officials, streamlining administration and delegating licensing authority to lower levels are deemed fundamental by central leaders.[108] By 2014, the State Council had cancelled and delegated 76 per cent of the original approval items for enterprise investment projects.[109] A few public officials would resist or even oppose the reform of administrative approval systems for their personal gains, but other officers are expected to promote the reform in the public interest.[110]

4.2.2. SOEs under the Jurisdiction of the Regulators

SOEs under the jurisdiction of the central regulators may be in favour of regulating inter-provincial establishment at central level. This is because the central regulatory agencies may use their business licensing power to prevent private firms from entering the market, thereby benefiting the SOE incumbents. It has been pointed out

104 人民日报, 涉企收费: 说不清的"费", 何时能杜绝, 2014年12月15日. People's Daily, When can Rampant Charges upon the Enterprises be Stopped, 15 December 2014.

105 王秀强, 国务院大力清理投资项目前置审批拟实行网上并联核, 21世纪经济报道, 015年1月9日-01-09, Xiuqiang Wang, State Council Checks up Approval Items Related to Investment and plans to establish an online combined approval system, 21st Century Business Herald, 9 January 2015.

106 *Ibid.*

107 廊坊市中级人民法院刘铁男涉嫌受贿一审判决书, the Judgment of the Langfang Intermediate People's Court on the Corruption Case of Liu Tienan.

108 简政放权铲除"审批腐败"土壤, 2014年11月24日, 中国纪检监察报, China Discipline Inspection News, Streamline Administration and Delegate Power to Lower Levels so as to eliminate the soil for corruption related to licensing, 24 November 2014.

109 *Ibid.*

110 宋世明, 实现取消和下放行政审批事项数量和质量的统一, Shiming Song, Cancelling and Delegating Administrative Licensing Items in real earnest, available at: <www.scopsr.gov.cn/xzspzd/pl/201312/t20131211_248060.html> (last accessed 17 April 2016).

that SOEs affiliated with the central departments profit from the protection of these agencies and usually establish monopolies over the respective economic sectors.[111] What is even worse, SOEs are often involved in 'regulatory capture'.[112] In practice, SOEs or stock-holding companies under the jurisdiction of the central ministries and subsidiaries of these firms benefit mostly from rents and privileges.[113] According to Yang, governmental officials do not always adhere to the principle of separation of the functions of the government from those of enterprises. Relying on administrative measures, officials still create entry barriers to private companies that may pose a threat to the monopoly power of SOEs. In monopoly industries, based on licensing, these barriers take various forms.[114]

There are examples that the central licensing agencies abuse licensing power to erect obstacles to the establishment of subsidiaries or branches by entrants, thereby profiting centrally-owned companies. In this section, cases are used from the civil aviation industry (i.e. establishing airline offices) and the petroleum retail industry (opening petrol stations).

In the civil aviation sector, the Civil Aviation Administration of China (CAAC) sometimes imposes stringent requirements on entrants looking to expand across provincial borders. In particular, entry barriers are often raised for entrant companies, when centrally-owned enterprises, as incumbents, encounter difficulties in their operation.

The restrictions to the expansion of new airlines were first provided in 2007. According to the Document No. 101 of CAAC, this authority would not accept applications for establishing airline offices before 2010.[115] With regard to the 15 applications already received by 2007, no permission was granted until 2010.[116] Moreover, airline corporations and branches can only be set up in the airports that would be listed by CAAC.[117]

As reported by the Shanghai Security News, the regulatory measures introduced by CAAC in 2007 gave rise to significant profits for the Big 3 (Air China, China Eastern and China Southern). These policies considered the market share these firms have captured and gave priority to the development of these firms. Due to these giant SOEs' advantages in terms of air routes etc., these companies can

111 Ngo 2009, p. 12.

112 Wang 2014b, p. 415.

113 Ngo 2009, p. 12.

114 Yang 2003a, p. 31.

115 民航总局关于调控航班总量、航空运输市场准入和运力增长的通知（2007）, the Notice of CAAC on Controlling flight volume, Market Access and Capacity Growth (2007).

116 张孜异，民航"禁令"2.0版：地方"航空梦"碎，21世纪经济报道，2010年10月28日，Ziyi Zhang, the Further Ban of CAAC: Prohibiting local Governments from entering into the Aviation Industry, 21st Century Business Herald, 28 October 2010.

117 民航总局关于调控航班总量、航空运输市场准入和运力增长的通知（2007）, the Notice of CAAC on Controlling flight volume, Market Access and Capacity Growth (2007).

secure their dominant positions. Generally, the strong policy support rendered for these big corporations can help them develop.[118]

As shown by the Security Daily, the financial account of the Big 3 swung into a deficit of almost 30 billion RMB in 2008, to which CAAC paid close attention. In the same year, this central regulator quickly offered relief measures to these operators.[119] These policies restricted entry into the market, according to the Guangzhou Daily. Among them, one provision imposed six requirements on airline offices looking to set up branches, e.g. having at least 3 years of operation experience and at least 10 aircraft. As a result, since most of privately funded entities consist of a fleet of less than 10 planes, such limitation made the establishment of branches extremely difficult.[120] Moreover, the national aviation regulator almost excluded the possibility that new entrants can form businesses in some of China's busiest airports. As provided by CAAC (2009), only 5 air offices can be established in airports that accommodate more than 10 million passengers each year.[121] However, 5 airline holding companies have already set up branches in Shanghai Pudong Airport that handled almost 30 million passengers in 2009.[122] According to Anbound Consulting, a research group, the policies proposed by CAAC, in fact, promoted the development of SOEs, but hindered private companies. It cannot be denied that the governmental policies, as one important factor, constrained privately funded firms from quickly growing their business.[123]

When SOEs suffer heavy losses, CAAC usually restricts private companies' expansion through making administrative rules. A case in point is the document of 2010 imposing tight restrictions on granting licenses to airlines.[124] As provided in this document, CAAC would continue to refuse to accept airlines' applications for opening subsidiaries. Moreover, this authority would stop considering further applications for forming branches. Furthermore, entry barriers would be increased that only airline holding firms with more than 20 airplanes can create one branch.[125] As far as one journalist knows, most private airlines did not have branches by the

118 胡昆明，行业调控有利于提升三大集团盈利能力，上海证券报，2007年9月7日，Kunming Hu, Regulatory Measures of CAAC can Benefit the Profitability of the 'Big Three', the Shanghai Security News, 7 September 2007.

119 证券日报, 2010航空业喜忧: 巨大的繁荣遭遇成长的烦恼, 2010年12月10日， the Security Daily, the Development of the Civil Aviation Industry, between Joy and Sorrow, 10 December 2010.

120 王飞, 民营航空还能走多远, 广州日报, 2009年3月18日， Fei Wang, the Future of the Private Airlines is Uncertain, Guangzhou Daily, 18 March 2009.

121 民航局关于航空公司设立分公司的管理意见（2011）, the Opinion of CAAC on the Establishment of Branches by Airlines (2011).

122 索佩敏，需备6条件，航企设分公司门槛抬高，2009年2月19日，上海证券报，Shanghai Securities News, Raising Entry Barriers for Branches in the Aviation Industry: the Establishment Needs to Meet 6 Requirements, 19 February 2009.

123 安邦集团研究总部，每日经济，Anbound Consulting, Economic Daily, available at: <www.northernint.com/files/upfile/20090220095815451.doc> (last accessed 1 January 2016).

124 邱林. 谁是压倒民营航空的最后一根稻草？，中华工商时报，2011年9月5日，Lin Qiu, Who Plays a Decisive Role in Ruining Private Airlines?, China Business Times, 5 September 2011.

125 陈嘉佳，航空公司设立分、子公司门槛提高， 中国民航报， 2010年10月21日，CAAC News, Raising Entry Barriers for Airlines, 21 October 2010.

year 2010. Since these carriers provided services for only a few years and owned a small number of airplanes, they would not get chances to establish branches or subsidiaries.[126] One senior manager from a private airline complains that these enterprises would face almost insuperable difficulties in expansion, due to the requirement made in 2010.[127]

In the petroleum industry, regulations created by central regulators for this sector prevent non-public enterprises from forming businesses to operate the oil wholesale and retail business. Departmental rules made by the national agencies in 2001 ban private oil companies from holding controlling shares in newly established petrol stations. Moreover, only Sinopec and PetroChina are allowed to apply for licenses to open processed oil wholesale firms.[128] Regulations subsequently promulgated only permit the two SOEs to open new petrol stations.[129]

According to the Unirule Institute of Economics, a Beijing-based think-tank, the above provision was made, when Sheng Huaren was in charge of one of the central departments. From 1990 to 1998, he managed Sinopec. Immediately after being transferred to the leadership of the national agency in 1998, he set an agenda for making these rules favouring the development of Sinopec. Almost in the same period, Sinopec and PetroChina performed badly, due to high crude oil prices, as a 1997 national economic survey shows.[130]

The rules presented increased the two oil majors' dominance of the petroleum wholesale and retail market.[131] The SOEs' monopoly in the oil sector is closely related to such requirements and other government restrictions on competition in this industry.[132] As Huang and others note, it was anticipated that the 2001 provision would completely get rid of private oil wholesale enterprises and considerably decrease the number of non-public retail businesses. In 1999, there were 88,000 petroleum stations in China, including privately-owned stations amounting to 87.6 per cent of the national total and accounting for 60 per cent of the national total retail volume. Up to mid-2003, with a 40 per cent fuel retail market share, non-public firms had 40,000 petrol stations (half of the petrol stations in

126 陈姗姗，控制扩张速度，民航局再次收紧新设航企申请，第一财经日报，2010年10月21日，Shanshan Chen, Limiting the Expansion of Airlines: CAAC Restricts the Establishment of Airlines Once More, China Business News, 21 October 2010.

127 胡潇滢, 2010航空业喜忧: 巨大的繁荣遭遇成长的烦恼, 证券日报，2010年12月10日, the Security Daily, the Development of the Civil Aviation Industry, between Joy and Sorrow, 10 December 2010.

128 国家经贸委, 关于进一步整顿和规范成品油市场秩序的意见（2001), the State Economy & Trade Commission, A Suggestion on Furthering to Clean up and Normalize Trade Order of Crude Oil and Petroleum Products (2001).

129 国家经贸委，关于严格控制新建加油站问题的通知（2001), the State Economy & Trade Commission, the Notice of Exercising Strict Control over the Opening of New Petrol Stations (2001).

130 天则经济研究所，我国石油产业体制的形成、现状及其性质，Unirule Institute of Economics, An Analysis of the Current Situation of the Oil Industry in China, available at: <www.china-review.com/eat.asp?id=32374> (last accessed 9 March 2015).

131 *Ibid.*

132 Wang 2012, p. 23.

China).[133] These requirements spelled doom for privately-owned fuel oil retailers and wholesalers, as one private investor in the fuel station sector demonstrates.[134]

5. Conclusion

Adopting the theoretical framework presented in chapter 5, this chapter offered a critical analysis of the regulation of cross-provincial establishment in China. The first issue treated in this chapter was to what extent regulating inter-provincial establishment by rules different from the regulation of general establishment serves public interest or private interest goals. There are valid reasons for regions with higher standards to impose stricter requirements on the inter-provincial establishment of companies, provided that they do not abuse this justification to limit competition. However, the enforcement of the regulation of inter-provincial establishment in many other situations is certainly not in the public interest. Instead, the exercise of business licensing power seems to primarily serve local officials' attempts to seek promotion and to extract bribes. Chapter 7 will discuss potential solutions to the licensing barriers, on the basis of studying the issue of whether the EU can be a source of inspiration to China.

This chapter also examined the extent to which regulating inter-provincial establishment at central level can be considered as serving the public interest or private interest purposes. From a public interest perspective, centralization of the regulation has its cons and pros. A negative aspect is the fact that the centralization cannot provide certain benefits that decentralization can provide. More specifically, giving local authorities the power to regulate inter-provincial establishment can meet the different needs of economic development in different regions. Moreover, local authorities are allowed to compete with (and learn from) each other and governments may remove unnecessary licensing barriers to establishment.

Through examining the economic arguments in favour of centralization, it is demonstrated that scale economies and transaction cost savings cannot provide strong support for regulating inter-provincial establishment at central level. Other arguments need to be considered more carefully. In practice, trans-boundary externalities occur in the form of inter-provincial pollution. Empirical evidence also shows that regions in Central China and Western China are engaged in a race to the bottom and relax environmental regulation on establishment to attract factories relocating from Eastern China to these regions. However, these environmental problems do not suggest that empowering central regulators to create licensing systems for inter-provincial establishment alone would be an optimal response. This is because the mere creation of licensing regimes for inter-provincial establishment does not guarantee that the centrally set environmental standards will be complied with at local level. If national authorities want to ensure local authorities' compliance with the standards, other measures need to be added. As demonstrated

133 Huang *et al.* 2010, p. 351.

134 黄小伟，石油业兼职成风中石化清理门户，南方周末，2006年11月09日，Xiaowei Huang, PetroChina Proposes Reducing Concurrent Posts, Southern Weekly, 9 November 2006.

in section 3.2, a solution could be to upgrade the regional centers for environmental protection to the branches of Ministry of Environmental Protection (MEP). As a result, these centers will shoulder the responsibilities of directly enforcing compliance with the central standards at local level.

The public choice analysis provided some plausible explanations for regulating the inter-provincial establishment of companies at central level. The central governmental agencies may seek to regulate this business activity, because this authority enables them to gain economic benefits and create opportunities for corruption. Another benefiting party can be state-owned enterprises under the jurisdiction of the central governmental departments. These companies may support the centralization of the regulation, since barriers to entry can be created.

Taking into account both the public interest and private interest analysis, regulating inter-provincial establishment at local level appears to be preferable, if the environmental problems can be curbed. As the literature suggests, improving the capacity building of the regional centers for environmental protection can solve the environmental issues caused by empowering local authorities to establish environmental licensing systems for inter-provincial establishment. However, MEP seems to have no intention of giving more power to these institutions for environmental protection.[135] Though a new environmental protection law came into force in 2015, the authority of these centers has not been increased. Improving their functions remains a problem.[136] Therefore, at present, without improving the capacity building of these centers, it is hard to say whether regulating cross-provincial establishment at local level would lead to socially optimal results. Obviously, there can be a fear that pollution in China may be aggravated, if local authorities are empowered to create environmental licensing systems for inter-provincial establishment. Currently, pollution already causes huge losses.[137]

135 Huan 2011, p. 157.

136 澎湃新聞，全國政協委員張泓銘：升格區域環境督查中心，管各地環保部門，The Paper, An Expert Suggests Improving the Capacity Building of 6 Regional Centers for Environmental Protection and Empowering them to Oversee Local Environmental Agencies, available at: <www.thepaper.cn/newsDetail_forward_1307371> (last accessed 6 March 2015).

137 Liu 2013, p. 8.

Chapter 7

REGULATION OF THE INTER-PROVINCIAL ESTABLISHMENT OF COMPANIES IN CHINA: LEARNING FROM EUROPE?

1. Introduction

Chapter 6 showed that local governments in China sometimes compete with each other to attract investment by providing more lenient rules on business establishment. In some cases this competition leads to a race to the bottom, but in other cases it results in learning effects. Of course, competition among local authorities also occurs in other federal jurisdictions, such as the EU. Considering the development of the internal market presented in Chapter 3, this chapter compares China with the EU, in order to see to what extent the EU can be a source of inspiration for China.

The EU and China may be incomparable, since the differences between these jurisdictions appear very distinct. One major difference relates to the institutional features of the European and Chinese legal regimes, which will be elaborated on in this chapter. Moreover, China has its own problems to establish a law-based order: 'a low level of legal consciousness; the lack of a robust civil society; the enduring influence of paternalistic traditions and a culture of deference to government authority; the fallout from the unfinished transition from a centrally planned economy to a market economy;' and so on.[1] Therefore, we should be aware of the limitations of comparing China with the EU, (due to the unique situation in China).

This chapter will focus on the particular institutional features of the European and Chinese systems, in order to find out whether China can learn something from the EU experience. Specifically, this chapter will point out how the differences in institutions in China and the EU influence the formation of barriers to freedom of establishment in these jurisdictions. Moreover, close attention will be paid to how these differences impact on choosing solutions to these obstacles.

Comparative law and economics will be employed in the analysis. Combining the analytic tools of these two disciplines, this methodology can serve the purpose to better see the reasons for existing provisions and institutions and of their changes

1 Peerenboom 2002, p. 12.

and development.[2] This chapter starts by presenting how this approach deals with the comparison of legal systems.

2. Comparative Law and Economics: The Importance of Considering Institutional Differences in Comparative Study

Comparative law and economics adopts a comparative approach and takes into account local institutional environments.[3] The subject of comparative law and economics is a comparative analysis of various legal rules embedded in different institutional frameworks.[4] Different rules and different institutions are discussed in the light of economic efficiency.[5]

Mattei shows that existing divergences between various legal systems do not mean some of the legal rules are inefficient. Different legal systems may opt for different solutions to common legal problems.[6] Alternative solutions may all appear to be efficient, when associated with different institutional contexts.[7] The fact that institutional frameworks depend on the different organizational structure of each society may in turn justify the differences among legal systems.[8]

It is also pointed out that transplanted law may have very different effects in transplant countries from those in origin countries.[9] Whether the same legal rule can function effectively depends greatly on the institutional framework where the provision is embedded.[10] A lesson of this is that limitations should be considered when transplanting foreign law.[11]

Comparative law and economics can play a key part in legal improvement. The combination of comparative and economic tools can provide a powerful analytic method for legal study. For instance, comparative law and economics might enable scholars to measure the efficiency of various institutional arrangements and legal rules. Moreover, this approach may help us with the identification of those elements of a legal system that stand in the way of successful legal transplants. Furthermore, we might be able to predict the long-term effects of a legal arrangement from the standpoint of efficiency.[12]

2 Mattei *et al.* 2000, p. 505.
3 *Ibid.*, p. 521.
4 Caterina 2006, p. 165.
5 *Ibid.*
6 Mattei *et al.* 2000, p. 509.
7 Mattei & Cafaggi 1998, p. 347.
8 Caterina 2006, p. 164.
9 *Ibid.*
10 Mattei & Cafaggi 1998, p. 347.
11 Siems 2014, p. 4.
12 Mattei *et al.* 2000, p. 509.

3. The EU Regulation of Cross-border Establishment

3.1. *Institutional Aspects*

The EU comprises currently 28 Member States and they have ceded some of their sovereign rights to the union.[13] The institutions of the EU have limited legislative competences granted by its Treaty.[14] Conferral is the principle that governs the limits of the competences.[15] As provided by Article 5(2) TEU, 'Under the principle of conferral, the Union shall act only within the limits of the competences conferred upon it by the Member States in the Treaties to attain the objectives set out therein.'

In most areas that come under EU competence, the EU holds concurrent legislative authority,[16] and the choice of who should act is governed by the subsidiarity principle. Article 5(3) TEU notes that '[I]n areas which do not fall within its exclusive competence, the Union shall act only if and in so far as the objectives of the proposed action cannot be sufficiently achieved by the Member States, either at central level or at regional and local level, but can rather, by reason of the scale or effects of the proposed action, be better achieved at Union level'.

In the case of the completion of the internal market, the EU legislature has competences to adopt directives and regulations that harmonize, replace, or add to national law.[17] The exercise of these competences, like other legislative actions undertaken by the EU institutions, must comply with the principles of conferral and subsidiarity.[18]

Moreover, the CJEU supervises Member States, applying the freedoms of goods, persons, services and capital to national law. Through the case law of the CJEU, the principle of four freedoms has developed, thereby removing constraints imposed by Member States on cross-border activities.[19] The four freedoms and the role of the CJEU in the integration were discussed in chapter 3.

Among the procedural avenues to the court, infringement proceedings can be started in the situation where Member States are in breach of EU law. For instance, Member States may be unable to implement directives within the given time limits or may produce national law contravening EU law.[20] As another important procedure, preliminary rulings enable national courts to make references over the interpretation or validity of EU law to the CJEU.[21] The most vital function of this process, as noted by the CJEU, is to ensure the uniform application of European law by national courts throughout the EU.[22] Based on preliminary rulings, the judiciary

13 Borchardt 2010, p. 11.
14 Weatherill 2011, p. 828.
15 Horsley 2012, p. 269.
16 Muir Watt 2004, p. 436.
17 Snell 2013 p. 519.
18 Muir Watt 2004, p. 436.
19 *Ibid.*
20 Albors-Llorens 2014, p. 284.
21 Carrubba & Murrah 2005, p. 399.
22 Albors-Llorens 2014, p. 284.

of Member States can enforce EU law over national legislation, so this procedure is central to European integration.[23]

3.2. *Remaining Barriers to Cross-border Establishment*

As demonstrated in Chapter 3, the EU has undertaken a major effort to promote the development of the internal market, but there remain barriers to the cross-border establishment of companies. Chapter 3 identified the existence of national regulatory autonomy in some matters as the main cause of the remaining barriers. A case in point is Member States' regulatory competence in the field of taxation. Complying with different national tax regimes and dealing with different national tax authorities in the EU can impose extra costs on firms establishing branches across borders.

3.3. *Ways to Tackle the Remaining Barriers*

According to Chapter 3, there are two ways to further promote market integration in the EU: political integration and judicial integration. It is shown that CJEU rulings seem better able to cope with the remaining obstacles to the cross-border establishment of companies than intergovernmental bargaining among Member States. In the field of taxation, CJEU judgments have removed certain tax barriers to cross-border establishment that cannot be erased through political bargains.

4. Regulation of Inter-provincial Establishment in China

4.1. *Institutional Aspects*

It is obvious that China has a very different institutional structure from the EU. In post-1949 China, the state created a highly centralized unitary state regime.[24] Scholars hold that China's legislative power-division has its characteristics. The National People's Congress, the national legislature of the state, and its Standing Committee take unified leadership in law making. To complement national law and to adapt to local conditions, it is reasonable to delegate certain law making power to local authorities.[25] Local laws, as provided by Article 72 of the Legislation Law (2015), shall not contradict national legislation.[26] Considering the legislative power that the central organs have, one can note that their legislative activities are unlikely to be subject to any severe restriction.

Compared to the EU legislature, its Chinese counterpart faces few difficulties in passing laws to regulate its internal market. However, Chinese courts, unlike the judiciary in the EU, can only play a limited role in promoting market integration.

23 Carrubba & Murrah 2005, p. 399.
24 Kin 2009, p. 528.
25 Tian 2004, p. 315.
26 立法法 (2015).

According to Item (4) of Article 12 of the Administrative Procedure Law (APL) (2015), courts should accept suits brought by legal persons against a refusal by an administrative organ to issue a permit or license, which the legal person considers themselves legally qualified to apply for, or the failure of that administrative agency to respond to the application.[27] Therefore, when local officials reject non-local firms' licensing applications for entering the local market, non-local firms can use this provision to challenge such decisions in courts.

Moreover, as provided by the 2015 amendment to the Administrative Procedure Law (APL), courts in China should accept suits against the abuse of administrative power to eliminate or restrict competition.[28] This provision may cause us to raise a question whether businesses can challenge the abuse of administrative authority to restrict inter-provincial establishment in courts. Until now, no judicial interpretation has answered this question. Also, there appears to be scarce literature on this issue.

However, it is impossible for Chinese courts to use the power of judicial review to strike down general rules. As pointed out in chapter 2, according to Article 13(2) of the APL (2015), courts are not entitled to deal with suits against administrative regulations, the rules of local governments, the rules of the departments under the State Council or decisions and orders with general binding force promulgated by administrative organs. Article 3 of the Judicial Interpretation for the APL (2000), explains what is meant by 'decisions and orders' as referred to in Article 13(2).[29] Administrative normative documents with the following characteristics fall into the definition: (1) those created by administrative authorities; (2) those regulating unspecified objects of laws; and (3) those that can be used repeatedly.

4.2. *Barriers to the Inter-provincial Establishment of Companies*

Chinese companies, either foreign-funded or domestic-invested, which want to expand across provincial borders, may encounter barriers to market entry that have been erected by local licensing authorities. The main cause of this problem is the under-enforcement of national law on granting business licenses, as illustrated in chapter 2.

Despite these obstacles, some local authorities, as shown by chapter 2, assist FIEs in obtaining licenses for their expansion. Moreover, literature demonstrates that less developed provinces engage in a race to the bottom and implement lax environmental regulation on business establishment, in order to attract plants relocating from Eastern China to Western China and Central China.

27 行政诉讼法 (2015).
28 Art. 12 of the APL (2015).
29 最高人民法院关于执行《中华人民共和国行政诉讼法》若干问题的解释 (2000).

4.3. *Existing Ways to Tackle the Barriers*

The 2008 Anti-Monopoly Law (AML) empowers some administrative agencies to cope with the imposition of restrictions on inter-provincial establishment. According to Articles 35 and 51 of the AML, when administrative agencies abuse their power to restrict non-local undertakings' establishment of branches and subsidiaries in their regions, the superior authority of these organizations should order them to rectify. Moreover, State Administration of Industry and Commerce (SAIC) or local Administrations for Industry and Commerce (AICs) can propose suggestions to the superior authority on how to deal with the matter.[30]

However, the sanctions proposed by the AML are deemed to be unable to effectively tackle administrative monopolies, as concluded by chapter 2. An explanation for this ineffectiveness is that higher and lower administrative departments are not independent of one another.[31] Therefore, higher organs are unlikely to order lower departments to rectify the abuse of administrative power. The inability of higher agencies to deal with administrative monopolies is pointed out as another reason.

Moreover, many scholars strongly criticize the absence of judicial review over the abuse of business licensing power. As discussed in chapter 2, some authorities tend to create unlawful licensing regimes through local legislation; as a result, barriers for inter-provincial establishment are erected. However, courts have no jurisdiction over the legislation.

5. Insights from Standards versus Rules Debate on China Learning from the EU

As shown by sections 3 and 4, the enforcement of the regulation on inter-provincial establishment is unsatisfactory in China due to its weak administrative and judicial systems, while a strong judicial mechanism is vital to ensure the freedom of establishment in Europe. Considering the different capacities in these jurisdictions, it may be misguided for China to take the same approach to regulate inter-provincial establishment as the EU. The reason is that the EU regulation of cross-border establishment appears to depend to a considerable degree on the existence of a strong judicial system.

In the field of law and economics, there is a debate exploring the circumstances in which ex ante rules provided by legislatures are better than standards created by judiciary or bureaucratic agencies.[32] We may use the conclusion drawn from this study to investigate whether China would be better advised to develop a standards-based system of inter-provincial establishment regulation that relies heavily on courts for specification of norms, or a rule-based system that concentrates more authority in the hands of legislators.

30 Art. 51 of the AML.

31 Wang 2009, p. 57.

32 Faure *et al.* 2010, p. 110.

In recent years, the law and economics literature has suggested that in countries with weak administrative capacities and inefficient judicial systems, rule-based systems are easier to manage. While rules have high initial costs, they possess enforcement and compliance cost advantages over standards. As a result, rule-based systems rather than standards-based systems may be recommendable to developing countries where limited administrative capacities are prevalent.[33]

Moreover, Posner argues that in countries whose judiciary suffers from weak capacities or the lack of judicial independence, rules have one advantage not available to standards, i.e. rules can decrease the likelihood of bribery and political influence on judicial decisions. With less discretion in law enforcement, it will be more difficult for judges to misuse law in rendering judgments, when rule-based systems are adopted.[34]

In applying these insights to regulatory design for cross-provincial establishment in China, it is better to adopt a rule-based system of regulation. There are two reasons for the recommendation: low-capacity administrative systems and the lack of judicial independence.

First, existing administrative organs appear to face difficulties in building capacities necessary for dealing with the abuse of administrative power by local governments. According to Liu, central governmental agencies shoulder the responsibilities of formulating policies and macro-plans, but their implementation usually does not fall within the power of the departments. Instead, local authorities play a vital part in enforcing laws and policies.[35] It is recognized that they lay down detailed rules to implement vaguely defined central mandates and legal norms.[36]

However, the enforcement of laws and policies by local governments turns out to be non-uniform and weak.[37] As summarized by Van Rooij and others, one can find a large literature arguing that in numerous fields of law and policy, enforcement of national provision is hampered by 'local protectionism'. The reason to hamper the implementation is that strong enforcement can harm the economic interests of local governments.[38] Based on a large body of literature on local governance in China, Ahlers and Schubert hold that local authorities, as implementers, sometimes even displace the objectives of central policies.[39] According to Huaide Ma, a leading scholar on Chinese administrative law, there are numerous cases where local officials disregard law tackling local protectionism in order to benefit local economic development.[40]

33 Schäfer 2006, p. 113 and 134.

34 Posner 1998, p. 5.

35 刘海波，我国中央与地方政治结构的分析与改进，改革内参，2006年第6期，Haibo Liu, An Analysis of Political Structure Between Central and Local Governments and its Improvement, No. 6, 2006, available at: <https://www.iolaw.org.cn/showArticle.asp?id=2050> (last accessed 23 August 2015).

36 Minzner 2009, p. 77 and 78.

37 Ma 2003, p. 157 and 158.

38 Van Rooij *et al.* 2015, p. 2.

39 Ahlers & Schubert 2014, p. 3.

40 Ma 2003, p. 157 and 158.

Second, scholars recognize local administrative interference in China's courts as the principal problem that influences their activities in handling administrative litigation cases.[41] Local administrative intervention in judicial decision-making remains acceptable and is even supported by party-state leaders.[42] Due to local governments' influence over the judiciary in various ways, China's judges cannot decide these cases according to law.[43] Although courts face fewer difficulties to deal with license denial cases than cases involving socio-economic rights, courts may still render rulings favouring local government in the first type of cases, due to local protectionism or government intervention.[44] It is pointed out that litigants have a very low likelihood of winning these lawsuits.[45] As revealed by one judge from the China Supreme Court, the winning rate for plaintiffs against the government in administrative litigation cases has decreased from 30 per cent in the 2000s to less than 10 per cent in recent years. The courts continue to be subject to the interference, since administrative litigation empowers civilians to dispute the administrative acts of local authorities.[46]

The reason why local governments are able to exert influence on the courts is that they control court finances and the appointment and removal of local judges.[47] Within the Party's own hierarchy, many local administrative officers are more powerful than judges at the same level.[48] According to Wang, Chinese local governments shoulder the responsibility of covering the costs of local courts at the corresponding territorial level. All the basic expenses of local courts, such as the fees for staffing, office equipment and court buildings, are funded by local governments.[49] Considering this relation, one cannot expect the judges to have the willingness to cope with local protectionism.[50] Moreover, since personal independence has not been granted to individual judges, some court presidents often interfere in judicial decisions in order to meet the needs of local officials.[51]

6. Conclusion

Based on an analysis of the institutional features of the European and Chinese regimes, this chapter studied whether lessons can be drawn for China from the European experience in promoting market integration. From an institutional perspective, we should pay attention to the fact that the EU consists of sovereign

41 Li 2013, p. 46.
42 Liebman 2007, p. 635.
43 Ma 2013, p. 8.
44 Peerenboom & He 2009, p. 47.
45 Pei 1997, p. 841.
46 大河报，中国司法尴尬现状: 民告官案原告胜诉率不到10%，A Less than 10% Likelihood of Winning Administrative lawsuits in China, available at: <http://news.qq.com/a/-20141105/006766.htm> (last accessed 14 August 2015).
47 Ma 2013, p. 8.
48 O'Brien & Li 2004, p. 84.
49 Wang 2013b, p. 48.
50 Liu 2002, p. 14.
51 Ma 2013, p. 8.

countries, while China is a unitary country. Unlike the EU lawmakers, Beijing faces few difficulties in legislating its internal market. However, a problem for China can be that law enforcement in this country may be ineffective at tackling local protectionism, due to low administrative capacities. Moreover, compared to their European counterparts, Chinese courts are not smooth-functioning and independent. Obviously, since administrative intervention in judgments often occurs, China's courts face difficulties in dealing with suits brought by firms against administrative organs who refuse to issue licenses. Another important issue is that the power of judicial review to strike down general rules has not been granted to the judiciary. At present, when courts consider that local law contradicts national law, they may submit to the Standing Committee of the National People's Congress (NPC) written suggestions for examination. Nevertheless, according to Xu, an expert on legislation law, the Standing Committee has not responded to any suggestions ever made.[52]

The institutional differences lead to different causes of barriers to cross-border establishment in the two jurisdictions. In the EU, the remaining barriers to cross-border establishment mainly arise from the existence of national regulatory autonomy in some matters. By contrast, in China, the enforcement of national law on granting licenses and dealing with administrative monopolies at local levels is far from satisfactory, which create troubles for businesses expanding across provincial borders.

The institutional differences also have a big impact on choosing solutions to the barriers in China and the EU. China should not adopt a standards-based system of regulation for cross-border establishment that is used in the EU. Precise rules defined by the legislative authority offer a better prospect of regulatory effectiveness for China whose administrative capacities are weak and courts are not independent.

52 Xu 2014, p. 14.

Chapter 8

CONCLUSIONS

1. Research Questions and Summary of Findings

In the introduction of this book, two main research questions were posed:

1. To what extent can regulation of inter-provincial establishment of companies in China be considered as serving public interest or private interest goals?
2. To what extent can we learn lessons from the economic theory and the EU experience for the regulation of inter-provincial establishment?

These main research questions were divided into a number of sub-questions. The following will first reproduce these sub-questions and then provide answers to them, divided into the respective parts of this dissertation.

Part I. Legal Analysis

Question 1: What regulations exist in China concerning the inter-provincial establishment of companies and how are they enforced?

Chinese authorities impose minimum capital requirements and licensing requirements on firms expanding across provinces. The establishment by companies across provinces can take the form of either subsidiaries or branches. Minimum capital requirements apply for subsidiaries, but not for branches. Apart from capitalization rules, it is also necessary to obtain an establishment registration license to open subsidiaries and branches in China. Other licensing obligations for inter-provincial establishment are presented as follows.

According to the Company Law (2005), domestic firms that want to form branches or subsidiaries in another province need to acquire permission 'if the business scope of these branches and subsidiaries contains any matter subject to approval'.[1] Moreover, if the incorporation of the branches and subsidiaries invested in is subject to approval, it is necessary to complete the relevant approval formalities before registering the establishment.[2]

1 Arts. 12 and 14 of the Company Law (2005).
2 *Ibid.*, Arts. 6 and 14.

In terms of the inter-provincial establishment by Foreign Invested Enterprises (FIEs), FIEs opening subsidiaries in designated 'restricted investment fields' also need to obtain approval from commercial agencies, in addition to registering their establishment.[3] Before permitting establishment, commercial authorities need to ask for the opinions of authorities administrating the fields these subsidiaries operate in.[4] When subsidiaries are established in 'permitted and encouraged fields', such establishment only needs to go through the registration procedure.[5] FIEs forming branches in any of the 'restricted, permitted or allowed fields' are asked to obtain project approval from the Development and Reform Commissions (DRCs) prior to registering their establishment.[6]

The Administrative License Law (ALL) (2003) provides which matters are subject to licensing. Article 12(6) of the ALL seems to allow administrative agencies to extend licensing systems to almost every matter. Therefore, there is a possibility that legal barriers can be erected for the inter-provincial establishment of companies.

The actual use of the legal rules on the inter-provincial establishment of companies set up significant obstacles to this establishment. Specifically, there are cases where the exercise of licensing power by local authorities creates barriers for domestic firms in some fields. Moreover, the licensing authority of both national and local departments is used to erect obstacles for Foreign Invested Enterprises (FIEs) to expand in different regions. However, in some other cases, local authorities rather support these industries in expanding across provinces.

Existing administrative remedies cannot deal with the imposition of restrictions on inter-provincial establishment. As provided by Articles 35 and 51 of the 2008 Anti-Monopoly Law (AML), in cases where administrative departments abuse their authority to restrict non-local undertakings' establishment of branches and subsidiaries in their regions, the superior authority of these organizations shall order them to rectify. However, mainly because higher and lower administrative departments are not independent of one another, the sanctions proposed by the AML cannot effectively cope with the abuse of administrative power.

Moreover, many scholars strongly criticize the absence of judicial review over the abuse of business licensing power. According to the Administrative Procedure Law (APL) (1989) and its judicial interpretation, where unlawful licensing regimes are established through local legislation, decisions or orders, such cases cannot be brought before courts. The absence of judicial control has been recognized as an important cause for the occurrence of barriers to the inter-provincial establishment of companies.

3 Art. 9 of the Provisional Regulations Governing Investment within the Territory by FIEs (外商投资企业境内投资的暂行规定) (2000) (hereinafter the Regulations for Reinvestment).

4 *Ibid.*, Art. 10.

5 *Ibid.*, Art. 7.

6 US Chamber of Commerce, China's Approval Process for Inbound Foreign Direct Investment: Impact on Market Access, National Treatment and Transparency, available at: <https://www.uschamber.com/sites/default/files/documents/files/020021_China_InboundInvestment_Cvr.pdf> (last accessed 4 February 2015).

Question 2: how does the EU regulate the cross-border establishment of companies?

The EU has undertaken a major effort to integrate markets across member countries. The European integration experience indicates that the CJEU and the Commission are major engines behind the market integration. Moreover, the internal market is established through both negative integration and positive integration.

The Treaty on the Functioning of the European Union (TFEU) provides the freedom of establishment for companies. This principle is reinforced by the CJEU through applying Articles 49 and 56 TFEU to national obstacles to this freedom. Moreover, on the basis of codifying the rulings of the court on the establishment of service providers, the Services Directive 2006/123 has further facilitated the cross-border establishment of companies.

As a result, today companies in the EU enjoy much more freedom to establish operations across borders, but barriers remain. The remaining barriers mainly arise from the exercise of national regulatory autonomy in certain fields such as company taxation. CJEU rulings seem better able to deal with these barriers than intergovernmental bargains among Member States.

Part II. Theoretical Framework

Question 3: what does the economic theory teach us about regulation of the cross-border establishment of companies in a multi-level jurisdiction?

The economic theory taught us two things about regulation of the cross-border establishment of companies in a multi-level jurisdiction. The first lesson concerns imposing different rules on cross-border establishment and regular establishment. It was shown that both public and private interest reasons can explain the creation of tougher conditions for cross-border establishment. On the one hand, making more stringent requirements for cross-border establishment can be justified on the grounds of information asymmetry between companies funded by non-local investors and local consumers. Compared to businesses established by local enterprises, local consumers may have more difficulties to find information about companies formed by non-local firms, such as company reputations. The difficulty of knowing the reputations of subsidiaries established by non-local firms can affect buyers' perception of the quality of these subsidiaries' new products and services. On the other hand, the danger exists that some interest groups, i.e. incumbents, local entrants and politicians and officials from states with higher standards, may profit from raising entry barriers to companies from jurisdictions with lower standards.

The second point learned from economic theory concerns the question whether cross-border business establishment should be regulated at central level or at local level. Following an economic approach, inefficiencies caused by inter-jurisdictional competition and scale economies in information were brought forward to support centralization of the regulation of cross-border establishment. However, whether a race to the bottom and transaction cost savings are arguments in favour of centralization needs to be evaluated on the basis of empirical evidence. In particular, benefits arising from the differentiation of the regulation of cross-border establishment may outweigh the reduction of transaction costs. Moreover, a public choice analysis demonstrated that some interest groups may have incentives to regulate cross-border business establishment at central level for private interests. Making the regulation at the federal level may serve the interests of politicians and officials of the central government to increase influence and power. Incumbent firms may also require centralized regulations in the field of cross-border business establishment, if barriers to entry can be created. The national policy makers and bureaucrats, as the third type of interest group, may favour their national interest groups and support the centralization of the regulation.

Part III. Economic Evaluation

Question 4: *to what extent can the regulation of inter-provincial establishment in China be considered as serving public interest or private interest purposes?*

In terms of making different rules for general establishment and inter-provincial establishment, some advanced areas in China, e.g. Beijing, created higher entry barriers for the latter. These barriers can be justified on the ground of the possible occurrence of externalities caused by lower standards in other regions, e.g. arising from lower quality standards. This argument turns out be valid, as long as the developed areas do not abuse this justification to limit competition. However, the enforcement of the regulation of inter-provincial establishment in many other situations certainly does not serve the public interests. A significant incentive for local officials to make more stringent requirements for inter-provincial establishment seems that they want to seek promotion and extract bribes.

Regarding the regulation of inter-provincial establishment at central level or at local level, there are some public interest arguments in favour of the centralization of the regulation of inter-provincial establishment. Empirical evidence demonstrates that trans-boundary externalities exist in the form of inter-provincial pollution. Moreover, regions in Central China and Western China engage in a race to the bottom in environmental standards to attract corporate relocations from Eastern China. However, empirical evidence was also provided that the private interest goals of the regulators for inter-provincial establishment and State Owned Enterprises (SOEs) under their jurisdiction may be achieved through regulating inter-provincial establishment at central level.

Question 5: is regulating inter-provincial establishment at central level or at local level to be preferred in China?

The inter-provincial pollution and the race to the bottom provide potential public interest justifications for regulating inter-provincial establishment at central level, but this does not mean that the centralization can achieve socially optimal results. The main drawbacks of the centralization are that, unlike decentralization of the regulation, it cannot provide some advantages. More specifically, empowering local authorities to regulate inter-provincial establishment enable them to create business licensing systems suitable for local economic development. The decentralization also allows local governments to compete with (and learn from) each other. As a consequence, they may remove overly restrictive licensing barriers to establishment. Moreover, a solution was found that can cope with the race to the bottom and the trans-boundary pollution arising from the competition. It was recommended that China should upgrade the regional centers for environmental protection to the branches of the Ministry of Environmental Protection (MEP). As a result, these centers will be empowered to directly enforce compliance with the centrally set environmental standards at local level.

Therefore, theoretically, decentralization of the regulation of inter-provincial establishment appears to be better, if the authority of these centers can be increased. However, in practice, since the capacity building of these institutions has not been improved, it is hard to say whether regulating cross-provincial establishment at local level would be socially optimal.

Question 6: to what extent can the EU experience in regulating the cross-border establishment of companies be a source of inspiration for China?

When learning lessons from the EU experience for the regulation of inter-provincial establishment in China, we should attach importance to the institutional features of these jurisdictions. Owing to the institutional differences between China and the EU, Chinese policymakers should not use a standards-based system of regulation that is adopted for cross-border establishment in the EU. Without high administrative capacities and independent courts, this nation is better advised to provide precise rules set by the legislature.

2. Policy Recommendations

Some policy recommendations are already apparent in the previous section presenting the main research findings of this dissertation. In addition to these specific suggestions, a number of recommendations of a more general nature will also be provided in this section.

First, the thesis suggests that inter-provincial establishment should be regulated at local level in China. Meanwhile, MEP should upgrade the regional centers for environmental protection to branch-level agencies, empowering these centers to directly assure compliance with the centrally issued environmental standards at local level. The reason for adopting these policy options is that regulating inter-provincial establishment at local level allows for competition among local authorities and a learning process. Moreover, upgrading the regional centers can help to cope with the negative effects of such regulatory competition, i.e. a race to the bottom in environmental standards and inter-provincial pollution. Obviously, improving the capacity building of these centers should not be considered a total remedy for environmental pollution in China. How to tackle the pollution problem is beyond the scope of this thesis.

Second, China should use a rule-based system of regulation for inter-provincial establishment. More specifically, legislative decision making in the setting of inter-provincial establishment should be taken at the central level. Moreover, national legislators should precisely and clearly prescribe which authorities are empowered to control inter-provincial establishment, and under what conditions,. It should be noted that the ALL (2003) clearly defines who can create licensing regimes, but the provision of this law about what matters can be licensing items, is vaguely formulated.

Because the rule-based regulation does not require strong capacities for enforcement, this form of regulation suits the legal and political situation in China. The reality in China shows that its administrative agencies lack capacities to tackle the problem of abuse of administrative power at local level. Moreover, Chinese courts continue to be subject to external controls that significantly reduce their ability to handle administrative cases.

Third, Chinese courts should be granted the power of judicial review to strike down general rules. The empirical evidence provided by this thesis revealed a paradox between the provision of the ALL (2003) and the implementation on licensing. From the relevant legal provisions, it follows that central government constrains the autonomy of licensing power owned by local authorities, so that local administrative agencies cannot abuse business licensing power. However, the actual use of licensing significantly departs from the regulation provided in the ALL (2003). More specifically, governmental agencies, other than the statutory licensing authorities, set up licensing regimes and determine what matters can be licensing items, apparently at random. As a result, the real application of licensing leads to considerable barriers in doing business. A significant cause of this paradoxical situation is that general rules cannot be challenged for their legality in China. This means that where unlawful licensing systems are created through local legislation, such cases cannot be brought before the courts. Of course, the creation of the right to institute suits against unlawful regulations would be a long march.

Fourth, Chinese courts should have independent finances. Even if the judiciary were granted the power to review general rules, it would be hard to expect local courts whose finances are controlled by local governments to strike down local legislation.

Fifth, China's efforts to curb corruption should not only focus on delegating business licensing power to governments at lower levels. As pointed out in section 9 of chapter 2, Premier Li Keqiang views delegating power to lower levels as a fundamental way to rule out corruption. However, as argued by many commentators, bribery in China was more frequent at local levels than at the central level.[7] Also, theoretically, it is unclear whether regulatory decentralization leads to a reduction in corruption in local governments.[8]

Sixth, local officials' ability to foster growth should not be regarded as the over-riding criterion for assessing their performance. A strong correlation between economic growth and career future has historically motivated local public servants to violate environmental and other laws viewed as impediments to economic goals.[9] In order to have better career outcomes, local public officers sometimes implement local protectionist measures that can increase local economic development in the short term. Therefore, local officials should also be held responsible for granting equal market access opportunities to non-local companies, rather than only promoting local economic growth.

7 Wong 2011, p. 143.
8 Fan *et al*. 2009, p. 18.
9 Wang 2013a, p. 380.

3. Academic Achievements

This dissertation used the private interest approach to regulation in explaining the existing regulation of the inter-provincial establishment of companies and its enforcement. The findings presented in this work, taken from existing sources and from the author's interviews with stakeholders, provided some support for Stigler's hypothesis that regulation is used as a barrier to entry, serving the interests of local companies. It also provided some support for the hypothesis that public officials do not (only) take into account social interests, but private interests as well, including their own.

Nevertheless, the explanations for existing licensing barriers in China do not seem to be entirely consistent with those suggested by the 'traditional' public choice theory. Although corruption, a central element in the 'tollbooth view' presented in chapter 3, explains some of the entry barriers experienced by non-local firms and FIEs, the 'vote motive' for re-election does not seem to be relevant in the Chinese context. A much more likely explanation for entry control is that it affects the behaviour of local officers seeking promotion, taking into account that career advancement within the CPC is to some extent linked to (local) GDP growth. This 'career advancement' motive creates a level of competition between local areas that has the potential to become destructive. Moreover, in combination with the often short-term tenure of local officials, and the goal of creating strong local industries (who in turn become strong lobbying groups), it provides incentives to create barriers to cross-provincial establishment.

The preceding paragraphs demonstrate that with considerable modifications and adapting to the political context, the private interest approach to regulation can be useful for explaining the regulation of inter-provincial establishment in China. Due to China's unique political institutions, promotion rather than the 'vote motive' drives local officials to introduce entry barriers. The political context also means that interest groups having close links to the government, such as SOEs, perhaps can play more vital roles in the formation of the regulation.

4. Limits

The limitations of this research are that it cannot provide one clear answer to some important questions. First, concerning the effect of the regulatory competition between local authorities, empirical evidence presented in this book cannot lead to one clear result. This thesis showed that local authorities in China sometimes compete with (and learn from) each other to relax rules on business establishment. As a result, overly restrictive licensing barriers to establishment in some regions have been erased. Nevertheless, sometimes this competition results in a race to the bottom, lowering the standards for the protection of the environment etc.

Second, it appears extremely difficult to predict local officers' behaviour. This thesis provided no empirical support that officials' quest for promotion necessarily leads to entry barriers to non-local companies. With the 'career advancement' motive, public officials may be responsive to the demands of local businesses, but they may also be responsive to non-local firms. In previous chapters, we saw many cases where entry barriers are erected for non-local industries, while in other cases, they receive support from local officers. Interviews with stakeholders, as well as other empirical studies, show that whether or not local governments attract the investment by non-local firms depends on various factors. For instance, if investment destinations are regions where government intervention in economic activities has been reduced, non-local investors may face fewer difficulties in establishing businesses. Moreover, it appears to be easier for companies having strong ties with the central government, in particular certain SOEs, to expand nationwide. Furthermore, if the market concerned is competitive or profitable, local governments are more likely to restrict the entry of non-local firms, in order to protect local industries.

5. Future Research

Based on the effects of the regulatory competition between local governments, directions for future research naturally include creating an institutional framework for competition among local authorities.

First, considering the positive effects of the regulatory competition, Chinese law should establish a legal framework that allows competition between local governments. A first step for achieving this goal can be creating scope for competition. Apparently, today regions or provinces in China have very limited regulatory competence. The ALL (2003) bans local authorities from passing licensing rules except licensing regulations managing their local affairs.

Second, Chinese law should also provide remedies to reduce the risk of a race to the bottom and deal with potential negative externalities across provincial borders. As the preceding sections suggest, reshaping the regional environmental protection centers to become branches of MEP can help to cope with a race to the bottom in environmental standards and inter-provincial pollution. However, MEP shows no willingness to do so. The question which follows, therefore, is why this authority has no intention of adopting this policy option.

Third, equally important is the establishment of a legal mechanism that aims to preserve the internal market. While regulatory competence granted to local authorities makes competition between them possible, their regulatory power can be used to protect local interests against competition. It was recommended that China should use precise rules set by the legislature to regulate inter-provincial establishment. However, this approach does not eliminate enforcement problems. Therefore, a future task is to study the issue of the enforcement of the rule-based legal norms, considering China's specific political and economic institutions.

VALORISATION ADDENDUM

1. Relevance: What is the social/economic relevance of the research results?
It is generally argued in the literature that protectionist measures are taken by local authorities, which lead to restrictions on the inter-provincial establishment of companies and to market segmentation. In China, local government may take disguised measures to restrict the entry of commodities and enterprises from other places to local areas, thereby abusing their power to grant licenses. As a result, market barriers are created. Existing empirical evidence, as well as my own interviews with stakeholders, confirm that Chinese companies, either foreign-funded or domestic-invested, which want to expand across provincial borders, sometimes encounter barriers to market entry that have been erected by local licensing authorities. In contrast to the creation of entry barriers, as discussed above, there may be destructive competition between provinces to attract investment by non-local businesses.

Based on the above observations, this research examined to what extent regulation of the inter-provincial establishment of companies in China can be considered as serving public interest or private interest goals. Moreover, this thesis studied the extent to which lessons can be learned from economic theory and past EU experience for the regulation of inter-provincial establishment.

Obviously, the research results have social/economic relevance. Firstly, this thesis answered the question whether China can learn something from the EU experience with market integration. Since the expansion of China's internal market is likely to become a more significant ingredient for China's future economic growth, this country would benefit from ensuring easier inter-provincial establishment.

Secondly, this dissertation pointed out that Chinese courts should be granted the power of judicial review to strike down general rules. Because general rules cannot be challenged for their legality in China, the real application of licensing leads to considerable barriers in doing business. Obviously, the establishment of judicial review over general rules can help curb the abuse of business licensing power and remove unnecessary entry barriers. As a result, both Chinese companies and international companies would profit from this suggestion.

Thirdly, this research studied the extent to which lessons can be learned from economic theory for the regulation of inter-provincial establishment. In the process of economic development, local governments in China sometimes create overly restrictive entry barriers to non-local firms, in order to protect local industries. In contrast to the erection of entry barriers, local authorities sometimes engage in destructive competition to attract investment by non-local businesses. It is obvious that both the creation of overly restrictive barriers and the destructive competition is socially inefficient. Therefore, the lessons learnt from economic theory can benefit China.

Fourthly, although this thesis studies the situation in China, the case studies presented in this book can be insightful for other countries. Regulatory competition in the business establishment field, as demonstrated by the Chinese experience, may lead to both positive effects and negative effects. This experience also shows that while there may be public interest arguments for licensing requirements concerning business establishment, interest groups sometimes abuse these arguments and introduce licensing regimes to benefit themselves. These lessons can be insightful for other countries in pointing to problems they may want to prevent.

2. Target groups: To whom, in addition to the academic community, are the research results of interest and why?

The results are of high importance for various groups. A first party can be companies, including international companies, doing business in China. The Administrative License Law (ALL) (2003) has explicitly restricted the establishment of licensing regimes by administrative agencies at random for a long time, but the provision of the ALL has no effect to curb the random creation of licensing systems. As a result, the real application of licensing leads to considerable barriers in doing business. A significant cause of this paradoxical situation is that general rules cannot be challenged for their legality.

This book is of relevance for Chinese policy makers too. Considering the development of the internal market of the EU, Chinese policy makers may wish to learn lessons from the EU experience for the regulation of inter-provincial establishment in China. As recommended by this thesis, China should not use a standards-based system of regulation that is adopted for cross-border establishment in the EU, due to the institutional differences between China and the EU.

Also, Chinese legislators can get good insights into the division of regulatory competences between Beijing and local governments. The ALL (2003) bans local authorities from passing licensing rules except licensing regulations managing their local affairs. Taking into account the positive effects of regulatory competition, Chinese lawmakers should consider creating scope for competition among local governments.

Moreover, the Chinese experience can be of importance for policy makers worldwide. As demonstrated in section 1, China has a large body of experience in regulating business establishment, this country can be chosen as a reference point.

Finally, this research can be of academic interest. The reason is that this book added value to law and economics research by examining the conditions under which Chinese local governments create entry barriers to non-local firms. A large body of literature exists on the effects of competition between jurisdictions on regulatory standards, but it is still unclear in which circumstances a race to the bottom or a race to the top will occur.

3. Activities/Products: Into which concrete products, services, processes, activities or commercial activities will your results be translated and shaped?
Firstly, the results of this research will be published in book form, which will offer a thorough analysis of regulation of business establishment in China and, more generally, the law and economics literature on business licensing.

Secondly, the author has continuously disseminated the research results, e.g. by presenting at workshops and conferences, and some parts of the book have already been published in a different form elsewhere. For instance, 'Regulation of the Inter-Provincial Establishment of Companies: Applying the Private Interest Approach to China' was published in the book 'Market Integration: The EU Experience and Implications for Regulatory Reform in China'. In addition to book chapters, there is a plan to convert the thesis into journal articles.

4. Innovation: To what degree can your results be called innovative in respect to the existing range of products, services, processes, activities and commercial activities?
This dissertation can be called innovative, since it adopted the private interest approach to regulation in explaining the existing regulation of inter-provincial establishment and its enforcement in China. This thesis demonstrated that with significant modifications, this approach can be useful for explaining the regulation of inter-provincial establishment in a setting that is different from the more traditional application of this theory to western democracies like the US and EU. Due to China's unique political institutions, the creation of entry barriers seems to primarily serve local officials' attempts to seek promotion.

Moreover, this book explored the circumstances under which local authorities in China erect entry barriers to non-local businesses and therefore contributed to the literature. As pointed out in section 2, no definite answer can be given to the question under which conditions a race to the bottom or a race to the top will occur.

5. Schedule & Implementation: How will these plans for valorization be shaped?
Presenting at conferences can make the research results available to the public. Some results have been presented at seminars and meetings, such as the 32nd Annual Conference of the European Association of Law and Economics in Vienna, the 10th Annual Conference of the European China Law Studies Association in Cologne and the seminar 'Market Integration: The EU experience and implications for regulatory reform in China' in Beijing. Moreover, the author will have the opportunity to speak at the annual conferences organized by the German Law and Economics Association and the Chinese Economic Association (UK/Europe).

In addition to academic presentations, there is a plan to provide legal advisors and chambers of commerce with handbooks created from this research. Focusing on offering deep insights into the reality of business establishment in China, these brochures can help attract the attention of the respective stakeholders.

BIBLIOGRAPHY

Adler 2012
Adler, J., 'Interstate Competition and the Race to the Top', *The Harvard Journal of Law & Public Policy*, 2012, Vol. 35(1), p. 89-99.

Ahlers & Schubert 2014
Ahlers, A.L. & Schubert, G., 'Effective Policy Implementation in China's Local State', *Modern China*, 2014, Vol. 17, p. 1-34.

Akerlof 1970
Akerlof, G., 'The Market for "Lemons": Quality and the Market Mechanism', *Quarterly Journal of Economics*, 1970, Vol. 84, p. 488-500.

Albors-Llorens 2014
Albors-Llorens, A., 'Judicial Protection before the Court of Justice of the European Union', in Barnard C. & Peers, S. (eds.), *European Union Law*, Oxford: Oxford University Press, 2014, p. 255-299.

Andvig *et al.* 2000
Andvig, J.C. *et al.*, *Research on Corruption: A Policy Oriented Survey*, Bergen: Chr. Michelsen Institute, 2000.

Armour 2000
Armour, J., 'Share Capital and Creditor Protection: Efficient Rules for a Modern Company Law', *Modern Law Review*, 2000, Vol. 63(3), p. 355-378.

Armour 2006
Armour, J., 'Legal Capital: An Outdated Concept?', *European Business Organization Law Review*, 2006, Vol. 7, p. 5-27.

Armour *et al.* 2009a
Armour, J. *et al.*, 'Agency Problems and Legal Strategies', in Kraakman, R. *et al.* (eds.), *The Anatomy of Corporate Law. A Comparative and Functional Approach*, Oxford: Oxford University Press, 2009, p. 36-54.

Armour *et al.* 2009b
Armour, J. *et al.*, 'What is Corporate Law', in Kraakman, R. *et al.* (eds.), *The Anatomy of Corporate Law. A Comparative and Functional Approach*, Oxford: Oxford University Press, 2009, p. 1-35.

Armour *et al.* 2009c
Armour, J. *et al.*, 'Transaction with Creditors', in Kraakman, R. *et al.* (eds.), *The Anatomy of Corporate Law. A Comparative and Functional Approach*, Oxford: Oxford University Press, 2009, p. 115-152.

Aubert & Laffont 2003
Aubert, C. & Laffont, J-J., 'Designing Infrastructure Regulation in Developing Countries', in Beato, P. & Laffont, J-J. (eds.), *Competition Policy in Regulated Industries: Approaches for Emerging Economies*, Washington DC: Interamerican Development Bank, 2003, p. 1-52.

Balcerowicz *et al.* 1998
Balcerowicz, E. *et al.* (eds.), *Barriers to Entry and Growth of Private Companies in Poland, the Czech Republic, Hungary, Albania and Lithuania*, Warsaw: CASE - Center for Social and Economic Research, 1998.

Baptista 2007
Baptista, R., 'Culture, Institutions and the Regulation of Entry', *Comparative Labor Law and Policy Journal*, 2007, Vol. 28, p. 785-815.

Barnard 2008
Barnard, C., 'Unraveling the Services Directive', *Common Market Law Review*, 2008, Vol. 45, p. 323-394.

Barnard 2010
Barnard, C., *The Substantive Law of the EU: The Four Freedoms*, Oxford: Oxford University Press, 2010.

Barnard & Deakin 2002
Barnard, C. & Deakin, S., 'Market Access and Regulatory Competition', in Barnard, C. & Scott, J. (eds.), *The Law of the Single European Market: Unpacking the Premises*, Portland, OR: Hart Publishing, 2002, p. 197-224.

Barnard & Snell 2014
Barnard, C. & Snell, J., 'Free Movement of Legal Persons and the Provisions of Services', in Barnard, C. & Peers, S. (eds.), *European Union Law*, Oxford: Oxford University Press, 2014, p. 403-442.

Becker 1983
Becker, G.S., 'A Theory of Competition among Pressure Groups for Political Influence', *Quarterly Journal of Economics*, 1983, Vol. 98(3), p. 371-400.

Bellingwout 2014
Bellingwout, J., 'Corporate Income Tax: Marking the Passage of Time', *European Taxation*, 2014, p. 171-177.

Bhagwati 1982
Bhagwati, J., 'Directly Unproductive, Profit-Seeking (DUP) Activities', *Journal of Political Economy*, 1982, Vol. 90(5), p. 988-1002.

Biermeyer 2015
Biermeyer, T., *Stakeholder Protection in Cross-Border Seat Transfer in the EU: Between Boundaries and Freedom*, Oisterwijk: Wolf Legal Publishers, 2015.

Blazey & Chan 2008
Blazey, P. & Chan, K-W., *The Chinese Commercial Legal System*, Sydney: Lawbook, 2008.

Boehm 2007
Boehm, F., Regulatory Capture Revisited – Lessons from Economics of Corruption, available at: <www.icgg.org/downloads/Boehm%20-%20Regulatory%20Capture-%20Revisited.pdf>, p. 7-8 (last accessed 8 May 2016).

Borchardt 2010
Borchardt, K-D., *The ABC of European Union Law*, Luxembourg: Publications Office of the European Union, 2010.

Bovenberg & De Jong 1997
Bovenberg, L. & De Jong, A.H.M., 'The Road to Economic and Monetary Union', Kyklos, 1997, Vol. 50(1), p. 83-109.

Bowman 2004
Bowman, A. O'M., 'Horizontal Federalism: Exploring Interstate Interactions', *Journal of Public Administration Research and Theory*, 2004, Vol. 14(4), p. 535-546.

Boyreau-Debray & Wei 2004
Boyreau-Debray, G. & Wei, S.-J., 'Can China Grow Faster? A Diagnosis of the Fragmentation of Its Domestic Capital Market', available at: <www.imf.org/external/pubs/ft/wp/2004/wp0476.pdf> (last accessed 5 May 2016).

Braun 1998
Braun, B., 'Locational Response of German Manufacturers to Environmental Standards', *Tijdschrift voor Economische en Eociale Geografie*, 1998, Vol. 89(3), p. 253-263.

Brisimi 2014
Brisimi, V., *The Interface between Competition and the Internal Market: Market Separation under Article 102 TFEU*, Portland, OR: Hart Publishing, 2014.

Buchanan & Tullock 1962
Buchanan, J.M. & Tullock, G., *The Calculus of Consent: Logical Foundations of Constitutional Democracy*, Ann Arbor: University of Michigan Press, 1962.

Buchanan *et al.* 1980
Buchanan, J.M. *et al.* (eds.), *Toward a Theory of the Rent-Seeking Society*, College Station: Texas A&M University Press, 1980.

Cabral & Cunha 2000
Cabral, P. & Cunha, P., '"Presumed Innocent": Companies and the Exercise of the Right of Establishment under Community Law', *European Law Review*, 2000, Vol. 25, p. 157-164.

Callaghan 2011
Callaghan, H., 'Constrain-thy-neighbor Effects as a Determinant of Transnational Interest Group Cohesion', *Comparative Political Studies*, 2011, Vol. 44, p. 1-22.

Cao & Wang 2012
Cao, L. & Wang, T., 'Thoughts and Modification on Administrative Authorization Establishment Power', *Academia Bimestrial*, 2012, Vol. 4, p. 130-133. （曹缪辉、王太高, 行政许可设定权的反思与重构, 学海, 2012年第4期，页130-133）.

Carrubba & Murraj 2005
Carrubba, C. & Murrah, L., 'Legal Integration and Use of the Preliminary Ruling Process in the European Union', *International Organization*, 2005, Vol. 59(2), p. 399-418.

Caterina 2006
Caterina, R., 'Comparative Law and Economics', in Smits, J. (ed.), *Elgar Encyclopedia of Comparative Law*, Massachusetts: Edward Elgar, 2006, p. 161-171.

Chalmers *et al.* 2014
Chalmers, D. *et al.*, *European Union Law: Text and Materials*, Cambridge: Cambridge University Press, 2014.

Chari & Gupta 2008
Chari, A. & Gupta, N., 'Incumbents and Protectionism: The Political Economy of Foreign Entry Liberalization', *Journal of Financial Economics*, 2008, Vol. 88(3), p. 633-656.

Chen 2004
Chen, D., 'Administrative License and Individual Freedom', *Legal Research*, 2004, Vol. 5, p. 25-35.（陈端洪, 行政许可与个人自由, 法学研究, 2004年第5期，页25-35）.

Chen 2008
Chen, H., *Research on the Implementation Situation of the ALL-Taking the enforcement of the ALL by Huaibei City, Anhui Province as an Example*, the East China University of Political Science and law, thesis for judicial master. （陈怀清，行政许可发实施状况研究——以安徽淮北市实施《行政许可法》为例，华东政法大学，专业硕士学位论文，2008).

Chou 2009
Chou, B.K.P., 'Regulatory Reform and Private Sector Development in China: A Case Study of Downsizing Administrative Licenses', in Mok, K.H. & Forrest, R. (eds.), *Changing Governance and Public Policy in East Asia*, London: Routledge, p. 159-182.

Christiansen & Smith 2012
Christiansen, V. & Smith, S., 'Externality Correcting Taxes and Regulation', *The Scandinavian Journal of Economics*, 2012, Vol. 114(2), p. 358-383.

Čiočys 2010
Čiočys, R., 'Freedom of Establishment after Cartesio: Absence of EC Incorporation Doctrine and Implications Thereof', *Teisė (Law)*, 2010, Vol. 75, p. 143-158.

Claessens 2008
Claessens, S., *Free Movement of Lawyers in the European Union*, Nijmegen: Wolf Legal Publishers, 2008.

Coase 1960
Coase, R.H., 'The Problem of Social Cost', *Journal of Law and Economics*, 1960, Vol. 3(1), p. 1-44.

Craig 2002
Craig, P., 'The Evolution of the Single Market', in Barnard, C. & Scott, J. (eds.), *The Law of the Single European Market: Unpacking the Premises*, Oxford: Hart Publishing, 2002, p. 1-40.

Craig 2004
Craig, P., 'Competence: Clarity, Containment and Considerations', *European Law Review*, 2004, Vol. 29(3), p. 323-344.

Craig 2010
Craig, P., *The Lisbon Treaty: Law, Politics, and Treaty Reform*, Oxford: Oxford University Press, 2010.

Craig & de Búrca 2011
Craig, P. & de Búrca, G., *EU Law: Text, Cases, and Materials*, Oxford: Oxford University Press, 2011.

Dahlman 1979
Dahlman, C.J., 'The Problem of Externality', *Journal of Law and Economics*, 1979, Vol. 22(1), p. 141-162.

Darby & Karni 1973
Darby, M. & Karni, E., 'Free Competition and the Optimal Amount of Fraud', *Journal of Law and Economics*, 1973, Vol. 16, p. 67-88.

Davies 2007
Davies, G.T., 'The Services Directive: Extending the Country of Origin Principle and Reforming Public Administration', *European Law Review*, 2007, Vol. 32, p. 232-245.

Deakin 2006
Deakin, S., 'Legal Diversity and Regulatory Competition: Which Model for Europe?', *European Law Journal*, 2006, Vol. 12(4), p. 440-454.

Dean & Brown 1995
Dean, T. & Brown, R., 'Pollution Regulation as a Barrier to New Firm Entry: Initial Evidence and Implications for Future Research', *The Academy of Management Journal*, 1995, Vol. 38(1), p. 288-303.

Delors 1994
Delors, J., 'The Maastricht Treaty', *IBRU Boundary and Security Bulletin*, 1994, Vol. 1(4), p. 45-47.

Demsetz1982
Demsetz, H., 'Barriers to Entry', *The American Economic Review*, 1982, Vol. 72(1), p. 47-57.

Deng 2003
Deng, D., 'Research on Regional Protectionism in the Period of Institutional Reform', *Journal of Guangdong Business College*, 2003, Vol. 1, p. 13-20. （邓大才，体制转轨时期的地方保护主义研究，广东商学院学报，2003 年第1 期）.

Den Hertog 2000
Den Hertog, J., 'General Theories of Regulation', in Bouckaert, B. & De Geest, G. (eds.), *Encyclopedia of Law and Economics, Volume III: The Regulation of Contracts*, Cheltenham: Edward Elgar, 2000, p. 223-270.

Den Hertog 2003
Den Hertog, J., *Public and Private Interests in Regulation: Essays in the Law and Economics of Regulation*, Utrecht University, doctoral dissertation, 2003.

De Waele 2010
De Waele, H., 'The Role of the European Court of Justice in the Integration Process: A Contemporary and Normative Assessment', *Hanse Law Review: The E-journal on European, International and Comparative Law*, 2010, Vol. 6, p. 3-26.

Dezan Shira & Associates 2011
Dezan Shira & Associates, *Setting up Joint Ventures in China*, Berlin: Springer-Verlag 2011.

Di Federico 2009
Di Federico, G., 'The New Anti-monopoly Law in China from a European Perspective', *World Competition*, 2009, Vol. 32(2), p. 249-270.

Djankow *et al.* 2002
Djankov, S. *et. al*, 'The Regulation of Entry', *Quarterly Journal of Economics*, 2002, Vol. 117(1), p. 1-37.

Doing Business 2014
Doing Business, *Why are Minimum Capital Requirements a Concern for Entrepreneurs?*, Washington DC: World Bank, 2014.

Dougan 2000
Dougan, M., 'Minimum Harmonization and the Internal Market', *Common Market Law Review*, 2000, Vol. 37, p. 853-885.

Dranove & Jin 2010
Dranove, D. & Jin, G.Z., 'Quality Disclosure and Certification: Theory and Practice', *Journal of Economic Literature*, 2010, Vol. 48(4), p. 935-963.

Dreher & Gassebner 2013
Dreher, A. & Gassebner, M., 'Greasing the Wheels of Entrepreneurship?: The Impact of Regulations and Corruption on Firm Entry', *Public Choice*, 2013, Vol. 155, p. 413-432.

Drezner 2006
Drezner, D., *The Race to the Bottom Hypothesis: an Empirical and Theoretical Review*, The Fletcher School, Tufts University, mimeo.

Duvivier & Xiong 2013
Duvivier, C. & Xiong, H., 'Transboundary Pollution in China : A Study of Polluting Firms' Location Choices in Hebei Province', *Environment and Development Economics*, 2013, Vol. 18(4), p. 459-483.

Easterbrook & Fischel 1996
Easterbrook, F.H. & Fischel, D.R., *The Economic Structure of Corporate Law*, Cambridge: Harvard University Press, 1996.

Eger & Schüller 2007
Eger, T. & Schüller, M., 'A Comparison of Chinese and European-Style Federalism from a Law and Economics Perspective', in Eger, T. *et al.* (eds.), *Economic Analysis of Law in China*, Cheltenham: Edward Elgar, 2007, p. 3-28.

Emery *et al.* 2000
Emery, J. ***et al.***, *Administrative Barriers to Foreign Investment: Reducing Red Tape in Africa*, Washington, D.C.: The World Bank, 2000.

Enriques 2006a
Enriques, L., 'Company Law Harmonization Reconsidered: What Role for the EC?', in Bartman, S.M. (ed.), *European Company Law in Accelerated Progress*, Alphen aan den Rijn: Kluwer Law International, 2006, p. 59-82.

Enriques 2006b
Enriques, L., 'EC Company Law Directives and Regulations: How Trivial are They?', *University of Pennsylvania Journal of International Economic Law*, 2006, Vol. 27(1), p. 1-78.

Enriques & Gatti 2006
Enriques, L. & Gatti, M., 'The Uneasy Case for Top-Down Corporate Law Harmonization in the European Union', *University of Pennsylvania Journal of International Economic Law*, 2006, Vol. 27, p. 939-998.

Enriques & Macey 2001
Enriques, L. & Macey, J.R., 'Creditors versus Capital Formation: The Case against the European Legal Capital Rules', *Cornell Law Review*, 2001, Vol. 86(6), p. 1165-1204.

Esty & Geradin 2000
Esty, D. & Geradin, D., 'Regulatory Co-opetition', *Journal of International Economic Law*, 2000, Vol. 3(2), p. 235-255.

Fan *et al.* 2007
Fan, G. *et al.*, *NERI Index of Marketization of China's Provinces 2006 Report*, Beijing: Economic Science Press, 2007. (樊纲、王小鲁、朱恒鹏, 中国市场化指数——各省区市场化相对进程2006 年度报告，北京：经济科学出版社).

Fan *et al.* 2009
Fan, C.S. *et al.*, 'Political Decentralization and Corruption: Evidence from around the World', *Journal of Public Economics*, 2009, Vol. 93(1-2), p. 14–34.

Fares & Abou Bakr 2013
Fares, A-R.F. & Abou-Bakr, E.A., 'Economics of Insurance against Natural Catastrophes: Over-Burdened Arab Insurers', *Review of Economics & Finance*, 2013, p. 95-105.

Faure 1998
Faure, M., 'Harmonization of Environmental Law and Market Integration: Harmonizing for the Wrong Reasons?', *European Energy and Environmental Law Review*,1998, Vol. 7(6), p. 169-175.

Faure 2001
Faure, M., 'Regulatory Competition v. Harmonization in EU Environmental Law', in Esty D. & Ger. (eds.), *Regulatory Competition and Economic Integration*, Oxford: Oxford University Press, 2001, p. 263-286.

Faure 2003
Faure, M., 'How Law and Economics May Contribute to the Harmonization of Tort Law in Europe', in Zimmermann R. (ed.), *Grundstrukturen des Europäischen Deliktsrechts*, Baden-Baden: Nomos, 2003, p. 31-82.

Faure 2008
Faure, M., 'Calabresi and Behavioural Tort Law and Economics', *Erasmus Law Review*, 2008, Vol. 1(4), p. 75-102.

Faure 2009
Faure, M., 'General Introduction', in Faure, M. (ed.), *Tort Law and Economics*, Cheltenham: Edward Elgar, 2009, p. xxi-xli.

Faure 2011
Faure, M., 'Does Environmental Law Matter?', in Faure M. & Smits, J. (eds.), *Does Law Matter? On Law and Economic Growth*, Cambridge: Intersentia, 2011, p. 385-416.

Faure 2012
Faure, M., 'Designing Incentives Regulation for the Environment', in Brousseau, E. *et al.* (eds.), *Global Environmental Commons: Analytical and Political Challenges in Building Governance Mechanisms*, Oxford: Oxford University Press, 2012, p. 275-307.

Faure 2014a
Faure, M., 'The Complementary Roles of Liability, Regulation and Insurance in Safety Management: Theory and Practice', *Journal of Risk Research*, 2014, Vol. 17(6), p. 689-707.

Faure 2014b
Faure, M., 'Transboundary Pollution', in Martella Jr., R.R. & Grosko, J.B. (eds.), *International Environmental Law, the Practitioner's Guide to the Laws of the Planet*, Chicago: American Bar Association, 2014, p. 235-267.

Faure & Bruggeman 2008
Faure, M. & Bruggeman, V., 'Catastrophic Risks and First-Party Insurance', *Connecticut Insurance Law Journal*, 2008, Vol. 15(1), p. 1-52.

Faure & Johnston 2009
Faure, M. & Johnston, J., 'The Law and Economics of Environmental Federalism: Europe and the United States Compared', *Virginia Environmental Law Journal*, 2009, Vol. 27(3), p. 205-274.

Faure & Wang 2003
Faure, M. & Wang, H., 'The International Regimes for the Compensation of Oil-Pollution Damage: Are they Effective?', *Review of European Community & International Environmental Law*, 2003, Vol. 12(3), p. 242-253.

Faure *et al.* 2006
Faure, M. *et al.*, 'Economic Instruments: Suited to Developing Countries?', in Faure M. & Niessen, N. (eds.), *Environmental Law in Development: Lessons from the Indonesian Experience*, Cheltenham: Edward Elgar, 2006, p. 218-262.

Faure *et al.* 2010
Faure, M. *et al.*, 'Bucking the Kuznets Curve: Designing Effective Environmental Regulation in Developing Countries', *Virginia Journal of International Law*, 2010, Vol. 51(1), p. 95-156.

Feldstein 2012
Feldstein, M., 'The Failure of the Euro', *Foreign Affairs*, 2012, Vol. 91(1), p. 105–116.

Fewsmith & Gao 2014
Fewsmith J. & Gao, X., 'Local Governance in China: Incentives and Tensions', *Daedalus*, 2014, Vol. 143(2), p. 170-183.

Franch & Torrelles 2012
Franch, M. & Torrelles, J., 'The Implementation of Services Directive in Spain, in Stelkens, U. *et al.* (eds.), *The Implementation of the EU Services Directive: Transposition, Problems and Strategies*, The Hague: T.M.C. Asser Press, 2012, p. 573-588.

Frankel 2010
Frankel, C., 'Market Making: The History of the Internal Market as Technicalization of Politicization of the Technical', in Guimarães, M.H. & Faria, A.P. (eds.), *Product Market Integration: A Multifaceted Approach*, Bingley: Emerald Group Publishing Limited, 2010, p. 37-47.

Gao 2009
Gao, Y., 'Thoughts on the Legal Regulation Situation of China's Administrative Monopolies', *Hebei Law Science*, 2009, Vol. 27(1), p. 112-116. （高雁，中国行政垄断法律规制的现状及思考, 河北法学, 009年1月，第27卷第1期）.

Gao 2011
Gao, Y., 'Government Intervention, Perceived Benefit, and Bribery of Firms in Transitional China', *Journal of Business Ethics*, 2011, Vol. 104, p. 175-184.

Garbarino 2012
Garbarino, C., 'Inter-country Equity and Intra-group Transactions at EU Level: An Analysis of the CCCTB Proposal and CJEU Tax Cases', *EC Tax Review*, 2012, Vol. 21(5), p. 248-261.

Garoupa 2004
Garoupa, N., 'Regulation of Professions in the US and Europe: A Comparative Analysis', Paper for American Law & Economics Association Annual Meetings, Berkeley, CA: the Berkeley Electronic Press, 2004.

Genschel & Jachtenfuchs 2011
Genschel, P. & Jachtenfuchs, M., 'How the European Union Constrains the State: Multilevel Governance of Taxation', *European Journal of Political Research*, 2011, Vol. 50(3), p. 293-314.

Geradin & McCahery 2004
Geradin, D. & McCahery, J., 'Regulatory Co-opetition: Transcending the Regulatory Competition Debate', in Jordana, J. & Levi-Faur, D. (eds.), *Politics of Regulation: Institutions and Regulatory Reforms for the Age of Governance*, Cheltenham: Elgar, 2004, p. 90-123.

Gu 2006
Gu, A., *Research into Reforming the System of Administrative Licenses*, Suzhou University (the PRC), doctoral dissertation, 2006. （顾爱平，行政许可制度改革研究，苏州大学, 博士论文, 2006年）.

Guo & Hu 2004
Guo, Y. & Hu, A, 'The Administrative Monopoly in China's Economic Transition', *Communist and Post-Communist Studies*, 2004, Vol. 37, p. 265-280.

Guo & Wu 2004
Guo, J. & Wu, N. 'The Anti-Monopoly Characteristic of the ALL and Remarks on it', *Journal of Yunnan Administration College*, 2004, Vol. 6, p. 84-86 （郭静, 吴宁, 行政许可法的反行政垄断特征及评析, 云南行政学院学报2004 年第6 期）.

Hahn *et al.* 2003
Hahn, R.W. *et al.*, 'Federalism and Regulation: An Overview', *Regulation*, 2003, Vol. 26(4), p. 46-50.

Hatzopoulos 2012
Hatzopoulos, V., *Regulating Services in the European Union*, Oxford: Oxford University Press, 2012.

Heremans 2012
Heremans, T., *Professional Services in the EU Internal Market: Quality Regulation and Self-Regulation*, Portland, OR: Hart Publishing, 2012.

Hertig & McCahery 2007
Hertig, G. & McCahery, J., 'Legal Options: Towards Better EC Company Law Regulation', in Weatherill, S. (ed.), *Better Regulation*, Portland, OR: Hart Publishing, 2007, p. 219-245.

Höpner & Schäfer 2015
Höpner, M. & Schäfer, A., 'Integration Among Unequals: How the Heterogeneity of European Varieties of Capitalism Shapes the Social and Democratic Potential of the EU', in Magone, J.M. (ed.), *Routledge Handbook of European Politics*, London: Routledge, 2015, p. 725-745.

Horsley 2012
Horsley, T., 'Subsidiarity and the European Court of Justice: Missing Pieces in the Subsidiarity Jigsaw?', *Journal of Common Market Studies*, 2012, Vol. 50(12), p. 267-282.

Hu & Jin 2005
Hu, J. & Jin, C., 'The Study on the Suggestion Right for Reviewing an Unconstitutional Regulation', *The Jurist*, 2005, Vol. 2, p. 133-139. (胡建淼、金承东, 论法规违宪审查建议权, 法学家, 2005年第2期).

Hu & Guo 2013
Hu, J. & Guo, F., 'Rent-Seeking, Bureaucratic Corruption and Market Segmentation', *Economic Management*, 2013, Vol. 11, p. 36-47. (胡军、郭峰, 企业寻租、官员腐败与市场分割, 经济管理, 2013第11期).

Huan 2011
Huan, Q., 'Regional Supervision Centres for Environmental Protection in China: Functions and Limitations', *Journal of Current Chinese Affairs*, 2011, Vol. 3, p. 139-162.

Huang 2010
Huang, Z., 'Explorations on Improving the Pre-administrative Registrations', *Study on China Administration for Industry & Commerce*, 2010, Vol. 9, p. 50-55 (黄晄晖, 完善注册登记前置许可制度探讨, 中国工商管理研究, 2010年第9期).

Huang *et al.* 2010
Huang,Y. *et al*, 'China's 2007 Anti-Monopoly Law: Competition and the Chinese Petroleum Industry', *Energy Law Journal*, 2010, Vol. 31(2), p. 337-370.

Hui & Hu 2007
Hui, H. & Hu, Y., 'Study on the Role of the ALL in the AML', *Journal of Henan Administrative Institute of Political Science and Law*, 2007, Vol. 2, p. 136-138 (黄辉, 胡楹楹, 行政许可法在反行政垄断中的地位研究, 河南政法管理学院学报, 2007年第2期).

Jeng 2011
Jeng, S-P, 'The Effect of Corporate Reputations on Customer Perceptions and Cross-buying Intentions', *The Service Industries Journal*, 2011, Vol. 31(6), p. 851-862.

Jiang 2009a
Jiang, B., 'The Administrative Procedure Law and Abstract Administrative Acts', *The Study on Administrative Law*, 2009, Vol. 3, p. 13-23 （江必新,《行政诉讼法》与抽象行政行为,《行政法学研究》2009年第3期）.

Jiang 2009b
Jiang, Y., *Hunting for the Chinese Dragon? – Study on China's Economic Security*, Beijing: Economic Science Press, 2009 （江涌, 猎杀"中国龙"？——中国经济安全透视，经济科学出版社, 2009).

Jiang & Li 2006
Jiang, P. & Li, G., *The Interpretation on Provisions of the Latest Company Law*, Beijing: People's Court Press, 2006 （江平、李国光, 最新公司法条文释义, 人民法院出版社, 2006).

Jiang & Chen 2010
Jiang, Q. & Chen, W., 'The Need for Reform of Approval System of Pre-administrative Licenses for Enterprises', *Study on China Administration for Industry and Commerce*, 2010, Vol. 7, p. 65-67 （姜庆宏、陈伟，企业注册登记前置审批制度亟待改革，中国工商管理研究，2010年第6期）.

Kaczorowska 2013
Kaczorowska, A., *European Union Law*, Abingdon: Routledge, 2013.

Kerber & Van den Bergh 2008
Kerber, W. & Van den Bergh, R., 'Mutual Recognition Revisited: Misunderstandings, Inconsistencies, and a Suggested Reinterpretation', Kyklos, 2008, Vol. 61(3), p. 447-465.

Kin 2009
Kin, L.W., 'The Relationship Between Central and Local Governments Under the Unitary State System of China', in Oliveira C.J. & Cardinal, P. (eds.), *One Country, Two Systems, Three Legal Orders – Perspectives of Evolution*, Berlin: Springer, 2009, p. 527-540.

Klein & Coffee 2004
Klein, W. & Coffee, J., *Business Organization and Finance: Legal and Economic Principles*, New York, NY: Foundation Press, 2004.

Klevorick 1996
Klevorick, A., 'The Race to the Bottom in a Federal System: Lessons from the World of Trade Policy', *Yale Law & Policy Review*, 1996, Vol. 14, p. 177-186.

Kobayashi & Ribstein 2007
Kobayashi, B. & Ribstein, L., 'The Introductory Essay for Economics of Federalism', in Kobayashi, B. & Ribstein, L. (eds,), *Economics of Federalism*, Cheltenham: Edward Elgar, 2007, p. i-xiii.

Kowalsky 2006
Kowalsky, W., 'The Services Directive: the Legislative Process Clears the First Hurdle, Transfer', *European Review of Labour and Research*, 2006, Vol. 12(2), p. 231-249.

Krueger 1974
Krueger, A., 'The Political Economy of the Rent-Seeking Society', *American Economic Review*, 1974,Vol. 64, p. 291-303.

Lamotte 2012
Lamotte, J., 'New EU Tax Challenges and Opportunities in a (C)CCTB World: Overview of the EU Commission Proposal for a Draft Directive for a Common Consolidated Corporate Tax Base', *European Taxation*, 2012, Vol. 6, p. 271-279.

Li 2003
Li, Y., 'Decrease and Regulate Administrative Approvals-a Good Point of the ALL', *Legal Science*, 2003, Vol. 10, p. 91-93（李援，减少和规范行政审批:〈行政许可法〉的亮点, 法学, 2003年第10期）.

Li 2006
Li, X., 'Thoughts on AICs' Check on Companies' Articles of Association', *Study on China Administration for Industry and Commerce*, 2006, Vol. 7, p. 38-40（李孝猛， 公司登记机关审查公司章程若干法律问题的思考, 中国工商管理研究, 2006年第7期）.

Li 2008
Li, S., 'Study on How to Optimize the Administrative License's Establishment Scope-the Critical Thinking of the Article 13 of the ALL', *The Study on Administrative Law*, 2008, Vol. 3 p. 69-73 （李诗林， 论行政许可设定范围的合理界定——对《行政许可法》第13条的批判性思考, 行政法学研究， 2008年第3期）.

Li 2013
Li, H., 'New Direction of China's Administrative Litigation System Development', *Administrative Law Review*, 2013, Vol, 1, p. 46-52 （李洪雷，行政法学研究，2013年第 1 期， 中国行政诉讼制度发展的新路向).

Li *et al.* 2005
Li, S. *et al.*, 'The Analysis on Survey of Local Protection in China Domestic Market: A Study Based on a Questionnaire Survey of Enterprises', *China Journal of Economics*, 2005, Vol. 1(2), p. 92-117 （李善同、刘云中、陈波， 中国国内， 地方保护问题的调查,分析——基于企业问卷调 查的研究，经济学报，2005年， 第1卷， 第2辑).

Liebman 2007
Liebman, B.L., 'China's Courts: Restricted Reform', *The China Quarterly*, 2007, Vol. 191, p. 620-638.

Liu 1999
Liu, J., 'On Judicial Examination of the Abstract Administrative Act in China', *Modern Law Science*, 1999, Vol. 21(6), p. 69-74. (刘俊祥, 论我国抽象行政行为的司法审查, 现代法学, 1999年12月第21卷第6期).

Liu 2002
Liu, H., 'Several Thought about Reforming the Current Court Management System', *Legal Studies*, 2002, Vol. 3, p. 12-20 （刘会生：人民法院管理体制改革的几点思考，法学研究，2002年第3期).

Liu 2006
Liu, W., 'The Control on Administrative Licensing by Local Legislation', *Legal Science Review*, 2006, Vol. 2, p. 85-93 (刘巍，行政许可之地方立法控制, 法学评论, 2006年第2期).

Liu 2013
Liu, J., *Compensating Ecological Damage: Comparative and Economic Observations*, Maastricht University, doctoral thesis, 2013.

Liu & Huang 2000
Liu, X. & Huang, J., 'Administrative Action Should Be Brought in to the Jurisdiction of Administrative Procedure', *Modern Law Science*, Vol. 22(3), p. 56-59 (刘德兴、黄基权, 抽象行政行为应纳入行政诉讼受案范围, 现代法学, 2000年4月第22卷第3期).

Loewenstein *et al.* 2013
Loewenstein, G. *et al.*, 'Consumers' Misunderstanding of Health Insurance', *Journal of Health Economics*, 2013, Vol. 32(5), p. 850–862.

Luth 2010
Luth, H.A., *Behavioral Economics in Consumer Policy: the Economic Analysis of Standard Terms in Consumer Contracts Revisited*, Erasmus University of Rotterdam, doctoral thesis, 2010.

Ma 2003
Ma, H., 'Causes of the Formation and Measures of the Resolution of Localism', *Tribune of Political Science and Law*, 2003, Vol. 21(6), p. 156-161 (马怀德, 地方保护主义的成因和解决之道, 政法论坛, 2003年第6期).

Ma 2013
Ma, H., 'The Aim of Reforming Administrative Litigation System is to Establish Courts for Administrative Litigation, *Journal of Law Application*, 2013, Vol. 7, p. 8-11 (马怀德, 行政审判体制改革的目标:设立行政法院, 法律适用，2013年07期).

Machado 2010
Machado, F.S., 'Effective Creditor Protection in Private Companies: Mandatory Minimum Capital Rules or Ex Post Mechanisms', *Revista de Direito das Sociedades*, 2010, Vol. 2(3-4), p. 681-718.

Maloney & McCormick 1982
Maloney, M.T. & McCormick, R., 'A Positive Theory of Environmental Quality Regulation', *Journal of Law and Economics*, 1982, Vol. 25(1), p. 99-123.

Mao 2005
Mao, M., 'Understanding of the Enacting Right in the Local Administrative License', *Tribune of Political Science and Law*, 2005, Vol. 23(1), p. 145-155 (茅铭晨, 对地方行政许可设定权的若干认识, 政法论坛, 2005年1 月， 第23 卷第1 期).

Martinez 2013
Martinez, G.A., *The Law and Economics of Eco-Labels*, Erasmus University Rotterdam, doctoral thesis, 2013.

Mattei & Cafaggi 1998
Mattei, U. & Cafaggi, F., 'Comparative Law and Economics', in Newman, P. (ed.), *The New Palgrave Dictionary of Economics and the Law (Vol. 1)*, London: Palgrave Macmillan, 1998, p. 340-352.

Mattei *et al.* 2000
Mattei, U. *et al.*, 'Comparative Law and Economics', in Bouckaert, B. & De Geest, G. (eds.), *Encyclopedia of Law and Economics: The History and Methodology of Law and Economics*, Cheltenham: Edward Elgar, 2000, p. 505-538.

McCahery *et al.* 2007
McCahery, J.A. *et al.*, 'Traditional and Innovative Approaches to Legal Reform: "The New Company Law"', *European Business Organization Law Review*, 2007, Vol. 8, p. 7-57.

McGee & Weatherill 1990
McGee, A. & Weatherill, S., ; The Evolution of the Single Market: Harmonization or Liberalization', *The Modern Law Review*, 1990, Vol. 53(3), p. 578-596.

Mehra & Meng 2008
Mehra, S. & Meng, Y., 'Against Antitrust Functionalism: Reconsidering China's Antimonopoly Law', *Virginia Journal of International Law*, 2008, Vol. 49(2), p. 380-429.

Mi 2008
Mi, X., *Legality Issues of Corporate Establishment, Renmin University of China*, doctoral thesis, 2008 (米兴平, 公司设立的合法性问题研究, 中国人民大学, 博士学位论文, 2008).

Miceli 2009
Miceli, T.J., *The Economic Approach to Law*, Redwood City, CA: Stanford University Press, 2009.

Milgrom & Roberts 1992
Milgrom, P. & Roberts, J., *Economics, Organization and Management*, Englewood Cliffs, NJ: Prentice-Hall International, 1992.

Minzner 2009
Minzner, C.F., 'Riots and Cover-ups: Counterproductive Control of Local Agents in China', *University of Pennsylvania Journal of International Law*, 2009, Vol. 31(1), p. 53-123.

Monti 2010
Monti, M., 'A New Strategy for the Single Market: At the Service of Europe's Economy and Society: A Report to the President of the European Commission', 9 May 2010.

Montinala *et al.* 1995
Montinala, G. *et al.*, 'Federalism, Chinese Style: the Political Basis for Economic Success in China', *World Politics*, 1995, Vol. 48(1), p. 55-81.

Moravcsik 1991
Moravcsik, A., 'Negotiating the Single European Act: National Interests and Conventional Statecraft in the European Community', *International Organization*, 1991, Vol. 45(1), p. 19-56.

Morisset & Pirnia 1999
Morisset, J. & Pirnia, N., *How Tax Policy and Incentives Affect Foreign Direct Investment: A Review*, Washington DC: World Bank, 1999.

Muir Watt 2004
Muir Watt, H., 'Experiences from Europe: Legal Diversity and the Internal Market', *Texas International Law Journal*, 2004, Vol. 39, p. 429-459.

Mukoyama & Popov 2014
Mukoyama, T. & Popov, L., 'The Political Economy of Entry Barriers', *Review of Economic Dynamics*, 2014, Vol. 17(3), p. 383-416.

Mulbert & Birke 2002
Mulbert, P.O. & Birke, M., 'Legal Capital – Is There a Case against the European Legal Capital Rules?', *European Business Organization Law Review*, 2002, Vol. 3, p. 695-732.

Munin 2011
Munin, N., 'Tax in Troubled Time: Is It the Time for A Common Corporate Tax Base in the EU?', *EC Tax Review*, 2011, Vol. 3, p. 121-133.

Mustilli & Pelkmans 2013
Mustilli, F. & Pelkmans, J., 'Access Barriers to Services Markets: Mapping, Tracing, Understanding and Measuring', Centre for European Policy Studies, Brussels, Special Report No. 77, 2013.

Naughton 2003
Naughton, B., 'How Much can Regional Integration do to Unify China's Markets?', in Hope N. *et al.* (eds.), *How Far Across the River? Chinese Policy Reform at the Millennium*, Redwood City, CA: Stanford University Press, 2003, p. 204-232.

Nello 2005
Nello, S.S., *The European Union: Economics, Policies and History*, Berkshire: The McGraw Hill Companies. 2005.

Nelson 1970
Nelson, P., 'Information and Consumer Behavior', *Journal of Political Economy*, 1970, Vol. 78(2), p. 311-329.

Ngo 2009
Ngo, T-W., 'The Policies of Rent Production', in Ngo, T-W. & Wu, Y. (eds.), *Rent Seeking in China*, Abingdon: Routledge, 2009, p. 1-21.

O'Brien & Li 1999
O'Brien, K.J. & Li, L., 'Selective Policy Implementation in Rural China', *Comparative Politics*, 1999, Vol. 31(2), p. 167-186.

O'Brien & Li 2004
O'Brien, K.J. & Li, L., 'Suing the Local State: Administrative Litigation in Rural China', *The China Journal*, 2004, Vol. 51, p. 75–96.

Oberholzer-Gee & Mitsunari 2006
Oberholzer-Gee, F. & Mitsunari, M., 'Information Regulation: Do the Victims of Externalities Pay Attention?', *Journal of Regulatory Economics*, 2006, Vol. 30(2), p. 141-158.

OECD 2002
OECD, *Alternatives to Traditional Regulation*, Paris: OECD Publishing, 2002.

OECD 2003
OECD, *China: Progress and Reform Challenges*, Paris: OECD Publishing, 2003.

OECD 2005
OECD, *The Business Registration Process in South East Europe: A Peer Review*, Paris: OECD Publishing, 2005.

OECD 2012
OECD, *Economic Surveys: European Union 2012*, Paris: OECD Publishing, 2012.

Ogus 1994
Ogus, A., *Regulation: Legal Form and Economic Theory*, Oxford: Clarendon Press, 1994.

Ogus 2007
Ogus, A., 'Regulatory Arrangements and Incentives for Opportunistic Behaviour', in Eger, T. *et al.* (eds.), *Economic Analysis of Law in China*, Cheltenham: Edward Elgar, 2007, p. 151-163.

Ogus & Zhang 2005
Ogus, A. & Zhang, Q., 'Licensing Regimes East and West', *International Review of Law and Economics*, 2005, Vol. 25, p. 124-142.

Oi 1995
Oi, J.C., 'The Role of the Local State in China's Transitional Economy', *The China Quarterly*, 1995, Vol. 144, p. 1132-1149.

Oksanen & Välimäki 2003
Oksanen V. & Välimäki, M., 'Some Economic Aspects of the European Harmonization of Intellectual Property Rights in Software and its Impact to Eastern EU', Warsaw: Paper for Conference on the Economic Integration of the Eastern EU, 2003.

Olson 1965
Olson, M., *The Logic of Collective Action: Public Goods and the Theory of Groups*, Cambridge: Harvard University Press, 1965.

Ommeslaghe 1969
Ommeslaghe, V., 'La Premiere Directive du Conseil du 9 Mars 1968 en Matière de Sociétés', *Cahiers de Droit Européen*, 1969, Vol. 233, p. 524-543.

Panayi 2012
Panayi, C.H., 'The Anti-Abuse Rules of the CCCTB', *Bulletin for International Taxation*, 2012, Vol. 66(4/5), p. 256-269.

Peerenboom 2001
Peerenboom, R., 'Globalization, Path Dependency and the Limits of Law: Administrative Law Reform and Rule of Law in the People's Republic of China', *Berkeley Journal of International Law*, 2001, Vol. 19(2), p. 161-264.

Peerenboom 2002
Peerenboom, R., *China's Long March toward Rule of Law*, Cambridge: Cambridge University Press, 2002.

Peerenboom & He 2009
Peerenboom, R. & He, X., 'Dispute Resolution in China: Patterns, Causes and Prognosis', *East Asia Law Review*, 2009, Vol. 4(1), p. 1-62.

Pei 1997
Pei, M., 'Citizens v. Mandarins: Administrative Litigation in China', *The China Quarterly*, 1997, Vol. 152, p. 832-862.

Pelkmans 2005
Pelkmans, J., 'Mutual Recognition in Goods and Services, and Economic Perspective', in Schioppa, F.K.P. (ed.), *The Principle of Mutual Recognition in the European Integration Process*, Basingstoke: Palgrave Macmillan, 2005, p. 85-128.

Pelkmans 2008
Pelkmans, J., 'Economic Approaches of the Internal Market', in Pelkmans, J., Chang, M. & Hanf, D., *The EU Internal Market in Comparative Perspective: Economic, Political and Legal Analyses*, Brussels: Peter Lang - International Academic Publishers, 2008, p. 29-76.

Pellé 2008
Pellé, P., 'Companies Crossing Borders Within Europe', *Utrecht Law Review*, 2008, Vol. 4(1), p. 6-12.

Peltzman 1976
Peltzman, S., 'Toward a More General Theory of Regulation', *Journal of Law and Economics*, 1976, Vol. 19, p. 211-240.

Petersen & Rajan 1997
Petersen, M. & Rajan, R., 'Trade Credit: Theories and Evidence', *Review of Financial Studies*, 1997, Vol. 10(3), p. 661-691.

Philipsen 2003
Philipsen, N.J., *Regulation of and by Pharmacists in the Netherlands in the Netherlands and Belgium: An Economic Approach*, Antwerp/Groningen: Intersentia, 2003.

Philipsen 2007
Philipsen, N.J., 'The Law and Economics of Professional Regulation: What Does the Theory Teach China?', in Eger T. *et al.* (eds.), *Economic Analysis of Law in China*, Cheltenham: Edward Elgar, 2007, p. 112-150.

Philipsen 2010
Philipsen, N.J., 'Regulation of Liberal Professions and Competition Policy: Developments in the EU and China', *Journal of Competition Law and Economics*, 2010, Vol. 6(2), p. 203-231.

Philipsen 2011
Philipsen, N.J., 'Professional Licensing and Self-regulation in Europe and China: A Law and Economics Perspective', in Faure M. & Zhang, X. (eds.), *Competition Policy and Regulation- Recent Developments in China, the US and Europe*, Cheltenham: Edward Elgar, 2011, p. 205-237.

Philipsen *et al.* 2016
Philipsen, N.J. *et al.* (eds.), *Market Integration: The EU Experience and Implications for Regulatory Reform in China*, Berlin: Springer-Verlag, 2016.

Pi 2008
Pi, J., 'Regional Market Integration under Inter-jurisdictional Competition in China: on the Role of the Chinese Central Government in Regional Market Integration', *Economic Research Journal*, 2008, Vol. 3, p. 115-124 (皮建才，中国地方政府间竞争下的区域市场整合, 经济研究, 2008年第3期).

Pistor *et al.* 2002
Pistor, K. *et al.*, 'The Evolution of Corporate Law: A Cross-Country Comparison', *University of Pennsylvanian Journal of International Economic Law*, 2002, Vol. 23(4), p. 791-872.

Polinsky & Shavell 2012
Polinsky, M. & Shavell, S., 'Mandatory versus Voluntary Disclosure of Product Risks', *Journal of Law, Economics and Organization*, 2012, Vol. 28, p. 360-379.

Porter 1980
Porter, M.E., *Competitive Strategy*, New York, NY: the Free Press, 1980.

Posner 1974
Posner, R., 'Theories of Economic Regulation', *Bell Journal of Economics and Management Science*, 1974, Vol. 5(2), p. 335-358.

Posner 1998
Posner, R., 'Creating a Legal Framework for Economic Development', *The World Bank Research Observer*, 1998, Vol. 13(1), p. 1-11.

Potters & Sloof 1996
Potters, J. & Sloof, R., 'Interest Groups, a Survey of Empirical Models That Try to Assess Their Influence', *European Journal of Political Economy*, 1996, Vol. 12, p. 403-442.

Ren 1987
Ren, J., 'An Essay on Environmental Regulation Made by Local Authorities', *Chinese Journal of Law*, 1987, Vol. 3, p. 22-26 (任进, 略论地方性环境法规, 法学研究, 1987年第3期).

Revesz 1992
Revesz, R.L., 'Rehabilitating Interstate Competition: Rethinking the Race-to-the-Bottom Rationale for Federal Environmental Regulation', *New York University Law Review*, 1992, Vol. 67(6), p. 1210-1255.

Rodden & Rose-Ackerman 1997
Rodden, J. & Rose-Ackerman, S., 'Does Federalism Preserve Markets?', *Virginia Law Review*, 1997, Vol. 83(7), p. 1521-1572.

Rose-Ackerman 1993
Rose-Ackerman, S., *Rethinking the Progressive Agenda: the Reform of the American Regulatory State*, New York, NY: the Free Press, 1993.

Ruhl 1988
Ruhl, J.B., 'Interstate Pollution Control and Resource Development Planning: Outmoded Approaches or Outmoded Politics?', *Natural Resources Journal*, 1988, Vol. 28, p. 293-314.

Saydé 2014
Saydé, A., *Abuse of EU Law and Regulation of the Internal Market*, Oxford: Hart Publishing, 2014.

Schäfer 2006
Schäfer, H-B., 'Rules Versus Standards in Rich and Poor Countries: Precise Legal Norms as Substitutes for Human Capital in Low-Income Countries', *Supreme Court Economic Review*, 2006, Vol. 14, p. 113-134.

Schafer 2014
Schafer, J., 'European Commission Officials' Policy Attitudes', *Journal of Common Market Studies*, 2014, Vol. 52(4), p. 911-927.

Schoen 2004
Schoen, W., 'The Future of Legal Capital', *European Business Organization Law Review*, 2004, Vol. 5(3), p. 429-448.

Shapiro 1986
Shapiro, C., 'Investment, Moral Hazard and Occupational Licensing', *Review of Economic Studies*, 1986, Vol. 53, p. 843-862.

Shavell 1984
Shavell, S., 'Liability for Harm versus Regulation of Safety', *Journal of Legal Studies*, 1984, Vol. 13, p. 357-374.

Shavell 2005
Shavell, S., ´Minimum Asset Requirements and Compulsory Liability Insurance as Solutions to the Judgment-proof Problem´, *RAND Journal of Economics*, 2005, Vol. 36(1), p. 63–77.

Shleifer & Vishny 1993
Shleifer, A. & Vishny, R., 'Corruption', *Quarterly Journal of Economics*, 1993, Vol. 108(3), p. 599-617.

Shleifer & Vishny 1994
Shleifer, A. & Vishny, R., 'Politicians and Firms', *Quarterly Journal of Economics*, 1994, Vol. 109(4), p. 995-1025.

Shughart II 2008
Shughart II, W.F., Public Choice, 2008. Available at: <www.econlib.org/library/Enc/PublicChoice.html> (last accessed 8 May 2016).

Siems 2014
Siems, M., *Comparative Law*, Cambridge: Cambridge University Press, 2014.

Smith 2013
Smith, G., 'Measurement, Promotions and Patterns of Behavior in Chinese Local Government', *Journal of Peasant Studies*, 2013, Vol. 40(6), p. 1027-1050.

Smits 2010
Smits, J., 'Full Harmonization of Consumer Law?, A Critique of the Draft Directive on Consumer Rights', *European Review of Private Law*, 2010, Vol. 18, p. 5-14.

Snell 2013
Snell, J., 'Book Review: The Law and Policy of Harmonisation in Europe's Internal Market', *Yearbook of European Law*, 2013, Vol. 32(1), p. 518-520.

Snell 2014
Snell, J., 'The Internal Market and the Philosophies of Market Integration', in Barnard, C. & Peers, S. (eds.), *European Union Law*, Oxford: Oxford University Press, 2014, p. 300-324.

Stigler 1971
Stigler, G.J., 'The Theory of Economic Regulation', *Bell Journal of Economics and Management Science*, 1971, Vol. 2, p. 3-21.

Stone 2007
Stone, K., 'A New Labor Law for a New World of Work: the Case for a Comparative-transnational Approach', *Comparative Labor Law & Policy Journal*, 2007, Vol. 28(3), p. 565-582.

Storm 2006
Storm, P., 'Cross-border Mergers, the Rule of Reason and Employee Participation', *European Company Law*, 2006, Vol. 3(3), p. 130-138.

Svorny 2000
Svorny, S., 'Licensing, Market Entry Regulation', in Bouckaert, B. & De Geest, G. (eds.), *Encyclopedia of Law and Economics, Volume III: The Regulation of Contracts*, Cheltenham: Edward Elgar, 2000, p. 296-328.

Tanzil 2000
Tanzil, V., 'Some Politically Incorrect Remarks on Decentralization and Public Finance', in Dethier, J.-J. (ed.), *Governance, Decentralization and Reform in China, India and Russia*, New York: Springer, 2000. p. 48-64.

Terleeka & King 2006
Terlaaka, A. & King, A., 'The Effect of Certification with the ISO 9000 Quality Management Standard: A Signaling Approach', *Journal of Economic Behavior & Organization*, 2006, Vol. 60(4), p. 579-602.

The Bureau of Industrial Economics 1996a
The Bureau of Industrial Economics (Australia), *Business Licenses: International Benchmarking*, Canberra: Australian Government Publishing Service, 1996.

The Bureau of Industrial Economics 1996b
The Bureau of Industrial Economics (Australia), *Business Licenses and Regulation Reform*, Canberra: Australian Government Publishing Service, 1996.

The Commission of the European Community 1992
The Commission of the European Community, *Towards a Single Market in Financial Services*, Luxemburg: Office for Official Publications of the European Community, 1992.

The World Bank 1994
The World Bank, *China: Internal Market Development and Regulation* (A World Bank country study), Washington DC: the World Bank, 1994.

The World Bank Group 2008
The World Bank Group, *Doing Business in China 2008* (English), Beijing: Social Sciences Academic Press, 2008.

Thieffry *et al.* 1989
Thieffry, J. *et al.*, 'The Single European Market: A Practitioner's Guide to 1992', *Boston College International and Comparative Law Review*, 1989, Vol. 12(2), p. 357-385.

Tian 2004
Tian, C., *The Theory and the Practice of Local Law Making*, Beijing: China Legal Publishing House (田成有，2004，地方立法的理论与实践, 北京: 中国法制出版社).

Tideman & Plassmann 2010
Tideman, T.N. & Plassmann, F., 'Pricing Externalities', *European Journal of Political Economy*, 2010, Vol. 26, p. 176-184.

Tiebout 1956
Tiebout, C., 'A Pure Theory of Local Expenditures', *The Journal of Political Economy*, 1956, Vol. 64, p. 416-424.

Tosiek 2008
Tosiek, P., 'The European Union after the Treaty of Lisbon - Still an Intergovernmental System', in Jańczak, J. (ed.), *Beyond Borders. External Relations of the European Union*, Poznań: Faculty of Political Science and Journalism, Adam Mickiewicz University, 2008, p. 1-16.

Trachtman 1993
Trachtman, J., 'International Regulatory Competition, Externalization, and Jurisdiction', *Harvard International Law Journal*, 1993, Vol. 34(1), p. 47-104.

Trillas 2011
Trillas, F., 'Regulatory Federalism in Telecommunications', *Cuadernos Económicos de ICE*, 2011, Vol. 81, p. 9-38.

Ulen & Cooter 2011
Ulen, T. & Cooter, R., *Law & Economics*, Boston: Addison-Wesley, 2011.

Valk 2010
Valk, O., 'C-210/06 Cartesio Increasing Corporate Mobility through Outbound Establishment', *Utrecht Law Review*, 2010, Vol. 6(1), p. 151-167.

Van den Bergh 1994
Van den Bergh, R., 'The Subsidiarity Principle in European Community Law: Some Insights from Law and Economics', *Maastricht Journal of European and Comparative Law*, 1994, Vol. 1, p. 337-366.

Van den Bergh 1998
Van den Bergh, R., 'Subsidiarity as an Economic Demarcation Principle and the Emergence of European Private Law', *Maastricht Journal of European and Comparative Law*, 1998, Vol. 5, p. 129-152.

Van den Bergh 2000
Van den Bergh, R., 'Towards an Institutional Legal Framework for Regulatory Competition in Europe', Kyklos, 2000, Vol. 53(4), p. 435-466.

Van den Bergh 2008
Van den Bergh, R., 'Economic Criteria for Applying the Subsidiarity Principle in European Environmental Law', in Revesz, R. *et al.* (eds.), *Environmental Law, the Economy, and Sustainable Development*, Cambridge: Cambridge University Press, 2008, p. 80-95.

Van den Bergh 2010
Van den Bergh, R., 'Private Law in a Globalizing World: Economic Criteria for Choosing the Optimal Regulatory Level in a Multi-level Government System', in Faure, M. & Van der Walt, A. (eds.), *Globalization and Private Law: The Way Forward*, Cheltenham: Edward Elgar, 2010, p. 57-96.

Van den Bergh & Visscher 2006
Van den Bergh, R. & Visscher, L., 'The Principle of European Tort Law: the Right Path to Harmonization?', *European Review of Private Law*, 2006, Vol. 4, p. 511-543.

Van Rooij *et al.* 2015
Van Rooij, B. *et al.*, 'Split Enforcement: How central local relations affect pollution law enforcement in China', Paper Presented at Brown University workshop on Central Local Relations and Environmental Governance, 2015.

Vanistendael 2003
Vanistendael, F., 'Bosal?!', *EC Tax Review*, 2003, Vol. 12(4), p. 192-193.

Vanistendael 2006
Vanistendael, F., 'The CJEU at the Crossroads: Balancing Tax Sovereignty against the Imperatives of the Single Market', *European Taxation*, 2006, Vol. 46(9), p. 413-420.

Vaubel 1994
Vaubel, R., 'The Political Economy of Centralization and the European Community', *Public Choice*, 1994, Vol. 81, p. 151-190.

Vihanto 1992
Vihanto, M., 'Competition between Local Governments as a Discovery Procedure', *Journal of Institutional and Theoretical Economics*, 1992, Vol. 148, p. 411-436.

Visscher 2012
Visscher, L., 'A Law and Economics View on Harmonization of Procedural Law', in Kramer, X.E. & Van Rhee, C.H. (eds.), *Civil Litigation in a Globalising World*, The Hague: T.M.C. Asser Press, 2012, p. 65-92.

Wagner 2009
Wagner, G., 'Tort Law and Liability Insurance', in Faure, M. (ed.), *Tort Law and Economics (Encyclopedia of Law and Economics)*, Cheltenham: Edward Elgar, 2009, p. 377-405.

Wagner 2011a
Wagner, H., 'Costs of Legal Uncertainty: Is Harmonization of Law a Good Solution?', in United Nations Commission on International Trade Law (ed.), *Modern Law for Global Commerce: Proceedings of the Congress of the United Nations Commission on International Trade Law Held on the Occasion of the Fourtienth Session of the Commission*, New York, NY: United Nations, 2011, p. 53-60.

Wagner 2011b
Wagner, W., 'Negative and Positive Integration in EU Criminal Law Co-operation', *European Integration online Papers* (EIoP), 2011, Vol. 15, <http://eiop.or.at/eiop/-texte/2011-003a.htm>.

Wang 1998
Wang, X., 'Industrial Monopolies and Regional Monopolies-Remarks on How to Regulate Administrative Acts Restricting Competition', *International Trade*, 1998, Vol. 4, p. 7-9（王晓晔, 条块垄断——论依法规范行政性限制竞争行为, 国际贸易, 1998年第4期）.

Wang 2007
Wang, K., 'To Reestablish the Relation Between Administrative Approval and Administrative License', *China Legal Science*, 2007, Vol. 4, p. 60-68 （王克稳, 我国行政审批与行政许可关系的重新梳理与规范, 中国法学，2007年第4期）.

Wang 2008
Wang, X., 'Highlights of China's New Anti-Monopoly Law', *Antitrust Law Journal*, 2008, Vol. 1, p. 133-150.

Wang 2009
Wang, X., 'Reconsideration on the Issue of Administrative Monopoly', *Journal of Graduate School of China Academy of Social Sciences*, 2009, Vol. 4, p. 49-58 (王晓晔, 行政垄断问题的再思考, 中国社会科学院研究生院学报, 2009年7月 第4期）.

Wang 2011
Wang, K., 'On the Administrative Franchise and its Difference with Common Administrative Permit', *Social Sciences in Nanjing*, 2011, Vol. 9, p. 83-87 (王克稳, 论行政特许及其与普通许可的区别, 南京社会科学, 2011年9期）.

Wang 2012
Wang, J., 'Anti-monopoly Issues in the Processed Oil Market in China', *Legal Science*, 2012, Vol. 2, p. 18-29 (王健， 我国成品油市场中的反垄断问题，《法学》 2012年第2期）.

Wang 2013a
Wang, A.L., 'The Search for Sustainable Legitimacy: Environmental Law and Bureaucracy in China', *Harvard Environmental Law Review*, 2013, Vol. 148, p. 365-440.

Wang 2013b
Wang, Y., 'Court Funding and Judicial Corruption in China', *The China Journal*, 2013, Vol. 69, p. 43-63.

Wang 2014a
Wang, K., 'Regulation of Administrative Licenses and the Reform of Administrative Licensing Systems in China', *Chinese Journal of Law*, 2014, Vol. 2, p. 3-18 (王克稳, 我国行政审批制度的改革及其法律规制, 法学研究，2014年第2期）.

Wang 2014b
Wang, X., 'China's Anti-Monopoly Law for Three Years: Achievements and Challenges', in Wang X. (ed.), *The Evolution of China's Anti-Monopoly Law*, Cheltenham: Edward Elgar Publishing, 2014, p. 401-418.

Wasserfallen 2013
Wasserfallen, F., 'Political and Economic Integration in the EU: The Case of Failed Tax Harmonization', *Journal of Common Market Studies*, 2013, Vol. 52(2), p. 1-16.

Weatherill 2011
Weatherill, S., 'The Limits of Legislative Harmonization Ten Years after Tobacco Advertising: How the Court's Case Law Has Become a "Drafting Guide"', *German Law Journal*, 2011, Vol. 12(3), p. 827-864.

Weatherill 2012
Weatherill, S., 'Maximum versus Minimum Harmonization: Choosing between Unity and Diversity in the Search for the Soul of the Internal Market', in Shuibhne, N.N. & Gormley, L.W. (eds.), *From Single Market to Economic Union: Essays in Memory of John A Usher*, Oxford: Oxford University Press, 2012, p. 172-199.

Wei & Bi 2011
Wei, W. & Bi, C., 'Environment Regulation, Interregional Industry Transfer and Pollution Heaven Effect in China: Empirical Analysis Based on Provincial Panel Poisson Model', *Jounal of Shanxi Finance and Economics University*, 2011, Vol. 33(8), p. 69-75 (魏玮、毕超, 环境规制、区际产业转移与污染避难所效应——基于省级面板Poisson模型的实证分析, 山西财经大学学报, 2011年, 第33卷, 第8期).

Weishaar 2011
Weishaar, S., 'Administrative Monopolies, State Aid, Barriers to Entry and Market Integration: Challenges for the Chinese Anti-Monopoly Law', in Faure M. & Zhang, X. (eds.), *Competition Policy and Regulation, Recent Development in China, the US and Europe*, Cheltenham: Edward Elgar, 2011, p. 98-129.

Weiss & Kaupa 2014
Weiss, F. & Kaupa, C., *European Union Internal Market Law*, Cambridge: Cambridge University Press, 2014.

Wong 2011
Wong, K.C., *Police Reform in China*, Boca Raton: CRC Press, 2011.

Wymeersch 2003
Wymeersch, E., 'The Transfer of the Company's Seat in European Company Law', *Common Market Law Review*, 2003, Vol. 40(3), p. 661-695.

Xia, Lu & Yu 2011
Xia, L., Lu, M. & Yu, W., 'Political Relations and Inter-provincial Investment-Empirical Evidence from Chinese Listed Companies', *Management World*, 2011, Vol. 7, p. 128-140 （夏立军、陆铭、余为政, 政企纽带与跨省投资—来自中国上市公司的经验证据, 《管理世界》2011年, 第7期）.

Xiao 2004
Xiao, J., 'The Index of Law-Ruling Government: Moderate Government and Uniform Government', *China Administration Management*, 2004, Vol. 10, p. 70-80 (肖金明, 法治政府指标: 适度政府与统一政府, 中国行政管理, 2004 年第10期）.

Xu 2011
Xu, C., 'The Fundamental Institutions of China's Reforms and Development', *Journal of Economic Literature*, 2011, Vol. 49(4), p. 1076-1151.

Xu 2014
Xu, X., 'Considering the Revision of Legislation Law from the Perspective of Governance Modernization', *SJTU Law Review*, 2014, Vol. 3, p. 10-17 (徐向华, 国家治理现代化视角下的《立法法》修改, 2014年第3期）.

Yang 2003a
Yang, T, 'An Essay on Institutional Barriers to the Development of Private Economy', *Reform*, 2003, Vol. 3, p. 29-33 (杨天宇, 民营经济发展的制度性障碍研究, 改革, 2003年第6期）.

Yang 2003b
Yang, T, 'The Economics Analysis of Administrative Licenses', *Economist*, 2003, Vol. 1, p. 28-31 （杨天宇, 政府行政审批制的经济学分析, 经济学家, 2003年第1期）.

Yang 2005
Yang, W., 'Problems and Methods in the Implementation of the ALL', *Study on China Administration for Industry and Commerce*, 2005, Vol. 7, p. 30-32 (杨卫东, 行政许可法实施中的问题与对策, 中国工商管理研究, 2005年第7期）.

Yang 2011
Yang, M., *Study on the Establishment of Administrative Licenses by the Provincial Governments through Making Local Rules*, the East China University of Political Science and law, master thesis, 2011 (杨敏, 省级政府规章行政许可设定研究, 华东政法大学, 2011年, 硕士学位论文).

Yang & Han 2006
Yang, Y. & Han, L., 'Difficulties in Implementing the Administrative Licensing Law', *Law Science Magazine*, 2006, Vol. 2, p. 17-20 (杨寅、韩磊, 行政许可法实施中的困境, 法学杂志, 2006年第2期）.

Yao & Zhang 2008
Yao, X. & Zhang, H., 'Education, Human Capital and Regional Economic Differentials', *Economic Research Journal*, 2008, Vol. 5, p. 47-57 (姚先国、张海峰, 教育、人力资本与地区经济差异, 经济研究, 2008年第5期).

Huang 2008
Huang, H., 'When Administrative Monopolies Meet Legal Challenges', *China Report*, 2008, Vol. 8, p. 92-93（黄勇， 当行政垄断遭遇法律"挑战", 中国报道, 2008年第08期）.

Yu 2006
Yu, Z., 'Study on the Enactment System of the Administrative Licensing', *Hebei Law Science*, 2006, Vol. 24(3), p. 72-75 (余正琨， 论行政许可设定制度, 河北法学, 2006年3月， 第24卷第3期）.

Zeng 2006
Zeng, X., 'Administrative Legislation and Rule of Wuwei', *Zhengfaluncong*, 2006, Vol. 10, p. 19-27 (曾祥华, 行政立法与无为而治, 政法论丛, 2006 年6 月第10期）.

Zhang 2004
Zhang, Y., 'The Implementation Reality of the ALL and Corresponding Suggestions', *National Judges College Law Journal*, 2004, Vol. 11, p. 80-81 (张韵声,《行政许可法》执行现状及相关对策, 法律适用， 2004年第11期）.

Zhang 2008a
Zhang, Q., 'The Better Use of Administrative Licenses', *The Study on Administrative Law*, 2008, Vol. 4, p. 101-109 （张卿, 论行政许可的优化使用——从法经济学角度进行分析, 行政法学研究， 2008 年第4 期）.

Zhang 2008b
Zhang, Z., 'The Study on the Right of Suggestion for Reviewing Unconstitutional Regulations', in He, H. (ed.), *The Development of Public Interest Litigation in China*, Beijing: China Social Sciences Press, 2008, p. 105-114（张卓明， 论法规合法性审查建议 权, 载贺海仁主编,《公益诉讼的新发展》, 中国社会科学出版社， 2008年版）.

Zhang 2011
Zhang, J., 'Interjurisdictional competition for FDI: the Case of China's "Development Zone Fever"', *Regional Science and Urban Economics*, 2011, Vol. 41(2), p. 145-159.

Zhang 2013
Zhang, G., 'Environmental Pollution and Inter-provincial Investment: An Analysis of the Data of Chinese Listed Companies in High-polluting Industries', *Communication of Finance and Accounting*, 2013, Vol. 6, p. 98-100 (张功富, 环境污染与企业跨省投资分析——基于重污染行业上市公司数据, 财会通讯, 2013年第6期）.

Zhang & Li 2003
Zhang, X. & Li, M., 'Legislation Thoughts and Some Defects on the Examination and Approval of Foreign Capital after China's Entry into the WTO', *Journal of Gansu Political Science and Law Institute*, 2003, Vol. 1, p. 5-8 (张晓东、李梅, 中国入世后外资审批中存在的问题及立法思考——从环保角度看外资审批, 甘肃政法学院学报2003年第1期).

Zhang & Ogus 2005
Zhang, Q. & Ogus, A., 'Licensing Procedures in Developing Countries: Should They Be Part of the Set-up Process?', *International Journal of Public Administration*, 2005, Vol. 29(12), p. 1091-1108.

Zhang & Zhang 2007
Zhang, X. & Zhang, V.Y., 'The Antimonopoly Law in China: Where Do We Stand?', *Competition Policy International*, 2007, Vol. 3(2), p. 185-201.

Zhang *et al.* 2007
Zhang, Y. *et al.*, 'Main issues Arising in Administrative Licensing and Administrative Approving and Methods to Deal with Them', *China Public Administration*, 2007, Vol. 4, p. 75-76 (张寅、孙如松、郑万城、张勇勤, 行政许可与行政审批中出现的主要问题与对策, 中国行政管理, 2007年第4期).

Zhang *et al.* 2013
Zhang, G. *et al.*, 'Local Protection, Corporate Investment and Corporate Competitive Advantage: Evidence from Chinese Manufacturing Listed Companies', *Economic Survey*, 2013, Vol. 5, p. 84-89 (张功富、王永强、刘振, 地方保护、企业投资与竞争优势——基于中国制造业上市公司面板数据的实证研究, 经济经纬, 2013年第5期).

Zhou 2001
Zhou, L.-A., 'The Incentive and Cooperation of Government Officials in Political Tournaments: An Interpretation of Prolonged Local Protectionism and Duplicative Investments in China', *Economic Research Journal*, 2001, Vol. 6, p. 30-40 (周黎安, 晋升博弈中政府官员的激励与合作：兼论我国地方保护主义和重复建设问题长期存在的原因, 经济研究, 2004年第6期).

Zhou 2007
Zhou, L.-A., 'Governing China's Local Officials: An Analysis of the Promotion Tournament Model', *Economic Research Journal*, 2007, Vol. 7, p. 36-50 (周黎安, 中国地方官员的晋升锦标赛模式研究, 经济研究, 2007年第7期).

Zhou 2010
Zhou, J., 'Thoughts on Improving Pre-administrative Licenses for Enterprises', *Study on China Administration for Industry and Commerce*, 2010, Vol. 6, p. 39-41 (周家东, 关于规范企业登记前置行政许可事项的思考, 中国工商管理研究, 2010年第6期).

Zhuo 2011
Zhuo, Y., 'The Behavioral Character of Government Approval and Possible Reasons for Excessive Approvals', *Journal of Jiangsu Administration Institute,* 2011, Vol. 3, p. 103-106 (卓越， 政府审批的行为特征与审批扩张的原因分析, 江苏行政学院学报, 2011 年第3 期).

CURRICULUM VITAE

Guang Shen was born in Shaoxing, Zhejiang Province, the PRC. He attended schools in Hangzhou and graduated from Xuejun High School in 2004. Upon graduation, he went to the China University of Political Science and Law (the CUPSL, Beijing) where he obtained the degree of Bachelor of Law and a Bachelor's degree in English. Afterwards he pursued postgraduate studies in Chinese law, European law and international law at the China-EU School of Law at the CUPSL. In September 2012 Guang started his PhD research into the regulation of cross-border establishment at Maastricht Institute for Transnational Legal Research (METRO). From 2014 until 2016, he was the faculty representative of Maastricht University in the PhD Council of the Ius Commune Research School.

IUS COMMUNE EUROPAEUM

A peer-reviewed book series in which the common foundations of the legal systems of the Member States of the European Union are the central focus.

The *Ius Commune Europaeum* series includes horizontal comparative legal studies as well as studies on the effect of treaties within the national legal systems. All the classic fields of law are covered. The books are published in various European languages under the auspices of METRO, the Institute for Transnational Legal Research at the Maastricht University.

Recently published:

Volume 139: *Evidence in Contemporary Civil Procedure. Fundamental Issues in a Comparative Perspective*, C.H. VAN RHEE and A. UZELAC (eds.)
Volume 140: *The Effect of D&O Insurance on Managerial Risk Taking*, M. GABER
Volume 141: *Information and Notification Duties*, I. SAMOY and M.B. LOOS (eds.)
Volume 142: *The Application of the Theory of Efficient Breach in Contract Law. A Comparative Law and Economics Perspective*, W. LIAO
Volume 143: *A European Legal Framework for Nuclear Liability. Rethinking Current Approaches*, T. HELDT
Volume 144: *The Development of European Private Law in a Multilevel Legal Order*, E.A.G. VAN SCHAGEN
Volume 145: *Property Law Perspectives IV*, D. GRUYAERT, E. RAMAEKERS and L. ROSTILL (eds.)
Volume 146: *The Citizen in European Private Law: Norm-setting, Enforcement and Choice*, C. CAUFFMAN and J. SMITS (eds.)
Volume 147: *Legal Certainty in Real Estate Transactions: A Comparison of England and France*, B. DU MARAIS and D. MARRANI (eds.)
Volume 148: *Scarcity and the State I. The Allocation of Limited Rights by the Administration*, P. ADRIAANSE, F. VAN OMMEREN, W. DEN OUDEN and J. WOLSWINKEL (eds.)
Volume 149: *Optional Instruments of the European Union. A Definitional, Normative and Explanatory Study*, W.A. BULL
Volume 150: *The European Union and National Civil Procedure. A Smooth Process or a Rocky Road for Member States?*, A. NYLUND and B.H. KRANS (eds.)
Volume 151: *Different Paths Towards Sustainable Biofuels? A Comparative Study of the International, EU, and Chinese Regulation of the Sustainability of Biofuels*, T. YUE

www.ingramcontent.com/pod-product-compliance
Ingram Content Group UK Ltd.
Pitfield, Milton Keynes, MK11 3LW, UK
UKHW051926100926
8556IPUK00022B/1392